Thought and Letters
in Western Europe

Thought and Letters in Western Europe

A.D. 500 TO 900

M. L. W. LAISTNER

Cornell Paperbacks

CORNELL UNIVERSITY PRESS

ITHACA AND LONDON

First published, Methuen & Co. Ltd., 1931
Revised edition, Methuen & Co. Ltd. and
Cornell University Press, 1957
First printing, Cornell Paperbacks, 1966
Second printing 1976
Published in the United Kingdom by Cornell University Press Ltd.,
2-4 Brook Street, London W1Y 1AA

International Standard Book Number 0-8014-9037-5
Printed in the United States of America

Preface to the First Edition

A book in English, which, within the moderate compass of a single volume, essays to describe and estimate thought and literature in Western Europe during the four centuries following the final collapse of the Roman Empire, should need no apology. For the period and the subject have been rather neglected as a whole by English scholars, although excellent studies have been made of special topics or authors, and there exist also some useful surveys of a more general character in works devoted to the whole medieval era. Nevertheless, it must be confessed that even good medievalists are at times prone to be somewhat cavalier towards anything prior to the eleventh century or to the rise of the universities. No reasonably informed person, it is true, any longer believes in the 'Dark Ages'—a prolonged period of hopeless barbarism succeeding on the fall of the Western Empire. But in the English-speaking countries at least, where so much has been published, whether of specialized research or of broader interpretation, on the later Middle Ages, the early centuries have attracted little attention. And yet, apart from the immense and obvious debt that we owe to the Carolingian Age for the preservation of classical and post-classical Latin literature, that era and the centuries that preceded it were a formative period without which it is impossible either to understand or to explain the full achievement of medieval culture at its zenith.

As to the arrangement of this book—the first three chapters do not pretend to be more than a brief survey to introduce the main subject which begins with Chapter IV. The literature and thought of the period beginning with Boethius and ending with Bede and Boniface have been treated regionally. In no other way would it have been possible to bring out the contrast between different areas of culture and the alternations of brilliance and obscurity that characterized them, nor yet to trace the evolution of a particular intellectual group—for example, the Irish in the sixth and seventh centuries—and its influence on other than its native area. On the other hand, from the time of Charlemagne to the end of the ninth century, in spite of the partial collapse of Charles's political empire, there existed a certain unity in religious observance, education, and the cultivation of letters, which justifies the application of the term, Carolingian, to the whole period. Moreover, after considering the several aspects of educational theory and practice, and closely allied topics, it seemed most convenient and most conducive to clearness to devote one of a series of chapters or part-chapters to each of the different branches of literature. The final chapter (XV) on vernacular literature is but a sketch for the convenience of the general reader or student. It is only with the greatest hesitation that I have ventured to include it in this volume, since, in writing it, I have rashly ventured into a field with which I am but imperfectly acquainted.

My debt to previous writers, which has necessarily been great throughout the composition of this book, will be apparent from the footnotes and from the select bibliography at the end. One work must, however, be singled out for special mention here, the monumental *Geschichte der lateinischen Literatur des Mittelalters* by Dr Max Manitius. The debt which scholars owe to him for that work, and for many papers and monographs on medieval Latin literature and on the transmission of the ancient classics into and through the Middle Ages, seems to me at least never to have been properly and adequately acknowledged either in his own or in other countries. And, with the expression of my gratitude for the help and inspiration that I have derived from this great scholar's writings, I would couple the earnest wish and hope that the third volume of his *History* may soon be given to the world.

My sincere thanks are due to Professor C. H. Beeson, of the University of Chicago, and to Mr R. A. B. Mynors, Fellow of Balliol College, Oxford, for kindly answering certain palaeographical queries. To my friend and colleague, Professor H. Caplan, I owe a debt of gratitude for patiently listening to and discussing many parts of this book during its composition.

Innocents' Day, 1930.   M. L. W. L.

Preface to the Second Edition

Twenty-five years have passed since the first edition of this book was published. During this interval, and despite the dislocation caused by six years of war, a good many books and innumerable articles on the period covered by this book have appeared. While I cannot pretend that I have read more than a portion of what has been written since 1931, it is my earnest hope that no important discovery or new interpretation of the evidence has been overlooked. Revision has entailed some additions and also some subtractions; but I have refrained deliberately from altering the scale of the book as a whole, since, whatever defects it may have in other respects, it has the merit of treating the subject within a moderate compass. The notes and bibliography have been drastically revised and brought up to date. Finally, I am most grateful to all those, too many to enumerate individually and some unhappily no longer with us, who were kind enough to send me copies of their books or offprints of articles or who corresponded with me on many points of detail.

December, 1955

M. L. W. L.

Contents

PART III

THE CAROLINGIAN AGE

List of Abbreviations

BOT   Charles W. Jones, *Bedae opera de temporibus.*

CLA   E. A. Lowe, *Codices latini antiquiores.*

Clavis   E. Dekkers and E. Gaar, *Clavis patrum latinorum (Sacris Erudiri* III, 1951).

CSEL   *Corpus scriptorum ecclesiasticorum latinorum.*

E.H.   Bede's *Ecclesiastical History.*

Kenney   J. F. Kenney, *Sources for the early history of Ireland,* Vol. I.

Manitius M. Manitius, *Geschichte der lateinischen Literatur des Mittelalters.* Three volumes.

MGH   *Monumenta Germaniae historica.* The different parts of this collection have been abbreviated as follows:

AA	Auctores antiquissimi.
Capit.	Capitula regum Francorum.
Chron. min.	Chronica minora.
Concil.	Concilia aevi Carolini.
Epist.	Epistulae.
Poet.	Poetae Latini aevi Carolini.
SS.	Scriptores.
Script. Langob.	Scriptores rerum Langobardicarum.
Script. Merov.	Scriptores rerum Merovingicarum.

PL   J. Migne, *Patrologiae cursus completus; series latina.*

RB   *Revue bénédictine.*

SMAH   A. Bruckner, *Scriptoria medii aevi Helvetica.*

ST   *Studi e Testi.*

PART I

Introductory: the Western Empire in the Fourth and Fifth Centuries

PART II

CHAPTER I

The Empire and the Church

(a) The Empire and its Invaders

To a contemporary observer the opening years of the third century of our era may well have seemed to promise fair for the future. Peace and unity once more reigned in an empire whose safety and prosperity had been imperilled for three decades by foreign aggressors without, and by civil war and misgovernment within. But the military autocracy perfected by Septimius Severus as a system of government was only effective temporarily; in the half-century following his death (211) it broke down disastrously. The majority of the soldiers was recruited from the frontier provinces. However considerable their merits as fighters, they were undisciplined, and, looking chiefly to their personal advantage, lacked loyalty to the Empire and even to their commanders-in-chief, if their demands for pay and spoil were not fully satisfied. It was in their power to make and to unmake emperors, and they used it. The constant civil wars of the third century, coupled with increasing pressure from the northern and north-eastern neighbours of the Empire, rendered large tracts of territory waste land. Whole provinces passed out of Roman control, and the economic condition of the civil population, bled white by a succession of despots, was pitiable. To have arrested the collapse, before it was completed, of the imperial structure, and, after chastising the barbarian enemy, to have recovered most of the lost dominions of Rome was the especial merit of Claudius Gothicus and of Aurelian. The slower but no less difficult task of reconstruction was carried through by Diocletian and after him by Constantine.

But the restored Empire of the fourth century was an organization very different from the Empire of the Caesars or the

Antonines. The principate in theory had never ceased to be elective; it was replaced by a quasi-Oriental despotism whose trappings recalled, if indeed they were not copied from, Sassanian Persia. A rigid system of castes, not springing from racial or religious institutions or taboos but imposed by the edicts of successive imperial rulers, who could devise no other method of holding together a decaying political structure, left no portion of society untouched. The same principle of compulsion, which gradually converted the free peasant into a serf bound to the soil that he tilled, was applied to the small landed proprietors (*curiales*) from whom the local councils and local magistracies of the numerous urban communities in the Empire were recruited. If these changes in general called forth no violent or organized resistance, although the attempt of Diocletian in 301 to regulate prices and wages led to serious riots in the eastern provinces, the main reason was that conditions which had steadily developed much earlier favoured the gradual encroachment of the imperial Government. Thus, in the imperial estates in North Africa and Egypt, and possibly also in Asia Minor, the free peasantry (*coloni*) had in practice, though not in law, become hereditary by the time of Marcus Aurelius. In the municipalities the central Government from the age of Trajan began to encroach, especially in the matter of taxation, on the local autonomy of magistrates and town-councils, and this supervision or interference, once begun, grew constantly more widespread. The associations (*collegia*) of merchants, shippers, and craftsmen of every kind, which had been formed in the earlier period of the Empire for religious and social ends, had begun in many instances to be utilized by the Government for its own purposes, primarily for securing the food and other essential supplies of the two capitals, Rome and Constantinople, and of the army. In return for this public service the members of the associations were granted certain privileges, as long as they continued to fulfil their contracts. From forbidding the members of those *collegia* to cease their membership it was but a further step to compel the son to follow his father's calling, until the free and voluntary associations which had been formed by the members themselves were changed into hereditary guilds rigidly controlled by imperial authority. The enormous burden of taxation, which crushed every class of the community, even if it pressed most pitilessly on the *curiales*, and the demands of the Government on the guilds, which constantly impeded private enterprise and the unrestricted development of industry and commerce, relentlessly furthered the impoverishment of the Empire. Infractions or evasions of the law, as can be seen from the edicts and ordinances of the *Theodosian Code*, were punished with ever-growing harshness. But, even after the utmost had been squeezed out of the civil population, it became increasingly difficult to meet the cost of maintaining a too numerous bureaucracy and the armies necessary to secure Rome from the enemies on her frontiers.

The danger of invasion from the North and the problem of defending an extended frontier had been the inevitable sequel of Roman expansion beyond the boundaries of Italy. At the end of the second century B.C. the attacks of the Cimbri, Teutones, and other tribes, which had threatened not only Italy but the recently acquired Roman province of Narbonese Gaul, were finally repulsed by Marius. In the hundred years that followed, the genius of Julius Caesar and of Augustus created a new frontier by enlarging Rome's dominions, and gave the capital and Italy greater security at the cost of vastly greater responsibilities. Caesar's conquest of Gaul, and the operations of Augustus' generals at intervals during a quarter of a century, advanced the Empire to the natural barriers of the Rhine and the Danube. The more ambitious plan of shortening the total line of defence by advancing the boundary eastwards from the Rhine to the Elbe proved impracticable and was abandoned by Augustus and Tiberius. But under their successors, from Vespasian to M. Aurelius, although no attempt was made to repeat in full the costly experiment of Augustus, a less ambitious rectification of the frontier was carried out by constructing a series of defence-works (the so-called *limes Germanicus* and *limes Raeticus*) running south-east and east from the Rhine opposite Cologne to Heinheim on the Danube. The total length of these fortifications was nearly three hundred and fifty miles. The winning of new territory beyond the Rhine which preceded these military works had not passed off without some fighting against Germanic tribes. But as these did not at that time succeed in forming any considerable coalition against Rome, the task of breaking down their opposition was relatively simple. On the Lower Danube the most notable event of these years was the conquest of Dacia completed by Trajan in A.D. 106. Some sixty years later the northern defences were put to the first severe test. The importance of the so-called Marcomannic Wars of Marcus Aurelius has sometimes been greatly underrated, mainly perhaps because reliable information about them is so scanty. But it seems clear that the incursions of Germanic tribes at various points into the Roman border provinces were to a great extent the result of concerted action and had as their cause the pressure exerted on the tribes nearest to the Danube by the extensive migrations of more northerly peoples. Of these the most considerable was that of the Goths. Tradition places their earliest home in southern Scandinavia; in the middle of the second century, however, they were settled on the Lower Vistula. By A.D. 200, or soon after, the whole nation was established in South Russia, and little more than a decade later they were the immediate neighbours of the Roman province of Dacia. Finally, in 270 prudence or necessity induced Aurelian to evacuate Dacia in face of the Gothic encroachments into the territory between the Theiss and the Pruth.

From the death of Septimius Severus to the reign of Aurelian the attacks of Germanic neighbours contributed not a little to the anarchic confusion which threatened to disrupt the Roman dominions. While Goths and Herulians raided the eastern Mediterranean coastlands, and Saxons made descents on the Gallic and British shores, the Alamanni and Franks pressed forward to the Upper and Lower Rhine. Meanwhile in 227 the Persian nobleman Ardashir, son of Sassan, instigated a rebellion against the last of the Parthian kings and became the founder of a new Persian dynasty. The Sassanid kings showed their warlike ardour and skill by robbing Rome of a part of her eastern possessions and even taking prisoner the Roman emperor, Valerian (259).

The relief from barbarian attacks which the emperors of the later third century and Constantine afforded to the harassed inhabitants of the Empire was only temporary. In the fourth and fifth centuries, while the Roman resources in men and material, and consequently the Roman power of resistance, steadily grew less, the forward movements of the northern peoples continued with increasing frequency. Nor was the experiment, tried by certain emperors, of enlisting some of the Germanic tribes as allies (*foederati*) of the Empire and obtaining their military services, particularly to secure the frontiers, in return for heavy subsidies of food or money, without its dangers. The precise date at which the Gothic nation was split into a western (Visigothic) and an eastern (Ostrogothic) group is uncertain; most probably it was the result, or at least an early sequel to, the series of migrations which took place during the last forty years of the second century. At all events their development in the period when their history was interwoven with that of Rome was independent, and shows a noteworthy difference in political organization. The Visigoths owed allegiance to no single monarch, at least until the very end of the fourth century, but were composed of a number of groups, each with its own chief. In questions affecting the people as a whole it was the chiefs who guided the deliberations of the nation and often determined the issue. And the special prestige of one chief would lead to his election as commander-in-chief in time of war, when single rather than divided authority was expedient, even as the Homeric Agamemnon, though no more than *primus inter pares*, owed his position to his paramount influence. The Ostrogoths in the third and fourth centuries were ruled by kings; of these the best known was Ermanaric, reputed to have created a great Gothic empire which collapsed before the assaults of the Huns in 370. When nearly forty years before that date Constantine came to a forced agreement with the Visigoths, and, in return for heavy subsidies, was able to enrol them as *foederati* of the Empire, both branches of the Gothic nation were still heathen. But in, or soon after 340, a Goth named Ulfilas, who had been reared in Cappadocia and later in Constantinople where he had been converted to Christianity, began to labour as a missionary in Dacia after he had been duly consecrated bishop by Eusebius of Nicomedia. The work of Ulfilas was in every way momentous. Although after a few years his labours as a missionary were cut short by persecutions instituted by Visigothic chiefs, so that the bishop and his converts were forced to seek refuge in Roman territory south of the Danube, the seed had been sown, and the conversion of the Goths and other Germanic peoples was then only a matter of time. Ulfilas translated the Scriptures into Gothic, after he had fashioned a Gothic alphabet derived partly from the Greek, partly from the runes of the Northmen. The extant Gothic Bible consists of substantial fragments from the Gospels and the thirteen Epistles of St Paul and some passages from the Book of Nehemiah. One further aspect of Ulfilas' mission is important. He had been taught the Arian creed and had been consecrated by an Arian bishop. Hence the Goths, and the related tribes to whom the new religion was spread from them, were won over to the Arian, not to the orthodox communion. This circumstance was to complicate their relations with the imperial Government by the superimposition of doctrinal on political differences. And there was also the further danger that Romans living in the border provinces might lapse into heresy under the influence of their Gothic neighbours. It is no accident that, a generation after Ulfilas, Niceta, the Catholic bishop of Remesiana (near the modern Nish), warned baptismal candidates especially against the false teaching of Arius.

Of the West German tribes the most formidable for many years were the Alamanni, a branch of the Suevic people, who had already threatened the Raetian frontier in the reign of Caracalla. Further assaults by them and by the Franks on the Lower Rhine followed later, so that by 260 the right bank of the river and all that lay east of it passed out of Roman control, after the elaborate defence-works forming the two *limites* had been destroyed. During the long reign of Constantius (337–61) the safety of Gaul was endangered by serious raids across the Rhine. The victory of the Caesar, Julian, over the Alamanni in 357 eased the pressure for only a few years. At the same time the Franks were compelled to submit to Roman suzerainty.

A new and unforeseen complication in Rome's problem of frontier defence arose in 370 owing to the arrival of a Mongolian people, the Huns, in South Russia. Unfortunately for themselves and for their neighbours, the Visigoths at that time were divided amongst themselves through the acute rivalry of their two most prominent chieftains, Athanaric and Fritigern. A united front presented to the Asiatic hordes by both the eastern and the western Goths might perhaps have stemmed the tide of invasion. But the kingdom of Ermanaric collapsed and the Ostrogoths with some neighbouring tribes became the subjects of the Hun. A few years later Athanaric and his followers after a severe defeat withdrew behind the barrier of the Carpathians. The rest of the Visigothic nation led by Fritigern applied to the emperor, Valens, in 376 for land on which they might make their homes. Permission to settle in Moesia was granted, but the process of settlement, especially when more and more fugitives including a part of the Ostrogoths appeared across the frontier, did not pass off without friction between the immigrants on the one hand and the Roman authorities and the older population on the other. Before the end of 376 the emperor found himself at war with the Goths and some lesser tribes. Simultaneously in the West Gratian had all that he could do to check a renewed assault of the Alamanni on the Upper Rhine. After two years of indecisive fighting Valens was disastrously defeated at the battle of Adrianople in which two-thirds of the Roman army perished. But the Goths failed to capture any of the fortified cities that they attacked, and by 382 Theodosius I was able to effect a settlement. The Visigoths became *foederati*, binding themselves to render military service for the emperor when required. In return they received land in Moesia as well as payments in kind or money. Thus a numerous Germanic people was installed within the Empire, and one on which Theodosius relied more and more to furnish troops for his later campaigns. Moreover, the permeation of the Empire with the Northerners went on apace, so that in the fifty years following many of the most powerful ministers of State and generals of the emperor in the West were of Germanic stock, for example, Arbogastes, Merobaudes, Stilicho, and Gainas. After the death of Theodosius I the disintegration of the western half of the Empire was greatly accelerated. It will suffice to point out the chief stages in the process of dismemberment.

In 395 the Visigoths, who had abandoned their former political organization and chosen a king, Alaric, openly revolted against Rome. For two years Alaric with his men overran and ravaged the Balkan peninsula. In 401, after four years of quiescence, he attacked Italy itself but was repulsed; once more he and his people withdrew for some years to Epirus. Meanwhile, as the danger to Italy from attacks on the north and north-east had been so recently demonstrated, Honorius and his advisers withdrew large bodies of troops from the Rhine defences in order to be secure nearer home. The opportunity was seized by the trans-Rhenane tribes. In 406 a great horde of Germans—Suevi, Asding Vandals and Siling Vandals—and the Alans, who originally were of Iranian stock and had, like the Goths, been driven by the Huns from their home in South Russia, crossed the Rhine and swarmed into Gaul. Two years later Alaric and his Visigoths descended anew on Italy, this time with disastrous success culminating in the capture and sack of Rome in 410. Alaric survived his triumph only a few months. His successors now turned their attention to Gaul and Spain; it was in Gaul that they were finally settled soon after 418 and technically they were still counted as *foederati* of the Empire. In the meantime the Vandals, Suevi, and Alans had pushed on across the Pyrenees and occupied the Spanish peninsula, a conquest which the emperor was powerless to prevent. In 429 the Vandals under their able, if ruthless, king, Gaiseric, evacuated southern Spain and invaded North Africa. Thus another Roman province passed into barbarian hands. For nearly two generations the Vandal kingdom of Africa, gradually enlarged by the addition of Corsica, Sardinia, the Balearic Islands, and Lilybaeum in the north-west corner of Sicily, was the most dangerous enemy of the reduced Roman Empire, the more so as the Vandals, unlike the other German invaders, took successfully to the sea, and their fleets harried the Mediterranean coasts and more than once threatened to starve out Rome and Italy.

Early in the fifth century the evacuation of Britain still further narrowed the territories of Rome. In the third decade of the same century the westward expansion of the Huns represented a new peril on the north-eastern boundaries of the Empire. Organized, it would seem, as a loose confederacy of tribes, the Huns owed their military successes primarily to their skill as mounted archers. Already greatly feared, alike by their Roman and Germanic neighbours, under several earlier chiefs, they attained to their

greatest power politically and controlled the widest territories
under the leadership of Attila (434–54). The real ruler in the
Western Empire at that time was the Master of both Services
(*magister utriusque militiae*), Aetius. Thanks to a good understanding with the Huns, and partly with their military help, he was
able to hold south-eastern and central Gaul for the Empire against
a ring of Germanic peoples; for the Visigoths occupied Aquitaine, the Burgundians were established in Savoy, and the Franks
held northern Gaul. But, when in 451 Valentinian III refused
the demands of Attila, who was then at the height of his power,
the Huns invaded Gaul. The skilful diplomacy of Aetius was now
demonstrated. He was able to enrol the Franks and Visigoths as
allies of Rome. Attila was checked near Orléans and then defeated near Troyes. In 452 he invaded northern Italy but was
induced to come to terms. In the next year he died and almost
at once the Hunnish empire collapsed; for in 454 a coalition of
German tribes who had lately been subjects of the Hun and had
fought for him, defeated the Hunnish forces. From this date the
Huns ceased to play any part in history. The peoples who had
conquered them settled partly north, partly south of the Danube.
Of special significance was the establishment of the Ostrogoths
in Pannonia, since this powerful nation was thus brought into
close proximity to Italy. The Western emperors were little more
than nominal rulers; the actual power from 456 to 472 was in the
hands of a Master of the soldiery, Ricimer, who, like so many
prominent officers before, was of Germanic descent. Four years
after his death a rising of Germanic troops, who asked for land
on which to settle in Italy, led to the establishment of their
leader, Odovacar, as ruler of Italy. The Eastern emperor, Zeno,
acquiesced in what he was powerless to prevent. While claiming
that his imperial authority extended also to the West, he recognized Odovacar as an imperial official by conferring on him the
title of Patrician of the Empire. Odovacar himself assumed the
royal style and ruled for seventeen years. Then the Ostrogothic
king, Theodoric, after five years of war, stepped into his place
and founded an Ostrogothic kingdom in Italy which endured for
nearly half a century (493–540). He, too, won imperial recognition from Constantinople. In the interval momentous changes

had taken place in what had once been the western provinces of the Roman Empire. While Raetia and Noricum were occupied by the Alamanni and other tribes, the Salic Franks under Clovis in 486 made themselves masters of that portion of Gaul which till then had still acknowledged the authority of Rome. Now the country contained two major Germanic kingdoms, the Frankish and the Visigothic, the River Loire forming the boundary between them, and the smaller Burgundian state. Before his death in 511 Clovis had wrested a good part of their Gaulish territory from the Visigoths and had compelled the Burgundians to accept his overlordship. One important fact remains to be noted. The Franks, who were the latest of the Germanic invaders to develop a powerful state, were also the only people who till the time of Clovis had continued to be faithful to their ancient gods. The conversion of Clovis and his people to Christianity was in itself a significant event; even more striking, however, was the circumstance that they accepted the Catholic, not the Arian confession. This fact was to have far-reaching consequences on the political history of Western Europe in the sixth and seventh centuries. It ensured the ultimate triumph of Catholic orthodoxy there; and the result was that, as existing antipathies were rapidly obliterated, the fusion of the Frankish people with the older Gallo-Roman population was gradually achieved. The more transitory character of the other Germanic states, save the Visigothic kingdom in Spain which ended by becoming orthodox, was due at least in part to doctrinal differences between the older inhabitants and the invaders, and this militated against the blending of the two elements into a homogeneous political whole.

It will be sufficiently clear from the brief sketch just given that there was nothing cataclysmic about the Germanic invasions. The decline and fall of the Western Empire was a gradual process lasting two centuries; and it is not unreasonable to assume that this process would have been even slower, but for the widespread disturbances caused by the Huns during the century or more that they terrorized Romans and Germans alike.[1] During these two hundred years the changes were not confined only to

---

[1] Cf. the interesting discussion in E. A. Thompson, *Attila and the Huns* (Oxford, 1948), pp. 209–15.

one side. All, or nearly all, the invaders had become familiar to some extent both with Roman institutions and with Roman culture. Many of them alternated between hostility to Rome and alliance with her as *foederati*. And, even when they were her political enemies and invaded her territories, they were filled with awe at her name and respected her venerable civilization. Men like Odovacar and Theodoric were quite content to recognize the titular authority of the emperor in Constantinople, provided that their own position as rulers under imperial licence was regularized. Nor did Clovis disdain to receive from the emperor in the East, Anastasius, the *insignia* of a Roman consul. We must also be on guard against the exaggerations of the contemporary Latin writers. Often where they relate the total destruction of a town by the barbarians, archaeological exploration has shown such narratives to be grossly overdrawn. Many sites suffered only partial damage and soon recovered some semblance of their old prosperity. Others, though they might be in ruins for a short time, were not permanently abandoned, but were resettled after a brief interval. In short, just as the Roman Empire had been permeated with Germanic blood long before its fall, so the German nations before and during their advance into the Empire became steadily and increasingly Romanized.

(b) The Church

The policy of religious toleration adopted by Constantine and Licinius radically altered the position of the Christian minorities in the Empire. The communities of the Faithful, which for three centuries had been either illicit organizations, or, even when tolerated by the highest authority, were without legal status, now came into the category of permitted associations. The Christians, who hitherto had always been liable to suffer individually or in groups because of occasional outbursts of popular hostility in the several provinces of the Roman world, and in whose lives for sixty years (251–311) a precarious toleration had alternated with rigorous persecution by the imperial Government, could now live in and by their faith without let or hindrance. Moreover, if religious differences provoked disturbances of the peace, the

Christians could, if wronged, claim the redress under the law that was the right of all citizens, whatever their religious beliefs. Within less than a decade from 313 the Church had secured from the emperor the right to corporate ownership of property, and like other lawful associations, could receive testamentary bequests. As a result the wealth of the Church grew with remarkable swiftness. Even if nothing further had developed from these changes they would have been noteworthy enough; actually the fourth century witnessed a transformation which deserves to be called revolutionary. With the exception of Julian, all the emperors from Constantine I were Christian rulers. The adherents of a religion which was not only permitted but fostered by the imperial family increased with such rapidity that at the death of Theodosius I in A.D. 395 the Christians in the Empire were in a marked majority. Constantine and his successors were not merely tolerant of Christianity and its adherents, but active proselytizers. Theodosius, whose early years were distinguished by a certain easy-going indifference, towards the end of his life displayed a very rigid and active orthodoxy. He took steps to suppress all pagan rites and sacrifices within the Empire. In Rome, Italy, and the West these coercive measures were on the whole attended by little disturbance. But in the East, especially in Syria and in Egypt where the cult of Sarapis was stamped out, they produced riots and not a little bloodshed. The imperial Government did not, however, like the Church Militant of a later date, attempt to dictate the beliefs of the individual, though Constantine and again Theodosius I ordered all copies of Porphyry's treatise against the Christians to be destroyed. Adherents of pagan religions, though gradually diminishing in number, continued to exist for many years. The schools of philosophy at Athens were not finally suppressed until the age of Justinian. In Italy the chief upholders of paganism in the later fourth and early fifth centuries were the members of the senatorial aristocracy. They strove to maintain the old Roman State religion and promoted the better preservation of Rome's literary heritage by fostering the copying and editing of Latin classics. In the country districts of the western provinces pagan superstitions and practices survived fitfully for centuries amongst a nominally Christian peasantry, and their eradication was a never-ending anxiety to the Church and her ministers.

Long before 313 the ecclesiastical organization had travelled a long way from the simple system of the primitive Church. The democratic election of elders by each congregation had been gradually superseded, as a purely parochial arrangement no longer sufficed for a steadily expanding body, by a monarchic method of government which developed side by side with the growth of a more elaborate hierarchy. In the fourth century this evolution became more rapid than before. The Church which waxed so quickly in size and authority began to derive inspiration from the civil law of the Empire for her own purposes. From this and from the decisions of councils and synods, over and above the authority of the Bible and tradition handed down from Apostolic times, there developed, slowly but steadily, the impressive body of canon law. So, too, in the matter of administration: the organization of the temporal State seems to have served as a model for the ecclesiastical. Moreover, the influence of the bishops was not restricted to the spiritual care of their flocks. Roman civil law had long recognized the settlement of suits by a private arbiter approved by both litigants. Between two Christians such differences most usually had been adjudicated by the religious head of the community. What before could, between Christians, only be an amicable but private arrangement between co-religionists, was approved *de iure* by Constantine. It was a far more radical innovation when a more general civil jurisdiction was entrusted to the bishops, which in theory put them on the same footing with civil officials charged with the administration of the law, while in practice, thanks to their prestige in their communities, their juridical authority tended to be more highly regarded and sought after than that of secular judges. The functions performed by such ecclesiastical tribunals became more and more important. Similarly one can trace the growth of episcopal influence and leadership in urban and municipal government throughout the Empire; and many instances could be cited to show how, during the stress of foreign invasions and in time of war, bishops took the lead in organizing the defence of towns and districts, displaying an exemplary devotion to the call of national patriotism as they did to the especial duties of their religious office. But, if there is much to admire in the growth to maturity of this still youthful organism, much, too, to reverence in the selfless dedication to the highest calls of religion not only of many leaders of the Church but of countless other Christian men, it cannot be disguised that there were also some much less pleasing aspects of ecclesiastical history during the fourth and fifth centuries.

The transmutation of a despised cult into a State religion was not effected without moral and spiritual loss. All too often worldliness and love of the good things of this life contrasted glaringly with the lofty ethics of the primitive Christian communities, even as they gave the lie to the efficacy of the Church's teaching whose moral standards had not been lowered. Not less painful is the effect produced by contemplating the disunion and often rancorous quarrels in the Christian body as a whole, and their concomitant religious intolerance. It is, nevertheless, as dangerous as it is unjustified to judge of these manifestations with a mind filled with modern liberalism, which is often no more than a polite name for indifference. The absence of a central ecclesiastical authority for the whole Christian world, as well as the attitude of the temporal power and its relations with the Church, were productive of various complications. Nor could the same acceptance of authority and the same unquestioning faith be expected in the sophisticated world of the Empire, in which half a hundred religions and philosophies had grown up and thrived for centuries, as in a simpler and untutored society like the Germanic peoples; and, as has been shown, their acceptance of Arianism proved to be a disruptive force, once the invaders settled as conquerors in Roman territory. As the ecclesiastical hierarchy developed, the bishops of provincial capitals, the so-called metropolitans, gradually acquired a certain pre-eminence over the other bishops in the province. Besides this, certain sees, whose origins, though simpler in form, went back to Apostolic or sub-Apostolic days, were invested with a special influence and sanctity. Such in the eastern half of the Empire were Antioch, Jerusalem, and Alexandria. These sees, together with Constantinople whose bishop, as exercising in the new Eastern capital his spiritual sway, soon claimed equal rank, have, under the more impressive title of patriarchates, retained their pre-eminence in the Eastern Church to this day. In the West, however, only the bishop of Rome could claim a similarly outstanding position. The further development in the East and the West was strikingly different. The emperors in Constantinople kept a controlling hand over the Church and the clergy and were, in effect, heads of both Church and State. In the West this Caesaropapism, as it has been called, could not develop. There the emperors during the fifth century were for the most part mere puppets; after 476 their place was taken by Germanic kings. Step by step, though not without occasional set-backs, the bishops of Rome acquired an ultimate supremacy in the West in all spiritual matters. Outstanding personalities, like Leo I or Gelasius in the fifth, or Gregory I in the later sixth century, exerted a leading influence in temporal affairs as well.

Almost from the first the emperor was drawn into religious controversy; for Constantine, soon after his final triumph over Licinius, intervened in the dispute between the opponents and the followers of Arius. The outcome of this was the first oecumenical council of the Church, held at Nicaea in 325 and probably resumed in 327, and the formulation of the orthodox confession which derives its name from it. But, although the emperors might take steps to convene a representative body of prelates to decide a question of faith or doctrine, they did not as a rule, attempt to impose their own will in spiritual questions; for the action of Constantius, when he intimidated the Synod of Milan into pronouncing the condemnation of Athanasius and his teaching, was exceptional. Similarly, the election of bishops was carried out by the leaders of the Church without interference from the secular power; for the occasional consecration of an imperial nominee does not invalidate the general truth of our contention. Again, the deposition of a bishop, which would only result from condemnation for a major offence, such as heresy, addiction to magic, or gross immorality, was effected by his peers. In short, the intervention of the Government normally occurred either at the request of the Church, where it had need of the secular arm, or, if an ecclesiastical offender was guilty of a crime against the

State. The position of bishops compared with that of laymen, even those of the highest rank, was undoubtedly privileged. A certain sacrosanctity enshrouded the spiritual leader, which the imperial official lacked. There are not a few examples of bishops speaking or acting unchecked with a freedom or even contumacy against the emperor which, coming from a layman, would have been followed by swift punishment. Yet even amongst the princes of the Church few dared to proceed with the boldness of Ambrose face to face with Theodosius I. Pagan rites were gradually suppressed and pagan temples closed, but the eradication of heresy and faction in the Church by the emperors was often less successful. The outstanding example of such failure was in North Africa, where no measures, however harsh, availed against the Donatists. Again, the blind zeal and partisanship with which the entire population of a province supported its leading prelate, as did the people of Alexandria and Egypt theirs, was a grave danger to the public peace, if that spiritual leader was engaged in embittered controversy with Antioch or Constantinople. The *Theodosian Code* contains a number of ordinances promulgated against heretical sects yet even the smaller were often able to maintain themselves for long periods. Even if no more active steps were taken to enforce the law, their members were penalized in various ways by the Government, for instance, by being excluded from office or Government employ, or by forfeiting their testamentary rights.

One special development within the Church which was to a great extent the outcome of that relaxation of ethical standards and decline from the pristine austerity of a persecuted Church was destined to have a profound and lasting effect. Asceticism, whether accompanied by withdrawal from all human society or practised with others in a communal fellowship, was far older than Christianity. While simplicity of life and abstention from worldly pleasures, especially the theatre and other popular shows, were general among the early Christians, there were always some from the very beginning who, without forsaking their communities, were distinguished by exceptional austerity and self-renunciation. There were also some sects, like the Montanists, whose tenets were unusually narrow and rigid. The beginnings of Christian monasticism, however, do not go back further than the concluding years of the third century. Egypt was the country of its origin and Saint Antony its founder. His younger contemporary, Pachomius, while animated by an equally intense desire to leave the world and for the abnegation of carnal things, formed a somewhat different conception of the monastic ideal. Whereas Antony was an eremite who in his desert retreat shunned the society of all men, even of other ascetics, the monastic settlements founded by Pachomius in Upper Egypt were in some degree cenobitic, that is to say, all the monks in them obeyed one superior and their life was not wholly solitary but communal in part. Both men had many disciples and imitators, so that before long the desert regions of Upper and Lower Egypt were thronged by thousands desirous, by fleeing from the temptations of this world and combining a life of prayer and contemplation with bodily privations and mortifications, to fit themselves for the bliss of the world to come. Monasticism had not long gained a footing in Egypt when similar scenes of renunciation were enacted in other regions of the Near East. In Syria the anchoretic type of monastic life predominated; at the same time the self-torture practised by the most fanatical of the solitaries far surpassed the severest austerities even of an Antony. So grotesque were some of these excesses that even a great Roman Catholic historian of the early Church was moved to compare them to the extravagances of Indian fakirs.[1]   In the rest of the Greek-speaking world, notably in Asia Minor, monasticism was inspired from Egypt and more especially by the practice of Pachomius. The lead in personal example and in organization was taken by Eustathius, and by Basil the Great. On the body of rules which bear Basil's name the monastic discipline of the Greek Church has ever since been based. The monasteries were cenobitic and the life in the religious community was austere; but Basil discouraged severe mortification, and, as he ordained that the brethren must engage in constant work, disapproved of any excessive asceticism that would interfere with their useful labours. Monasticism was introduced in the West by Athanasius and received a great stimulus from the example of St Martin, who

[1] L. Duchesne, *Histoire ancienne de l'église*, II, p. 516.

founded settlements first at Ligugé near Poitiers and later at
Tours. Their practice was more eremitical than cenobitic. Each
monk had his own cell and only foregathered with his fellows for
prayer on stated occasions. Monastic foundations quickly
multiplied in other parts of Gaul and were established in Italy
also. The house of St Victor at Marseilles and the monastic
settlements at Lérins exerted a specially wide influence. At Lérins
the example and precepts of John Cassian entitle him to rank
among the foremost promoters of the religious life. He found his
ideal in the monasticism of Egypt, where he himself had passed
a decade in a community of monks, and in his own convent the
anchoretic was combined with the cenobitic life, the former being
regarded as the more perfect form of renunciation practised by
the older brethren. Cassian's influence after his death became
widespread in the West through his writings on the institution
and practice of monasticism and on the eight mortal sins.[1] Nor
must the great influence of Jerome be overlooked. He had
embraced the religious life before he was thirty, and from 385
to his death in 419 remained continuously in the convent that he
had founded at Bethlehem. While in Rome he had inspired with
his own religious zeal a group of cultured women who thereupon
vowed themselves to a life of virginity and renunciation of the
world. The passionate ardour of Jerome met with not a little
opposition in Rome. While he condemned in unequivocal
language the luxurious self-indulgence of the age, which was
nowise in keeping with the teaching of Christ or of His Church,
there were some who were rash enough, like Helvidius, Jovinian,
and Vigilantius, to take up their pens against him and the
asceticism that he preached. The treatises in which Jerome
replied to his several opponents, inasmuch as they defended
asceticism and glorified especially the life of virginity, served to
set his ideals more clearly before the world. But the violence of
the polemic passages, particularly in the treatises against Jovinian,
shocked some of Jerome's admirers, and the zeal of the saint
to some extent overshot the mark. Of more constructive value
for the cause which he had so deeply at heart was his Latin
version of the *Rules* of Pachomius. In this way a work of basic

[1] Cf. the admirable study by Owen Chadwick, *John Cassian*.

importance—it is the earliest of all monastic rules—became accessible to the Latin-speaking West.[1] It was perhaps inevitable that
a new institution and one, moreover, which grew with astonishing rapidity, should also attract unworthy persons and should be
marred by excesses. In the time of Benedict of Nursia and again
in that of Gregory I, there were many complaints of irregularities
and laxity in monastic houses. Nevertheless, not only was
monasticism in the West destined to a long life, but its devoted
followers performed a unique service for civilization during
centuries to come.

[1] On Jerome cf. the various essays in *A Monument to St Jerome* (London and
New York, 1952).

CHAPTER II

Pagan Education and the Christians

(a) Pagan Education and Letters

The Roman system of elementary and higher education, in spite of minor modifications, remained essentially unchanged for many centuries. In the first century of our era boys received their earliest grounding in the school of a *litterator*, who was commonly a slave or a freedman; but the children of the wealthy often learnt the elements from a tutor at home. The second stage of a boy's education began when, at the age of about twelve, he attended the classes of the *grammaticus*, both Greek and Latin. It is immaterial for our purpose whether instruction in both languages was given in the same or in two separate establishments. The curriculum consisted in studying Greek and Latin literature, mainly the poets, together with grammar, syntax, and some tuition in history, mythology, and elementary mathematics (arithmetic). The third step was the study of rhetoric. Two observations are necessary in connexion with the second and third stages of educational progress. Attendance at the schools of the *grammatici* and of the rhetoricians was confined to a minority, to the sons of parents who, in an economic sense, might be said to belong to the middle and upper classes. Again, although the threefold division is convenient, it is not wholly accurate because there does not seem always to have been a sharp separation between the work done with the *grammaticus* and the introductory lessons in rhetoric. Quintilian (*Inst. orat.*, ii, 1, 1–13) wished the spheres of the teacher of literature and of the *rhetor* to be kept strictly apart, but he writes as if in contemporary practice the separation was not always observed; and, although after his time there is far less evidence for the West, it is unlikely that conditions there differed greatly from those in the eastern

half of the Empire, where certainly there was much overlapping.[1]
The age at which boys began the study of rhetoric varied a good
deal, though the normal was probably fourteen to fifteen. The
study of prose writers, which formed the most advanced part of
the curriculum with the *grammaticus* together with some practice
in composition, prepared the way for the studies carried on with
the *rhetor*. With him a more intensive application to the prose
writers, and especially to the orators, would be a necessary
preparation for elaborate spoken and written exercises of different
types (*suasoriae* and *controversiae*). Philosophy, the sciences, and
jurisprudence were advanced subjects, commonly lying outside
the regular curriculum. The profoundest theorists on education,
like Cicero and Quintilian, might indeed maintain that the perfect
'orator' must not pass by any of the branches of human knowledge. But in practice philosophy and science were neglected in
the Latin-speaking portions of the Empire. The study of law,
on the other hand, was vocationally important for the sons of the
upper classes, who planned to make a career in the imperial civil
service. The third century, which otherwise was so unproductive
of new ideas, was the great age of classical Roman jurisprudence,
and during the later Empire the great centres for legal studies
were Rome in the West and Constantinople and Berytus in the
East. Greek rhetoric, which had special periods of florescence in
the second, and again in the fourth, century, maintained its
vitality to the age of Justinian. But Roman rhetoric declined
after A.D. 100. It produced no outstanding teachers like Quintilian and, in the sphere of public lectures and declamations, the
Latin *rhetores* could not hold their own against their Greek rivals.
Apuleius of Madaura in North Africa was, indeed, a solitary
figure in the second century. His prose is essentially an attempt
to reproduce in Latin the rhetorical displays of the Greek
Sophists. Like them he travelled to various cities, giving public
addresses and declamations. He is easily the most interesting
literary personage of the Antonine Age, but as a successful Latin
Sophist he remained an isolated figure.

The second century was not free from preciosity. In Roman
Republican days schoolboys were taught from the early poets of

[1] Cf. Peter Wolf, *Vom Schulwesen der Spätantike* (Baden-Baden, 1952), pp. 36 ff.

Rome, Livius Andronicus, Naevius, and Ennius. From the
Augustan Age on, authors like Horace and especially Virgil
replaced the early poets in the schoolroom. A little later Lucan's
Pharsalia shared a similar fate, while Statius in his lifetime
anticipated that his *Thebaid* would become a school-text. Similarly
the more recent ousted the older writers of prose, the popularity
of Cicero deservedly putting him in the first place. The pupils
doubtless found the change from archaic and in part uncouth
authors to those who were contemporary or nearly so an agreeable
experience. But in the second century there was a curious reaction
which affected Latin literature as well as school practice. This
was the cultivation of a wilful archaism. The Augustan and post-
Augustan poets, with the exception of Virgil whose position was
unassailable from the first, were set aside, and it became fashion-
able to take down from dusty shelves and to praise extravagantly
authors like Ennius, and the earliest writers of prose also came
into fashion again. When Hadrian's preference of Ennius and
Cato the Censor to Virgil and Cicero became known, admiring or
obsequious subjects could scarcely do less than copy the imperial
taste. But this archaistic craze was not merely found in court
circles, but radically affected the prose writers of the later second
century. Apuleius, Fronto, Aulus Gellius, all employ unusual,
sometimes strange-sounding, words, some of which were certainly taken over from the vernacular into the literary language,
while others must undoubtedly be regarded as archaizing revival.
In addition, the works of Fronto and Gellius abound with
citations from the early Latin authors. Edward Gibbon in a
classic passage composed a panegyric on the period of the
Antonines as the golden age of the Roman world, and this
estimate has often been repeated. But it was intellectually arid
and, as far as works composed in Latin are concerned, wellnigh
barren of creative literature. Men lived in the past and inspiration
was for the most part dead. Public taste as a whole was satisfied
with the showy but often vapid declamations of the Greek
Sophists. The intellectual decline which began in the age of the
Antonines continued in the following century, when social and
political conditions were far less favourable to literary production
than in the days of Antoninus and of Marcus Aurelius. Yet there

are certain tendencies and a number of works, which may be uninteresting and unoriginal in themselves, but cannot be disregarded by any student of early medieval thought and education.

We may begin with historical composition With the exception of Ammianus Marcellinus, who flourished in the second half of the fourth century, the Roman world produced no historical writer of the first rank after the death of Tacitus (c. 118). Historians who composed in Greek there continued to be, but even Cassius Dio (c. 220), who was the best of them, is hardly more than mediocre. But in the Latin-speaking world there was even less. Popular taste, too, found the standard histories of an earlier age too long. Abbreviations were demanded and a supply was soon forthcoming. Epitomes of Livy, like that compiled by Florus in the age of Hadrian, show that the demand for 'potted' history began early. Others followed Florus' example. Slightly more original minds put together brief historical summaries from several sources. Others, with their eyes on the schools of rhetoric, where such morsels could be successfully utilized to deck out declamations, enlivened dry chronological accounts by the addition of 'chatty' anecdotes, which sometimes were not even historical but fictitious. In this style, too, the example had already been set in the first century by Valerius Maximus (c. 30). There was thus a body of so-called historical works of various dates— Valerius, the Lives of Nepos, Florus, Eutropius (fourth century), Aurelius Victor (fourth century), and an anonymous adaptation of Victor made in the fifth century—which are important for our purpose; for it was these, and not the works of Livy or Tacitus, that, with rare exceptions, supplied the early Middle Ages with their information about Roman and pre-Christian history. It is the same with geography, ethnography, and kindred studies. The Natural History by Pliny the Elder may be an amorphous and unoriginal work; but it is a storehouse of facts. Yet the number of medieval scholars who knew Pliny at first hand was very small. Much more popular was the work of Solinus (third century). It was short and at the same time catered to popular taste because it contained many stories of fabulous men or beasts. The brief geography by Julius Honorius, of which several versions survive, did for that science what the epitomators did for history.

Grammar and the study of language had flourished in Alexandria during the Hellenistic Age, when the contemporary literature was undistinguished in comparison with what had been produced in the preceding centuries—Pindar, the Attic dramatists and orators, Herodotus, Thucydides, and Plato. So, too, during the later Roman Empire, when pagan literature was at its lowest ebb, a wealth of grammatical treatises and other school-books was put out. Many of these were transmitted to the Middle Ages and determined the character of much of the instruction given in the medieval schools. We cannot do more than indicate a few of the more noteworthy of these books. Amongst the commentators on classical authors the best were Porphyrio on Horace, Donatus on Terence, and, above all, Servius on Virgil. Of the treatise on Latin words (*De verborum significatu*) by Festus, who like the commentators flourished in the fourth century, only a small part has survived; for the rest we depend on an abbreviation made by Paul the Deacon four hundred years later. Festus' book is valuable chiefly because it was based on the work of the learned Verrius Flaccus, the contemporary of Augustus. From Festus much linguistic and antiquarian lore passed into early medieval glossaries, whence it found its way into the teaching and writings of monastic scholars. The *Compendiosa doctrina* of Nonius Marcellus (early fifth century) may be described as half grammar, half dictionary. It is badly arranged and not the work of a very intelligent man. But it was popular in some regions during the Middle Ages, just as it is of some importance to modern philologists because of the numerous quotations from lost authors that it contains. The writers on grammar and syntax were many, but it must suffice to name three. Marius Victorinus, who was born in North Africa in the early fourth century, was already well advanced in years when he migrated to Rome. There his success as a *rhetor* was phenomenal, and we are told that the enthusiastic Romans set up a statue to him in the forum of Trajan. He became a convert to Christianity and for that reason was obliged to abandon his profession in 362, when Julian prohibited Christians from teaching in the schools. His declining years Victorinus spent in composing polemical works against the Arians and other opponents of orthodox Trinitarian doctrine;

and he was also the first Latin writer to comment on the Pauline Epistles. Of this lengthy exposition only the sections on Galatians, Ephesians, and Philippians survive. Unlike the majority of *rhetores* at that date, Victorinus was interested in philosophy, translating the *Isagoge* of the Neoplatonist Porphyry and writing commentaries on certain works of Aristotle and Cicero. Finally, he was the author of an *Ars grammatica*, which only attained to a limited circulation in the Middle Ages, because it was quite outshone by the two treatises of Aelius Donatus, to whose commentary on Terence allusion has already been made. Donatus, who has the distinction of having St Jerome as a pupil, besides his success as a teacher in Rome, became famous as the author of two grammatical works. The *Ars minor* was an elementary grammar for schoolboys, which retained its popularity in the schools until the sixteenth century. The *Ars maior* was no less successful, but, being an advanced treatise on grammar, syntax, and the figures of speech, it was not copied in the Middle Ages as often as the elementary text. Although much later in date, the grammar of Priscian (sixth century) may conveniently be mentioned here; for, next to the two *artes* by Donatus, it became the most frequently consulted grammatical work of the medieval period. Its many Greek quotations, as will appear later, made it particularly valuable in those monastic centres where some interest in that language was revived at least for a time.

We turn to four works by pagan authors of the later Empire: The so-called *Disticha Catonis* seem to have been put together by a Latin *rhetor* before the end of the third century and are a collection of ethical maxims or precepts. The book was from the first intended for use in the schools, and the pupils were expected to memorize its contents. Few books have had a greater success. The moral teaching conveyed in hexameter couplets and couched in tersely idiomatic Latin was suitable for even the most austerely brought-up monastery pupils. Two versions of the *Disticha* survive, one in a Verona codex of the early ninth century, the other in numerous manuscripts of various dates. Very popular also was a poem of 205 lines, *Praecepta vivendi per singulos versus quae monosticha dicuntur*. It is not a version of the *Disticha*, but an independent poem composed by Alcuin in the late eighth century;

but it was inspired by the *Disticha* and contains many reminiscences of them.[1] An all but unique influence was exercised
through the Middle Ages by the treatise entitled *The nuptials of
Mercury and Philology*. Its author, Martianus Capella, seems to have
been an advocate by profession and to have composed the book
in his old age. Various dates have been suggested for its composition, the most probable being the first third of the fifth
century. It is divided into nine books and is in essence a treatise
on the seven liberal arts. But it was made more attractive to the
taste of the time by being cast into the form of a mythological
story and by being decked out with much allegory which strikes
the modern reader as exceedingly fantastic. The language is
highly ornate and full of sophistic conceits. Nevertheless the core
is sound, so that the student who has succeeded in disregarding
the meretricious adornments of the book and in mastering the
eccentricities of style and language, will find the embedded teaching,
especially in the sections on grammar, rhetoric, and dialectic, far
from contemptible. The men of the Middle Ages at least had this
experience; for, even if the form of the work also appealed to them
in a way which to us is surprising, they would not have assigned
to it a supremacy in the schools, if it had not had solid merits.

The allusion just made to the seven liberal arts requires a word
of comment. This scholastic canon, which historically can be
traced right back to the educational programme of Isocrates in
the fourth century B.C., embraced grammar, rhetoric, dialectic,
arithmetic, music, geometry, and astronomy. In this precise form
the canon first appears in Augustine although the so-called
Ambrosiaster a little earlier lists six out of the seven.[2] But four
centuries earlier Varro had grouped together and had elucidated
nine 'arts' or 'disciplines', namely, the seven given above together with medicine and architecture. Cicero uses the terms *artes*

---

[1] For the two versions of the *Disticha* see Marcus Boas, *Disticha Catonis*
(Amsterdam, 1952), which supersedes all earlier editions. For the *Monosticha* cf. M. Boas, *Alcuin und Cato* (Leyden, 1937).

[2] *PL*, 17, col. 55. This passage appears to have been generally overlooked: Sapientes autem illos dixit qui mundanis rationibus eruditi, sapientes
vocantur in saeculo; dum aut siderum speculatores sunt, aut mensuris aut
numeris aut arti grammaticae student, rhetoricae aut musicae. His omnibus
ostendit nihil haec prodesse nec vere sapientes esse nisi credant in Christum.

liberales and *liberalis disciplina,* but offers his readers no complete list in any one passage. A generation or two later Philo Judaeus reproduces in the form of a Biblical allegory the Stoic teaching that a study of the liberal arts must precede the study of philosophy:[1]

> Grammar teaches us to study literature in the poets and historians, and will thus produce intelligence and wealth of knowledge. * * * Music will charm away the unrhythmic, the inharmonious by its harmony. * * * Geometry will sow in the soul that loves to learn the seeds of equality and proportion, and by the charm of its logical continuity will raise from those seeds a zeal for justice. Rhetoric sharpening the mind to the observation of facts, and training and welding thought to expression, will make the man a true master of words and thoughts. * * * Dialectic, the sister and twin, as some have said, of Rhetoric, distinguishes true argument from false and convicts the plausibilities of sophistry.

Other writers, for example Vitruvius and Galen, drew up lists differing somewhat from Varro's, but it was not till late in the fourth century that the canonical number was fixed as well as the separate subjects. Established firmly by Martianus and approved by notable successors—especially Cassiodorus and Isidore—the grouping of subjects which were believed to ensure a liberal education was transmitted to the Middle Ages. In time it became customary to distinguish the first three from the later four, and to regard the first group as preparatory to the second. The *trivium* was equivalent to the more elementary curriculum taught to all who came to school, while the *quadrivium* comprised the more advanced subjects which would be attempted only by the more apt pupils. Two reservations must be made: though Boethius employs the term *quadruvium* (corrupted later into *quadrivium*), *trivium* does not appear to be older than the age of Charlemagne. In the second place, the educational curriculum laid down in the *trivium*, to be followed by the *quadrivium*, seems to have remained largely theoretical. In actual practice, at least in the earlier Middle Ages, the teaching given in most monastic schools was far more restricted.[2]

[1] *On Mating with the Preliminary Studies,* 4, 15 ff. (IV, p. 464, in the Loeb Library edition of Philo).

[2] See Charles W. Jones, *Saints' Lives and Chronicles in Early England* (Ithaca, N.Y., 1947), pp. 200–1.

Two other authors of the later imperial age must be mentioned. Next to nothing is known about Fulgentius, unless the unlikely identification of him with Fulgentius, bishop of Ruspe, be accepted. None of the four short 'pagan' works that have survived have any great intrinsic value. They are the *Mitologiae* in three books, the *Expositio sermonum antiquorum*, the *Expositio Virgilianae continentiae*, and the *De aetatibus mundi et hominis*. All are distinguished by their fantastic vocabulary and tortured periods, and all make extensive use of allegory, but Fulgentius was a popular writer in the eighth and ninth centuries.[1] Macrobius is an author of much higher rank. His chief work, entitled *Saturnalia*, is composed in the form of a dialogue and divided into seven books, of which substantial portions are now lost. Many subjects are discussed, antiquarian and religious topics, social customs, and literature, no less than four books (3 to 6 inclusive) being devoted to the poet Virgil. The value of the *Saturnalia* to the better scholars of the Middle Ages, who used it as the inferior ones did not, lay in the multiplicity of the subjects discussed and of the information offered. The fact that most of what the books contained was taken over by Macrobius from a relatively small number of earlier authors gave them additional authority, and it is also the main reason why they still retain their interest. Macrobius also wrote a commentary on a Ciceronian work, the *Dream of Scipio*, which was originally a digression in the sixth book of the treatise *On the Commonwealth*, but early came into circulation as a separate essay. Macrobius' elucidations are chiefly valuable because he had studied the Neoplatonist philosophy in some detail and reproduces many of its doctrines. It has, however, been shown that, though he had some familiarity with the early Neoplatonists, he relied heavily on the later exponents of this philosophy.[2]

[1] All four works have been edited by R. Helm (Teubner). On the great popularity of Fulgentius in the Carolingian Age see Laistner in *Mélanges Hrouchevsky* (Ukrainian Academy of Sciences; Kiev, 1928), pp. 445ff. But my attribution of the *Super Thebaiden* to Fulgentius has been disproved by Bernhard Bischoff in *Byzantinische Zeitschrift*, 44 (1951), p. 51, n. 3.

[2] See the valuable summary of Macrobius' literary and philosophical sources in P. Courcelle, *Les lettres grecques en occident* (ed. 2; Paris, 1948), Chapter 1.

Africa, Gaul, and Spain, as they became romanized, took over the Roman practice of education. No town of any size was without its *grammatici*, and teachers of rhetoric, at least for a time, were almost as ubiquitous. This did not mean that the tuition was everywhere equally good. Thus, in the fourth century, Augustine, who began his schooling in his native Tagaste, was soon sent to Madaura, and finally to Carthage. Again, Ausonius bears testimony to the existence of schools at Autun, Lyons, Toulouse, Narbonne, Poitiers, and other towns in Gaul; but they were surpassed as cultural and educational centres by Trèves and Bordeaux. The decline of Greek in that century and the next throughout the Western Empire was also very noticeable. Augustine relates that he was forced with many pains and penalties to learn the rudiments of Greek at school. But he did not continue his study of that language and so never mastered it completely, although his later writings show that after many years he again took up Greek so that he might read Greek theological works in the original.[1] Jerome, educated mainly in Rome, did not acquire the second language until he went to the East. When a rescript addressed in 376 by Gratian to the prefect of Gaul authorized the appointment of a Greek rhetorician in Trèves, with the proviso, 'if any person worthy (of the post) can be found', it implied a difficulty in finding a suitable man, and indirectly shows us that the supply must have been small.[2] Several authors of the period, notably Ausonius, allude, it is true, not infrequently to Greek as a school subject and to teachers of it. Some of these had gone far afield in the course of their careers. Thus, Minervius and Arborius, besides scholastic experience in Rome and in Spain respectively, had both practised their profession in Constantinople. But it must be remembered that at Bordeaux, and also in the chief cities of the old province of Gallia Narbonensis, whose prosperity depended largely on maritime trade, not a little of which was with the Greek-speaking half of the Empire, the language survived longest, in some instances

---

[1] Augustine's knowledge of Greek has been the subject of much recent controversy. Cf. H. I. Marrou, *Saint Augustin et la fin de la culture antique* (ed. 2; Paris, 1949), pp. 27–46 and 631–7.

[2] *Codex Theodosianus* (edd. Mommsen and Krüger), XIII, 3, 11.

well into the sixth century. But it was not fostered in the monasteries of Gaul, since even the more scholarly inmates were satisfied if they could interpret such nouns, proper names, and short phrases as occurred in the Latin versions of the Bible or in the liturgy. And, to refer once more to Ausonius, although he appears to have been a good Greek scholar himself, his habit of introducing Greek tags into his poems, pedantic in itself, becomes ludicrous in those where he appends a Latin version for the benefit of his readers.[1] At any rate, he does not expect the majority of his readers to understand his incursions into the tongue of Homer and Menander.

We may conclude with the observation that the only two pagan Latin poets of the later Empire who wrote some verse of enduring merit, Ausonius and Claudian, seem to have enjoyed little vogue in the earlier part of the Middle Ages.

(b) The Christian Attitude to Pagan Learning[2]

The attitude of Christian thinkers to pagan education and literature, which brought in its train the problem how best to instruct the children of Christians, is a question of some complexity. The development of Latin Christian writings was slow, for until the beginning of the third century the literature of the Faithful was in Greek. Thus it is hardly surprising that nothing is heard at this time, or indeed much later, of separate Christian schools. Clearly provision must have been made from the first for religious instruction to converts. A considerable body of catechetical literature, both Greek and Latin, has survived but no part of it antedates the third century. Still, one can assume that some of the general principles laid down in these writings, based as they were on the precepts of the Bible, had been applied long before. It was the general custom to delay baptism until

[1] See, for example, the ten poems which make up the thirteenth book of his verse, entitled Ludus.

[2] The general topic of this section has been discussed by the writer in Christianity and Pagan Culture in the Later Roman Empire (Ithaca, N.Y., 1951), pp. 49–73, and in Liber Floridus: Festschrift Paul Lehmann (Eosverlag, St Ottilien, 1950), pp. 47–61. For Augustine see the book by Marrou cited above, and for Jerome the excellent essay by E. A. Quain in A Monument to St Jerome, pp. 201–32.

well on in adult life. Only after he had been baptized did the convert become a full member of the Christian community and a partaker of the Eucharist. The probationary period for catechumens lasted for several years, although there was some variation in different localities. Ultimately the catechumens were divided into an upper and a lower grade. Those of the upper group who had signified their wish to be baptized were then given intensive instruction in the chief articles of the Christian faith during the Lenten period, preparatory to their baptism at Easter. Such training was a thing apart and quite distinct from secular education at whatever level. When Christianity early in the fourth century became 'a lawful religion', there would indeed have been no danger or illegality in the establishment of specifically Christian schools; but there were nevertheless in practice very real difficulties to overcome, especially in the western half of the Empire. Although the Latin Church by then could boast of Tertullian, Cyprian, Victorinus of Pettau, Arnobius, and Lactantius, their writings were not suitable as school-books. There were no treatises on grammar, rhetoric, or any of the liberal arts save those by pagan authors; and, while there was no danger to orthodoxy in declensions, conjugations, and, in short, the rules of idiomatic language and composition, the illustrations from literature which were sown broadcast through the more popular text-books of grammar and rhetoric were from infidel prose writers and poets. At every turn the Christian boy or youth was familiarized with pagan mythology, and with aspects of pagan literature and thought which the leaders of the Church were bound to disapprove. Thus there existed a dilemma from which there was no escape for those who were willing to seek a compromise.

The extreme attitude in the earlier period is well exemplified by Tertullian who fiercely attacked pagan letters. His famous aphorism, 'the philosophers are the patriarchs of the heretics', illustrates the danger to which, in his view, well-to-do Christians were exposed if they were subjected to the higher education of the day. He would have liked, too, to forbid Christians to teach the literature of the heathen; yet he was bound to advise sending children to school. This could only mean handing them over to the *litterator* or *grammaticus*, in other words, giving them the same education as their pagan contemporaries. How far the safeguard which he advocates, that the young should first have received some religious instruction at home, was effective, it would be rash to surmise. And in at least one passage Tertullian admits that the study of philosophy might have some value and that ignorance can be more dangerous than knowledge. The Greek Fathers of the third and fourth centuries were more lenient. A catechetical school in Alexandria, whose beginnings go back to *c.* A.D. 180, under Clement and particularly under Origen seems to have developed into a school of higher Christian education and continued to function in some fashion at least till the time of Eusebius (*c.* 324). Origen, after his departure from Alexandria, resided some twenty years in Caesarea and there continued his teaching with great success. Methodius' treatise, *The Banquet: On Chastity* (*c.* 280?), in language and style is modelled on Plato's *Symposium*. In the fourth century John Chrysostom, whether or not he was the pupil of Libanius, Basil the Great, and Gregory of Nazianzus, all sanctioned contemporary higher education as a preparation for the Christian teacher and theologian. Of the three, Chrysostom is perhaps the most critical in his attitude to pagan letters, although the classical purity of his style bears witness to the thoroughness of his own early training. Basil is the author of a short address to young men, in which he expounds to them the advantages to be derived from the perusal of pagan literature and the lives of virtuous pagans in the past. Gregory, who like Basil had been educated in the Sophists' lecture-halls of Constantinople and Athens, has perhaps the most humanistic outlook of all the Greek Fathers. His namesake, Gregory of Nyssa, the younger brother of Basil, shows in his writings the profound influence exerted on his thought by Philo Judaeus and the Neoplatonists.

In the West it was only with the spread of monasticism that a more general movement towards substituting for the traditional a more specifically Christian education began. The primary aim of monastic schools was to train those who chose to become monks, and amongst these would be the oblate children dedicated at an early age by their parents to a religious life. But it must not be forgotten that many of the leaders of the Church were, at least in part, alumni of monastic centres. Especially in Gaul during the fifth and early sixth centuries we find a whole series of eminent Churchmen—John Cassian, Hilary of Arles, Faustus of Riez, Lupus of Troyes, Eucherius, Caesarius—who had passed some of their early years in St Victor at Marseilles or at Lérins. Amongst the children educated in the monasteries there were always some who were destined for secular life. In the practice followed by many bishops of gathering round them young students to be trained for orders may be found the germ from which grew the cathedral schools of later date. But it is clear, both from their own writings and from what their biographers relate of them, that the distinguished bishops just named had also bene-fited by the study of pagan rhetoric. Their attitude subsequently was far from uniform, and one may note the extreme of tolerance and even approval of the liberal arts on the one hand and un-compromising condemnation on the other, as well as a position intermediate between the two. We shall have occasion to observe this contrast more in detail in sixth-century Gaul and Italy.

Both Jerome and Augustine had pondered more deeply on educational theory and practice, and on the place of non-Christian literature in a scheme of Christian education. Both men had enjoyed the best secular education available in their day, Jerome in Rome, Augustine at Madaura and in Carthage, whose schools were reputed amongst the best in the Empire. Both again were experienced teachers. Jerome during his second stay in Rome (382–5) was the admired tutor of a number of women in high station, who at his behest devoted themselves to a life of virginity and under his guidance studied the Scriptures and the languages in which they were written. In his monastery at Bethlehem, from 386 to his death in 419, in addition to his unceasing labours as a commentator, translator, and theological controversialist, he instructed the inmates of the monastery in both religious and secular subjects. Much can be gleaned from his abundant corre-spondence about his methods as a teacher and expositor, and much from his writings as a whole concerning his attitude to pagan authors. After he had left the West for good he still corresponded with his female disciples on learned subjects; and, if these were more commonly questions of Biblical interpretation, they were not exclusively so. In one and the same letter (33) he discusses the writings of Origen and of Varro, the two most learned men produced respectively by the Christian East and Pagan Rome. Twice, in a letter to Laeta (107) and again in one to Gaudentius (128), he describes with much elaboration the best method of educating Christian virgins, starting with the elementary instruction of early childhood; and he begins his remarks by repeating some of the precepts of Quintilian. Besides their historic importance, since they were long used in some nunneries during the Middle Ages as a guide in the training of novices, these two epistles contain educational principles and betray an understanding of child psychology which seem to stamp Jerome a man far in advance of his age. His predilection in youth for Cicero, Virgil, and other Roman authors, and his famous dream in *Epistle* 22 when he first entered on a life of extreme asceticism, are well known. What is sometimes forgotten is that his renunciation of the classics was never complete and that, as he grew older, his attitude again became more tolerant. Quotations from pagan authors are found in his letters at all periods of his life. Writing in 397 to the Roman *rhetor*, Magnus (70), he defends the practice of citing non-Christian authors and points out that with few exceptions—Epicurus is one—Christians can learn something from their perusal. The beautiful letter of condolence addressed to Heliodorus in the previous year contains (60) noteworthy allusions to Jerome's earlier studies in secular literature, while that written to Domnio (50) is full of biting contempt for an illiterate monk who had found fault with Jerome's writings. In a letter to Paulinus of Nola (53) he outlines a system of Christian hermeneutics, and it is implicit in his argument that to interpret the Bible correctly the expositor must previously have had a thorough education similar to Jerome's own. Even in those of his Biblical commentaries which he composed in old age citations from Virgil, Plautus, and Horace are by no means rare. In general one may stress, first, that Jerome himself was so steeped in the classics that quoting them became second nature to him, while his own fluent style plainly demonstrates his familiarity with them. Secondly, his was essentially a scholar's nature, so that, even during that part of his life when his views were most austere, his strictures were qualified, not absolute. At the worst a study of pagan authors and the pagan education were a means to an end.

[Paul] had read in Deuteronomy (xxi, 10–13) the command given by the voice of the Lord that when a captive woman had had her head shaved, her eyebrows and all her hair cut off, and her nails pared, she might then be taken to wife. Is it surprising that I too, admiring the fairness of her form and the grace of her eloquence, desire to make that secular wisdom, which is my captive and my handmaid, a matron of the true Israel? Or that shaving off and cutting away all in her that is dead, whether this be idolatry, pleasure, error, or lust, I take her to myself clean and pure and beget by her servants for the Lord of Sabaoth? (*Epist.*, 70, 2.)

But during the greater part of Jerome's life the humanist maintained a not unequal contest with the theologian.

Augustine, like Jerome, had passed with distinction through the schools of the *grammaticus* and *rhetor*; but unlike his older contemporary, he was himself for a decade a teacher of rhetoric in Africa, in Rome, and finally in Milan. From several of his works it is possible to ascertain with some distinctness his earlier and his later views on the education of a Christian. He himself has recorded the profound impression left upon his youthful mind—he was nineteen years old at the time—by the study of Cicero's *Hortensius*. The purpose of this treatise, which has not survived, was to serve as an introduction to the study of philosophy (and, more particularly, to Cicero's own works in this field), and at the same time to combat prevailing misconceptions about the value of philosophical speculations. The effect of its perusal on the young Augustine was far-reaching. It was an antidote to the one-sided rhetorical training which had hitherto fallen to his lot. It started that deep admiration for Cicero which remained with him to the end of his life. It gave a new direction to his intellectual activity by leading him to some interest in science and to a study of philosophy, particularly Neoplatonism. The steadily deepening understanding which came to him from constant application to these subjects ultimately caused him to reject the Manichaean heresy to which he had adhered for a few years. The treatise, *De ordine*, composed in 386 at Cassiciacum near Milan, a retreat to which he had withdrawn with a few friends after his conversion to the orthodox Faith, is a dialogue having as its theme the order existing in the Universe, and the position and significance of evil therein. The existence of order and method throughout the Universe is illustrated incidentally from divers human examples, amongst others from the liberal arts. As one would expect from a Ciceronian and an ex-teacher, his attitude is liberal and even enthusiastic:[1]

> Seeing that all those liberal arts, [he observes,] are learnt partly for the conduct of life, partly for the understanding and contemplation of the Universe, the attainment of their (proper) use is extremely difficult save for one who, being endowed with the best natural gifts, has from earliest youth devoted himself to them with the greatest application and unswerving assiduity.

In 387, when his opinions on education were still the same, he conceived the plan and began the execution of an encyclopedia of the liberal arts (disciplinarum libri). But only a small portion of the whole was ever completed; for more vital matters engaged his attention after his return to Africa in the same year. When he again turned his thoughts to educational questions, both his point of view and his purpose had deepened. The book, De catechizandis rudibus (c. 400), although it deals with a specialized type of instruction, the preparation of catechumens, contains profound reflections applicable to any kind of teaching. To deal with each convert individually, since neither the disposition nor the mental capacity nor the previous education of any two persons are precisely alike, in actual teaching to limit the subject and to teach a little thoroughly, and so to order the material handled that, even while some parts are dealt with fully, others more cursorily, the whole forms a unity in which the leading principles are never lost to view—these are counsels of perfection to which modern educators and teachers pay repeated lip-service (some would call them trite maxims), yet none but a few have ever attained in practice.

But Augustine's most elaborate contribution to educational theory is the long treatise, De doctrina Christiana. It was composed at different times, for Books I, II, and part of III belong to the year 397, whereas the remainder of III and the whole of IV were

[1] De ordine (CSEL, 63), II, 44.

not completed until 426. Although by that time the earlier portions were already known, the author then brought out a revised redaction of the entire work, and it is this that has survived in the extant manuscripts. Augustine's two main theses are how best to interpret Holy Writ (Hermeneutics) and how to impart it to Christian men (Homiletics). But in the end he went far beyond this, so that there was incorporated in the complete treatise a reasoned course of study for the training of the Christian priest and preacher. Our concern, however, is only with Augustine's attitude to pagan letters. It had been greatly modified since the days of Cassiciacum. In his *Retractations*, written in 427, three years before his death, he subjects his early works to severe criticism. He refers thus to the *De ordine*:

> At the same time, in fact amongst the books written about the Academics, I also wrote two books, *De ordine*, in which an important question is discussed, namely whether the order of divine Providence embraces all good and evil. Yet, when I saw that this topic which is difficult to grasp could only be transmitted very inadequately by disputation to the understanding of my friends, I preferred to speak about the order of studying, seeing that it is possible to advance from corporeal to incorporeal things. Now in these books I disapprove both of my frequent use of the word 'fortune' and of my omission of the word 'body' when I refer to bodily senses; further (I disapprove) of the emphasis that I laid on the liberal arts, of which many saints are greatly ignorant, whilst some who are familiar with them are not saints; and of my mentioning the Muses as goddesses of a kind, even though it was in jest; and of having called wonder (*admirationem*) a fault, and of asserting that philosophers who were not endowed with true piety shone with the light of virtue.[1]

There are many passages in the *De doctrina Christiana* which show Augustine striving for some mean between practical necessity and orthodoxy. He deserves all credit for being the first to write a comprehensive guide for the education of the Christian teacher; a book, moreover, which became a standard work in the Middle Ages. At the same time those parts which deal with the liberal arts, in which the standard of attainment regarded as needful is still elementary, reflect the low level to which the intellectual life of the later Empire had declined. One

[1] *Retract.* (*CSEL*, 36), I, 3.

may also wonder whether, if he had completed his encyclopedia of the liberal arts, the treatment of each subject and the standard aimed at would have been more exacting; and whether such a work would have been able to displace the older pagan treatises in the monasteries and Christian schools of the earlier Middle Ages. In Books II and III Augustine is fain to admit the need of the liberal arts but, like other Christian thinkers before him, he urges that their study should cease as early as possible; and science —he is thinking particularly of astronomy—is dangerous because it may lead the student to belief in astrology which was so prevalent during the later Empire.[1] In Book IV, written a year before the *Retractations*, he tries to prove that there is no necessity for profane literature in training the Christian preacher or orator, because the Scriptures provide all necessary material for illustration. Several observations may here be made. Augustine admits that the Christian preacher to maintain his thesis must make use of rhetoric; yet he would restrict its study to the years of adolescence, and he propounds views which could never hold good save in special cases. 'Men of quick intellect,' he remarks, 'and glowing temperament find it easier to become eloquent by reading and listening to eloquent speakers than by following rules of eloquence.'[2] Again, he cites from St Paul, Ambrose, and Cyprian to illustrate the oratorical mastery attained by great Christian teachers. Yet Jerome had justified his own use of pagan quotations by instancing the similar practice of St Paul. Ambrose, intended at first for a career in the imperial service, had passed through the usual curriculum in pagan schools and his philosophical studies, as has recently been shown, extended to the *Enneads* of Plotinus himself.[3] Cyprian, like Augustine, in his early manhood had taught rhetoric. Finally, what did Augustine himself do in composing Book IV of the *De doctrina Christiana*? He adapted Cicero's *Orator* to Christian needs, even as the first Latin treatise on Christian ethics, Ambrose's *De officiis*, was modelled on Cicero's dialogue of the same name. Augustine took

---

[1] Cf. Laistner in *Harvard Theol. Rev.*, 34 (1941), pp. 251–75.

[2] *De doctr. Christ.*, IV, 3.

[3] See P. Courcelle in *Revue philologique*, 24 (1950), pp. 29–56, and *Recherches sur les confessions de Saint Augustin* (Paris, 1950), pp. 106 ff.

his illustrations from Christian authors, but the framework of the whole is closely modelled on the *Orator*. Thus the love and admiration for Rome's greatest orator was never quenched in Augustine's heart. And the noble and impressive chapters which conclude the *De doctrina Christiana* (IV, 28 and 29) are the utterance not of a narrow doctrinaire but of a man who can recognize and welcome truth wheresoever he may find it.

CHAPTER III

Christian Literature during the Fourth
and Fifth Centuries

Secular Latin literature was at a very low ebb in the fourth and fifth centuries. What was produced was, with scarcely an exception, lacking in originality. Tired minds were content to copy or abbreviate the works of a mentally more vigorous age. Indeed one may agree with the caustic verdict passed by a recent critic on pagan literature after Fronto. 'Quand', he remarks, 'ils ne sont plus soutenus par les faits qu'ils racontent, ils n'ont rien ou presque rien à dire.'[1] It was far different with the Christian writers. Indebted only for their technique to pagan teaching, they were filled with new ideals that fructified their spoken and written words. A Church recently freed from bondage, but at first still weaker numerically than its opponents, was fortunate in having amongst her spokesmen for decades to come a succession of the most original and able minds; unfortunate, however, in seeing her unity constantly threatened and sometimes broken by the embittered dissensions of her members. The writings of the Christians during those two centuries were almost wholly in the service of religion. Paganism in its various forms and heresy were the two enemies against which the champions of orthodoxy were pitted. But there was this difference: whereas the adherents of the older religions and the devotees of philosophy were fighting a losing battle from the first, there were among the Christian heresiarchs men as able as amongst the orthodox, which led them more than once to a temporary triumph over their adversaries. The nobility of Julian's life and character must not blind us to the fact that towards the end of his life he rivalled his extremest opponents in fanaticism, and that his writings produced

[1] P. de Labriolle, *Histoire de la littérature latine chrétienne* (ed. 3, 1947), p. 15.

no permanent effect. But Arius or Donatus and their followers, Pelagius, or Nestorius caused schisms in the Church which endured for many years, or, in one instance, Nestorianism, permanently. The bulk of the prose literature can be broadly classified under one of four headings—dogmatic treatises, including most of the controversial literature, exegetical and hermeneutical writings, homiletics and pastoral dissertations, and apologetics. Besides these there are some historical works and some important collections of letters. The division cannot, however, be kept too rigidly, since a particular book may have a composite character. Augustine's greatest work is the supreme example of Christian apologetics; it is also not a little polemical in character. Or again, some of the exegetical works of Jerome contain controversial matter, because Christian scholars were sharply divided on the question of Biblical interpretation.

The elucidation of dogma might be regarded *per se* as a necessary task undertaken by the leaders of the Church to instruct the Faithful. Actually the abundant dogmatic literature produced both in the East and in the West was to a great extent the outcome of doctrinal disputes between prominent Churchmen themselves, which took on a more serious complexion when the rank and file of Christian men took sides with either party. Of the various heresies prevalent in the fourth and fifth centuries which called forth a great mass of writings, partly intended to define dogma, partly to confound opponents, some affected the eastern and the western halves of the Empire alike, some were confined to one or the other, or even to a single country only. We are here concerned solely with those heresies which took a firm hold in the West and thereby led to a Latin Christian literature on the subject. The Trinitarian controversy deserves first place. The orthodox definition of the three Persons had first been clearly formulated in 325 at the Council of Nicaea. Its purpose was to crush once and for always the false teaching of Arius, who had defined the Second Person of the Trinity as having been created by the Father and therefore not of the same nature with Him. Arianism, however, had a long life. It won many adherents in the East because Constantine's successor, Constantius, accepted its teaching; while for the future it was assured a long life, particularly in the West, because the Germanic neighbours of the Empire, when they abandoned heathendom, were converted to the Arian form of Christianity. But the Christological controversies concerning the single or double nature of Christ, which from the end of the fourth century agitated clergy and laity alike in the East, had only slight repercussions in the West, where they produced no more than an isolated treatise here and there. Of all the defenders of orthodoxy against Arianism in the West the most remarkable was Hilary (c. 315–67). He had already been bishop of Poitiers for some years, when the condemnation of Athanasius and his defence of the Nicene confession by the Synod of Milan in 355 was followed by the attempt of the metropolitan bishop of Arles, Saturninus, and of others, to establish the Arian creed in Gaul. Hilary led the opposition with such vigour and effect that he was banished by the emperor in 356 and was not allowed to return home till 361. These six years were exceedingly valuable to his development, since he became acquainted with many leading Churchmen and theologians as well as with Greek theological literature, and thus obtained a deeper insight into the doctrinal question that was disturbing all Christendom to its depths. On returning to Gaul he was received with widespread acclamation and laboured so successfully, until his comparatively early death, to root out Arianism there that half a century later a chronicler could write: 'it is a fact universally agreed that thanks to the good work of Hilary alone our country of Gaul was freed from the defilement of heresy'.[1] Hilary's masterpiece, which was the direct outcome of the dogmatic questions to solve which he devoted his life, was the treatise in twelve books, De Trinitate. The oldest surviving manuscript of it is a venerable codex copied c. 500 and contains in all probability, marginal notes in the hand of Fulgentius of Ruspe.[2] Nearly half of the treatise (Books 4 to 7 and 9) is controversial in the sense that this part aims specifically at countering and destroying the arguments of his Arian opponents. The rest is devoted to a constructive justification of orthodox belief. Thus he treats of the mystery of the divine birth

---

[1] Sulpicius Severus, Chron., II, 45, 7.

[2] For MS. Basilicanus, D 182, see CLA, I, 1a–c, and A. Wilmart in Studies in honor of E. K. Rand (New York, 1938), pp. 293–305.

of the Son (Book 2); he sets out to show that the divinity of the Son does not contradict the unity of the Godhead (Book 8); and he strives to bring certain passages in the New Testament, which seem to imply the subordination of the Second to the First Person of the Trinity, into harmony with the belief in the divinity of Christ (Books 10 and 11). A kind of appendix to this work was an open letter to the bishops of Gaul, Britain, and the Rhine provinces, entitled *De synodis seu de fide orientalium*, in which Hilary explains for the benefit of his readers the general course of the Trinitarian disputes in the East, giving translations of half a dozen confessions promulgated between 341 and 358. The writings of the Arians in defence of their position have mostly perished, and doubtless did so at an early date, owing to the ultimate triumph of orthodoxy. Amongst those who, besides Hilary, published attacks against them or defences of the Catholic claims were the extremist Lucifer of Calaris, who ended by becoming a schismatic himself, Ambrose in his treatise, *De fide*, written at the invitation of and dedicated to Gratian, Marius Victorinus who composed a number of anti-Arian or Trinitarian tracts, only three of which have survived, and Augustine. In addition to penning two shorter controversial pamphlets against the Arians, Augustine was engaged off and on for many years on his *De Trinitate*. This long work, divided into fifteen books, was the profoundest study yet made in the West of the central mystery of the Christian faith. It was at once accepted as authoritative and its influence through the Middle Ages can be gauged not only from quotations in medieval authors but particularly from the very great number of extant manuscripts.[1] But the bulk of Augustine's controversial writings was evoked by the Donatist schism, by the Manichaean religion which in the western half of the Empire won adherents chiefly in Africa, and by Pelagianism.

If the immediate cause of the formation of the Donatist Church in North Africa was the result of a bitter dispute concerning Church organization, it must be remembered that personal issues and doctrinal questions complicated the controversy and made possible the permanent separation of the Donatists from the Catholic Church. Furthermore, it is most probable that, in the

[1] Cf. A. Wilmart in *Miscellanea Agostiniana* (Rome, 1931), pp. 257–315.

last analysis, economic and racial differences, even if at first obscured, contributed greatly to the growth and persistence of the Donatist schism.[1] In 307 the see of Carthage, which had been vacant for nearly a year, was filled by the appointment of the first deacon, Caecilianus. The bishop, Felix of Aptunga, who consecrated him was, however, believed by many to have betrayed his Faith and the Church by handing over Christian writings and Church property to the imperial authorities during the recent Diocletianic persecution. This circumstance was utilized by the opponents of Caecilianus, and a synod of seventy bishops found Felix unworthy of the episcopal office, at the same time declaring his consecration of Caecilianus null and void. They then proceeded to elect a certain Majorinus as bishop of Carthage. But Caecilianus had many supporters who were not prepared to see him thus cavalierly set aside. The decision of a Roman synod in his favour in 313, and the subsequent efforts of Constantine in the same sense, only intensified the bitterness. Africa was distracted by civil war in which the whole population took sides for one or other of the episcopal claimants. All the horrors of religious persecution were re-enacted amongst two groups of citizens who had but lately suffered in common at the hands of a pagan emperor. The further history of the Donatist sect, which derived its name from Donatus, the successor of Majorinus, lies outside our subject, but the abundant literature that was evoked by the dispute merits a brief notice. As usual, it is mainly the orthodox writings which have survived, while those of the Donatists have mostly perished.

Among the earlier Latin Fathers none was more universally revered, above all in his native Africa, than the martyred Cyprian (c. 200–58). The extreme rigour of his orthodoxy, however, had brought him shortly before his death into conflict with the bishop of Rome. It is generally supposed that the death of both men and the diversion caused by the Valerian persecution, whose victim Cyprian had become, averted a schism in the African Church at

[1] See now the valuable monograph, *The Donatist Church* by W. H. C. Frend (Oxford, 1952). The Donatists were strongest in the rural areas, particularly of southern Numidia, the orthodox Catholics being primarily in the towns. Thus there is much to be said for the view that it was a conflict between Latin and native Libyan (i.e. Berber) civilization.

that time. The question at issue between the two bishops was the necessity of second baptism. Cyprian, true to his rigid interpretation of what was meant by the Church universal, required all persons, who had been baptized as members of a Christian sect and subsequently had returned to the orthodox communion, to undergo the sacrament of baptism a second time. His view, it may be added, coincided with that of his older fellow-countryman, Tertullian. Stephen, the bishop of Rome, following the traditional and more liberal view, had ruled that any baptism performed in the name of the three Persons of the Trinity was valid, and rebaptism neither necessary nor permissible. This anabaptist doctrine was taken over by the Donatists and applied by them to all outside their communion. Only the pure could be members of the true Church of Christ; they only could bestow the rite of baptism on the impure. And who was more unclean than the betrayers (*traditores*), as the Donatists charitably called the adherents of the Catholic Church in Africa? The same principle was applied to other sacraments, which were only efficacious if he who administered them was a member of the true (*i.e.* the Donatist) Church. Thus questions of doctrine were introduced into a controversy which began over a matter of Church organization, that in itself was called forth by personal antipathies and rivalries. Of those who waged war with the pen rather than with the sword and the stave it will suffice to name two Donatists and two of their opponents. The writings of Parmenianus, the successor of Donatus, are lost, but they can be partly reconstructed from the reply of the orthodox Optatus, bishop of Mileve in Numidia. Optatus' treatise in six books, to which a seventh was added when the work appeared in revised form, deals with historical material in so far as it traces the history of the Donatist schism (Book 1), vindicates the Catholic party from the charge of being responsible for the measures taken against the Donatists by the imperial authorities (Book 3), and enumerates the destruction of Catholic property wrought by their adversaries (Book 6). The remaining books are a reply to the various accusations and claims of the Donatists, the whole of Book 5 being devoted to the baptismal question and to the rebuttal of the Donatist interpretation of sacramental acts and their operation.

The contemporary of these two men, Tyconius, though a Donatist, was expelled from their communion by Parmenianus. Basing
his opposition on a detailed interpretation of the Scriptures, he
refused to approve the intolerant claims of his co-religionists to be
the only true Church. It is, however, on his work in hermeneutics
that Tyconius' reputation subsequently rested. This will be more
fully explained below. Augustine between 393 and 420 published
no less than twelve different treatises against the Donatists. Again
the works of his later opponents are lost, but they can be reconstructed to some extent from his quotations. Nothing proves
more clearly how deep-seated and incurable the rupture was in
his day than the amount of time and labour that the bishop of
Hippo found it needful to expend on his anti-Donatist essays.
As far as the root problems are concerned, he envisaged them as
two, when, in the most brilliant of these tractates, he addressed
his opponents with the words: 'we charge you with two errors;
first that you are wrong on the question of baptism, and, second,
that you set yourselves apart from those who hold the true view
of this matter'.[1]

Manichaeanism need not detain us long. In the Greek-speaking
East it had won many adherents and for a time its success in North
Africa was far from negligible. In the western provinces it had
less appeal and its direct influence seems to have been slight. Yet
Priscillianism, which was localized in Spain and southern Gaul,
had features derived from it; and it is noteworthy that, as late as
the sixth century, Caesarius of Arles warned his congregation
against the Manichaeans' rejection of the Old Testament, while
in the canons of the first Council of Braga (561) the Manichaean
and the Priscillianist heresies are regularly named and condemned
together. The religion founded by the Persian, Manes, was
essentially an attempt to combine the dualism of the Persian
religion and its two coeternal powers of Light or Good (Ahura
Mazda) and Darkness or Evil (Ahriman) with certain parts of the
Christian teaching. But the Manichaeans rejected the Old Testament as irreconcilable with the New, and went so far as to regard
the Old Testament as the work of the power of Darkness. If it
be added that to them Jesus during his earthly life was a mere

[1] *Contra Cresconium grammaticum* (CSEL, 52), 3, 3.

phantasm, while Manes was the Messiah foretold by Him, it becomes clear that the Manichaean scarcely deserves the name of a Christian sect at all. In the later fourth century there were many Manichaeans in North Africa, and the young Augustine, to the distress of his mother, Monnica, became one of them. But his disappointment when he met and heard the celebrated Manichaean teacher, Faustus, coming, as it did, at the end of several years devoted to philosophical and scientific studies, which had seriously undermined his belief in the doctrines that he had so lightly embraced, led him in 383 to sever his connexion with the sect. Between 389 and 405 he published thirteen anti-Manichaean works. The most elaborate was the treatise *Against Faustus*, in which the arguments of Faustus alternate with the refutations of Augustine. Its main thesis is the defence of the Old Testament.

Of all the lapses from orthodoxy that which from the fourth to the sixth century produced the greatest stir in the West was undoubtedly the heretical teaching of Pelagius. A native of either Ireland or of the Roman province of Britain he appeared in Rome at the end of the fourth century. As one of the refugees who fled in 410 at the time of Alaric's march on the capital he first visited North Africa and then Palestine. By that time he had already formulated the doctrines named after him. Although he was able to exculpate himself at two Palestinian synods held in 415, his teaching was condemned in Africa, and two years later he and his disciple, Caelestius, were excommunicated by Innocent I. Pope Zosimus was inclined to be more lenient, but ultimately confirmed his predecessor's decision after the temporal power had issued a rescript banishing Pelagius from Rome. Pelagius himself is heard of no more after 417; but his views had brought him not a few supporters, the chief being Julian, till then bishop of Aeclanum in Apulia. At the Council of Ephesus in 431 the condemnation of Pelagianism was formally pronounced. Nevertheless, a modified form of it, commonly called Semipelagianism, continued for a century to find adherents in the West, until it too was condemned in 529 by the second Synod of Orange. The essential feature of Pelagius' teaching was his rejection of the doctrines of Predestination and Original Sin. He denied that the sin of Adam and Eve was transmitted to all their posterity, and he claimed for each human being an unqualified freedom of the will which enabled him to choose between good and evil. It followed that a completely sinless life was possible without the operation of Divine Grace. Pelagius' views are known not only from the works of his chief opponents, Augustine and Jerome, but from a number of letters and short treatises which have been identified as his, although they have been transmitted either anonymously or else under the name of others.[1] His denial of the doctrine of Original Sin is also apparent in his extended commentary on the Pauline Epistles. In its original form the work survives in only two manuscripts, but interpolated versions of it enjoyed considerable popularity in the Middle Ages, mainly perhaps because Jerome's name became attached to them. Yet another version, begun by Cassiodorus and completed by his associates from which heretical opinions had been carefully expunged, was frequently quoted by Biblical scholars in the ninth century.[2] It can occasion no surprise that Pelagianism met with strong opposition from the orthodox, and that in its extreme form it was short-lived because both Jerome and Augustine condemned its tenets outright. Jerome, who was an old man at the time, would hardly have entered the lists, had not Pelagius in the course of his travels visited Palestine. But then, when the poisonous teaching was, as it were, brought to his own door, Jerome launched a treatise in three books, *Dialogi contra Pelagianos*, in which he displayed all his old powers as a controversialist and had no difficulty in rebutting the main arguments of the heresiarch. The anti-Pelagian writings of Augustine, on the other hand, were not merely skilful examples of dialectic. The doctrines of Predestination and of Divine Grace were two fundamental concepts of Augustinian theology, so that the fifteen treatises against Pelagianism, which he composed between 415 and 430,

---

[1] See particularly G. de Plinval, *Pélage* (Lausanne, 1943) and *Essai sur le style et la langue de Pélage* (Fribourg, 1947). Plinval assigns twelve short compositions with certainty to Pelagius and regards seven others as possibly or probably his. One of these last is printed for the first time as an appendix in Plinval's *Essai*.

[2] Cf. A. Souter, *The Earliest Latin Commentaries on the Epistles of St Paul* (Oxford, 1927), pp. 205–13, and his masterly edition of the *Commentary* (Cambridge, Eng., 1922–26).

are not merely a refutation of what he regarded as a pestilent heresy, but are constructive, inasmuch as in them he elaborates first principles on which his theologico-philosophic system was based. There was also a more personal reason for Augustine's fulminations against Pelagianism. In his *Confessions* he has recorded with a unique self-revelation his own religious experience. He had relapsed many times from the true path, and on each occasion had only found it again not by his own free will, but by the Grace of God causing his will to choose aright. But, although he killed Pelagianism, he was in a sense responsible for Semi-pelagianism. By enunciating his views on Predestination and Free Will with the complete rigour of a relentless logic, he invited strong opposition. To many the belief that a majority of mankind were marked out for eternal damnation, while only a minority would attain to salvation, especially also the inclusion among the damned of young children who had died before baptism, must have been, at least secretly, repugnant. Even amongst theologians, whose written utterances were more cautious, there were those who sought to vindicate to some extent the freedom of the will. These Semipelagians were particularly active in Gaul. Thus John Cassian (*c.* 360–435) wrote:

> But that it may be still clearer that, through the excellence of nature which is granted by the goodness of the Creator, sometimes the first beginnings of good will arise, which however cannot attain to the complete performance of what is good unless it is guided by the Lord, the Apostle bears witness and says (Rom. vii, 18): 'for to will is present with me, but to perform what is good I find not'.[1]

Other dissenters from this part of Augustinian teaching were Vincent of Lérins and Faustus of Riez who died at an advanced age some time after 485. Vincent in his much admired *Commonitorium* (434) elaborated the doctrine of the Church's authority in defining dogma and stressed the importance of tradition. He denied that the Bible was the sole criterion for Christian belief, since it could and had been interpreted in different ways. The real criterion, he argued, is the teaching of the Church which embodies universally accepted beliefs and which in

[1] *Collationes* 13, 9, translated by C. S. Gibson in *Select Library of Nicene and Post-Nicene Fathers*, second series, XI.

disputed matters appeals to tradition, or, where that is not enough, has recourse to the opinion of a majority of bishops and Christian teachers or to an oecumenical council.[1] To Vincent the views of Augustine relative to Predestination and Free Will were heretical or, more precisely, the opinions of an individual who in that instance was at variance with the teaching of the Church. Even in Gaul, however, Augustine had staunch adherents like Prosper of Aquitaine (c. 390–463). Among many others who continued to support or propagate his views on Predestination were Marius Mercator and particularly Fulgentius, bishop of Ruspe (c. 467–532). Enough has been said to show that Pelagius started doctrinal questions which engaged many of the best minds in the Church and evoked an extensive literature, partly dogmatic, partly polemical.

From the beginning of the third to the end of the fifth century a great number of expository and hortatory writings saw the light. It will be enough to explain briefly the salient characteristics of these works and to refer specifically only to those which exerted a marked influence and thus have a special importance for the student of medieval thought. In the matter of expounding the Scriptures the Latin West once more stood to the Greek East in the relation of pupil to master. Among the Greek Fathers who turned their attention to exegesis, Origen towers head and shoulders over all others. It is no exaggeration to say that his influence was universal, since even those who opposed his methods or rejected his conclusions were compelled in the process to deepen their own researches and to seek a solution for problems which, but for him, they might never have envisaged. His learning and his literary output were immense. His work as a textual critic was of inestimable value. His outstanding achievement in that field was the so-called *Hexapla*, an edition of the Old Testament in which the Hebrew Text in Hebrew characters, the same in Greek characters, the Septuagint, and three other Greek translations (Aquila, Symmachus, and Theodotion) were arranged in six parallel columns. In the fifth column, which contained the

---

[1] Cf. his famous definition (2, 3): 'in ipsa item catholica ecclesia magnopere curandum est ut id teneamus quod ubique, quod semper, quod ab omnibus creditum est'.

Septuagint, divergences of that translation from the original text were carefully obelized. At the same time *lacunae* in the Septuagint were emended with the help of the other Greek versions. This vast work, which, owing to its huge bulk, can never have been duplicated as a whole, was preserved in the library at Caesarea, where more than a century after Origen's time it was consulted by Jerome.

Origen's method of interpreting the Bible, both in his homilies and in his commentaries, was the allegorical. Although this type of hermeneutics was much older than Christianity and Origen himself was acquainted with and indebted to the writings of Philo the Jew, he must be regarded as the father of allegorical interpretation in the Christian Church. To him the literal or historical sense of a passage was of secondary importance, and sometimes he disregarded it altogether. In setting forth his method he postulates a threefold sense of Scripture, which he calls the somatic, the psychic, and the pneumatic. This division has its analogy in the three constituents of man, body, soul, and spirit. In practice, however, he rarely succeeds in forcing a given passage to bear all three meanings; in general he is content with a twofold mystical or allegorical interpretation, the one having reference to Christian life on earth, the other to the life hereafter. Later expositors, especially among the Latin writers, introduced various changes or modifications in the manner of interpreting Holy Writ other than literally.[1] But it is from Origen that the method of allegorizing ultimately derives. In the East the strongest opposition came from the Antiochene school of commentators who insisted primarily on the literal or historic sense and assigned to allegory a second place. The influence of this school in the West was not negligible, being furthered partly by Latin renderings of works by John Chrysostom and Theodore of Mopsuestia, partly by the treatise of Junillus.[2] Nevertheless in the earlier Middle Ages the authority of Jerome, and even more of Gregory

[1] For the methods of Scriptural interpretation with special reference to medieval practice in the West, see H. Caplan in *Speculum*, 4 (1929), pp. 282–90, and Beryl Smalley, *The Study of the Bible in the Middle Ages* (ed. 2, Oxford, 1952), pp. 1–13.

[2] Cf. Smalley, *op. cit.*, pp. 14ff., and Laistner in *Harvard Theol. Rev.*, 40 (1947), pp. 19–31. For Junillus see below, p. 115.

the Great, was paramount among the great majority of Churchmen.

Hilary of Poitiers in his commentaries on St Matthew and on the Psalms, and Ambrose in his lengthy exposition of the opening chapters of Genesis (*Hexaemeron*) and of St Luke, as well as in some shorter tractates, were the chief Latin precursors of Jerome in the task of expounding portions of the Bible. Hilary tries to keep the balance between literal interpretation and allegory; Ambrose, though he also strives after mystic or esoteric meanings in the words of Scripture, his chief guides being Origen and Philo Judaeus, is most concerned with moralizing them. Both Ambrosian commentaries enjoyed considerable popularity in later ages, but it is in the realm of homiletics and as a preacher that he shone especially. This is apparent also in his commentaries; for these, in fact, grew out of homilies which he had delivered on various occasions.

As a work of Biblical scholarship the commentary on the thirteen Epistles of St Paul—the Epistle to the Hebrews is not included—wrongly included among the works of Ambrose and generally referred to as Ambrosiaster stands much higher. Although various conjectures have been made, its authorship is still uncertain, but its date can be fixed within narrow limits. Internal evidence proves that it was composed between 366 and 384. The commentary is remarkable because its author is one of the very few Latin writers—Jerome and, to a limited extent, Augustine are the others—who was interested in and understood textual criticism.[1] He tries, and with success, to explain the meaning of the Apostle's words in straightforward language and without recourse to mystical interpretation. He is thoroughly familiar with all parts of the Bible, alludes frequently to heretical beliefs current in his own day, and shows some knowledge of pagan religions and institutions.[2] He can be witty and even satirical, as when he comments on the words of St Paul (I Cor. xiv, 14), 'for if I pray in an (unknown) tongue, my spirit prayeth, but my understanding is unfruitful'.

[1] Cf., for example, *PL*, 17, col. 96B; 159A; 293C; *CSEL*, 50, p. 425, 13.

[2] For instance, he is aware (*PL*, 17, col. 137B–C) that Pharaoh is not a name but a royal title, and compares it to Augustus, the title assumed by the Roman emperors.

It is obvious that our mind is in ignorance if it should speak in a tongue which it does not know. It is like Latin (speaking) men who make a practice of chanting in Greek; they are charmed by the sound of the words, but they do not know what they are saying.[1]

The same qualities of mind and style are apparent also in a collection of essays in which Ambrosiaster discusses specific passages in the Old and the New Testaments.[2]

A singularly interesting, though isolated figure, contemporary with Jerome and Ambrosiaster, is Tyconius. Apart from his Donatist writings, he was the author of two works which, with certain reservations, won the approval even of his Catholic opponents, notably Augustine. The first is entitled *Liber Regularum* and lays down seven rules for discovering the meaning of Scripture, each being elucidated in detail with the help of ample illustrations. In general Tyconius is concerned with two senses of Holy Writ, the historical and the typical. By typical he meant the reference of Biblical passages to the Church. Augustine, who admired Tyconius greatly, while he regretted and warned against his Donatist views, ensured a wider publicity for this book by including the essential parts of its teaching in the third book of *De doctrina Christiana*. Tyconius' other expository work was a commentary on the Apocalypse. It, too, was much admired; to it many later commentaries on this book of the New Testament were indebted directly or indirectly. In consequence, although no manuscript of it has survived, it has been possible to reconstruct it in large part from later commentators, like Bede and Beatus of Liébana.[3]

It would be difficult to exaggerate the importance of Jerome's work as a translator, textual critic, and commentator. Of all his undertakings that for which he is most justly and universally famed is his translation of the Bible. When he began his labours there was no standard version of the Old and New Testaments in

---

[1] *PL*, 17, col. 255B: 'manifestum est ignorare animum nostrum, si lingua loquatur quam nescit, sicut adsolent Latini homines Graece cantare, oblectati sono verborum, nescientes tamen quid dicant'.

[2] These *Quaestiones veteris et novi testamenti*, which in the manuscripts are wrongly attributed to Augustine, have been edited by A. Souter in *CSEL*, 50.

[3] For the *Liber Regularum* see the edition by F. C. Burkitt in *Cambridge Texts and Studies*, II, 1 (1894); for the commentary cf. Traugott Hahn, *Tyconius Studien* (Leipzig, 1900)

Latin. Various translations existed and had existed for some time, and our knowledge of them depends partly on surviving manuscripts of certain books of the Bible in one or other of these versions, partly on quotations from the Bible in Christian writers before Jerome's time. The earliest Greek translation of the Old Testament, called the Septuagint, which had usurped the place of the Hebrew even amongst the majority of Jews, to the Christians had all the authority of an original text. To Jerome an undertaking which might at first seem to be relatively simple, if laborious, only gradually took on a more complex aspect when his occupation with the Septuagint and later Greek versions ceased to satisfy the demands of his scholarship and led him to the original language in which the Jewish Scriptures were composed. His first translation, begun by him at the request of Pope Damasus in 383, was a comparatively easy task. It consisted in revising the Four Gospels in the Old Latin version used in Rome at that date; but there is some doubt whether he extended his revision also to the other books of the New Testament. In course of time many corruptions had crept into the text, which Jerome emended with the help of Greek manuscripts, without departing more than necessary from a version which age and religious conservatism had hallowed. Jerome's translation of the New Testament rapidly passed into general use. It is disputed whether the version of the Psalter known as the *Psalterium Romanum* is from Jerome's hand; but it was used in Rome until the latter part of the sixteenth century and parts of it are still preserved in the Roman Breviary. After Jerome had become acquainted with Origen's *Hexapla* he began a new revision of the Old Testament, utilizing not merely the Greek versions but the Hebrew text. Only the Psalms have survived in this version and have remained in use in the Roman Church to this day. Its usual name, *Psalterium Gallicanum*, arose from the fact that it came into common use in Gaul. Great as Jerome's second undertaking was, he had not yet completed it when he decided to make a new Latin translation of as many books of the Old Testament as possible direct from such Hebrew (or Aramaic) manuscripts as were accessible to him. Although this version was Jerome's greatest achievement as a translator, it only won adequate recognition slowly. Religious conservatism delayed its use in place of the venerated *Vetus Latina*, so that it was not until the end of the seventh century that it was generally adopted. And even after that date the older Latin versions were still used sporadically. This third version by Jerome, the so-called Vulgate, has remained in use in the Roman Catholic Church ever since. Only the new translation of the Psalter was set aside in favour of the more familiar *Psalterium Gallicanum*. Those books of the Apocrypha which Jerome did not translate or revise—for instance, I and II Maccabees, Wisdom, and Ecclesiasticus— continued to be read in the older Latin version. By universal consent the Vulgate, judged as a whole, is a model of exact and elegant translation; for Jerome combined deep erudition, bred of a constant study of the Bible, with a rare gift of being faithful to the original in spirit, even if the divergent idioms of the two languages sometimes necessitated some freedom in the letter.

The earliest of Jerome's commentaries are those on the Epistles of St Paul to the Galatians, the Ephesians, Titus, and Philemon. With the exception of the commentary on St Matthew, which he dictated in a fortnight in 398, all his expository work from 389 to his death was done on the books of the Old Testament. The result was commentaries on Genesis, the Psalms, Ecclesiastes, and all the major and minor prophets. There is, however, much variation in the scope and treatment, and consequently in the value, of these numerous expositions. Some were written, or rather dictated, very rapidly, and the handling of the subject-matter was correspondingly superficial. Others were elaborated with much more care. It is in the commentaries on Habbakuk, Daniel, Isaiah, Ezekiel, and Jeremiah, the last named being unfinished at Jerome's death, that his best exegetical work is to be found. Although he himself defined the function of the ideal Biblical commentator as 'erecting on the foundation of history a spiritual edifice',[1] it is noticeable that many of his own commentaries, and amongst them some of his best, confined themselves almost wholly to the historical elucidation of the text. Furthermore, what gave them a peculiar value to his contemporaries and to posterity was that their composition went hand in hand with

[1] Preface to the sixth book of the commentary on Isaiah (*PL*, 24, col. 205C): 'super fundamenta historiae spiritale exstruere aedificium'.

his work as a translator and textual critic; for, in addition to expounding his author's meaning, Jerome constantly took note of the various Greek translations and of the Hebrew original as well. We have seen that he used Origen's *Hexapla*; but Origen is also the predecessor to whom Jerome is most constantly indebted in his exposition of the Old and the New Testaments.

The expository works of Augustine form a conspicuous contrast to those of Jerome. His ignorance of Hebrew and imperfect knowledge of Greek precluded success in the sphere in which Jerome, the *vir trilinguis*, particularly shone. Again, like Ambrose's commentaries, many of Augustine's are essentially the work of a preacher. Their value lay first and foremost in the ethical teaching which he put before his readers in the course of expounding passages in the Scriptures. Thus his homilies on the Psalms and on the Fourth Gospel were particularly valued in the Middle Ages. Both Ambrose and Augustine took their pastoral duties very seriously and for the guidance of their flock composed many shorter treatises dealing with particular moral questions. As a preacher Augustine surpassed even Ambrose, and posterity has assigned to him the first place among Christian orators in the West, even as it has placed John Chrysostom first among the Greeks.

It is indicative of the changed position of Christianity after the final triumph of Constantine that the need and therefore also the output of apologetic literature dwindled away, whereas in the previous century the defence of Christianity, be it against the Government or against pagan philosophers engaged the attention of the best writers. Among them Tertullian, Arnobius, and Lactantius may be named. In the early fifth century, however, owing to the political circumstances of the time, two remarkable works of this class were given to the world, Augustine's *City of God* and Salvian's *Governance of God*.

In the earlier centuries of the Empire national or regional calamities were often attributed by the Romans and their provincial subjects to the anger of the Roman deities at the new religion, if not to the baleful power of the Christians and their God; and at times popular resentment led to persecution and pogroms. At the beginning of the fifth century, under the influence of the catastrophic attacks launched against Italy by the Visigoths which culminated in the capture of Rome by Alaric in 410, there was a recrudescence of these anti-Christian feelings. Many fugitives from the capital found their way to North Africa. Among them were some who were still faithful to pagan divinities, and who loudly voiced their opinion that all the disasters which had befallen the Empire and had not even spared the venerated city of Rome, were due to the wrath of the gods neglected in favour of Christ. To these charges Augustine undertook to reply, but the masterpiece which resulted took more than a dozen years to complete (413–26). It is clear that its author had envisaged from the first the general plan of the whole work which, when complete, comprised twenty-two books. Of these the first ten are, in the proper sense of the term, apologetic; for they refute in detail the accusations of the pagans. The remaining books, on the other hand, are constructive and contain Augustine's own philosophic theory. Although he never loses sight of the main argument, the work contains a great number of digressions. The whole in consequence has the appearance of being rather loosely constructed. The brief analysis, included in the *Retractations*, of what his purpose and meaning in composing the *De civitate Dei* were, is so illuminating that it deserves quotation:

> Meantime Rome was overthrown by an assault of the Goths under their king, Alaric, and by the onset of a great calamity. The city's overthrow, the worshippers of many false gods, whom we call by a name in general use, pagans, tried to attribute to the Christian religion, and began to blaspheme the true God more sharply and bitterly than usual. At this I was fired with *zeal for the house of God* (Ps. lxix, 9) and set myself to compose the books concerning the City of God against their blasphemies and errors. This work occupied me for a number of years, because many other avocations which I might not put off intervened, and their completion took precedence of it. But at length this voluminous work concerning the City of God was brought to its conclusion in twenty-two books. The first five of these refute those whose view of human prosperity is such that, to ensure it, they deem the worship of many gods whom the pagans are wont to worship to be essential, and who maintain that our present ills have arisen and multiplied because those gods are banned. The next five books are addressed to those who, while admitting that mortal men have never been and never will be without

these misfortunes, which, now great, now little, vary in place, season, and in the persons affected, argue that the cult of many gods in the form of sacrifice to them will be useful on account of the life after death. Thus in these ten books those two opinions, which are idle and hostile to the Christian religion, are rebutted. But lest we might be reproved for having merely refuted the views of others without having set forth our own, the second part of this work, extending to twelve books, meets that demand, although, where necessary, in the first ten books we may state our views and in the last twelve may reply to opposing arguments. Of the twelve books, then, that follow on the first ten, the first four contain the origin of the two Cities, that of God and that of this world; the next four their continuation or advance, the remaining four their merited end. All the twenty-two books, although they were written about both cities, received their name from the better city and so are entitled, concerning the City of God.[1]

The term, *civitas Dei*, with which is contrasted the *civitas terrena* or *civitas huius mundi*, was not new. Augustine himself alludes to its occurrence in Psalms lxxxvii, 3. He contrasts the city of Jerusalem with Babylon, and, in an allegorical sense, while Jerusalem stands for the city of all the saints, Babylon is equivalent to the city of all the sinners. But Augustine was familiar, as we saw, with Tyconius; and he had already contrasted the *civitas Dei* with the *civitas diaboli*. Of these two 'the one yearns to serve Christ, the other to serve the world, the one desires to rule in the world, the other to fly from the world'. Augustine's use of the phrase is then akin to that of Tyconius, although in amplifying it he assigned to it a deeper, and in part a new, significance. Briefly stated, the philosophy of history laid down by Augustine consists in demonstrating how God's Purpose has through the ages been worked out in human society. The City of God is everlastingly being revealed in the world, whereas the States of men, the sum of which is equivalent to the City of the World, are mutable and perish from time to time. Though there cannot but be interaction here below between the *civitas Dei* and the *civitas terrena*, they, like their aims, are essentially different; for, while the one looks to eternity, the aims of the other are ephemeral and directed only to earthly well-being. In philosophical terms the struggle, which will only cease on the Day of Judgment, is one

[1] *Retract.*, II, 69.

between belief and unbelief; and, just as the *civitas terrena* does not correspond to any historical kingdom or empire on earth, so the *civitas Dei* is not to be identified with the Church. The ultimate triumph of the City of God whose fulfilment will bring about peace everlasting, is the hope which renders the earthly City intelligible, since it will bring the realization that the constant growth and decline of human commonwealths and empires were but the preparation for the *civitas Dei*.

Parenthetically we must here refer to a book which was a sublunary amplification of one aspect of Augustine's masterpiece. Paulus Orosius was a Spanish priest. He became the disciple of Augustine, at whose instigation he wrote a work, *Historiarum adversum paganos libri septem*, which, though called a *History*, belongs rather to apologetic than to historical literature. Books I to IV sketch the history of the Mediterranean World and Persia, V to VII are assigned to the history of Rome from 146 B.C. to the author's own time. As a reply to the pagan charge that the disasters of Rome at the beginning of the fifth century were due to her desertion of her old gods and to the spread of Christianity, Augustine's pupil sets out to show from past history that the centuries which preceded the establishment of Christianity had been marked by wars and devastations and multiple miseries. Those years, he argued, were not merely as disastrous as his own times, but were worse than these the further back in history we proceed. A history written deliberately to prove a certain thesis under the most favourable conditions would leave much to be desired as a historical source. But Orosius' compilation has other faults besides, and recent efforts to rate his performance more highly fail to convince. The book was hastily put together by a man of mediocre ability and education. There is a considerable parade of sources, but in reality the author relies for the most part on epitomes of earlier histories. He refers to Livy, but it is more than doubtful whether he ever set eyes on the original. Similarly he alludes to Pompeius Trogus, whose work he knew only through Justin's meagre abbreviation; and he frequently misunderstands the sources that he did use and so makes ludicrous mistakes. But although a modern critic may rate Orosius' performance very low, his contemporaries and the generations that followed thought differently. Few works were more popular in the Middle Ages than this history, which was regarded as authoritative by scholars like Gregory of Tours, Isidore, Bede, and Paul the Deacon. Extant manuscripts number nearly two hundred, the earliest being a fragment copied in the sixth century, and the *History* also appears in well over a hundred medieval library catalogues.[1]

The treatise of Salvian (*c.* 390–470) was, like Augustine's *City of God*, called forth by the political circumstances of the time, that is to say, by the coming of the Germanic invaders who during Salvian's day overran and occupied the greater part of Gaul. It sets out to defend the Divine Purpose against the accusations levelled against it by those who saw destruction and the ruin of the Empire taking place all round them. After proving in Books I and II, by appeals to reason, to the Scriptures, and to the past history of the Church, that God's Providence does rule the world, Salvian goes on to expose the corrupt habits and morals of Christian society. The overthrow of the Roman Empire by the barbarians is the retribution which its government and its inhabitants are paying for their unchristian way of life. Then Salvian proceeds, in what has become the most famous part of his book, to draw an elaborate parallel between the Romans and the invaders, both those who were still heathen and those who were Arians. His comparison is all in favour of the barbarian peoples whose purity of manners is contrasted with what Salvian in a previous passage had drastically described as the 'morass of vices' among the inhabitants of the Empire. Historians have differed in their estimate of the judgment passed by Salvian on two types of society. Wholesale condemnations of an entire people on the ground of corrupt manners have been made at all periods of history and are never true historically; and Salvian, who minimizes or ignores the horrors of invasion and of the Vandal persecution in Africa, is not free from the suspicion of what would now be called 'collaborationism'.[2] A more charitable

[1] The best text is that by C. Zangemeister in *CSEL*, 5; for a fuller discussion of Orosius as a historian cf. Laistner in *Classical Philology*, 35 (1940), pp. 250–4.

[2] Cf. P. Courcelle, *Histoire littéraire des grandes invasions germaniques* (Paris, 1948), p. 127.

judgment will attribute his *saeva indignatio* to an impassioned faith, and will regard the contrast that he draws between two groups of people, the one cultured but effete, the other vigorous but relatively rude, as true in part and stated in a style and language of a very high order.

In historical writing the Latin West lagged far behind the Greek East. It was the merit of Jerome and of Rufinus, once devoted friends and later bitter enemies, to make the epochal work in ecclesiastical history done by Eusebius accessible to the Latin-speaking world. Jerome translated the *Chronicle* of Eusebius, making some additions especially with reference to Roman history, while Rufinus rendered the same author's *Ecclesiastical History* into Latin. Both men followed up their translations by writing independent continuations; for Jerome compiled a *Chronicle* of the period from 325 to 378, while Rufinus composed what was the first ecclesiastical history written in the West, extending from 324 to the death of Theodosius I (395).[1] While neither writer's work could compare with that of Eusebius, both were widely used, Jerome's *Chronicle* especially becoming a standard work of reference in the West. Very different was the fate of Sulpicius Severus' *Chronicle* which was published in or soon after 403. Its style is clear and incisive, the work of a man who in his youth had been trained in the law. It was compiled with great care; for Sulpicius consulted various earlier sources and paid great attention to chronology to ensure the greatest possible accuracy. But the book met with little appreciation, probably because it contained veiled criticisms of the contemporary clergy in Gaul, and it seems to have been rarely used by medieval students.[2] In the fifth century Prosper of Aquitaine and the Spanish writer Hydatius composed continuations of Jerome's *Chronicle*. The Vandal persecution of the Catholic Church in Africa was described by Victor of Vita. It is a highly coloured record of atrocities whose value derives from the fact that two-thirds of the book is the account of an eye-witness. Hagiography was not

[1] The theory that Rufinus' continuation of Eusebius is not his own work but copied from Gelasius of Caesarea is now rather discredited.

[2] Only a single manuscript of the *Chronicle* survives (Vatican, *Pal. lat.*, 824 of the eleventh century). For Sulpicius as a historical authority cf. *Classical Philology*, 35 (1940), pp. 247–50. See also *Clavis*, No. 474.

neglected, although what was produced in this genre was of very unequal merit. The finest achievement was the *Life of St Martin of Tours* by Sulpicius Severus, which, unlike the same author's *Chronicle*, had an immediate and lasting success. Jerome's *De viris illustribus*, beginning with St Peter and ending with Jerome himself, was the first attempt made to write a history of Christian literature. Though marred by errors due to hasty composition and, in general, somewhat sketchy in treatment, it was a pioneer work and contained much valuable material. A continuation with the same title was published in the fifth century by Gennadius of Marseilles, and we shall meet with later continuations completed in the seventh century. Lastly we may refer to the survival of many letters. Two collections stand out, because they are not merely of superlative value as source material of the history of the period, but deserve to be reckoned some of the most remarkable literary productions of the time. The collected correspondence of Jerome contains more than one hundred and fifty, that of Augustine nearly three hundred epistles. These figures include some letters addressed to Jerome or Augustine by other correspondents.

Already during the fourth century the separation, in respect of language, of the western from the eastern half of the Empire had made great progress. In little more than a hundred years after the death of Theodosius I (395), which had been followed by the partition of his empire between his two sons, this linguistic divorce, save in a few isolated instances, became complete. The result, as is well known, was that during the earlier Middle Ages the ability to read and understand a Greek author was a rare accomplishment. But it would be a mistake to assume therefore that the thought of the Greek Fathers remained wholly unfamiliar to the West; for a substantial number of Greek works was available in Latin translations, even if the total formed only a fraction of Greek Patristic literature. That so much of Origen became known in the West was due to Rufinus and to Jerome; and, it may be added, the value of these Latin translations has continued to our own time because in many instances the Greek original is lost or fragmentary. Between them Rufinus and Jerome translated nearly two hundred homilies by Origen. Both men translated

Origen's *De principiis*, the first systematic treatise on Christian dogma. But Jerome's version which, ironically enough, had been undertaken deliberately because he found the translation by Rufinus marred by many inaccuracies and numerous omissions, has not survived. Rufinus' other translations included parts of Origen's commentaries on the Song of Songs and on the Epistle to the Romans; nine homilies and a letter by Gregory of Nazianzus; eight homilies and two monastic rules by Basil the Great; and the Christian romance known to scholars as the *pseudo-Clementine Recognitions*. The original text of Didymus' treatise on the Holy Spirit is lost, but the Latin version by Jerome survives. In the fifth century translations of other Greek works were made, although their translators cannot always be identified, and in the sixth there were further important additions. Thus the West became familiar with nine homilies on Genesis by Basil in the version of Eustathius (*c.* 440), more than a hundred homilies, though not all have survived, some short tracts, and the treatise *On the Priesthood*, by John Chrysostom, Theodore of Mopsuestia's commentary on Psalms, Hesychius' exposition of Leviticus, and Philo of Carpasia's commentary on the Song of Songs. A Latin version of sundry homilies by Ephraem was made from a Greek translation of the Syriac original. The one major figure in Greek theology who was unrepresented, save for Evagrius' translation of the *Life of St Antony* and for one or two letters, was Athanasius; for, as it now universally recognized, no part of the Latin treatise on the Trinity in twelve books is by him. It is a composite work by several hands and not even Book XII, called specifically *De Trinitate et Spiritu Sancto*, is by Athanasius, although the unknown author was clearly familiar with some parts of Athanasius' teaching. A very considerable body of material bearing on canon law and the Acts of Greek Church Councils also became available in Latin dress during the course of the sixth century, but, with the exception of Dionysius Exiguus, the translators are unknown.

Although there are some notable exceptions, Latin Christian poetry taken as a whole, if judged solely on its poetic merits, rarely rises above mediocrity. There are several good reasons for this. The most original minds used prose as a vehicle for their ideas. The only models which the writer of verse could study were the works of pagan poets. But language and metre, which in the right hands were adapted for singing the exploits or the loves of the heroes of classical mythology, became intractable and ill suited for telling the story of Genesis or of the Gospels. Phraseology, which had, so to speak, become standardized as epic diction might easily sound ludicrous or even profane if applied to Bible stories. Moreover, if the material for a poem were taken from the Scriptures, especially from the New Testament, the Christian poet would be obliged to reproduce the language of the Bible as faithfully as possible, unless he wished to incur the stigma of impiety. But a prose translation of St Matthew or of Acts could not easily or satisfactorily be forced into heroic hexameters. Close acquaintance with pagan poets, manifesting itself in echoes of Virgilian or Ovidian phraseology, and less frequently in reminiscences of Horace or Lucan, is observable in most of the Christian poets, and the importance of Virgil as a model far surpassed that of any other classical writer of verse. Juvencus' poem on the story of the Gospels (*Evangeliorum libri*) is illuminating for our purpose. Composed in dactylic hexameters, it was published *c.* 330. In more than three thousand lines he described the earthly life of Christ, basing his narrative mainly on the First Gospel, but making occasional additions from the other Evangelists. He had read widely in classical Latin poetry and knew the four poets mentioned above as well as some others. His hexameters are metrically correct, although here and there one can detect traces of accentual in place of quantitative scansion. Since he tried to keep as near as possible to the words of the Gospels, not merely in the conversational but even in the descriptive passages, his feat of versification was an impressive achievement. But it was at the cost of real poetic inspiration; and at the same time the recollection and the reproduction of names and phrases from the pagan epics must strike a modern reader as incongruous. But the poem had a striking success and was studied throughout the Middle Ages, being especially popular in the Carolingian epoch. Long before that it had received the doubtful honour of becoming a quarry from which grammarians extracted tags to illustrate their desiccated rules. The fashion in choice of subject set by Juvencus found many imitators. In the first half of the fifth century, for instance, Sedulius composed his *Paschal Poem* in five books. Its main theme is the miracles and the Passion of Jesus. Matthew and Luke were his chief sources. Like Juvencus he was familiar with the classical poets, particularly Virgil, and wrote correct quantitative hexameters, although occasional licences can be found.[1] Sedulius also was greatly admired and often quoted in the medieval period. In the sixth century we shall find Arator taking the story of Acts as the subject-matter for a poem. Among tales from the Old Testament the story of the Creation was much favoured by poets. Thus the most successful portion of the poem, *In praise of God*, by the African Dracontius (end of the fifth century) is worked up elaborately from the material provided by the opening chapters of Genesis.

Both poetically and formally the poetry of Paulinus of Nola (353–431) stands much higher. A native of Bordeaux, the pupil and friend of Ausonius, he had had an exceptionally thorough training in letters. He was a Christian from birth; in 390 he was baptized and soon after renounced all his worldly goods to live a life of poverty and asceticism, first in Spain, and, after *c.* 396, at Nola in Italy. He was consecrated bishop of that see in 409. The bulk of his poetry is composed in hexameters, but he also essayed elegiac couplets with success, and even iambic verse.[2] Among his earlier poems perhaps the best known is the versified letter addressed to Ausonius in reply to four verse epistles which he had received from his old teacher to dissuade him from his renunciation of the world. Of purely religious content are a panegyric on John the Baptist, based on the Gospels, and several paraphrases of the Psalms. After settling in Nola he composed a series of poems in honour of St Felix of Nola, whom he had chosen as his patron saint. Two other poems, describing the basilica of the saint, for the restoration of which Paulinus was responsible, are of some interest, especially to the student of early Christian art. Yet another is an attack on pagan religion and mythology. There are also a good many occasional pieces and some metrical

[1] Juvencus and Sedulius have been edited by J. Huemer in *CSEL*, 24 and 10.

[2] See the edition by W. von Hartel in *CSEL*, 30, xxxiii is composed in iambic trimeters, xxiv in alternating iambic trimeters and dimeters acatalectic.

epigrams. In short, Paulinus' muse was inspired by a diversity of circumstances. His verse, as one would expect from a pupil of Ausonius, is elegant and full of classical reminiscences, but there is often a lack of inspiration. Only occasionally, as in some of the poems glorifying St Felix, does he betray real depth of feeling. Though he stands second among the Christian poets of the later Empire, he is at all points inferior to the Spanish Prudentius, who is incomparably the greatest of them all, even as he is superior to Ausonius and Claudian. He was born in 348. Fifty-seven years later he published a collection of his poems. From the Preface it appears that he had followed an official career and finally had attained to a position of some importance in the imperial service. How soon after 405 he died is unknown. His poetic output comprises four long poems, three running to a thousand lines each or over, the fourth, in two books, to nearly two thousand; two books of shorter poems and hymns in lyric metres; and one book of forty-eight little four-line poems describing scenes or episodes from the Old or the New Testament. Of the long poems the two books, *Against Symmachus*, are partly an attack on various heathen cults, partly a reply to Symmachus' plea for the toleration of paganism. Prudentius, though he rebuts the proposal of Symmachus, concludes the first book with a noble eulogy of the man. In the *Apotheosis* he defends Catholic orthodoxy against various heresies and in the *Hamartigenia* refutes the Gnostics. The *Psychomachia* is an allegorical poem and the first of its kind to be composed in the West. To most modern readers it will appeal less than the other poems, but in the Middle Ages it was the most popular of Prudentius' works. The first of the two collections of lyrics (*Cathemerinon*) contains twelve hymns, all of considerable length, the other (*Peristephanon*) is made up of fourteen poems in honour of martyrs. Their length varies greatly, the shortest consisting of only eighteen lines, the longest of eleven hundred and forty. Prudentius was a skilled artist in metre. Besides dactylic hexameters and elegiacs, he experimented successfully with fifteen other verse forms, such as sapphics, hendecasyllabics, the lesser asclepiad, anapaestic dimeters, dactylic trimeters, trochaic tetrameters, and several variants of the iambic line. Most of these metrical schemes are found in the

Cathemerinon and *Peristephanon*; but the long poems in hexameters are introduced by prefaces composed in iambic trimeters or in the lesser asclepiad. He was widely read in both pagan and Christian poetry, as well as in Christian theologians, like Tertullian, Cyprian, and Lactantius. The many echoes of Virgil and other classical poets are so much a part of his thought that they do not give the impression of mere imitation.[1] Certain weaknesses are undeniable. Prudentius has not wholly freed himself from the literary affectations of his age. He tends to overload his verse with poetic imagery and there are too many echoes of the rhetorical schools. Like Propertius, he sometimes allows his erudition to swamp his poetic gifts, to the annoyance of the reader who is neither a theologian nor an antiquarian. In those poems whose purpose is polemic or apologetic the dialectician occasionally triumphs over the poet. Yet two characteristics of Prudentius atone for much and must strike every reader of his poems—a burning patriotism for Rome, her history, her institutions, and her civilizing mission, and an intense Christian fervour. These qualities combined with an exceptional literary training produced a poet whose work stands alone because it is a wellnigh harmonious blend of the best in pagan culture with the purest Christian inspiration.

There were other Christian poets or versifiers during the decline of the Empire, but their productions do not call for special mention in a short survey. There was, however, one genre of verse which cannot be passed over, since it was the most original poetic contribution made by Christian writers. The two earliest composers of hymns, Hilary of Poitiers and Ambrose, in simple beauty and depth of religious feeling, set a standard which was rarely equalled and never surpassed. Unfortunately Hilary's *Liber hymnorum* has disappeared except for the fragments of three hymns; for the attribution to him of some others is disputed. But his religious poetry does not seem to have met with the success that it deserved and none of his hymns appear to have come into general use in the liturgy. The result is that Ambrose is commonly regarded as the founder of Christian hymnology.

[1] Cf. the index of imitations in Bergman's admirable edition (*CSEL*, 61, pp. 455–69).

Yet it is uncertain how many Ambrosian hymns are genuinely his. The authenticity of four is unquestioned. These are the morning hymn, *Aeterne rerum conditor*, the evening hymn, *Deus creator omnium*, one intended to be sung at tierce, *Iam surgit hora tertia*, and the Christmas song, *Intende qui regis Israel*. Of fourteen others eight almost certainly are also by Ambrose. Hilary had tried his hand at several classical metres. But Ambrose, bearing in mind the needs and limitations of large congregations, chose the simplest metrical form that he could, the iambic dimeter acatalectic. The scansion is still quantitative, not accentual, but there is occasional rhyme. Paulinus of Nola is credited by Gennadius with the writing of hymns, but they have not come down to us. The poems on St Felix of Nola, however, partake somewhat of the character of hymns, but they were not suitable for general use in the liturgy. Some of the hymns in Prudentius' *Cathemerinon* are exquisite, but the diction is too elaborate to make them suited for large congregations. Some, moreover, have the additional disadvantage of being composed in metres which would be unfamiliar save to a highly educated minority of churchgoers. Thus, although the fine hymn (*Cathem.* 1) beginning, *Ales diei nuntius*, is in the simple metre favoured by Ambrose, two others of unusual charm are composed respectively in the lesser asclepiad and in anapaestic dimeter catalectic.[1] The fifth century produced little that was remarkable in this class of poetry with the honourable exception of Sedulius' famous hymn, *A solis ortus cardine*. This very soon came into general use in the Church. Apart from this, it was not until the sixth century that there appeared in the person of Fortunatus a worthy successor to Ambrose and Prudentius.

[1] Namely No. 5 (*Inventor rutili, dux bone, luminis*) and No. 10 (*Deus ignee fons animarum*).

PART II

From the beginning of the Sixth to the Middle of the Eighth Century

PART II

From the beginnings of life to the dawn of science

CHAPTER IV

From Boethius to Isidore

(a) Italy

If a man's eminence is to be estimated by the influence which his work or thoughts have exercised on succeeding generations, then assuredly Italy in the sixth century produced four men, each of whom deserves a niche in any hall of Fame. And, though the achievement of Boethius, Benedict of Nursia, Cassiodorus, and Gregory I would be reckoned noteworthy in any age, it stands out with conspicuous brightness because the fifty years which followed the death of Jerome and Augustine was one of intellectual decline throughout the Western Empire.

Anicius Manlius Severinus Boethius was born *c*. 480. He was the scion of a senatorial family, many of whose members had in the past held high office in the State. His father became consul in 487, an honour which Boethius himself enjoyed in 510, while twelve years later the dignity was conferred on his two sons before they had attained to manhood. The events that led to the execution of Boethius and the date of his death are still matters of controversy because the contemporary sources are insufficient and to some extent contradictory. According to the most probable interpretation of the evidence Boethius in 523 or 524 defended a prominent senator of consular rank, Albinus, who was accused of plotting with the Byzantine government against Theodoric. This action brought upon him the wrath of the monarch whose favour he had long enjoyed and whom on his part he had hitherto served faithfully. He was arrested and imprisoned, perhaps for several months, before being brought to trial and executed in 524 or 525. It has often been assumed that Boethius himself was innocent of treason and Theodoric has been blamed for a judicial murder. Doubtless the king, though usually a clement as well as a shrewd ruler, was, like Theodosius I, not free from the momentary passion of the despot. But it is more than questionable whether Boethius was a martyr, as he has so often been called; for it is probable that he was directly implicated in the treasonable dealings with Byzantium and in consequence Theodoric was justified in suspecting the loyalty of certain senators of whom Boethius was the most illustrious. Thus political fear, not religious animosity of an Arian prince towards a Catholic senate was responsible for the severity of Boethius' punishment.[1]

In the course of a short life he accomplished astonishingly much; for, although little is known of his official duties, they were undoubtedly heavy and took up much of his time. He also set himself vast literary and scientific projects, only a part of which he lived to complete. His training must have been unusually thorough, being by no means restricted to the customary rhetorical studies. A sound mastery of Greek, such as he acquired, was by this time a rare accomplishment in the West. No less uncommon was his acquaintance with later Greek philosophy, particularly Neoplatonism, so that there is much to be said in favour of the assumption that he had studied for a time in Alexandria. His earliest extant writings, the treatises, *De musica* and *De arithmetica*, as well as the lost *De geometria*, were the immediate outcome of his occupation with the subjects of the *quadrivium*. His subsequent studies were more ambitious and more profound; for he says that he planned to make the works of Aristotle and of Plato available in Latin. Actually only a small portion of this undertaking was finished, partly owing to his premature death, partly because, not content to be a translator, he undertook the role of expositor. Of Aristotle's works only the logical treatises were rendered into Latin by him; and of these the *Categories* and *De interpretatione*

[1] For this interpretation of the evidence see especially W. C. Bark in *American Hist. Rev.*, 49 (1944), pp. 410–26 and *Speculum*, 21 (1946), pp. 312–17. In a recent article, 'The Fall of Boethius; his character', C. H. Coster would bring the fall and punishment of Boethius into connexion with the Arian persecutions instituted by the Emperor Justin and would place the death of Boethius as late as 526. See *Annuaire de L'Institut de Philologie et d'Histoire orientales et slaves*, 12 (1952), pp. 45–81.

alone have survived.[1] He composed a commentary on the first and two on the second of these works. Similarly he translated the *Isagoge* of Porphyrius, the Neoplatonist, and wrote two explanatory treatises on it, the one in connexion with his own translation, the other to correct mistakes in the earlier version by Victorinus, which Boethius found to be faulty. A commentary on Cicero's *Topica*, of which only a part is now extant, and five independent essays on logic make up the impressive total of his logical works. There is, it is true, less originality in them than used to be supposed; for the commentary on the *Categories* and the two on *De interpretatione* are free adaptations of Porphyrius and of Boethius' older contemporary, Ammonius of Alexandria.[2] But though derivative, they are of unique importance. It was from them that the Western world derived its knowedge of Aristotle for the next six centuries, a knowledge not entirely restricted to the Aristotelian system of logic, since the longer commentary on *De interpretatione* contains many quotations from other writings of Aristotle and also some from Plato. Again, Boethius provided the scholars of succeeding generations with a technical terminology and many definitions which became classic and were ultimately approved and taken over by the Schoolmen. It would be fascinating to speculate on the development of medieval thought which might have resulted had Boethius lived to complete his task of making the entire corpus of Aristotelian and Platonic writings available in Latin dress.

That Boethius combined Christian orthodoxy with the pursuit of philosophy there was never adequate reason to doubt, and the authenticity of four out of five of the theological tractates going under his name, vouched for, as it is, by Cassiodorus, may be regarded as established. They deal with the Trinitarian doctrine, with Being and the Good, and with the Eutychian or Monophysite heresy. Whether the remaining tractate, *De fide catholica*, which shows some stylistic, though no doctrinal differences from

---

[1] The other translations going under Boethius' name are not by him. The printed translation of the *Categories* probably originated in the tenth century. The genuine translation survives in two manuscripts, now in Venice and in Paris. See L. Minio-Paluello in *Medieval and Renaissance Studies*, I (1943), pp. 151–77.

[2] See P. Courcelle, *Les lettres grecques en occident*, pp. 264 ff.

the other four, is by Boethius is a moot point. Modern criticism has, in general, denied its genuineness.[1] But, while in the four other tractates Boethius is a Greek-trained logician dealing with questions of dogma, so as to harmonize reason and orthodoxy, the *De fide catholica* contains a profession of Catholic belief as a whole. This difference in subject helps to explain a difference in style. Besides, it is a fact which has generally been overlooked that most of the less common words, which occur only in this and not in the other tractates or in the *Consolatio philosophiae*, can be found in the Vulgate. Familiarity with the Bible was to be expected of every orthodox and educated Christian—and Boethius was one—and echoes of it are natural enough in a treatise like the *De fide catholica* in which the author's approach is theological, not philosophic. Once the linguistic differences of this tractate are thus explained, the main argument against Boethian authorship falls to the ground and one is disposed to include it amongst his genuine works.

In his last and most widely known book, composed during the captivity which preceded his execution, Boethius appears once more as the devoted servant of philosophy. The literary form of the *Consolatio philosophiae*, with its intermingling of prose and verse, had been familiar to Roman readers ever since the time of Varro's *Menippean Satires*, and more recently it had been adopted by Martianus Capella for his fantastic treatise. The plan of the book is simple: as the prisoner in his confinement is engaged in composing, at the dictation of the Muses, elegiac couplets on old age and death, a woman of commanding aspect, with eyes shining like fire, having the vigour of youth, yet seeming so old as to belong to another age, appears before him. Driving the Muses away with contumely, the visitor, after some questioning, is recognized by Boethius as his old friend and guide, Philosophy. In the dialogue that follows—interrupted from time to time by a poetic interlude—Boethius recalls, with more than one tilt at the fickleness of Fortune, some of his experiences in public life, especially the circumstances which led up to his disgrace and

---

[1] On the genuineness of *De fide* see Dom Cappuyns in *Dictionnaire d'histoire et de géographie ecclésiastiques*, 9, col. 371 ff., and W. C. Bark in *Harvard Theol. Rev.*, 39 (1946), pp. 55–69.

imprisonment. Philosophy, after reminding him of his former devotion to her, gradually leads him from despair to resignation, then from resignation to disregard of human pains and pleasures, and lastly to the true contentment which reason allied with virtue alone can give. In the last chapter of Book V Philosophy utters a sublime passage, which, so far from being out of keeping with the rest of the book, in reality expresses Boethius' mature view how reason and faith may be reconciled, and philosophy and religion, so far from being antagonistic, may combine to attain the same end. After bringing the belief in Providence into harmony with the freedom of the human will, the speaker concludes thus:

> For this force of the divine knowledge comprehending all things with a present notion appointeth to everything its measure and receiveth nothing from ensuing accidents. All which being so, the free will of mortal men remaineth unviolated, neither are the laws unjust which propose punishments and rewards to our wills, which are free from all necessity. There remaineth also a beholder of all things which is God, who foreseeth all things, and the eternity of His vision, which is always present, concurreth with the future quality of our actions, distributing rewards to the good and punishment to the evil. Neither do we in vain put our hope in God or pray to Him; for if we do this well and as we ought, we shall not lose our labour or be without effect. Wherefore fly vices, embrace virtues, possess your minds with worthy hopes, offer up humble prayers to your highest Prince. There is, if you will not dissemble, a great necessity of doing well imposed upon you, since you live in the sight of your Judge, who beholdeth all things.[1]

The *Consolatio philosophiae* contains no new philosophical theory, and the echoes of Aristotle and later Greek philosophers may be many and constant. But it is surely idle to judge the book as if it were a treatise composed by the author in his study with all the resources of an ample library. The prisoner in his dungeon had few, if any, books; and in this, his last work, as he reflects on the eternal problem of human happiness and human suffering, he is reproducing consciously or unconsciously, much that in more prosperous days his memory had absorbed in the prolonged study of the Greek thinkers. The work has had its admirers in all

[1] This and the following citations are taken from the seventeenth-century version by I. T., revised by Stewart and Rand.

ages, for its appeal is many-sided. As sincere as the *Meditations* of Marcus Aurelius, it is free from the pessimism of the Roman Stoic, having rather the same power of comforting the afflicted that many have found in Thomas à Kempis. Its literary art, the skill with which the argument is made to progress, make us overlook the occasional rhetorical artifice, and, whilst admiring the dramatic qualities of the work, ponder the philosophical reflections it provides. The medieval biographer who said of it that Boethius in it so excelled in both prose and verse that he was not inferior to Cicero in one medium or to Virgil (in another version, to Homer) in the other, was not wholly wide of the mark.[1] No one indeed would now agree that such praise for the poetical passages is warranted, but the comparison to Cicero is more justified; for, if the *Hortensius* could inspire not merely Minucius Felix, but it and the rhetorical works of Cicero could win the deep admiration of Augustine, the *Consolatio* was an inspiration to Dante as well as to countless lesser medieval men. And, if we extend the comparison to the Boethian writings as a whole, then there is this further reason for seeing a likeness between Cicero and Boethius. Just as Cicero transmitted the post-Aristotelian systems of philosophy to his countrymen, and, in so doing, enriched the Latin language with many new terms, so Boethius gave posterity a logical system of enduring value and a philosophical vocabulary in which to expound it.

The theological tractates enjoyed a wide popularity at least from the ninth century onwards; the *Consolatio* was the favourite philosophical treatise of the Middle Ages. Medieval commentaries on both works survive.[2] The *Consolatio* was translated into Old English by Alfred in the ninth century and into Old High German by Notker the German in the tenth. The extant manuscripts of the tractates number about one hundred and seventy,

---

[1] Cf. Peiper's edition of the *Consolatio* (Teubner, 1871), pp. xxxi and xxxiii.

[2] Cf. P. Courcelle in *Archives d'histoire doctrinale et littéraire du moyen âge*, 14 (1939), pp. 5–140; E. T. Silk, *Saeculi noni auctoris in Boethii consolationem philosophiae commentarius* (Papers and Monographs of the American Academy in Rome, 1935). But Mr Silk has abandoned his earlier attribution of this commentary to John Scotus. See his recent article in *Mediaeval and Renaissance Studies*, 3 (1954), pp. 1–40, in which he criticizes and corrects some of Courcelle's conclusions.

those containing the *Consolatio* nearly four hundred; and the manuscripts of both works vary in date from the ninth to the fifteenth century. In addition, library catalogues show that the *Consolatio* was to be found in several monastic libraries of northern France in the eighth. From both the theological tractates and the *Consolatio* definitions and judgments were gathered, whose authority might be said almost to rival that of the Fathers. Of such we may instance the definition of Person, 'The individual substance of a rational nature'; of Providence, 'Providence is the very divine reason itself, seated in the highest Prince, which disposeth all things'; and of eternity, 'Eternity is a perfect possession altogether of an endless life.'[1] If the modern reader should find less of interest in those dicta which especially engaged the attention of medieval schoolmen and theologians, he will still find many a wise and pithy utterance to arrest and stimulate his thoughts. 'For in other living creatures the ignorance of themselves is nature, but in men it is vice'; 'Finally prosperity with her flatterings withdraweth men from true goodness, adversity recalleth and reclaimeth them many times by force to true happiness'; 'But whom prosperity maketh our friend, adversity will make our enemy'; 'But esteem the goods of the body as much as you will, so that you acknowledge this, that whatsoever you admire may be dissolved with the burning of an ague of three days.'[2]

Far less is known of the life of Benedict than of the lives of his three eminent contemporaries. He wrote nothing but his *Rule*, which may in part illumine the author's character but contains no details of his career; while the only biographical source of value, the second book of Gregory's *Dialogues*, is intended mainly to illustrate the miraculous powers of the saint. Benedict was born (*c.* 480) at Nursia in Umbria. His parents being in good

---

[1] *Tract.*, V, 3—Persona est naturae rationalis individua substantia; *Cons.*, IV, 6—Providentia est ipsa illa divina ratio in summo omnium principe constituta, quae cuncta disponit; *ibid.*, V, 6—Aeternitas igitur est interminabilis vitae tota simul et perfecta possessio.

[2] *Cons.*, II, 5—Nam ceteris animantibus sese ignorare naturae est; hominibus vitio venit; II, 8—Postremo felix a vero bono devios blanditiis trahit, adversa plerumque ad vera bona reduces unco retrahit; III, 4—Sed quem felicitas amicum fecit, infortunium faciet inimicum; III, 7—Sed aestimate quam vultis nimio corporis bona, dum sciatis hoc quodcumque miramini triduanae febris igniculo posse dissolvi.

circumstances in due course sent the boy to Rome for his education. At what age he came and how long he tarried there is not known, but before his training was completed, and when he had scarcely attained to manhood, he broke away and retired to a cave near Subiaco, there for a space to live the life of a hermit. Disgust with the depraved habits and pleasures of his compeers in Rome was the cause of this decision, says the biographer, giving a single reason for an action proceeding from a complex mental process. A yearning for religion and a mystic craving to serve God by sacrificing the goods of this world are a spiritual experience through which many a youth has passed. But what with the majority is a passing phase for a few determines the whole course of their lives; and so it was with Benedict. In time disciples came to live in his vicinity, so that ultimately he established twelve small religious communities, each of twelve monks, close by the cave to which he had first retired. About 520 he left Subiaco and proceeded to Monte Cassino in Campania, where he founded a larger monastery. Not many years later he began the composition of his *Rule* which was probably published *c.* 526. In 542 he was visited by an illustrious personage, the Ostrogothic king Totila. The date of his death is uncertain but most likely falls in 550 or soon after.[1]

The *Rule* contains a preface and seventy-three chapters, most of them brief. The monasticism there portrayed is the perfect communal life of the older and younger brethren who form, as it were, a large family, owing complete and unquestioning obedience to the *Rule* and the abbot, who rules with paternal autocracy. None may have any private possessions, while the conduct of monks who have leave temporarily to absent themselves from the monastery is strictly regulated.[2] The novice having passed through a full year's probation,

> when he is to be received into the community, is to make his vows
> in the oratory before all concerning his stability and monastic

---

[1] This account is indebted to *Saint Benedict and the Sixth Century* by the late Dom John Chapman, a number of whose conclusions have been adopted above. For recent works on Benedict cf. B. Altaner, *Patrologie* (ed. 2; Freiburg i. B., 1950), pp. 433–5.

[2] Briefly the *Rule* is made up as follows: Chapter 1, the four types of monk; 2–3, the abbot; 4–7, the instruments of good works, the monastic virtues of

observance in his conduct (*conversatione morum suorum*) and is to promise obedience before God and His saints to the end that, if he shall ever act contrary thereto, he may know that he stand condemned by Him whom he mocks.[1]

The daily life of the brethren consists of the proper performance of the canonical office, manual occupations, and devotional reading. The proportion of time allotted daily to each of these duties varies to some extent according to the season of the year. Apart from the instructions to set aside a portion of the day for reading and to appoint a weekly *lector*, who shall read aloud at meal-times,[2] there are no regulations about intellectual pursuits. A proper procedure for the admission of boy oblates is laid down, and, though nothing is said of their training, they must have received education sufficient to enable them to take part intelligently in the divine services and to read the Scriptures. The reason why nothing further is specified concerning education, copying of manuscripts, or the details of each monk's daily labours, whether in handicrafts or in 'brain-work', will become apparent when the purpose of the *Rule* has been explained.

Benedict, it is true, never finished his education, but it would be a mistake to interpret Gregory's dictum about him—"scienter nescius et sapienter indoctus"—too literally. He knew his Bible well. The works named by him specifically in the *Rule* are not many—the *Collations* of John Cassian, the *Lives of the Fathers*, the *Rule* of St Basil; but it has been shown that he had read other writings on monasticism as well as some of the works of Jerome

obedience, taciturnity, and humility; 8–18, liturgical chapters giving minute directions for the services at the canonical hours and for the proper psalms and lessons at each; 19–20, chapters supplementary to the preceding and laying down the proper spirit to be observed in psalmody and prayer. The remaining chapters deal with the organization and discipline of the religious community, the admission of oblates, of priests who desire to live in the monastery, and of travelling monks, and the election of the abbot and of the prior or provost (*praepositus*).

[1] *Regula* 58. The meaning of the Latin words cited in brackets has been explained by Chapman, *op. cit.*, Chapter XII; but there seems no reason for changing the manuscript reading *conversatione* to *conversationem*, as he has done. The sense in either case remains the same.

[2] *Regula* 42.—legat unus Collationes vel Vitas Patrum aut certe aliud quod aedificet audientes—non autem Eptaticum aut Regum quia infirmis intellectibus non erit utile illa hora hanc Scripturam audire.

and Augustine.[1] The latinity of the *Regula* must not be used as proof of Benedict's poor education. Much of it is colloquial, especially the liturgical chapters which it would be incumbent on every monk thoroughly to know and understand, although indeed he had to be familiar with the *Rule* as a whole; and it is this use of the vulgar tongue, with its breakdown of inflexions and its unclassical constructions which the stylist trained in literary Latin glibly labels ungrammatical.[2] Benedict does not appear to have known Greek, for, with a single exception, all the Greek words and the few Greek constructions used by him had long before become an integral part of the vocabulary usual in Latin theological authors. Furthermore, Chapman has given cogent reasons for believing that Benedict was familiar with a collection of canons translated from the Greek by Dionysius Exiguus, and has stressed the legalistic tone and phraseology of the *Rule*. We are thus brought face to face with the question, which has been answered in several, mutually irreconcilable ways, what was the occasion and purpose of the Benedictine *Regula*? It has been held that it was composed specifically for Monte Cassino, but its wording contradicts that hypothesis in a number of places. The objections to the view that it was framed for Monte Cassino and such other houses as Benedict may have intended to found are no less decisive. Moreover, one of its noteworthy features is the reference to abuses and, considering its brevity, the great amount of space devoted to penal enactments. In other words, the purpose of the *Rule* is not to lay down ordinances for a new foundation or even for a new monastic order, but to amend laxity in observance and to introduce uniform practice in existing monasteries. Thus one may agree with Chapman that Benedict drew up the *Rule* not merely for the monasteries of Italy but as a general monastic rule for Western Christendom. Chapman's arguments, drawn from the *Rule* itself, are strengthened by further evidence, which shows

---

[1] Cf. the copious references in the third edition (Freiburg i. B., 1935) of Dom Cuthbert Butler's edition of the *Rule*.

[2] Cf. the text of the *Rule* with a full linguistic commentary by B. Linderbauer. Published originally at Metten in 1922, it was reissued with corrections as Heft 17 of the *Florilegium patristicum* at Bonn in 1928. On the latinity of the *Rule* and its use in establishing the superiority of MS. *Sangallensis*, 914 see Christine Mohrmann in *RB*, 62 (1952), pp. 108–39.

that, within a very few years of its composition, it had become known in North Africa and southern Gaul and was probably utilized by Justinian in certain monastic regulations embodied in that emperor's *Novellae.*

The great merit, then, of the *Rule* is its simplicity and an elasticity that permitted its use by men living in different ages and under different social and climatic conditions. As far as it goes it was intended by Benedict to be obeyed absolutely. Beyond that the widest possible discretion is left to the abbot. It is this happy combination of authority in certain basic principles with great latitude in dealing with matters of detail and with circumstances that would vary from country to country, which ensured the success of Benedict's work and made the Benedictine Rule all but universal in the West by the Carolingian Age. And it may be questioned whether any book, except the Bible, has been re-printed so often and in so many different languages as the *Regula.*[1]

The career of Cassiodorus—his full name was Flavius Magnus Aurelius Cassiodorus Senator—was, in spite of certain similarities, in strange contrast to that of Boethius. Like Boethius, he came of a good family whose members had held high office, and he himself had a distinguished official career. He was born *c.* 490 at Scyllacium in southern Italy, was quaestor soon after 507, consul in 514, and before 526 had become *magister officiorum.* Finally, in 533, he attained to the dignity of Praetorian Prefect. He thus filled important posts under three Ostrogothic kings, Theodoric, Athalaric, and Vitiges; yet not all his energies were given to the arduous duties of his office, since from 519 onwards he found time for research and composition. Unlike his older contemporary he retained the confidence of his masters throughout the thirty years or so of his administrative life. This may have been in part a fortunate accident; but mainly Cassiodorus' success may be attributed to his own temperament and inclinations. Eminently practical as he was, he had a genuine admiration for the new masters of Rome, and loyally promoted the policy of the Ostrogothic rulers so to harmonize Gothic and Roman interests

[1] For the spread of the *Rule* since the discovery of printing cf. the superb volume, *Bibliografia de la Regla Benedictina* (Montserrat, 1933), by the present Prefect of the Vatican Library, Anselm M. Albareda.

as to form an inwardly united body politic. His intellectual pursuits or recreation, too, followed a different line to those of Boethius; for, if we except the short treatise, *On the soul*, none of his writings deal with philosophical subjects. But he had a profound interest in Higher Education, regretting especially the absence of facilities for studying and teaching Christian literature in the thorough way that had long been applied to pagan authors. Cassiodorus had seemingly assembled a large library which in these war years was lost or dispersed. To Pope Agapetus he had unfolded a scheme for founding a school or university of Christian studies at Rome. But this plan could not be carried out owing to the disturbed condition of Italy during the short reign of Vitiges which culminated in the collapse of Ostrogothic rule in Italy (540). Cassiodorus seems to have retired into private life a year or two before this catastrophe, but for more than a decade information about him is lacking. Then, from an allusion to him in a letter of Pope Vigilius, we learn that he was in Constantinople in 550, but at what date he had left Italy and in what year he returned there is uncertain. He may have withdrawn to his ancestral home in Bruttium already in 538 and have given effect soon after in a modified form to his educational plans by establishing a monastic community; for it is no more than a guess that the inspiration for this undertaking came from what he learnt during his stay in Constantinople from the quaestor Junillus about the theological school in Nisibis.[1] The name given to this monastic settlement near Scyllacium, whether its foundation took place *c.* 540 or not till *c.* 553, was Vivarium and was derived from the fish-ponds (*vivaria*) that were one of the attractive features of the site. Cassiodorus himself has left some description of it. Such were its allurements that, not without a touch of humour, he thus counselled his monks:

> Thus it chances that your monastery is sought out by others rather than that you can justifiably yearn for the outer world. But these (amenities of the monastery), as you know, are the delight of temporal things, not the future hope of the faithful; the former will pass

[1] The theory that Vivarium was not established until after Cassiodorus' return from Constantinople is based on a passage in the Preface to the *Institutiones* (p. 3, 8–10, ed. Mynors); but the only certain conclusions to be drawn from Cassiodorus' words is that the Preface was written after 550.

away, the latter will abide without end. But placed there (at Vivarium) we will more readily transfer our longing to those things which will make us to reign with Christ.[1]

In this community Cassiodorus remained till his death at the advanced age of over ninety, indefatigably engaged in the two-fold project of furthering his educational ideals and, with admirable farsightedness, of collecting manuscripts of the great literature of the past, Greek and Latin, pagan as well as Christian. And he continued to be busy as a writer and an editor. The works which he had given to the world during his public life were historical. A chronicle, which appeared in 519, is, save for the latest years, a compilation from Jerome and other early sources; it does not appear ever to have become popular. His *History of the Goths* in twelve books was a more ambitious undertaking, published between 526 and 533, for which he used both Greek authorities and the treatise of the Gothic author, Ablavius. In 551 the Goth Jordanes brought out a shorter *History of the Goths*, which was little more than an abbreviation of Cassiodorus. It is very regrettable that Jordanes has survived while Cassiodorus' *History*, partly perhaps because of its length, was lost at quite an early date. In 537 Cassiodorus issued his *Variae*, a collection of letters and communications written by him during thirty years in the name of his royal masters, as well as his own official correspondence when he was Praetorian Prefect. These four hundred and sixty-eight documents form a historical source of first-rate importance, though their turgid style makes them difficult reading and at times obscures the sense.[2] The short treatise, *On the soul*, was apparently composed within a year or two of his retirement. Cassiodorus' interest in historical writing continued, but his own compositions during the rest of his life dealt with education or theology. First in importance is his book,

---

[1] *Inst.*, I, i, 29 (p. 73, 20–6).

[2] Cassiodorus' style is typical of his time. The epistolary style of the Romans from the time of the younger Pliny tended, in accordance with the taste of the educated class, to be florid and artificial, while the language of official documents became more and more elaborated and overladen with high-sounding phrases. This can be studied in many of the inscriptions from the later second century on, and, above all, in the *Theodosian Code* (A.D. 438). Apart from the ornate Prefaces, Cassiodorus in his later works is clear and easily intelligible.

Institutiones divinarum lectionum, and the less notable continuation, *Institutiones saecularium lectionum*. Composed not later than *c.* 562, the *Institutiones* were intended to explain Cassiodorus' educational programme to the monks of Vivarium.[1] Comparing the ascent to a proper understanding of the Scriptures to Jacob's ladder, the rungs being the writings of the Fathers, he in *Institutiones*, Book I, lays down his plan of study in some detail. 'Read assiduously, diligently return to your reading; for constant and intent meditation is the mother of understanding', he advises. Then, after referring to his own Biblical studies and to his work of collating the most ancient manuscripts of the Bible that he was able to obtain, he describes the contents of each of the nine volumes which make up the monastery copy of the Old and New Testaments. Furthermore, he explains which are the best commentaries on each book, for example, Augustine and Ambrose on Genesis, Hilary, Ambrose, Jerome, and Augustine on the Psalms, Jerome and Hilary on Matthew, Ambrose on Luke, and Augustine on the Fourth Gospel. There may be some good even in heretical writers. Cassiodorus, doubtless following Augustine, points out that some parts of the commentary on the Apocalypse by Tyconius are profitable reading, 'other observations in truth that he interspersed are the very dregs of his poisonous teaching'; and we shall see that the works of Pelagius also engaged his attention. Next he passes on to some explanatory remarks about the four chief councils of the Church—Nicaea, Constantinople, Ephesus, and Chalcedon—and after that he gives some account of Jerome's and Augustine's division of the Scriptures together with some notes on the Greek and Old Latin versions. There follows a most interesting section in which he lays down the methods to be followed in emending the Sacred Writings where a manuscript is corrupt, and so forth. Unusual phrases are to be left untouched, even if they do not conform to the Latin usage of Cassiodorus' own day. Hebrew names are to be left undeclined. Only obvious spelling mistakes—v for b, n for m—shall be corrected. One piece of advice the modern critic and palaeographer must reprehend: emendations in the text are to be as well written

---

[1] The two books are commonly referred to as *Institutiones* I and II. There is a new text-critical edition by R. A. B. Mynors (Oxford, 1937).

as the original, 'that they rather be thought to have been written by the ancients' (*i.e.* the original scribes). After a chapter devoted to praise of the Bible he proceeds to give a kind of syllabus of other authors whose study he would advocate. The list includes a good selection of historians, mainly ecclesiastical, some works on geography, and a number of agricultural and medical treatises. Above all, Cassiodorus stresses the need for acquaintance with the liberal arts: 'the knowledge of those subjects—the Fathers of the Church were also of this opinion—is undoubtedly useful and not to be shunned, since you find that it is everywhere diffused in the Sacred Writings, as though it were in the fountain-head of general and perfect wisdom'. In justifying the study of secular literature as a means to an end, Cassiodorus is in line with Jerome, Augustine, or Basil; but some of his contemporaries were more rigorist. The promise that he gave to attempt a more detailed treatment of the liberal arts is fulfilled in the *Institutiones saecularium lectionum*. This book, though extensively used in later centuries, is a mere compilation. Its general scheme, as Courcelle has shown, is borrowed from Ammonius of Alexandria, while the material in each section is derived partly from Greek, partly from Latin sources.[1] Grammar, rhetoric, and dialectic are discussed at fair length, but the other four arts receive very brief treatment. Near the end of his life Cassiodorus composed a separate treatise on orthography; this also, though it enjoyed great popularity in the Middle Ages, contains little or nothing that is original.

Cassiodorus' Biblical studies resulted in the composition of several exegetical works, namely, the lengthy *Commenta psalterii*, which is heavily indebted to Augustine, and the sketchy *Complexiones* on the Pauline and Pastoral Epistles, Acts, and Revelation. To these books we may add the commentary on the Pauline Epistles which has come down to us under the name of Primasius, bishop of Hadrumetum in Africa. The true history of this work and Cassiodorus' share in it have been unravelled with masterly skill by Alexander Souter, who has shown that it is an expurgated version of Pelagius' exposition. The commentary on Romans was purged by Cassiodorus himself of the heretical portions and augmented by him with other passages taken from Augustine,

[1] *Les lettres grecques en occident*, pp. 322 ff.

Jerome, and some other authors. The task of freeing the other Epistles from unorthodox doctrine was carried out by Cassiodorus' helpers, and it is worthy of note that great care was taken by both master and pupils to correct the text of the New Testament in the original commentary so as to make it agree with the Vulgate.[1] One of Cassiodorus' assistants, Bellator, also compiled commentaries on several books of the Bible, but, as they have not survived, no opinion about their merit can be formed.

Another activity of the band of scholars in Vivarium which is alluded to in the *Institutiones* (I, 17) was the translation of Greek writers into Latin. The famous *Tripartite History*, to which Cassiodorus wrote an introduction, was a Latin version by Epiphanius Scholasticus of the ecclesiastical histories of Socrates, Sozomen, and Theodoret. Much of the Greek originals was omitted, as the history in its Latin form was compressed into a single volume. The selection and arrangement, which shows more care than has commonly been admitted, was in all likelihood supervised by Cassiodorus himself The translation is uneven and Epiphanius sometimes made serious mistakes. In justice to him, however, one must remember that parts of the Greek originals were exceptionally difficult to render into Latin, and also that the Greek texts at his disposal in Vivarium were already in some degree corrupt. No less valuable was a Latin rendering of Josephus' *Antiquities of the Jews* and his *Treatise against Apion*, but we do not know the name of the translator. The scholars in Vivarium also turned several Greek commentaries on the Bible into Latin. The version of John Chrysostom's *Homilies on the Epistle to the Hebrews* by Mutianus is the most important of these historically, because it was widely read in the Middle Ages and underlies later expositions of this Epistle.[2]

[1] See A. Souter, *Pelagius' Exposition of Thirteen Epistles of St Paul* in two volumes (Cambridge, England, 1922–26). For the Cassiodorus commentary see I, p. 15 and pp. 318 ff.

[2] For the *Historia Tripartita* see Laistner in *Harvard Theol. Rev.*, 41 (1948), pp. 51–67; a new text-critical edition has recently appeared as *CSEL*, 71. For the Latin Josephus cf. Franz Blatt in *Classica et Medievalia*, I (1938), pp. 228–33. On the influence of Mutianus' translation of Chrysostom see E. Riggenbach, *Die ältesten lateinischen Kommentare zum Hebräerbrief* (Leipzig, 1907), pp. 11 ff.

Although there is no positive evidence that Cassiodorus knew Benedict, it is possible that he was familiar with the *Rule*, and that the organization of Vivarium was in general accord with Benedict's ordinances. But the problem of Cassiodorus' acquaintance with the *Rule* has become part of a larger question. A lively controversy has arisen in recent years over the relationship of the *Regula Benedicti* to an anonymous monastic *Rule*, the so-called *Regula Magistri*, which survives wholly or in part in several early manuscripts. A number of scholars have tried to prove that this anonymous work was used by Benedict in framing his own *Rule*, but majority opinion still rightly upholds the priority of the *Regula Benedicti*. The fact that the *Regula Magistri* agrees in many passages with the later, interpolated version of the *Regula Benedicti* would seem to be conclusive.[1] Attempts have also been made to assign the *Regula Magistri* to a known author; of several proposals the most attractive is that of Cappuyns who would attribute this *Rule* to Cassiodorus, though the evidence is not conclusive.[2] But if the precise organization of Vivarium is uncertain, there is no doubt that Cassiodorus, baulked of his scheme to establish a Christian university in Rome, carried out his plans on a smaller scale in southern Italy. His community was one of Christian scribes and scholars for whom, as we have seen, he drew up a careful plan of studies. Those not fitted for intellectual pursuits might work in the fields and orchards of the monastery. In the centuries following his death monasteries became the sole repositories of culture and education in Western Europe; the same period saw the general adoption of the Benedictine *Rule*, a gradual but sure process. The fact that these developments could hardly have been as wide-spread or as successful as they were without the support and encouragement of enlightened temporal rulers does not detract from the greatness or the importance of Cassiodorus' life-work in setting so inspiring an example and so high a standard of achievement for later generations to emulate. Yet the

[1] For recent literature on the *Regula Magistri* cf. RB, 59 (1949), p. 166* and the penetrating essay by Ezio Franceschini in *Liber Floridus: Festschrift Paul Lehmann* (Eosverlag, St Ottilien, 1950), pp. 95–119.

[2] See M. Cappuyns in *Recherches de théologie ancienne et médiévale*, 15 (1948), pp. 209–68; cf. also Franceschini, *op. cit.*, p. 117, note 103 and F. Vandenbroucke in *RB*, 62 (1952), pp. 216–73.

fate of Cassiodorus' own works during the earlier Middle Ages is curious and still in part unexplained. The commentary on the Psalms, which is an adaptation from Augustine and others, was widely known by the eighth century, as is shown by extant manuscripts and by the use made of it by Bede at all times of his life.[1] Again the second book of the *Institutiones* and the *De orthographia* became very popular, although they are mere compilations from earlier sources. But Book I of the *Institutiones*, which sets out so clearly Cassiodorus' educational aims and methods and which was fitted to be an invaluable guide for all Christian students, remained relatively neglected. Extant manuscripts show that the transmission of Books I and II was very different. Book II was often copied alone and, in addition to the original text, two interpolated versions of later date survive. Leading men of letters, like Isidore, Bede, or Alcuin were familiar with it, but do not seem to have been familiar with Book I.[2]

The most obvious debt of posterity to Cassiodorus is the preservation of ancient writings, sacred and profane, which would have perished in those disturbed days but for his zeal in bringing together as large and diversified a library as possible. The result was impressive and, in spite of gaps, a very representative collection. Besides most of Ambrose, Augustine, and Jerome, and the chief works of Hilary and John Cassian, there were many less known treatises and commentaries, such as Primasius on the Apocalypse, Pelagius' Exposition of the Pauline Epistles, or the works of Tyconius. Greek theology was represented by homilies or commentaries of Origen, and small portions of the writings of Athanasius, Clement and Cyril of Alexandria, and John Chrysostom, and by Latin translations of some Greek works made before Cassiodorus' time. There was a good selection of historical works,

---

[1] Cf. *Harvard Theol. Rev.*, 41, p. 58, note 12; Bede quotes the commentary in his exposition of the Apocalypse, a very early work, and also in his *Retractatio*, composed near the end of his life.

[2] On the manuscript transmission see the Introduction to Mynors' edition and, for more recent contributions, the articles listed in *Clavis*, No. 906. Courcelle's arguments to show that Bede knew *Institutiones* I are attractive but insufficient to prove his point. See his *Les lettres grecques en occident*, pp. 374-5.

both pagan and Christian. Philosophy was chiefly represented by the translations and commentaries of Boethius. A large collection of grammatical works, but few rhetorical treatises—though Quintilian was among them—some Ciceronian speeches, Virgil, Horace, Lucan, and, finally, some medical and agricultural handbooks made up a library of remarkable richness in that age, as well as one admirably adapted to those purposes which Cassiodorus had in view.[1]

It was probably in the very year in which Belisarius made himself master of Ravenna and took Vitiges prisoner (540) that the future Pope Gregory I was born. Little is recorded of his early life. His parents were both members of good Roman families, and their son presumably enjoyed the usual education of his class. He was destined for an administrative career and advanced so far that he became *praetor urbanus* at Rome in or shortly before 573. When his father died not long afterwards, Gregory used his ample fortune to found seven religious houses, six in Sicily and one dedicated to St Andrew in his father's mansion in Rome. To this he himself retired as a monk. His exceptional talents must, however, have become well known; for much against his will he was compelled to abandon his cloistered life, first to become seventh deacon of Rome, and then to take the very responsible post of papal nuncio (*apocrisiarius*) in Constantinople. This position he appears to have filled for six years (579–85?). On returning to Rome he was elected abbot of St Andrew's. In 589, on the death from pestilence of Pelagius II, Gregory, in spite of his strong protests, was chosen to succeed him. His formal installation was carried out on September 3, 590, after the Emperor's sanction had been obtained from Constantinople.

Few men placed in a position of the highest authority have lived through times as difficult and troubled as were the fourteen years during which Gregory occupied the chair of Peter. By virtue of its patrimony the Roman see was now the greatest land-owner in Italy, and, in addition, held much property in other parts of the Empire. Even with an efficient staff of helpers the proper direction

---

[1] For the library cf. Courcelle, *op. cit.*, pp. 342 ff., but some of his conclusions are open to doubt. Cf., for example, *CLA*, IV, p. xxvii, and *CLA*, I, p. 34, with Courcelle, *op. cit.*, pp. 350–1.

of the resulting business was a heavy burden. The maintenance of good relations with the Temporal Power—the Emperor at Constantinople and his representative in Italy, the Exarch of Ravenna—was at times a difficult task. Frequent plagues and famines and the constant attacks of the Lombards drained Italy of her people and her resources, and entailed frightful misery for the survivors. It was to the Pope that men looked first of all to guide them, succour them, and help them through these calamitous years. Even a robust man might have quailed at the labour and the responsibility. Gregory fulfilled his high destiny with such success that his papacy became a model for future incumbents in the Roman see; in addition he found some time for authorship, although throughout his tenure of the papacy to his death in 604 he was constantly racked by a painful malady. Of his official actions the one fated to have the most weighty consequences in the history of culture was the dispatch in 596 of a mission under Augustine, a monk of St Andrew's, to convert the English, a project which he had apparently thought of some time before he became Pope. Hardly less momentous were his untiring efforts to establish Western monasticism on a secure foundation. An intense admirer of St Benedict, Gregory strove to increase the number of religious houses not only in Italy and Sicily, but wherever his authority was of sufficient weight, to remedy abuses in existing monasteries and convents, and to secure the general adoption of the Benedictine *Rule*. The fullest source for the history of these endeavours as for his multifarious administrative duties is a collection of his letters numbering 854 all told.

It is, however, with his teaching as found in his other writings that we are here concerned. Although all his genuine works were published after 590, the longest, his exposition in thirty-five books of the Book of Job, had been begun years before when he was residing in Constantinople. It was finally given to the world in 595. The *Dialogues* had appeared in the previous year. The forty *Homilies on the Gospel* seem to have been delivered by himself or read for him by notaries during 590 and 591. They were followed by twenty-two *Homilies on Ezekiel*. The official versions of these two sets of homilies were published in 592 and in 601 or 602.

Finally the *Liber Regulae Pastoralis* or *Pastoral Rule* was issued by Gregory at the very beginning of his papacy.[1]

His longest work, *Moralia in Iob*, can hardly be called a commentary; for the explanation of the literal or historic sense of the book forms but a small fraction of the whole. Gregory's purpose was to expound with great fullness the allegorical and moral senses, the result being a combination of mystical interpretation with lengthy disputations on Christian ethics, which to most modern tastes is exceedingly far-fetched and tiresome. A typical example of this exegesis will best explain Gregory's method. The following is his disquisition on the words (Job xxx, 4) 'and the root of junipers was their food':

> (*Heretics*) *seek the gain of this life alone.* The juniper tree has pricks at the point of its leaves. The leaves it puts forth are so rough that like thorns they avail to prick him who handles them. Now every sin is a thorn, because, while it draws to pleasure, it as it were by its pricking lacerates the mind. Hence the voice of the just and penitent man saith (Psalms xxxi, 4): *I have communed with my grief while it is broken by a thorn,* because verily the mind turns to lament so that by repentance the pricking of sin may be broken. However, in another translation the reading is not 'broken by' but 'impaled on' a thorn, a version which really signifies the same because the penitent's mind is drawn to grief, while the fault committed is impaled and held fast in his mind. By the juniper root therefore what else is meant save avarice, from which the thorn of all sins is produced. Concerning which Paul saith (I Timothy vi, 10): *The love of money is the root of all evil.* Avarice arises in the mind secretly, but openly it brings forth in its works the pricks of all sins. It is these pricks in sooth that rise up from this root to which the admirable preacher alludes, when he adds (*ibid.*): *which while some coveted after, they have erred from the faith and pierced themselves through with many sorrows;* for, in speaking of many sorrows, he has, so to say, indicated the pricks that are born from this root. Therefore by junipers, yea and by the root of junipers, what else do we understand than avarice, that is, the substance of sins? Since, then, heretics for the most part in their words pursue worldly gains alone, and, knowing full well that they are

---

[1] An allegorical exposition of I Samuel included among the printed works of Gregory has been labelled spurious by most scholars; but Chapman (*op. cit.*, pp. 200–1) and Capelle (*RB*, 41, p. 205) believe that it is a genuine work of Gregory's which has been worked over by another hand. In the same article Capelle has also demonstrated the authenticity of two homilies on the opening verses of the Song of Songs.

raising up perversity, nevertheless do not forsake the teachings of errors, while they wish to gain the rewards of would-be learned men, a holy man has now well said concerning them: *and the root of junipers was their food;* inasmuch as, while they ponder avarice with all the senses of their mind, they, as it were, feed on that food from which undoubtedly the pricks of ensuing sins are born. And these men, if ever they wisely find aught in the sacred words, while they understand them not, imagine that they support their own assertions; and then with noisy clamour they scatter these words on their unhappy hearers for whose substance, not their souls, they hunger.[1]

The work was not intended by its author for the general public. Hearing that the archbishop of Ravenna had directed passages from it to be read to the congregation, he wrote to the sub-deacon there:

> I have not welcomed the information which has come to me from the account of certain persons, that my reverend brother and fellow bishop, Marinianus, is causing my commentary on the blessed Job to be read publicly at Vigils; for that work is not popular, and to uninstructed hearers is productive of hindrance rather than of help. . . . I do not wish, while I am in this flesh, that whatever it has fallen to me to have said, should be generally made known to men.[2]

This process of 'stripping off the bark of the letter to find a deeper and more sacred meaning in the pith of the spiritual sense',[3] is not confined to Gregory's esoteric writings. We meet it constantly in his sermons, even in those on the New Testament which are far more popular in tone than the *Homilies on Ezekiel*;[4] nor is it wholly absent from the *Pastoral Rule* and the *Dialogues*.

Gregory was a great preacher, though he lacks the polished elegance of an Ambrose, a Chrysostom, or an Augustine. In one respect at least he was an innovator, for frequently near the end of his discourse he introduces some story with which to keep his hearers' interest alive and from which to point a moral. As for their content, the chief interest of the *Homilies* today lies in the picture they afford of the unhappy political and social conditions of that age. The four books of *Dialogues* form a collection of miracles, visions, and prophecies. Beyond the fact that Books 1

---

[1] *PL*, 76, col. 150A–C.   [2] *Epist.*, 12, 6.

[3] 'Retecto cortice literae, altius aliud et sacratius in medulla sensus spiritalis invenire', Bede, Preface to the commentary on Ezra (*PL*, 91, col. 808B).

[4] Cf., e.g., *PL*, 76, coll. 883B and 1082C–D.

and 3 are mainly devoted to miraculous events—raising from the dead, healing, expulsion of unclean spirits, and so forth—while Book 4 chiefly relates to dreams and visions and 2 is concerned entirely with Benedict of Nursia, there is no particular arrangement or unity in the work. The treatise of Gregory which displays most originality, because it is based on his personal experience, is his *Pastoral Rule*. It is divided into four books. In the first Gregory, likening the bishop's work to that of the physician, describes it as the healing of souls, a metaphor which, as applied to the philosopher, is at least as old as the Platonic Socrates.[1] The bishop must be specially suited by nature and training for his task, and reluctant to undertake it, but not beyond a certain point. We are given a careful description of the character of one fitted for the episcopate and then of one who is not. Both chapters are remarkable for their insight. The second book deals with the bishop's life, that is to say, just as Book 1 discusses him as a personality, so Book 2 treats of him in relation to his fellowmen, and particularly to those placed under his spiritual charge. He must be a good psychologist, so as to distinguish sham from real goodness. He must be practical, too, yet not so as to pay too much attention to mundane affairs. In one of his sermons, indeed, Gregory deplores the excessive worldliness of bishops in his day.[2] In the third book preaching and teaching are considered, and Gregory, emphasizing that the bishop's instruction must always be suited to his hearers, distinguishes no less than thirty-six types of person to whose different needs his advice and exhortation must be adapted. The brief fourth book is a reminder to the bishop to know himself, or, in Gregory's own words:

He must take great care to bite himself with the laceration of fear, lest he, who by healing other men's wounds, recalls them to health, may himself swell up through neglect of his own safety, may while helping others forsake himself, may fall whilst raising others up.[3]

All the works of Gregory, 'the Fourth Doctor of the Latin Church', enjoyed unrivalled popularity and exerted a profound

---

[1] Cf. Plato, *Politicus* 293A, 295–6; *Sophist* 230C. In one instance the art of the statesman, in the other the art of the educator is compared to the physician's.

[2] *PL*, 76, col. 1146A–D. [3] *PL*, 77, col. 125B.

influence throughout the Middle Ages. One or more of his works might be expected in any monastic library, as is shown by library catalogues from the eighth century on. The number of extant manuscripts is exceedingly great. More than a dozen chrestomathies are known compiled from the *Moralia* or other Gregorian works, the earliest in date being that compiled by the monk Paterius, a younger contemporary of the Pope. The seventh book of Bede's commentary on the Song of Songs is a cento of extracts from Gregory's works. He was used and quoted, with or without acknowledgement, during the succeeding centuries with as much constancy as Jerome or Augustine. His *Pastoral Rule* was cited as authoritative in several councils of the Carolingian Age, which shows that this book had attained a quasi-canonical standing; indeed, it became for the secular clergy what the *Rule* of St Benedict was for the monastic orders. This same book was translated into Greek by Anastasius of Antioch in Gregory's lifetime and in the eighth century a Greek version of the *Dialogues* was composed by Pope Zacharias. When the vernacular tongue began to be used as a literary medium in England, works by Gregory were among the first to be translated; for the *Regula Pastoralis* and *Dialogues* were rendered into Old English by Alfred and his helpers. Nearly a hundred years later Aelfric translated some forty homilies by Latin authors, among them being several of Gregory's. At St Gall his contemporary, Notker Labeo, translated portions of the *Moralia* into Old High German, while the survival of sundry manuscripts of the *Dialogues* and *Homilies* with Old High German glosses is a further proof of the zeal with which their author was studied. A thirteenth-century manuscript in Berne (*Bernensis*, 79) contains an Old French rendering of the first twelve *Homilies on Ezekiel*.

Gregory was neither a profound nor an original thinker. His spiritual master was Augustine whose teaching and doctrines he assimilated with rare thoroughness, yet without sounding completely the depths of Augustine's thought. Compared with Boethius or Cassiodorus, or with the great theologians of the fourth century, he lacks distinction as a writer, as well as width of culture. The Bible, which he must have known wellnigh by heart, is almost the sole source from which he introduces citations into his writings, and he does so constantly. His attitude to pagan letters, as expressed in the preface to the *Moralia* and in his famous letter to Bishop Desiderius of Vienne, has often been discussed though not always with real insight; for in reproving the Gallican bishop for lecturing on profane authors Gregory doubtless had in mind, first and foremost, that a bishop, to be true to his high office, could and should have no time for anything else. Yet he adds:

> For the same mouth cannot sing the praises of Jupiter and the praises of Christ. Consider yourself how offensive, how abominable a thing it is for a bishop to recite verses which are unfit to be recited even by a religious layman.[1]

This shows his general disapproval of secular literature. The reason for his attitude is obvious. Social conditions in his time were very different from what they had been one hundred and fifty years before. The decline of general culture in Italy and beyond, which had resulted from the unstable political conditions accompanied by much social and economic distress, produced a lowering of moral standards, and at the same time promoted the growth of popular superstitions. The man who would reform moral laxity and transform superstition into beliefs sanctioned by the Church would see in pagan literature his worst enemy. The condemnation of rhetoric and grammatical composition, on the other hand, must not be taken too seriously. Who can blame Gregory for condemning in those who wrote on sacred subjects the type of literary preciosity which in the previous century had produced the letters of Apollinaris Sidonius? But Gregory himself is not as uncouth an author as he would have us believe. He is the man who penned that very paragraph in the preface to the *Moralia* which has just been considered; who could describe St Benedict (Pref. to *Dialog.*, II) as 'scienter nescius et sapienter indoctus'; who could compose a passage like the following, in which each half sentence perfectly balances the other:

> Sit rector bene agentibus per humilitatum socius, contra delin-
> quentium vitia per zelum iustitiae erectus; ut et bonis in nullo se
> praeferat, et cum pravoram culpa exigit, potestatum protinus sui
> prioratus agnoscat, quatenus et honore suppresso aequalem se

[1] *Epist.*, 11, 34. The translation is by F. H. Dudden.

subditis bene viventibus deputet, et erga perversos iura rectitudinis exercere formidet.[1]

Is it not evident that in his youth he had studied at least the first three of the liberal arts to some purpose? The most remarkable gap in Gregory's education is his ignorance of Greek. If he did not himself assure us of this, we should find it difficult to believe that he could reside six years in Constantinople without acquiring some knowledge of that language. Gregory was above all a practical man and an organizer. If, as can scarcely be doubted, he had more than a little imperiousness in his nature, he had learnt as a monk and as an abbot first to obey, then to command. To such a man authority and faith were of more weight than reason. For authority there were two sources, Holy Writ and Tradition. Nor had Gregory the Pope lost the austerity of Gregory the monk. He was thoroughly consistent, therefore, in stressing the need of penance, and in elaborating the doctrine of purgatory, which in itself was not new, and elevating it to the dignity of a Church dogma, which was new. Gregory's God, one is tempted to observe, is the stern Jehovah of the Pentateuch and the Prophets rather than the God of Love of the New Testament. Yet, just as his letters reveal him labouring amid war, pestilence, famine, and flood for the bodily welfare of his people, so in the sermons and *Dialogues* he provided them with the spiritual food which they could best assimilate. The popular belief of that age in all varieties of supernatural phenomena, and not least in the malignant agency of evil spirits, belief which often had its deepest roots in pagan cults, no man, not even Gregory, could have suppressed. But he could and did transform or harness it to serve the ends of Christian dogma. His teaching is the primary source of those practices and doctrines, which are so inseparable from the religious life of the Middle Ages—the worship of saints, the veneration of relics, the doctrine of demons and angels who often intervene directly in human affairs.

His influence on Church organization and on the development of the Church's authority was no less profound. The tropological or moral interpretation of the Scriptures has its most thorough-going exponent in him; and what is its purpose? To interpret any

[1] *PL*, 77, col. 34B.

given passage in the Bible as referring to individual Christians and still more to the Church of Christ. His attitude to heretics is unrelenting, even to the point of what the Germans call 'Schadenfreude'. There is only one Church in which man can hope to find salvation.

> For it is the Church alone through which God willingly accepts a sacrifice, the Church alone which intercedes with confidence for those that are in error. The true Sacrifice of the Redeemer is offered only in the one Catholic Church. It is the Church alone in which a good work is fruitfully carried on. It is the Church alone which guards those who are within it by the strong bond of charity. It is the Church alone in which we truly contemplate heavenly mysteries. For truth shines forth from the Catholic Church alone.[1]

The Church is the sole authority on doctrine. The Temporal Power, though it may be required to intervene against the enemies of the Church, has no right to meddle with spiritual matters or with the affairs of the Church. But, unlike the great popes of later ages, Gregory deprecates the interference of the Church or its ministers in secular business; nor is there any hint that the ecclesiastical authority should ever usurp the powers of the State. The 'consul of God'[2] might write fearlessly to the emperor, but he did not challenge his supremacy. Finally, Gregory reformed and fixed the text of the Roman Mass and revised the texts of those portions of the services that were sung; but that he was the author also of the melodic part, that is to say, the author of the so-called Gregorian chant, is a later legend.[3]

In Italy during the first half of the sixth century it was not merely in Rome that secular letters were still cultivated; for there were schools of rhetoric both in Milan and in Ravenna. It was in the capital of the exarchate that Venantius Fortunatus received his early training, while Milan could boast of several teachers who were also authors. Ennodius, though a native of Arles, was educated at Milan in the school of Deuterius. He later entered

---

[1] *PL*, 76, col. 756C–D. The translation is by F. H. Dudden.

[2] See the last couplet of Gregory's epitaph in Bede, *E.H.*, 2, 1:

> Hisque Dei consul factus laetare triumphis;
> Nam mercedem operum iam sine fine tenes.

[3] For the *Sacramentarium Gregorianum* and the *Antiphonarium* see the bibliographies in Altaner, *op. cit.*, p. 421, and *Clavis*, Nos. 1902–4.

the Church, ultimately to become bishop of Pavia (513). His writings in prose and verse are characteristically turgid and artificial, giving abundant proof of his acquaintance and sympathy with profane literature, but they lack ideas and make irksome reading. Still, it is remarkable to find a highly placed ecclesiastic warmly advocating the study of the liberal arts in a letter to two young men. Later in life, while convalescing from a serious illness, the bishop regretted his former worldliness as an author:

> Thus while the glamour of superabundant harmony in the fields of rhetoric and poetry were agitating me, I had strayed from true wisdom to follow the false, desiring only to mount the breezes of vain panegyric and to acquire disdain for orisons (*orandi*), the while I was enthralled by the yearning for perorations (*perorandi*).[1]

Arator was his protégé and at first his pupil; later he continued his studies under Parthenius. He became an advocate, and then entered the Government service. Finally he withdrew from public life to become a sub-deacon of Rome. The only certain date in his life is the year 544, in which he presented to Pope Vigilius his poem in two books on the Acts of the Apostles.[2] Unhappily, not content with singing the achievements of Peter and of Paul, Arator tried also to shine as a commentator. But this attempt to combine an epic narrative with an exposition of Acts destroys the unity of the poem and impairs it as a work of art. He was evidently well read in the chief classical and the earlier Christian poets. Yet his mastery over the hexameter is not perfect, nor can his ear have been very sensitive to rhythm, seeing that we find as many as eleven consecutive lines (i, 695–705) with the same caesura. The modern reader is also likely to be wearied by the poet's fondness for allegorical interpretation. To the Middle Ages, however, this feature would be an added recommendation, and the popularity of the poem was great. It reached Britain early, being cited by Aldhelm and still more by Bede. Later it became favourite literature with the authors of the Carolingian Age. In Italy itself it seems to have had little vogue, and still less

---

[1] For the letter see *MGH*, AA, VII, pp. 310–15. The quotation is on p. 310, 22–26.

[2] For the poem see *CSEL*, 72 (Vienna, 1952), edited by A. P. McKinlay, which supersedes all earlier editions.

in Spain. In monastic circles intellectual occupation centred mainly in theology. Eugippius, abbot of the monastery of St Severinus near Naples, which was noted for the activity of its *scriptorium* and the richness of its library, is characterized by Cassiodorus as remarkable more for his knowledge of Scripture than for his acquaintance with secular authors. A biography by him of St Severinus, the apostle of Noricum, whose companion Eugippius had been in his youth, and a massive chrestomathy compiled by him from the works of Augustine, are extant.

(b) North Africa, Spain, and Gaul

Conditions in North Africa, Spain, and Gaul during the sixth century were far less favourable to culture and intellectual life than in contemporary Italy, where the rapid decline only set in after the destruction of the Ostrogothic kingdom, whereas in the other countries wars, invasions, and the misery that came in their train, filled the entire century.

In Africa, so long a home of secular culture and a nursery of great theologians, a feeble flame of learning continued to flicker. Perhaps the most interesting figure is Flavius Cresconius Corippus, who by profession was a teacher. He had probably reached middle life when he published his epic poem in eight cantos on Justinian's general Johannis and his successful campaign against the Moors (546-8). It is not only a valuable historical source but a work of marked poetic merit. The author was steeped in the poety of earlier ages—Virgil, Ovid, Lucan, Claudian, as well as some of the Christian poets—and reminiscences, especially from the *Aeneid*, abound on every page. But, if Corippus owes a heavy debt to others for the language and cadences of his poem, he has at least thoroughly absorbed what those masters could teach him, and he is a far more skilled versifier than his contemporary, Arator. The *Iohannis* is sustained at a surprisingly high level, and some passages in it little deserve the neglect with which the work is habitually treated. The battle descriptions are full of spirit (e.g. IV, 136–90), the speeches are natural and free from the artificiality of the *rhetor* (e.g. I, 377–410 or II, 357–413), and there are true grandeur and pathos in the description of the gallant captain who, after sustaining a magnificent fight against a host of enemies, perishes with his steed in a marsh. It may be quoted as a specimen of Corippus' art at its best:

> Est locus in mediis longe praeruptus harenis,
> fluminis in morem pelagi quem margine fluctus
> alluit atque undis agros concludit amaris
> egrediens: quibus alga locis limusque relabens
> atque altum tremulo putret sub gurgite caenum.
> Huc ubi pervenit, nigras equus horruit algas
> et pavidus post terga redit. Tunc naribus afflans
> erexit geminas (signum formidinis) aures,
> datque latus spumatque ferox oculosque retorquet
> prospiciens, nec dirum audet temptare periclum.
> Finierat spatium vitaeque viaeque repugnans
> dux, heu, magnanimus. Sequitur clamoribus hostis
> densus agens turbansque virum. Tunc calce frequenti
> pulsat equum geminans et magnos concutit armos.
> Exsilit impulsus sonipes cursuque negatam
> temptat adire viam, absorptusque voragine mersit
> ipse cadens, dominumque super gluttivit hiatu
> terra nefanda fero, rapuitque ex hoste receptum
> suscipiens fortuna virum, ne staret inermis
> aut humilis precibusque rogans, tribuitque sepulcrum,
> ne nudum in Libycis iacuisset corpus harenis.[1]

Corippus gave a successful public recitation of his poem at Carthage, which shows that there at least this popular form of entertainment still survived in spite of the clash of arms and the surrounding desolation. His more tangible reward was a post in the imperial civil service at Constantinople. His other work, a panegyric on the Emperor Justin II, published c. 567, is a bombastic and wearisome composition.

With the exception of Victor of Tonnenna, who compiled a chronicle extending from 444 to 567 and devoted almost wholly to ecclesiastical affairs, the African prose writers were all theological. Primasius, bishop of Hadrumetum, was the author of a commentary on Revelation which enjoyed some popularity in later centuries. To modern scholars it is of some interest, because it is one of the works from which the lost commentary of Tyconius, from whom Primasius borrowed freely, can be partly reconstructed. Verecundus wrote an exposition of nine canticles in the

[1] *Iohannis*, VI, 753–74.

Old Testament, while Junillus, a protégé of Primasius, composed an introduction to the study of the Bible (*Instituta regularia divinae legis*) which was a Latin version of a treatise by the Persian, Paul of Nisibis. Since Paul was influenced by the works of Theodore of Mopsuestia, the *Instituta* helped to make the West familiar with the Antiochene school of exegesis.[1] The middle of the century saw an embittered theological controversy caused by the action of Pope Vigilius in condemning, in deference to the importunate demands of Justinian, the so-called Three Chapters.[2] In Africa Vigilius' conduct was viewed with especial disfavour and provoked both polemic and expository writings. Ferrandus (died *c.* 546) is best known as the author of a life of Fulgentius of Ruspe and as the first scholar in Africa to put together a collection of canons (*breviatio canonum*), partly Eastern, partly African. A number of his letters has also survived. One of them, addressed to two deacons in Rome, deals with the doctrinal controversy just named, and condemns the decision of Justinian on the ground that it is a direct attack on the Council of Chalcedon. A younger contemporary, Facundus, composed an elaborate treatise, *In defence of the Three Chapters* (*c.* 550). It was followed some years later by a short but virulent diatribe, *Against Mocianus*, and a pamphlet entitled, *Letter of the Catholic Faith in defence of the Three Chapters*. The *Breviarium causae Nestorianorum et Eutychianorum*, compiled between 555 and 567 by a deacon of Carthage, Liberatus, was very timely; for it provided in a convenient form a summary of the Christological disputes which had agitated the Eastern, and to some extent the Western, Church from the patriarchate of Nestorius (428–31) to the Fifth Oecumenical Council (553). The writer, who consulted good sources and presented his material clearly, was himself a staunch defender of Chalcedon and the Three Chapters.

Spain, once one of the most cultured as it was one of the most prosperous provinces of the Roman Empire, had fallen on evil days. In the first half of the sixth century the Visigothic kingdom had declined in power and territory before the attacks of

---

[1] Cf. Laistner in *Harvard Theol. Rev.*, 40 (1947), pp. 19–31.

[2] Cf. T. G. Jalland, *The Church and the Papacy* (London, 1944), pp. 341 ff.; E. L. E. Caspar, *Geschichte des Papsttums*, II, pp. 234 ff.

Byzantine commanders in the south and of the Franks in the north. The Suevic kingdom had shrunk till it embraced no more than the north-western corner of the peninsula. Difference of creed was a no less potent factor of disruption than difference of race or of political allegiance; for the struggle between orthodoxy and Arianism was nowhere more acute than there. With the accession of Leovigild (567–86) Visigothic fortunes revived. He recovered important centres like Malaga and Corduba from the Byzantines, wrested Narbonne from the Franks, and made himself master of the Suevic kingdom. A staunch Arian, he took measures to repress Catholic orthodoxy, and banished its most prominent adherents. But his successor, Reccared, adopted the Catholic faith and a new era of orthodoxy was ushered in by the Third Council of Toledo (589). The Catholic rulers of Visigothic Spain not only took strong measures to suppress Arianism but, unlike their Arian predecessors, were most intolerant of the Jews. For more than a century they pursued a policy of extreme severity against them with the aim of bringing about their forcible conversion or else expulsion from the kingdom.[1]

The number of writers in sixth-century Spain was small; most of them are little more than names recorded in Isidore of Seville's short literary history, De viris illustribus, intended as a continuation of the works with the same title of Jerome and Gennadius. Justus, bishop of Urgel, whose name appears among the signatories of the Second Council of Toledo (531) and of the Council of Lerida (524), was the author of a short commentary on the Song of Songs, in which the interpretation is wholly allegorical. It seems to have enjoyed some popularity in the eighth and ninth centuries, but thereafter was forgotten.[2] His brother, Justinian, bishop of Valentia, composed a treatise, now lost, in which five questions of dogma were expounded according to orthodox teaching. Their contemporary, Apringius, bishop of Pace, compiled a commentary on the Apocalypse of which only fragments remain. Of far greater distinction was Martin. 'He was a native of Pannonia, whence he set forth for the East to visit holy places,

---

[1] Cf. the excellent summary in S. Katz, The Jews in the Visigothic and Frankish Kingdoms of Spain and Gaul (Cambridge, Mass., 1937), pp. 11–22.

[2] Cf. Laistner in Harvard Theol. Rev., 46 (1953), p. 40.

and became so well versed in letters that he was held second to none among the men of his day.'[1] From the Orient Martin found his way to Spain (c. 550) for reasons and in circumstances that are unknown. In Galicia he founded an abbey at Dumio and became its first abbot. Somewhat later he was consecrated bishop of Braga, a position that he filled till his death in 579. His chief fame rests on his missionary labours which brought about the conversion of the Suevi from the Arian to the Catholic belief, a work that had already been begun but had not greatly advanced before Martin's arrival in Spain. His extant works, though all brief, give proof of his zeal and ability, and bear out the general truth of the eulogy pronounced by Gregory of Tours. Martin's strenuous work as an ecclesiastical administrator is illustrated by two tracts on baptism and on the paschal question, as well as by the prominent part which he played at the First and Second Councils of Braga (561 and 572). His authorship of ten chapters submitted and approved in 572 is certain and there is little doubt that he also compiled the Acts of both Councils. The knowledge of Greek acquired in the East he put to use for the benefit of his monks by translating into Latin a collection of 109 sayings attributed to Egyptian abbots, while, at his instigation, the monk Paschasius who had been taught Greek by him produced a rendering of a similar collection, entitled *Verba seniorum*. Of greater interest are two ethical treatises composed by Martin in the last decade of his life, *De ira* and *Formula vitae honestae*, not because they show any originality, but because both are adapted and abbreviated from works of the younger Seneca, the one from Seneca's essay of the same name, the other from a treatise now lost. Martin's two tracts are valuable evidence that some at least of Seneca's writings were still available in the land of his birth during the sixth century. Three other short essays of ethical content, as Martin's latest editor has shown conclusively, reveal his familiarity with the works of John Cassian.[2]

That a missionary and reforming bishop should cultivate the

[1] Gregory of Tours, *History of the Franks*, V, 27 (37).

[2] Cf. C. W. Barlow, *Martini episcopi Bracarensis opera omnia* (New Haven, 1950), p. 53; for the *De correctione rusticorum* see pp. 159 ff. and the dissertation *Paganism and Pagan Survivals in Spain*, by Stephen McKenna (Washington, 1938).

art of preaching might have been safely assumed even without concrete proof. His *De correctione rusticorum* is a sermon in the form of a letter addressed to his fellow-bishop, Polemius of Asturica, at some date between 572 and 574. As a popular exposition expressed in simple Latin with a strong colloquial tinge it has an individual character of its own, even though its author has clearly been influenced by some sermons of Caesarius of Arles. Its main purpose is to combat the idolatry and pagan practices which were still rife among the peasants of his day. Martin begins by discoursing on the origin of idolatry and the belief in pagan gods. From this he passes to the life and Passion of Christ who was sent to redeem the world and to the Last Judgment In the second part of his address he reminds his hearers of the promises that they had made at baptism, and demonstrates how their heathenish practices and superstitions are in direct contradiction to their former professions. A general exhortation to persist in good works and orthodox belief, and especially to keep Sunday holy, brings this notable composition to a close. The allusions to all manner of rustic superstitions are of particular interest. We hear how the country folk kept days of moths and mice or lit candles by rocks, trees, fountains, and at cross-roads; how they observed pagan rites on the first day of the month or celebrated the Volcanalia; how it was the custom to drop bread into wells, to wreathe houses in laurel, to make offerings to trees, and to follow other abominable practices. Thus the sermon, even if in part derived from Caesarius' similar outbursts against paganism in Gaul, throws a vivid light on the beliefs of the common folk, beliefs which were widely prevalent all over the West and which, in spite of the efforts of the Church, lingered on for centuries. Thus, nine years after Martin's sermon we read in the sixteenth chapter of the Third Council of Toledo:

Whereas throughout almost the whole of Spain and Gaul idolatry has flourished, the holy synod, with the consent of the most glorious king, has decreed thus: that every bishop in his diocese, together with the judge of the territory, shall most sedulously seek out the aforenamed sacrilege, and, when he has discovered it, shall not delay to stamp it out.[1]

[1] Mansi, *Concilia*, IX, p. 996.

Martin's warnings were repeated by Eligius of Noyon and by Pirmin in the eighth century, and the penitential literature of the earlier Middle Ages is full of references to such relics of paganism.[1]

Martin of Braga was not the only Spanish prelate in this age who knew the Byzantine world. His younger contemporary, the Goth, John of Biclaro, spent some time in Constantinople *c.* 573. Six years later he was back in Spain; but, being a Catholic, he was exiled by the command of Leovigild. After the king's death (586) he founded the monastery after which he is named; it seems to have been in Catalonia, but its site has not been identified. In 591 John was raised to the see of Gerona, which he administered until his death about thirty years afterwards. He has left us a chronicle which begins at the point where Victor of Tonnenna's leaves off, and which covers a period of nearly a quarter of a century (567-90). In a truly Thucydidean spirit he informs his readers that the events narrated were either experienced by himself or learnt by him from the lips of reliable witnesses. The one written source which he appears to have consulted was the Acts of the Third Council of Toledo. His chronicle has been generally recognized as a valuable and trustworthy source, the more so as he succeeds in being impartial where we should least expect it. He fully admits the greatness of Leovigild's achievements and omits all reference to the religious persecution of which he was himself a victim.[2]

The summit of scholarly achievement in Spain was attained by Isidore of Seville. His elder brother, Leander, who became bishop of Seville *c.* 576 and was himself a respectable scholar, owing to the early death of their father was responsible for the boy's upbringing. Presumably Isidore from the first was destined for the Church and became deacon and priest at the earliest canonical date; for when he was only about thirty years of age (in 599 or 600) he succeeded his brother as bishop of Seville, occupying that see until his death in 636. He presided at a council

[1] Cf. Laistner in *Harvard Theol. Rev.*, 31 (1938), pp. 269-72, and J. T. McNeill and Helena M. Gamer, *Medieval Handbooks of Penance* (New York, 1938), pp. 38 ff. and elsewhere.

[2] For the chronicle see *MGH*, AA, XI, 1, 207 ff.

held in Seville in 619 and at the Fourth Council of Toledo in 633. No other trustworthy facts are recorded of his life which was mainly given over to scholarship. Amongst his friends and correspondents the chief was Braulio, bishop of Saragossa, who edited Isidore's last and greatest work and composed a short biography, in which he enumerated, probably in chronological order, the many writings of his friend.

Isidore was a polymath whose literary pursuits touched every branch of human knowledge. The variety of the subjects on which he wrote and the width of his reading entailed thereby demonstrate the comparative richness of the library at Seville as late as the early seventh century. He appears before us in all his works—with the possible exception of the *Synonyma*—as a compiler. But, if he made no original contributions either to theological thought or to secular learning, his most ambitious compilation became a standard work of reference for centuries to come.[1] We may first take note of his theological works. The *Quaestiones in Vetus Testamentum* are an exposition of certain books of the Old Testament based almost wholly on earlier commentators. While the treatment of the Hexateuch, especially Genesis, runs to some length, the sections on I and II Samuel, I and II Kings, Esdras and Maccabees are exceedingly brief. Isidore indicates his sources at the beginning; they are Ambrose, Jerome, Augustine, Fulgentius, Cassian, Rufinus' translation of homilies by Origen, Victorinus, and Gregory the Great His chief debt is to Augustine and Gregory in this work as also in his *Sententiae*, in which he expounds the nature of the Trinity and of the Angels, and various parts of Christian dogma. The earthly life and Passion of Christ form the subject of the first book of the *De fide catholica contra Iudaeos*, the second book being a polemic against the Jews whose treatment of the Saviour was punished by the destruction and desolation of Jerusalem, while they themselves have been crushed or dispersed. In his *De ecclesiasticis officiis* and his *Regula monachorum* the author deals very fully with the different parts of

---

[1] The complete works of Isidore, reprinted from the edition of Arévalo, will be found in *PL*, 81–4. For the *Chronicle* and the *History of the Visigoths* Mommsen's edition (*MGH*, Chron. min. ii) should be used, for the *Etymologies* the edition by W. M. Lindsay (Oxford, 1911).

Christian worship and the duties of Christian men, and lays down wholesome precepts for the guidance of those devoted to a Christian life. In these works also Isidore largely reproduces the teaching of earlier theologians. He follows Gregory the Great, for whom he feels the greatest veneration, in emphasizing the importance of interpreting the Bible allegorically and in teaching a threefold sense of Scripture. The *Regula* shows marked Augustinian influence, and it is questionable whether Isidore knew the *Rule* of St Benedict.[1] In view of his own predilection for secular learning, one is surprised at his instructions to monastic readers. His attitude recalls that of Gregory rather than the broader outlook of Cassiodorus. 'Let the monk beware of reading the books of gentiles and heretics. It is better for him to be ignorant of their pernicious doctrines than through making acquaintance with them to be enmeshed in error.'[2] His further instructions would delight the heart of any librarian; manuscripts are to be borrowed at the beginning of each day, late-comers not receiving one, and shall be returned after vespers. The two treatises, *De ecclesiasticis officiis* and *Regula monachorum*, represent only a small portion of the unusually influential and important work accomplished by Isidore during his long tenure of the episcopacy in the difficult but necessary field of canon law and ecclesiastical government. He was not only unwearied in improving the organization of the Church in Spain and regularizing both the conduct and lives of the clergy and striving for uniformity in liturgical observance; he also played a momentous part as a canonist. It seems probable that the codification of ecclesiastical law embodied in councils and decretals, which goes under the name of the *collectio Hispana* or *Isidoriana*, was partly his work, or at least was carried out under his general supervision. It is not wonderful, therefore, that his subsequent influence was very great; for it was not only in Spain that his dogmatic and ecclesiastical authority carried weight. It was also invoked in the Frankish Empire, notably at the Council of Aix in 816, the *acta* being full of citations from our author, while the monastic rule of Isidore was one of the works consulted

[1] See Sister Patrick Jerome Mullins, *The Spiritual Life According to St Isidore* (Washington, 1940), pp. 68–75.
[2] PL, 83, col. 877C.

at the same date by Benedict of Aniane when he was engaged in his monastic reforms.[1]

The so-called *Synonyma* is a devotional work, a lamentation for the sorrows of the world, followed by exhortation and counsel how to live like a true Christian, thereby winning the reward of divine forgiveness and ensuring the true happiness of a spiritual life.

From the bishop's historical studies there resulted a *Chronicle*, extant in two recensions, and a *History of the Visigoths*, to which are appended brief accounts of the Vandals and Suevi. This work is prefaced by a short panegyric on Spain, apostrophized by the author in the second person. Neither of these compositions, put together as they are from many earlier histories and chronicles, has any marked historical or literary value. The *Chronicle* was frequently copied, and a century later was used by Bede, whose greatly superior work to a considerable extent superseded Isidore's. The literary history, *De viris illustribus*, which contains some additions by Braulio, is a very slight performance. Far more influential after Isidore's time were the cosmographical treatises *De natura rerum*, and, above all, the *Etymologiae* or *Origines*. *De natura rerum* is dedicated to King Sisebut. It begins with various divisions of time and then passes on to the Sun, Moon, planets, and fixed stars. It ends with short sections describing different natural phenomena, the sea and the River Nile, earthquakes, and Mount Etna. In the main Isidore again copies his predecessors, the astronomical treatise of Hyginus, the pseudo-Clementine *Recognitions* in Rufinus' translation, Ambrose's *Hexaemeron*, Augustine, and some others. But here, as in his *Etymologiae*, it is sometimes doubtful whether Isidore's use of an author is direct or at a second or third hand. Still, the little book had a marked success, although the astronomical portions, judged from a scientific standpoint, compare unfavourably with the less-known treatise by Gregory of Tours. For general use, moreover, one may suspect that it was completely overshadowed by the relevant

---

[1] For Isidore's activities and later influence in canon law see Dom P. Séjourné, *Saint Isidore de Séville: son rôle dans l'histoire du droit canonique* (Paris, 1929); for more recent contributions cf. Altaner, *op. cit.*, p. 213, and *Clavis*, No. 1790.

parts of his encyclopedic work. The *Etymologiae*, which the author did not live to revise, was edited and divided into twenty books or sections by Braulio. A list of these will give some notion of the all-embracing character of this compilation. The first three books are devoted to the seven liberal arts, Grammar in Book I, Rhetoric and Dialectic in Book II, Arithmetic, Geometry, Music, and Astronomy in Book III. The contents of the remaining books are as follows: IV—Medicine; V, 1–27—Law; V, 28–39—Divisions of time and chronology; VI—The books of the Bible and its interpreters; canons, and ecclesiastical offices; VII—God, the Angels and Saints; VIII—The Church and the Sects; IX—Languages, races, kingdoms, the army, citizens, and kinship; X—Etymological word-list arranged under the initial letter, but not in closer alphabetical order; XI—Men and fabulous monsters; XII—Animals; XIII—The Universe and its parts; XIV—The Earth and its parts; XV—Buildings and lands; XVI—Stones and metals; XVII—Agriculture and botany; XVIII—War, games, and pastimes; XIX—Ships, building materials, dress; XX—Food and drink; furniture.

It is easy to sneer at the *Etymologiae* and to point to single items in the book which strike a modern reader as puerile. But it was assuredly no small achievement to put together a compendious encyclopedia of the arts and sciences from many sources, at a time when the larger works of earlier authors on different branches of human knowledge were accessible in very few places, and when few men, in any event, would have been capable of studying them. The fact that Isidore's approach is linguistic, and that he generally introduces each item with an etymological explanation that is often fanciful, if not absurd, has tended to obscure the substantial merits and accuracy of much of his information. Much has been written in recent years on Isidore's plan and method of composition and on his sources; yet it must be admitted that both topics are still to some extent obscure; and it is often easier to be certain of what he did not do than of what he did do.[1] Since many of the items in the *Etymologiae* are found in substantially the same

---

[1] Isidore was long supposed to have made extensive use of lost works by Suetonius. This hypothesis was finally exploded by P. Wessner in *Hermes*, 52 (1917), pp. 201–92.

form in other Isidorian works, notably scientific information appearing both in *De natura rerum* and in Books III, V, and XIII of the encyclopedia, it may be assumed that the author had formed a large collection of excerpts grouped under their appropriate headings, even as a modern compiler might devote his earlier labours to making a card-index. The sources on which Isidore drew are numerous, but he rarely indicates them by name. Where he cites an author verbally, giving also his name, the quotation is, more often than not, taken from an intermediate source. In short, the sources on which he relied were for the most part relatively recent. Patristic literature is represented by Tertullian, Lactantius, Jerome, Augustine, and Gregory, secular literature by the elder Pliny, Solinus, Orosius, Servius' commentary on Virgil and other Virgilian *scholia*, Hyginus' *Astronomica* and the *scholia* on Germanicus' *Aratea*, Placidus, Donatus, Cassiodorus' *Institutiones saecularium lectionum*, and other writers on the *trivium*, logical or scientific writings by Marius Victorinus and Boethius, Latin translations of Greek medical authors, and Gargilius Martialis, Palladius, and the *Agrimensores* on agriculture and kindred topics. As for the numerous citations from the poets and from prose writers of the Roman Republic and early Empire, while Isidore was familiar with some at first hand, like Virgil and Lucan, and perhaps Ovid, Juvenal, Martial, and Sallust, the rest, especially quotations from early authors like Ennius, Plautus, the Roman writers of tragedy, Lucilius, and Cato, were copied by him from his sources.[1]

Although most of Isidore's works were in great demand in the centuries following, the *Etymologiae* far surpassed any other of his books in popularity; for this encyclopedia was a *sine qua non* in every monastic library of any pretensions. Its use by a long list of writers from the seventh to the tenth century is easily demonstrable, it appears constantly in medieval library catalogues, and the number of extant manuscripts is exceedingly great.[2]

[1] See the convenient conspectus of the quotations at the end of Volume 2 of Lindsay's edition.

[2] C. H. Beeson, *Isidorstudien* (Munich, 1913) gives a nearly complete list of extant manuscripts, other than those copied in Spain, down to the middle of the ninth century. For some additional manuscripts or fragments see *Clavis*, Nos. 1186–1206.

In conclusion, mention must be made of a collection of twenty-seven brief poems—all save one in elegiac couplets—whose Isidorian authorship there is no adequate reason for doubting. They were inscribed above the bookcases in the library at Seville and praise the various authors whose works were there preserved. Their only interest lies in the fact that they corroborate the evidence of Isidore's writings regarding the contents of the episcopal library in Seville, for they have no poetic merit. The lines on Augustine may serve as a specimen of the bishop's ability as a versifier:

> Mentitur qui te totum legisse fatetur;
>   Aut quis cuncta tua lector habere potest?
> Namque voluminibus mille, Augustine, refulges;
>   Testantur libri quod loquor ipse tui.
> Quamvis multorum placeant praesentia libris,
>   Si Augustinus adest, sufficit ipse tibi.[1]

At the death of Clovis in 511 the kingdom of the Franks included all of Gaul from the Rhine to the Pyrenees except Provence and Septimania in the south-east. Owing to the Frankish practice of dividing the kingdom on the death of the ruler equally amongst his sons the unity of Gaul was at once weakened. The rivalry and individual ambitions of the sons and grandsons of Clovis plunged the country into unceasing warfare. After the death of three of the sons, the realm, which since 537 had been enlarged by the addition of Provence, was once more united under the sway of a single monarch. Lothar I reigned for sixteen years (545–61); but then his dominions were divided into four parts among his sons, so that the evils of civil war which had ensued on the death of Clovis were renewed with redoubled force.

The contrast between toleration or even approval of pagan literature and the unqualified condemnation of it which has already been noted in sixth-century Italy, is well illustrated in contemporary Gaul by the attitude of Avitus, bishop of Vienne (c. 450–518), and Caesarius, bishop of Arles (c. 470–543). Avitus, it is true, proved his staunch orthodoxy not only by his deeds but in treatises directed against the Eutychian and the Arian heresies.

[1] See Beeson, op. cit., p. 159; for a translation of the poem see the Appendix.

Yet a thorough training in the type of rhetoric admired in his day produced a notably artificial style, while his poetry—a poem in praise of virginity and a lengthy versification in five books of certain portions of Genesis—betrays intimate familiarity with Virgil. Caesarius' change of heart, on the other hand, is mirrored in the story related by his biographer. As a youth Caesarius was persuaded by friends to study with the noted African *rhetor*, Julianus Pomerius. This teacher had settled in Gaul and was the author of a treatise on the contemplative life which, though commonly and wrongly attributed to Prosper of Aquitaine, was widely read throughout the Middle Ages.[1] In due course Caesarius, even like Jerome, experienced a vivid dream which led him to abandon his study of secular literature and to devote himself wholly to religion and ascetic practices.[2] Later, as bishop, he worked indefatigably for the spiritual welfare of clergy and laity alike. His own disciples found in him a teacher of wonderful power who sedulously urged them to ask questions:

> I know you do not understand all; why do you not ask that you may comprehend? Cows do not always run to their calves, but at times the calves hasten to the cows, so that they can appease their hunger at the mother's udders.[3]

But Caesarius' greatest success was as a preacher. As such his influence was important and profound, even as was that of Gregory the Great in Italy fifty years later. The number of illiterate and quasi-illiterate persons was by this time so great that an able preacher could and did become the real teacher of his flock. Though there is little direct information about schools and education in sixth-century Gaul, the liberal arts were studied only by a small minority. In the monasteries studies were wholly theological, as was the training of lectors and clergy in the bishop's household, which was the earliest form of the cathedral school.[4] In 529 the Council of Vaison approved of priests in country districts taking in and training young lectors, some, if

[1] For Pomerius cf. Laistner in *ST*, 122 (1946), pp. 344–58.

[2] *MGH*, Script. Merov., III, p. 460, 13 ff.

[3] *ibid.*, p. 477, 14 ff.

[4] Cf. Mansi, *op. cit.*, VIII, 726—boys intended for orders shall be educated 'in domo ecclesiae, sub episcopali praesentia'.

not all, of whom would later become priests. In these conditions it became the task of the senior clergy not merely to edify but to educate their congregations. Caesarius made the laity in church join in singing hymns and psalms, so that they should not join in idle chatter during the service. His sermons were popular in the best sense of the word.[1] Steeped in Augustinian theology, he did not hesitate to borrow freely from this and other Latin Fathers; but he adapted and simplified his material so that it could be assimilated by the least cultured of his hearers. His frequent condemnation of rustic superstitions and of contemporary morals form an interesting commentary on the manners and customs of the age.

The example of Desiderius, bishop of Vienne, who incurred the displeasure of Gregory I, shows how even in the second half of the sixth century there were prelates who in their love of secular authors followed the example of an Avitus or a Sidonius. In the same period Gaul could boast of two writers of major stature, Fortunatus, and Gregory of Tours.

Fortunatus was, as we saw, a product of the Italian schools, since he had received his education, including some training in law, at Ravenna. In 565, when he was a little past thirty, he left his native land to visit the tomb of St Martin at Tours and to seek his fortune in a foreign country. His journey appears to have lasted nearly two years. He travelled in leisurely fashion by way of the Upper Danube and the Rhine, visiting Mayence, Cologne, Metz, Verdun, Rheims, and Paris, before he finally arrived in Tours. An agreeable manner coupled with a remarkable facility in inditing occasional verse in honour of the great ones of the earth, procured him a friendly reception wherever he fared. In 567 he ended his travels at Poitiers. Here he passed the next twenty years of his life as the friend and adviser of St Rhadegund, the widowed queen of Lothar I, whose austere life in the nunnery to which she had retired and whose piety and good works were famous throughout Gaul, and of her foster-daughter, the young abbess, Agnes. At some date during these years Fortunatus took

[1] For Caesarius' sermons and other writings see now the superb edition by G. Morin (Maredsous, 1937–42); reissued in the *Corpus Patrum Christianorum* (Turnhout, 1953).

orders. In 587, after the death of St Rhadegund, he again travelled for a spell. The latest of his poems that can be dated was composed in honour of a new bishop of Poitiers, Plato, who was consecrated in 591. On the decease of this prelate Fortunatus succeeded to the bishopric. He appears to have survived into the early years of the seventh century. Fortunatus was a prolific writer. His prose works, which include a life of St Rhadegund and biographies of several other saints, are negligible as literature. His reputation as a man of letters rests wholly on his verse. His eleven books of poems exhibit a marvellous variety in their subject-matter.[1] There are complimentary poems, panegyrics on lords temporal and spiritual, epitaphs, epithalamia, letters in verse, and, in addition, a great number of less formal compositions, abounding in pleasing descriptions of scenery and affording many glimpses of the social life of the time. Save in a very few instances the poet used the elegiac couplet. His one long poem, a life of St Martin of Tours, running to more than two thousand lines, is composed in hexameters. Of the ten hymns that have come down to us bearing his name three are certainly genuine. Two of these were included in the Roman Breviary not long after the poet's death, namely, that beginning *Pange lingua gloriosi* in trochaic tetrameters, and that written in iambic dimeters, *Vexilla regis prodeunt*. These and the hymn beginning *Agnoscat omne saeculum* have since been familiar to thousands to whom Fortunatus' other poems are wholly unknown. For their genuine feeling, expressed in simple but melodious diction, they deserve to be set side by side with the hymns of Ambrose. Modern estimates of Fortunatus' verse—apart from the universally admired hymns—have differed widely, the unfavourable predominating. Judged in bulk, and divorced from the time and circumstances in which it was written, it will assuredly not rank very high in the poetical literature of the world. But in the age in which he lived it is difficult to say which was more remarkable, Fortunatus' poetry or the appreciation with which it was received by princes and nobles whose manly qualities were undeniable, but to whom

[1] For his works see *MGH*, AA, IV. Books I to VIII of the poetry were published *c.* 576, Book IX eight years later. Books X and XI seem to have appeared posthumously.

artistic and intellectual tastes have commonly been denied. A greater poet would have failed to win a hearing in Merovingian society. But the facile troubadour,[1] who in correct and often elegant verse, and in language which was pointed, witty, and singularly free from the bombast and mannerisms of the schools, and often with a real sense for beauty or with a genuine note of pathos, could improvise his pieces for the most diverse occasions, correctly gauging the tastes and mentality of his audience, won a great reputation in his lifetime and still deserves his meed of praise for having kept some appreciation of literature alive in an all but illiterate age.

It is to Fortunatus' great contemporary that we primarily owe our knowledge of the earlier period of Merovingian history. Georgius Florentius, who was born in Auvergne in 538, was descended from an old patrician, Gallo-Roman stock. Ancestors and relatives on both sides of his family had been princes of the Church. He himself adopted the name of Gregory in memory of his maternal great-grandfather, Gregory, bishop of Langres, and was in due course ordained deacon (c. 563?). In 573, on the death of his cousin Eufronius, he was chosen bishop of Tours, a see which he filled until his death in 594. His pride in his ancestry is illustrated by his comment on the up-start priest, Riculf, 'the wretch was ignorant that all the bishops but five who held the see of Tours were connected with my family'. His education, which was as good as could be acquired in Gaul at that time, was, judged by earlier standards, modest enough. The only secular author with whom he shows a good deal of familiarity was Virgil. His two references to Sallust's *Catiline* are doubtless reminiscences of an ever-popular school-text; and his allusions to Martianus Capella leave no doubt that he knew the standard treatise on the liberal arts, even if he had not studied it profoundly.[2] Other isolated references to pagan authors do not prove that he was really familiar with them and may come from late Roman grammarians whom he had had to read as a boy. He himself in more than one place laments or apologizes for his rustic speech, but

---

[1] 'Une vie de troubadour errante' Labriolle calls Fortunatus' career.

[2] *History of the Franks*, V, 49 (Dalton's translation); IV, 8 and VII, 1; X, 31.

such modesty had become a common literary convention. One can but be grateful that he chose to write in the vernacular Latin of his day in preference to affecting the tortured 'literary' language, which was so popular in Gaul and elsewhere with the generations immediately preceding his own. The least known of all his works, the short essay entitled *De cursibus ecclesiasticis*, has a twofold interest: it shows that Gregory had some acquaintance with the subjects of the *quadrivium*, and it affords some indication of scientific knowledge of his day. The book was composed to provide the clergy with such astronomical information as would help them to tell the time at night by correct observation of the constellations and thus enable them all through the year to perform the night offices at the proper hour. The introductory chapters enumerate with short descriptions seven wonders of the world worked by the hand of man, and seven worked by God. From this he passes to his main subject, which is to describe the commoner stars and constellations together with the usual time of their rising and setting.[1] Instead of giving them their classical names he explains their appearance in terms which would be intelligible to persons not familiar with classical mythology. He then adds instructions applying this astronomical lore to the practical purpose for which the pamphlet was written. It must have been a very serviceable manual, and its scientific good sense fills one with respect for its compiler. Gregory's knowledge of the Bible was respectable. His quotations often diverge from Jerome's Vulgate. Sometimes this may be due to the fact that he is quoting from memory, but there is no doubt that he also used one or more of the Old Latin versions. He had also read extensively in Latin hagiographical literature. While he had acquired

---

[1] The seven man-made wonders are: Noah's ark, Babylon, Solomon's temple, 'tomb of a Persian king' (presumably the Mausoleum at Halicarnassus), the colossus at Rhodes, the theatre at Heraclea, the pharus at Alexandria. The seven divine wonders are: the tides, the growth of plants, the phoenix, Etna, the hot springs at Barthélémy near Grenoble, the course of the sun, and the phases of the moon. The following are among the constellations described: Arcturus, Corona, Lyra, Cycnus, Delphinus, Aquila, Auriga with Capella and the Kids, Gemini, Pleiades, Hyades, Canis major and minor, Ursa major. For further details cf. the notes of the German astronomer Galle in Krusch's edition of the treatise (*MGH*, Script. Merov., VII).

a good grasp of the canons of the Church, there is nothing to prove his familiarity with the great theologians of the third and fourth centuries. The early part of his work was based on Rufinus' translations of Eusebius, Jerome's *Chronicle*, and Orosius. The plan of the *History of the Franks* is as follows: Books I and II are introductory to the main work and briefly sketch events from the creation of the world to A.D. 511. The next two narrate the history of the Frankish kingdom to *c.* 573. The remainder, Books V to X, depict in far greater detail the years 573 to 591, during which Gregory was himself premier bishop in Gaul and thereby one of the outstanding figures in the political and ecclesiastical world. One must comprehend certain characteristics of the man to estimate him rightly as a writer and to explain the excellence of his work. In the first place, though he is extremely proud of his descent, he betrays no contempt or dislike for the Frankish conquerors of Gaul. In the Gaul of his day the older Gallo-Roman and the more recent Teutonic elements of society have been fused and there is none of the opposition and animosity between two racial and cultural groups which was so marked in the days of Sidonius. In the second place, Gregory was staunchly orthodox. Kindly and generous as he unconsciously reveals himself in the *History* to have been, he is ready to believe the worst of any heretic. His hatred of Arians was especially intense. He records long conversations with heretics and with a Jew; but modern readers will hardly be as convinced that Gregory had the best of the argument as he himself was.[1] His preposterous account of Theodoric and the Ostrogoths in Italy was no doubt due not merely to ignorance and inadequate sources, but to religious animosity; yet, when he had access to fuller historical material, his innate love of truth could triumph over prejudice. Thus his information about the Visigoths, who were also Arians, is usually accurate. His piety and faith were boundless; at the same time the quality of his faith, while eminently characteristic of his time, was of a kind which in the present age it is not easy to understand.[2] His unquestioning belief in miracles

[1] Cf. *Hist. Franc.*, V, 31 (43); VI, 5; VI, 26 (40).
[2] Cf. the admirable remarks of S. Dill, *Roman Society in Gaul in the Merovingian Age* (London, 1926), pp. 394–438.

and in the wonder-working powers of saints and relics, which is manifested on almost every page of his *History*, had even fuller scope in his other writings, a life of St Martin of Tours, a life of St Julian of Brioude, and several books of shorter lives recording the achievements of Gallic saints and martyrs.[1] He was also responsible for the earliest version in Latin of the legend of the seven sleepers and for free Latin adaptations of two other eastern pieces of hagiography, *The miracles of St Andrew* and *The passion and miracles of St Thomas*. It is one of Gregory's greatest merits that he is very careful, when recording the history of his own times, to give precise information and to acquaint his readers with his sources, where he is indebted to others for the statements in his narrative. This care he also displays, like Gregory the Great in his *Dialogues*, when he chronicles miraculous events. Some, like certain miracles performed at the tomb of St Médard or St Martin of Tours, were witnessed by Gregory himself, others he learnt from what he judged to be reliable informants. A deaf and dumb man who had been cured by the anchorite Hospicius, gave the bishop a long account of the life and marvellous powers of that strange man. Other valued informants were Tatto, who had been cured by the saintly Aredius, and Vulfolaic who had much to relate of the wonders of St Martin.[2] Gregory often introduces lists of portents which occurred in a given year, a procedure which recalls the practice of the great pagan historian of Rome.[3] That swindlers tried to impose on the people in an age when the miraculous was constantly expected is not surprising. On such quacks Gregory passes severe judgment;[4] when found out they were liable to receive short shrift. Where the issue was not serious, the bishop was merely contemptuous, as in his answer

[1] Gregory refers to the four books of the life of St Martin, the life of St Julian, the *Liber in gloria martyrum beatorum* and the *Liber in gloria confessorum* as his seven books of miracles. To these must be added the *Vitae patrum*. For the text see *MGH*, Script. Merov., I, p. 2.

[2] *Hist. Franc.*, VI, 6; X, 29 and VIII, 16.

[3] e.g., *ibid.*, V, 30 (41); VI, 8 (14); VI, 14 (21); VI, 31 (44); IX, 5. The lists of portents in Livy are most common in the books of the third decade which relate the stress of the Second Punic War when there were occasional outbursts of popular hysteria (*lascivia*).

[4] *Hist. Franc.*, IX, 6.

to Guntram Boso who believed what a certain prophetess told him:

> I laughed at his folly and said: 'Of God alone are these things to be obtained; the promises of the Evil One may not be believed.' When he had withdrawn in much confusion, I laughed heartily at this man who deemed such tales worthy of belief.[1]

Though free from personal vanity, Gregory had a very high conception of the importance of the episcopal office. The justified conviction that the Church and its leaders both as a political and a cultural force were of vital moment to the Frankish kingdom, is an ever-present thought in the *History*, which knits together and gives a certain unity to a work which is otherwise discursive, 'episodic', and chronologically somewhat confused. The deeper-lying causes of political events, the growth of institutions, the difficulties attendant on the fusion of Gallo-Roman with Frankish custom and law, Gregory comprehended very imperfectly. He is a truthful chronicler with a strong dramatic sense and much knowledge of men, but not a philosophic nor even a dispassionate historian. His insistence on the reality and frequency of miracles, not merely in the *History* but still more in his other works, made him one of the most influential writers for the development of hagiography in the West. 'He is the precursor of a great effort of systematic hagiography which extended roughly from the sixth to the tenth century.'[2] Thus he gave to the Middle Ages some of the best examples of a type of literature at once edifying and readable, because it satisfied the common human love for a good story and at the same time took men's thoughts away for a spell from the violence and sordid reality of their mundane existence. To the modern reader Gregory appeals primarily because of his dramatic quality and because he is most successful with the biographical part of history. Many of his portraits and pen pictures are unforgettable. Chilperic, morally the worst of the sons of Lothar I, and one of the few major characters in the *History* whom Gregory roundly condemns, is brought before us as the very personification of treachery and cruelty. Yet, like Nero to whom the historian compares him, he

---

[1] *ibid.*, V, 8 (14) in Dalton's translation.   [2] S. Dill, *op. cit.*, p. 396.

had a fondness for literature and tried his own hand at poetry, even hymns, which were perhaps not quite so contemptible as Gregory suggests. Like another Roman emperor, Claudius, Chilperic ventured into the field of philology, giving orders that four new letters be added to the alphabet to represent the sounds, long o, ae, th, and w, and that the innovation be taught to the young and the needful alterations be made in all books.[1] His brother, Guntram, is a no less living person in the *History*. In spite of sudden fits of passion and occasional outbursts of cruelty, he was a more amiable monarch and more easily appeased. It may be that Gregory, who was on very friendly terms with this king, in his portrait errs on the side of partiality. The queen, Fredegund, who in a ruthless age surpassed all her contemporaries of either sex in pitiless ferocity, who used to give her emissaries of death a potion to hearten them for their fell work,[2] and tried to break her daughter's neck by forcing down on it the lid of a large chest,[3] is shown by Gregory to have had on rare occasions a softer side to her nature. On the death of a son even this tigress had human feelings:

> The queen now took and burned all the valuable things that had belonged to her dead boy, precious objects and garments of silk and furs; it is said that they filled four carts. The gold and silver was melted down and so kept, that nothing might remain intact to recall the days of her mourning for her son.[4]

A host of minor characters, all equally real, people Gregory's book, while his powers as a narrator are seen at their best in the story of his ancestor Attalus' flight from serfdom, in the account of the career of Leudast, or in the description of the siege of Convenae and the death of its defender, Gundovald.[5] When Fortunatus, who was on the friendliest terms with his great contemporary and addressed many graceful poems to him, once

---

[1] For Chilperic's philological reforms and Gregory's judgment of his character cf. *Hist. Franc.*, VI, 32-3 (44-6).

[2] *ibid.*, VIII, 29. Fredegund's procedure recalls the methods of the famous 'Old Man of the Mountain' and his no less famous emissaries, the Assassins, a western corruption of Hashishin, that being the drug which they were given. See E. G. Browne, *A Literary History of Persia*, 2 (London, 1906), pp. 204-11.

[3] *Hist. Franc.*, IX, 34.

[4] *ibid.*, VI, 25 (35).

[5] *ibid.*, III, 15; V, 32 (48); VII, 34-8.

saluted him as *lumen generale*, he spoke the unvarnished truth;[1] for no one acquainted with the bishop's works, and with his *History* first and foremost, can fail to realize that Gregory is a figure unique in the Merovingian Age. His works are not listed in many of the earlier library catalogues, down to and including the tenth century.[2] But the fact that the *History* was used by a number of early medieval writers, for instance, Bede in his *Retractation*, the so-called Fredegarius, and Paul the Deacon, and that sundry extant manuscripts of early date survive, is sufficient proof that so remarkable a book was not neglected.

[1] Book VIII, 14; in the next poem he is called *celsum et generale cacumen*.

[2] For example at Reichenau (Lehmann, *Bibl.*, I, 248, 4) and at St Riquier (Becker, Nos. 11, 117). The manuscript listed in the ninth-century catalogue of Lorsch (Becker, Nos. 37, 87) is now in the Vatican Library (*Pat. lat.*, 966). See *CLA*, I, No. 98. For two other early codices cf. *CLA*, V, Nos. 670 and 671.

CHAPTER V

Irish and English Scholars and Missionaries
to the Death of Bede

While during the seventh century the continent of Western Europe was withered by a blight of intellectual sterility, a fresh and vigorous growth of culture was maturing in Ireland and Britain. The earlier history of Christianity in those islands is exceedingly obscure. Traditions of later date seem to imply that in Britain Christianity was fairly established by A.D. 200, but the first clear piece of evidence is the undoubted presence of three British bishops at the Council of Arles in 314. Again, in 359, at the Council of Rimini the British Church was represented by several prelates. It is thus apparent that during the third century, at any rate, the new faith had made considerable headway in the most northerly of the Roman provinces. Christian inscriptions found in Britain are notoriously few in number; nor do any appear to be earlier than the fourth century. Furthermore, it is impossible to determine how far Christianity was confined to the thoroughly Romanized portions of the province and how far the native population abandoned its old religious practices in favour of it. It is probable, moreover, that the work of conversion had been carried out chiefly from Gaul; and in the fifth century when the heads of the British Church were much disturbed at the growth in the island of the Pelagian heresy, it was from Gaul that they obtained help to combat it. Two Gallican bishops, Germanus of Auxerre and Lupus of Troyes, visited Britain in 529, but their orthodox teaching seems to have been only temporarily effective. In 547 Germanus returned to the island, accompanied on this occasion by Severus of Trèves. Britain had, however, long since ceased to be a Roman province, and during the second half of the century the progress of the

German invaders in the West and South-west was rapid. The picture of Church and society in sixth-century Britain portrayed in the *De excidio et conquestu Britanniae* going under the name of Gildas is one of unrelieved gloom. The work falls into two very unequal parts. The one (Chapters 2–26) gives a sketch of British history during and after the Roman occupation, but in all probability is a later interpolation which was not put together until the beginning of the eighth century. The second and longer section is a diatribe in which the writer laments the corruption and demoralization of temporal and spiritual rulers and of the people in the island. The date of this part is more doubtful; for, while some scholars still regard it as a product of the later sixth century, others would assign it to the same period as the preceding historical section. In the absence of other evidence—for Bede, when he deals with this period of British history, merely copies his predecessor—it is impossible to determine the accuracy of Gildas' description. The book itself affords proof that the older culture, though not wholly destroyed, was moribund. The style and language are pretentious and clumsy. The writer's sources were mainly oral, but he shows some acquaintance with Jerome's *Chronicle* and *Letters*, Orosius, and Rufinus' *Ecclesiastical History*. He cites Virgil incorrectly several times; his allusions to other pagan poets are more doubtful. In short, we are left with the impression that his knowledge of earlier authors was slight, and that such training in the arts as he had received was not of a high order. Additional testimony to a survival of secular learning in south-western Britain is perhaps provided by the so-called *Hisperica Famina*. The longest version of this strange example of perverted ingenuity consists of 612 rhythmic lines couched in a language of studied obscurity; for the vocabulary is made up predominantly of rare or even invented words, together with a sprinkling of Greek and Hebrew vocables. Portions of two other versions also exist, and, in addition, a glossary of Hisperic words. The contents stamp it as the product of a school, the variant versions being most readily explained, if we suppose that the different pupils were all given the same material to use, and utilizing this were set to describe the different occupations during the day of a young monastic scholar, articles of daily use, the wooden church, features of the landscape, like the sea and sky, and other topics or short tales. Besides this there are several shorter poems, of which the best known is the *Lorica*, whose vocabulary is similar in character.[1]

Ireland had never formed a part of the Roman Empire. The date at which the first converts to Christianity were made there cannot be determined. But there were already some Christians in Ireland, when Patrick began his missionary labours (*c.* 431?). That earliest work of conversion is perhaps more likely to have been carried out from Wales than from Gaul. The extent and success of Patrick's mission have been variously estimated. The earliest extant lives of the saint were not composed until near the end of the seventh century and already contain much legendary material. Contemporary evidence is lacking except for what little can be gleaned from Patrick's own writings. These are the so-called *Confessio*, a defence of his career in which the historical allusions are vague, and a letter addressed to the soldiers of Coroticus. This man may have been a Welsh chieftain or else the ruler of Britains in Strathclyde, some of whose retainers had raided the Irish coast and massacred or enslaved a number of Christian converts. Patrick's letter is a strongly worded protest against this outrage. In addition a few brief sayings and some ecclesiastical ordinances bearing the names of Patrick and two other bishops are probably genuine. Patrick describes himself as 'most rustic'. His Latin, though in general it conforms to the vulgar Latin of the period, is imperfect, because, as he says himself (*Confess.*, 9), he had never properly mastered this foreign tongue. Such literary and theological training as he had received was probably acquired in Gaul. This can be deduced both from his own vague allusions and from his Biblical quotations. These are principally drawn from the New Testament and have the closest textual affinity to Old Latin versions then in use in the Gallican Church. Neither the *Confession* nor the *Letter* lends support to the view that the greater part of Ireland was converted

[1] The *Hisperica Famina* and other poems have been edited by F. H. Jenkinson (Cambridge, 1908). See also Kenney, pp. 255–8 and 270–2. On the latinity cf. E. K. Rand in *Ehrengabe für Karl Strecker* (Dresden, 1931), pp. 134–42, and, for a new interpretation, P. W. Damon in *Amer. Journ. Phil.*, 74 (1953), pp. 398–406.

by him, nor yet that an elaborately organized Church existed there. On the contrary, his own words are significant:

> I confess that I have been appointed a bishop in Ireland. Most assuredly I deem that I have received from God what I am. And so I dwell in the midst of barbarous heathen, a stranger and exile for the love of God.

At the same time he speaks of having converted many thousands and having ordained many clergy.[1] It seems likely that Patrick's pre-eminent position as a saint and as the apostle of Ireland must be attributed to the zeal of Irish hagiographers in the eighth and following centuries.

Whatever the condition of the Church in Ireland may have been on Patrick's death (461?), there is no doubt that in the following century numerous monasteries had come into existence in various parts of the country—Kilmacduagh in the far west; Clonard in County Meath and Clonmacnois on the Shannon; Derry, Durrow, Moville, and Bangor in the north and north-east, and others of lesser note. This development was largely due to influences from southern and south-western Gaul. The Irish Church developed undisturbed by foreign invaders and had certain characteristic features both in organization and in observance. It was a monastic Church whose arrangement was adapted to existing social and political conditions. In a country where no towns existed and society was divided into a great number of clans, the monastery became the religious and educational centre of the clan. The abbot was elected by the clan and the upkeep of the monastery likewise was the concern of the clansmen. In return, the spiritual care of the social group, lay as well as religious, was undertaken by the abbot and his monks. The abbot, who sometimes held the ecclesiastical rank of bishop, sometimes only that of priest, was the spiritual head of the whole community. It followed that there was as yet no diocesan organization. The duties of bishops who were not also abbots were purely

[1] Cf. *Confess.*, 50. The text of the two letters has been edited with an elaborate linguistic commentary by Ludwig Bieler in *Classica et Medievalia*, 11 (1950), pp. 1–150, and 12 (1951), pp. 78–214. For the ordinances or canons see J. T. McNeill and Helena M. Gamer, *Medieval Handbooks of Penance* (New York, 1938), pp. 76–80. For Patrick in general cf. the excellent study by Bieler, *The life and legend of St Patrick* (Dublin, 1949).

ceremonial and liturgical; no central direction knitted together these numerous groups. In matters of observance the points of difference from the other Western Churches were the divergent reckoning of the Easter celebration, the tonsure from ear to ear, the consecration of a bishop by a single bishop, and a number of liturgical variations, for example, in the Mass and the baptismal rite. It is beyond dispute that from the sixth century the Irish monasteries cultivated both secular and theological learning and that for three centuries they produced a series of remarkable men who exerted a profound influence on thought and letters in Western Europe, even though we can no longer discern the earlier stages of this conspicuous intellectual growth. Manuscripts of the Bible, of theological and liturgical works, and, in a less measure, of the writings of secular authors had been brought into the country during the fifth and sixth centuries. These must have been written in half-uncial script—a circumstance pointing strongly to connexion with southern and western Gaul—since it was the half-uncial which the Irish scribes adopted and modified until they had evolved a characteristic hand of their own. Whereas the Irish half-uncial was long used for the more costly codices, which the Irish also learnt to illuminate with exemplary skill, there was also developed an Irish minuscule script for copying less valuable works. In time this became a national script which, having become fixed in the twelfth century, has survived with some modifications to the present day. Extant works written in Latin by Irish scholars of the sixth century are exceedingly scanty. Moreover, it must be remembered that the Irish vernacular was never ousted either as the medium for common speech or for written composition. Hence Latin even to the Irish monks was a book language laboriously acquired. Surviving Latin manuscripts frequently demonstrate the fact that they were copied by Irishmen not merely by the script but by the presence of glosses written in the vernacular. Belonging to the sixth century are the *Penitential* which has been attributed to Bishop Finnian of Moville (died 589) but which is more probably by Finnian of Clonard (died *c.* 550), and some Latin hymns assigned to various authors.[1]

---

[1] For the *Penitential* cf. McNeill and Gamer, *op. cit.*, pp. 86 ff. and for the hymns Kenney, pp. 261 ff.

But the characteristic of Irish monks at this time which had the most far-reaching influence on the development of European culture was their zeal for missionary work. According to a reasonable tradition, the first efforts at converting the southern Picts and the Britons of Galloway and Strathclyde were made by Ninian soon after 400.[1] The evidence of St Patrick's letter, however, suggests that some at least of the inhabitants of those regions had soon relapsed again into heathenism. Archaeological evidence, on the other hand, points to the fact that Christianity survived there precariously from c. 450 onwards.[2] A more permanent work of conversion was effected by the Irish Columba (Colum-cille). When he crossed over to Scotland c. 565, and, receiving the island of Iona (Hy) from a native chief, founded his famous monastery there, some of the islands and adjacent coastal strips had already been settled by *Scotti* from Ireland.[3] The task of conversion amongst the northern Picts and, somewhat later, the reconversion of the heathen amongst their southern neighbours, progressed apace. Many monastic settlements were made but, in marked contrast to the Irish system at home, where each monastery was independent and self-governing, the religious houses in Caledonia were all, as it were, colonies of Iona, and its abbot wielded authority similar to that of a metropolitan over all monasteries, churches, and clerics of every degree.

While the missionary work of the Irish was thus prospering in Scotland, a body of Irish monks, twelve in number, led by Columban (c. 560–615) made their way across the water to Britanny and thence into Burgundia, where they seem to have arrived c. 590. Granted land by King Guntram, the pilgrims founded a monastery at Annegray in the Vosges. With a passionate desire for spreading Christianity in heathen lands, Columban and his companions combined a rigid asceticism, which not only regulated their own lives but filled them with the wish to reform the abuses and moral laxity apparent to them in

[1] Bede, *E.H.*, 3, 4; for Ninian cf. W. Levison in *Antiquity*, 14 (1940), pp. 280–91 and W. D. Simpson, *St Ninian and the Origins of the Christian Church in Scotland* (Edinburgh, 1940). Simpson unfortunately ignored the eighth-century Ninian poems.

[2] Cf. C. A. R. Radford in *Antiquity*, 27 (1953), pp. 154–5.

[3] *Scottus* or *Scotus* always means Irish in the early Middle Ages.

Merovingian Gaul. Disciples flocked to the new religious centre in such numbers that two further abbeys were settled by the Irish within a few years, at Luxeuil and at Fontaines. The queen, Brunhild, is generally made responsible for Columban's ultimate expulsion from Burgundy because of his uncompromising condemnation of court life.[1] But it must not be forgotten that there was a strong contributory cause, the hostility which the Irish saint and missionary aroused by refusing to compromise with the leaders of the Church in Gaul either in the matter of observance or of discipline, or to acknowledge the authority of the Frankish bishops over his monasteries. After some stay in Austrasia, where he was joined by fugitive monks from Luxeuil, and in Alemannia, Columban finally found his way into northern Italy. There with the permission of the Lombard ruler he founded a new monastery at Bobbio near the river Trebbia and close to the northern end of the Apennines (c. 614). In the following year he died. One of his disciples, Gallus, whom he had left in Alemannia, c. 613 took up his abode with one or two companions in a small hermitage situated in the Alps of north-eastern Switzerland. So simple were the beginnings of the monastery of St Gall which was to become one of the most famous of medieval abbeys.

Whereas the only work which can reasonably be attributed to the founder of Iona is the poem, *Altus prosator*,[2] the literary output of Columban, in spite of his tireless life as a missionary and organizer was considerable, although only a portion of it has survived. Of five genuine letters, that addressed to Gregory the Great is of special interest; for in it Columban defends the Irish manner of reckoning Easter in a manner at once respectful and firmly independent.[3] Similar independence of judgment distinguishes a later letter, addressed to Pope Boniface, on the controversies aroused by the Three Chapters. His other extant writings may be regarded as the direct outcome of his work as an

[1] Cf. O. M. Dalton, *Gregory of Tours*, I, pp. 71 and 243. R. R. Bezzola in *Les origines et la formation de la littérature courtoise én occident* (Paris, 1944), p. 82, observes merely that Columban's asceticism fell foul of the Austrasian court.

[2] See *Irish Liber Hymnorum*, I, pp. 66–81; English translation, *ibid.*, II, pp. 150–3.

[3] See *MGH*, Epist., III, pp. 154ff. The sixth letter, though accepted by Kenney, is spurious. Cf. C. W. Jones, *BOT*, pp. 108–10.

abbot and religious reformer and ascetic. They are: a short penitential, which adds little to the *Penitential* of Finnian, four brief addresses to monks, and a monastic rule. The last named falls into two parts. The first portion is a rule properly so called, instructing his monks on ten topics in as many chapters, to wit, obedience, silence, food and drink, poverty, vanity, chastity, religious duties, discretion, mortification, and monastic perfection. The second part—*regula coenobialis patrum*—gives with much detail the mortifications and punishments for various offences. It contains clauses applicable to laymen as well as those intended specifically for monks. The distinguishing feature of Columban's ordinances and of his ethical teaching is their extreme rigour, manifested both in the exceptionally self-denying life which he advocates and in the severity of the punishments which he imposes, amongst which flagellation has a foremost place.[1] Although Columban himself had been forced to leave Burgundy, the influence of twenty years' work there and of his disciplinary writings was profound. Not only those Irish who remained behind but many converts, amongst them not a few of the Frankish nobility, successfully propagated the ascetic ideals of Luxeuil. New monasteries were founded on the Irish model. Monks of Luxeuil were installed as abbots in existing houses or in new foundations which were not actually the work of the *Scotti*. Thus the first abbot of Corbie, in Picardy, founded about the middle of the seventh century, came from Columban's foundation. Again, the *Rule* of Columban was followed in some communities jointly with the Benedictine.

The literary output in Western Europe during the seventh century may have lacked originality, but it is now certain that the Irish kept up the tradition of learning, especially in theology; and, apart from the works of the English Aldhelm, the most

[1] These prose works have all been well edited by Seebass in the *Zeitschrift für Kirchengeschichte*, namely: addresses to monks, 14 (1894), pp. 76–92; penitential, *ibid.*, pp. 430–48; the two recensions of the *Rule*, 15 (1895), pp. 366–86 and 17 (1897), pp. 218–34. English translation of the *Penitential* and part of the *Rule* in McNeill and Gamer, *op. cit.*, pp. 249–65. Parts of a Latin adaptation of Theodore of Mopsuestia's commentary on the Psalms, which used to be attributed to Columban, is in all probability the work of Julian of Aeclanum.

interesting treatises of this age are by two Irish scholars. The short *De duodecim abusivis saeculi* was composed in Ireland between 630 and 650 by an unknown writer. It begins abruptly:

> Twelve are the abuses of the age, that is: the scholar without works, the old man without religion, the young man without obedience, the rich man who giveth not alms, the woman without modesty, the master without virtue, the contentious Christian, the proud poor man, the unjust king, the negligent bishop, the common folk without discipline, the people without law.[1]

A section is then assigned to each of these in turn. The writer's style and treatment of his subject and the partly religious, partly ethical approach are best conveyed by actual quotation. The chapter on the Unjust King reads thus:

> The ninth class of perversion is the unjust king. He, whereas it hath behoved him to straighten unjust men, keepeth not in himself the dignity of his name; for the name of king rightly understood implieth this, that he fulfil over all his subjects the duty of a ruler. Yet in what manner will he be able to amend others who amendeth not his own manners that they be not unjust? Inasmuch as in justice the king's throne is exalted and in truth is firmly set the governance of peoples. The justice of a king meaneth, to oppress no man unjustly by the exercise of power; to judge without favour of persons between this man and his neighbour; to defend strangers, wards, and widows; to restrain thieves, to chastise adulterers; not to exalt unjust men nor give sustenance to the shameless and to mummers; to destroy the godless from the earth; to bring death to the parricide and the perjurer; to protect churches; to cherish the poor with alms; to set just men over the affairs of the realm; to take as counsellors old men, wise and temperate; to give no countenance to the superstitions of wizards, soothsayers, and witches; to put off anger; to defend his country bravely and righteously against its adversaries; to trust in God in all things; to be not puffed up at prosperity; to bear patiently all adversities; to believe in God according to the Catholic Faith; not to suffer his sons to act impiously; to attend to prayers at the hours fixed; to taste no food before the proper hours. 'Woe to the land where the king is a child and whose nobles feast in the morning!' (Ecclesiasticus x, 16). Those be the qualities that in the present secure the prosperity of the realm and lead the king to the better heavenly realms.

[1] Text edited with a valuable introduction by S. Hellmann in *Texte und Untersuchungen zur Geschichte der altchristlichen Literatur* (edd. A. Harnack und C. Schmidt), ser. III, 4 (Leipzig, 1909), pp. 1–62.

He who doth not administer his realm according to this law verily suffereth many adversities of his governance. For on that account often the peace of peoples is broken and disturbances take their rise from within the realm; the fruits also of the earth are diminished and the enslavement of peoples is hastened on; the deaths of relatives and children bring sadness; the invasions of enemies bring desolation on provinces far and wide; wild beasts rend the herds of cattle and flocks of sheep; hurricanes and stormy winters forbid the earth's fertility and the sea's good gifts, and at times the strokes of lightning burn up crops and the flowers of fruit trees and the vines. But above all the injustice of a king not merely maketh dim the face of his own governance, it darkeneth also his sons' and grandsons' that they inherit not the realm after him. For because of Solomon's sin the Lord scattered the realm of the house of Israel from the hands of his sons, and because of the justice of king David He left for ever a lamp from his seed in Jerusalem (cf. I Kings xi, 11–13). Behold to them that see is clearly manifested the worth of a king's justice to the age. It meaneth the peace of peoples, the guardianship of a country, the defence of the common folk, the bulwark of the race, the care of afflictions, the joy of men, a calm atmosphere and a serene sea, the fertility of the earth, the comfort of the poor, inheritance of his sons, and for himself hope of future blessedness. Moreover the king must know that even as he hath been set up on the throne as the first of mankind, so, if he shall fail to act justly, he shall be assigned the first place in punishment. For, as many as are the sinners that he hath had beneath him in the present, he shall have over him by way of torment in that future punishment.

The writer shows familiarity with the Vulgate, with the Benedictine *Rule*, and with Isidore of Seville, and his work has many points of contact with an Irish collection of canons made in the seventh century, the compiler of which knew Gregory's *Pastoral Rule*, five pseudo-Augustinian homilies, of which four are by Caesarius of Arles, and several of Jerome's Biblical commentaries. The latinity of the treatise is correct and even graphic, although the careful balancing of the clauses and the recurrence of similar rhythmic endings produces a certain monotony. This little tract, moreover, deserves more notice than it has commonly received, not merely for its own merits, but because it enjoyed much popularity in the Carolingian Age and after. Especially the section on the Unjust King engaged the attention of those writers of the later eighth and the ninth centuries—Kathvulf, Jonas of Orléans,

Sedulius Scotus, Hincmar—who themselves reflected on the theory of government and the relation of the spiritual to the temporal power, and wrote treatises on monarchic rule. It was also quoted in the records of Church councils and synods held during the ninth century, and doubtless owed its authority to the fact that it was commonly attributed to Cyprian and occasionally to Augustine.

The preoccupation of Irish scholars with Biblical exegesis, which had sometimes been assumed without adequate proof, has very recently been placed beyond doubt and shown to have been intense and widespread.[1] Many Biblical commentaries were composed by them during the seventh and eighth centuries, but most of them survive in only a single manuscript and most are anonymous. Only a few, because at one time or another they were attributed to authorities, like Jerome or Gregory I, seem to have attained to a wider circulation. Since, moreover, the extant manuscripts for the most part are not in Irish script, it is clear that these commentaries were brought to the Continent and for a time enjoyed some vogue. There is also reason for believing that a few commentators of the ninth century, for example, Radbert and Christian of Stavelot, knew and used some of these earlier works of exegesis. Many of these productions of the Irish show certain traits in common. Characteristic phrases recur, there is a fondness for displaying erudition by explaining the sense of words or names in Latin, Greek, and Hebrew. Above all, many stress the literal interpretation of the Bible, a fact which to a great extent explains their ultimate disappearance, because by the ninth century the predominant trend in exegesis was to follow Gregory and Bede and to lay the chief emphasis on the allegorical and moral sense of Scripture. Besides the usual Patristic authors we find traces of the use of rarer works, like the pseudepigraphical Gospel according to the Hebrews, Aponius' commentary on the Song of Songs, and the *Chronicle* of Sulpicius Severus. Although most of these compositions are anonymous, one or two can be assigned with some probability to a particular writer. Thus a commentary on Mark printed among the supposititious works of Jerome is probably by the same Cummian who *c.* 632 composed a letter on

[1] See B. Bischoff in *Sacris Erudiri*, VI (1954), pp. 189–281.

the Paschal controversy.[1] Less certain is the attribution of a gloss on the Bible, of which only parts are extant, to Cadac-Andreas, a contemporary of Charlemagne, who was involved in a controversy with Theodulf of Orléans.

One other Irish author merits attention. Adamnan, abbot of Iona for twenty-five years (679–704), seems to have been a native of Donegal who at an early age became a monk in Iona. He revisited Ireland three times and after 685 stayed more than once at the court of his old pupil Aldfrith, the Northumbrian king, to whom he also presented his *De locis sanctis*. This was a treatise on the holy places in Jerusalem and Palestine with a concluding portion on Constantinople. It was based on the oral account which he had received from a Frankish bishop, Arculf, who had spent nine months in Jerusalem; but Adamnan checked Arculf's statements by occasionally referring to Jerome, Hegesippus, Eucherius, or Sulpicius Severus. The fact that he is mainly recording Arculf's conversation, who had also made sketches on a wax tablet, gives the book a freshness which a narrative derived entirely from written sources would lack. The bishop, although his chief attention was properly focused on the holy places and the numerous churches and relics which he beheld, also has an eye for scenery and for eastern life. Thus he gave Adamnan a vivid description of the crowds of men and beasts thronging the streets of Jerusalem on September 15 (more correctly 13), when the camels, horses, donkeys, mules, and cattle produced an indescribable stench and filth in the holy city, which was cleansed away by a miraculous rainstorm on the day following. He noted that the only trees growing on the Mount of Olives were vines and olives, though wheat and barley also did well there. He observed that carts and carriages were rare in Judaea, where the bulk of the transport was carried by camels, and that the poor lived on locusts cooked in oil. The waters of the Jordan being of a different colour, can be clearly distinguished for some distance from those of the Dead Sea, after the stream has entered it. The orchards lying outside the city walls of Damascus delighted Arculf, and he was impressed by the fortifications of Constantinople no less than by the story of their origin related to him by the inhabitants.

[1] For the letter see Jones, *BOT*, pp. 89–98.

Adamnan's second work, the *Life of Columba*, is by general consent one of the finest examples of medieval hagiography. It is not, properly speaking, a biography at all, but a collection of the saint's prophetic utterances (Book I), his miracles (Book II), and the visions that appeared to him (Book III). The work thus belongs to the same genre as Gregory of Tours' 'biographies' of Saint Julian of Brioude and Saint Martin of Tours. The sources for Adamnan's book are the precious traditions of their founder preserved orally by the monks of Iona. Adamnan's purpose was to leave an eloquent record of the sanctity and superhuman powers of the saint. His skill as a narrator, however, was such that he also brings vividly before his readers the purely human characteristics of Columba. He was of handsome aspect and endowed with an exceptionally powerful voice. He had much practical good sense which showed itself in day-by-day events and, one may add, was readily given a miraculous interpretation by his followers. He was filled with compassion for those suffering unjust treatment in the world, and for a woman in the extreme agonies of childbirth. He was broadminded enough, though regretful to do so, to relax a strict fast for the sake of a visiting stranger. He shrewdly distinguishes the generous giver from the miser who was presumably shamed into giving. Lastly his kindness to dumb creatures is shown by the moving tale of the white horse which came to take a last leave of his master shortly before Columba's death.[1]

These two works by Adamnan are a clear proof of the excellence of the Irish monastic education. Both the style and the historic method—especially in the *De locis sanctis*—are highly praiseworthy. The author has a varied vocabulary; he seems to have had a smattering of Greek, since he has a fondness for introducing Greek words into his narrative.[2] A third work, which is almost certainly by Adamnan, was more directly the outcome of his interest in the liberal arts. He appears to have compiled a

[1] The tale of the horse (*Life*, ed. J. T. Fowler, III, 23) is so naturally related that it reads like an actual occurrence. Anton Mayer, however, regards it as a piece of Indo-Germanic folk-lore. See his article in *Liber Floridus: Festschrift Paul Lehmann*, pp. 131–51.

[2] Cf. Gertrud Brüning in *Zeitschrift für keltische Philologie*, 11 (1917), pp. 211–314, and Kenney, pp. 429–33.

commentary on Virgil's *Eclogues* and *Georgics* by abbreviating the works of three earlier writers, Philargyrius, Titus Gallus, and Gaudentius, and adding some observations of his own. Several copies, some fuller, some more meagre, of the notes made by pupils have survived.[1]

The untiring activity of the Irish in Scotland and on the continent of Europe synchronized with the conversion of the English by missionaries sent from Rome. When, at the bidding of Gregory the Great, Augustine, the prior of the monastery of St Andrew at Rome, landed in Kent with his companions in 597, only Wales, West Wales (*i.e.* Cornwall and part of Devon), and Strathclyde were still in the hands of the Britons and a Christian area. The rest of the island had gradually passed under the control of the Germanic invaders, who at this time were grouped into seven or eight kingdoms. In religion all alike were uncompromising heathen. Augustine during the six years of his missionary labours effected the conversion of Kent and a part of Essex. His two attempts to reach an understanding with the British Church in the West, so that its members should conform to the Roman ritual and celebration of Easter, failed. During the sixty years following the death of Augustine the Roman Church in England remained in a precarious situation. The crushing victory won at Chester in 616 by Ethelfrith, the heathen king of Northumbria, over the Britons in the West reduced their territory to such an extent that the dwellers in Strathclyde were cut completely off from their kinsmen in Wales. The success of Edwin *c.* 617 in dispossessing Ethelfrith and making himself master of Northumbria and then advancing his authority both southwards and westwards, followed, as it was, by his marriage in 625 to the Christian princess of Kent, Ethelburga, created more favourable conditions for promoting the spread of Christianity. Paulinus, consecrated first bishop of York, did a great work in winning over Northumbria and then East Anglia to the Faith. But the death of Edwin in 633 was followed by a strong pagan reaction. Paulinus narrowly escaped with his life, to pass the rest of his days as bishop of Rochester. In the next year Oswald, the second son of Ethelfrith, who had spent his earlier years as an exile in

[1] Cf. Kenney, pp. 286–7.

Iona, where he had received an excellent education, after a great victory over the British Caedwalla, secured the Northumbrian throne. A genuine, God-fearing ruler, he naturally desired that all his subjects should become Christians. It was no less natural that he should turn for help to the Irish Church in Scotland rather than to the English Church in Kent. Thus, since the labours of Paulinus in the North had been undone, it was Irish missionaries —Aidan was the most important—who during the next three decades achieved the permanent conversion of northern England. The religious centre of this new Celtic Church was the monastery founded at Lindisfarne (now Holy Island). The good work continued under Oswald's successor, Oswiu. Essex and Mercia were won over to Christianity, and numerous monasteries were founded. The conversion of the West Saxons seems also to have been mainly achieved by the Celtic Church. With the growth in influence of the English Wilfrith, who had become a staunch adherent of the Roman observance and had secured its adoption in his own monastery at Ripon, the question of a union between the two Churches in Britain again came to the fore. In 664 King Oswiu called together a synod at Whitby, at which various points of difference, especially the correct date of Easter, were discussed.[1] While Wilfrith with great eloquence and adroitness represented the Roman case, the chief spokesman of the Celtic Church was Colman, bishop of Lindisfarne. Oswiu and his people decided for Wilfrith and Rome, and the Irish bishops and priests with some natives who remained faithful to them withdrew to Iona.

Thus Northumbria, Mercia, and Essex, were brought into line with Kent. But almost immediately the country was visited by a pestilence which not only carried away all the bishops save one, but in places led many of the people to relapse into pagan worship. The kings of Northumbria and Kent, fearing that the Church denuded of its leaders would rapidly disintegrate, jointly applied to Rome for aid and for a new primate. But it was not till 669 that the Greek monk, Theodore of Tarsus, consecrated Archbishop of Canterbury by Pope Vitalian himself, arrived in England. During

---

[1] For the date, 664, not 663 as proposed by Lane Poole and Stenton, see W. Levison, *England and the Continent in the Eighth Century*, pp. 265 ff. and C. W. Jones, *Saints' Lives and Chronicles*, p. 47.

the twenty-one years of Theodore's episcopate (died in 690) the organization and unification of the English Church under the primacy of Canterbury were assured.

This [says Bede] was the first archbishop whom all the English Church obeyed. And forasmuch as both of them (Theodore and abbot Hadrian) were, as has been said before, well read both in sacred and in secular literature, they gathered a crowd of disciples, and there daily flowed from them rivers of knowledge to water the hearts of their hearers; and, together with the book of Holy Writ, they also taught them the arts of ecclesiastical poetry, astronomy and arithmetic. A testimony of which is, that there are still living at this day, some of their scholars, who are as well versed in the Greek and Latin tongues as in their own, in which they were born.[1]

The school of Canterbury, under the guidance of Theodore and of Hadrian, once abbot of Nividanum near Monte Cassino, and from 671 installed as abbot of the abbey of St Peter and St Paul at Canterbury, became a leading centre of education and of letters, while the library, enriched by the codices brought by Theodore and Hadrian, now contained many works, both theological and profane, which had hitherto been unknown in the island. Important light has recently been thrown on the teaching of these two men and on their theological background by the recovery of glosses on the Pentateuch and Gospels which survive in a manuscript of the eleventh century now in Milan. The glosses reflect the writer's personal knowledge of conditions in the Near East and his use of Greek authorities. Of most of these no Old Latin version exists, while the interpretation is predominantly literal or 'historical', not allegorical.[2] Two other men stand out at this time for their efforts in founding monastic communities and furthering religious education and learning, Wilfrith, who had been the dominant personality at Whitby in 664, and Benedict Biscop. Both men travelled extensively, for Wilfrith had made three journeys to Rome before his death in 710, while Benedict visited that city no less than six times. Whatever view may be taken of Wilfrith's ecclesiastical career and his disagreements with

[1] Bede, *E.H.*, 4, 2 (Giles's translation).
[2] See Bischoff, *op. cit.*, pp. 192–5, who promises a fuller treatment of these glosses.

Theodore and others,[1] there is no doubt that both as the founder of many religious houses organized on the Roman model and of churches in various parts of the country, and as the missionary who stamped out heathen worship in Sussex and the Isle of Wight, he deserves to be regarded as one of the founders of the English Church and of English culture.

Benedict Biscop, who died in 690, is best known as the founder of the monasteries of Wearmouth (674) and Jarrow (682) in Northumbria, which he enriched with many manuscripts, treasures, and relics gathered by him on his continental journeys. Ceolfrith, his successor as abbot (died 716), carried on Benedict's work in the same spirit, and further additions were made to the library of the combined monasteries. Both Wilfrith and Benedict Biscop were convinced upholders of the authority of the Roman see. Both had acquired extensive knowledge of the older Churches of Italy and Gaul. In addition, Benedict Biscop had taken the tonsure and received his training at Lérins. Nevertheless, though in such matters as the Easter reckoning and the tonsure and the monastic rule followed in religious houses Rome had triumphed, the Celtic teachers who had previously laboured there left a lasting impress on education and intellectual life in all those regions of England which they had visited.[2] Perhaps the most tangible proof of this influence is the script written in Anglo-Saxon *scriptoria*; for it is a modification of the Irish script and it lasted on for centuries after the Carolingian minuscule had superseded

[1] For Wilfrith see the *Life* by Eddius (Aedda) edited by W. Levison in *MGH*, Script. Merov., VI, pp. 163 ff. and by B. Colgrave (Cambridge, Eng., 1927).

[2] The date of the introduction of Benedict's *Rule* into England and of its adoption in different houses are matters still under dispute. Since Dom Chapman (*St Benedict and the Sixth Century*, pp. 197 ff.) has shown that the *Rule* was in general use in Italy and Sicily at the end of the sixth century and was the rule followed by Gregory the Great, it would be familiar to Augustine, prior of Gregory's own monastery of St Andrew, and would be used by him in the abbey of St Peter and St Paul at Canterbury. We know from Bede (*Hist. Abbat.*, 11; 16) that Benedict Biscop regarded St Benedict and his *Rule* with deep veneration and that the *Rule* was observed in Wearmouth and Jarrow, though possibly with some modifications, called for by the different conditions under which the Northumbrian monks lived. Finally, it is significant that the oldest extant manuscript of the *Rule*, belonging to the interpolated class, was written in uncials by an Anglo-Saxon scribe, *c.* 700, probably at Canterbury. See *CLA*, II, No. 240.

earlier hands on the Continent. The oldest extant manuscripts copied by Anglo-Saxon scribes are, even to the trained eye of the palaeographer, scarcely distinguishable from contemporary Irish codices.[1] There is a symbolic significance, too, in the first important literary figure produced by the young and vigorous English Church. In the south of England only two monasteries founded by Irishmen are on record, at Bosham in Sussex and at Malmesbury in Wessex. The community at Bosham seems soon to have languished, but Malmesbury was destined for greatness.

The West Saxon, Aldhelm, who was born *c.* 639, received his early education at Malmesbury under its first abbot and founder, the Irish Mailduib (Maildufus). At the age of thirty or thereabouts Aldhelm went to Kent where he became for some years a pupil of Theodore and Hadrian. Returning to Malmesbury *c.* 674 he was ordained priest, and already in the next year succeeded his old teacher as abbot. Later in life he made a pilgrimage to Rome at the invitation of Pope Sergius. In 705 he was consecrated bishop of Sherborne. Four years later he died. Himself a Saxon of noble birth, Aldhelm was intellectually a product of Celtic and Roman training. That the Roman influence was the stronger and was more permanent is shown by the fact that, when he became abbot of Malmesbury, he reorganized the monastery on lines which would be approved by Theodore, and by the tone of his own writings. These include compositions in both prose and verse. His chief work, *De Virginitate*, appeared first as a treatise in prose, but he followed it up by producing a metrical paraphrase of it. Further, he brought out a composition written in prose on rhythm and metrics, in which are incorporated one hundred riddles in verse, the whole work being dedicated to Acircius, who is to be identified with the Northumbrian king, Aldfrith. Lastly he is the author of a number of miscellaneous poems and of several important letters, one of which throws some interesting side-lights on our author. While at Canterbury much of his time was devoted to secular studies—Roman law, metrics and versification, arithmetic and astronomy. The man of over thirty has gone to school again and applies to himself a phrase of Jerome: 'I, who thought myself a scholar, am beginning again to be a

[1] See the valuable comments by E. A. Lowe in *CLA*, II, pp. xi–xii.

pupil.'[1] To one correspondent Aldhelm expressly states that cultivation of the liberal arts is indeed necessary, but must only be ancillary to the study of theology. This is, of course, the familiar doctrine formulated long since by Jerome and other Christian writers. Aldhelm is anxious lest another correspondent, who is going to Ireland to study, may spend too much time on pagan mythology. His letter to Eahfrith lauds the superiority of Hadrian and Theodore over Irish scholars. The latest editor of Aldhelm was the first to explain the real point of Aldhelm's letter. Although all of his prose is highly artificial and abounds in rare words and turgid diction, this letter far surpasses in this respect anything else that he has written. Its vocabulary, which is derived from glossaries, and has points of similarity to the language of the *Hisperica Famina*, its constant alliteration—the epistle opens with fifteen words, each beginning with the letter P—and the frequent introduction of Greek words, are meant to demonstrate to the recipient that all the conceits and stylistic mannerisms of Irish scholarship can be acquired in England, and that there is no need to cross the sea to learn them. The letter should not, therefore, be interpreted as a depreciation of Irish scholars; for, although Aldhelm reserves his highest praise for Theodore and Hadrian, he assuredly had not acquired his own high-flown style from them. The letter is designed to show that the English pupils have outgrown their pupilage and can rival their Irish masters in their own speciality.

It must be confessed that Aldhelm's works, though much admired in and after his day, are utterly unpalatable to a modern taste. In prose he seems incapable of writing a sentence that is readily intelligible. While the hortatory part of the *De Virginitate* does not contain a great deal which had not already been expressed more attractively elsewhere—for example, by Cyprian and Augustine, to both of whom Aldhelm is indebted—the illustrative material, drawn from the New Testament, the lives of the Fathers, and numerous early lives of saints and martyrs, is of great interest because we can see here very plainly the width of Aldhelm's reading. The poetic version, because it is phrased in

[1] *Epist.*, 8 in the edition by R. Ehwald in *MGH*, AA, XV. For Ehwald's note on the letter to Eahfrith see page 487 of his edition.

simpler language, is far more readable. Here he is heavily indebted to Virgil and Sedulius for his diction. Although his hexameters are free from licence, and, as we should expect in one so steeped in the formal rules of versification, metrically correct, they are monotonous because he has introduced so little variety in the matter of caesuras and pauses. His riddles, for which Symphosius, who flourished in the later fourth or early fifth century, was his model, merit attention both because they show considerable ingenuity and because they set a fashion in such literary *jeux d'esprit* which had a long history. The following is a good example of this type of poem. The answer to the riddle is *sanguisuga*, the leech.

> Lurida per latices cenosas lustro paludes;
> Nam mihi composuit nomen fortuna cruentum,
> Rubro dum bibulis vescor de sanguine buccis.
> Ossibus et pedibus geminisque carebo lacertis,
> Corpora vulneribus sed mordeo dira trisulcis
> Atque salutiferis sic curam praesto labellis.[1]

However alien from modern taste Aldhelm's compositions may be, it would be a serious error to underestimate or depreciate his significance as a writer or the greatness of his achievement. He is the first of a line of scholars trained in the monasteries of England. Even after every allowance has been made for the fact that some of his quotations from earlier literature are derived not from the works themselves but from an intermediate source, the width of his reading is still most remarkable. Some of the authors he had no doubt first studied with his Irish teacher; more, we may suspect, became accessible to him in the library at Canterbury of which he must have been one of the first men to make a thorough use. He was acquainted with Virgil, Lucan, Juvenal, Juvencus, Prosper's epigrams, and Sedulius' *Paschal Poem*; several grammatical treatises of the later Roman imperial age; some writings of Augustine and much of Jerome; the *Collationes* of Cassian; Gregory the Great and Isidore; Rufinus' translation of various Greek

[1] *Epist.*, 43 (Ehwald, p. 116). 'A lurid shape in the water I haunt muddy lakes. A name of blood was fortune's gift to me, as I feed on red blood with thirsty cheeks. Bones, feet, and twin arms I lack, but dreaded by men I bite their bodies with three-furrowed wound, and thus with health-bringing lips I afford them cure.'

theological works and a considerable body of hagiographical literature. These are the authors whom he most frequently cited or used;[1] but there are others from whom he quotes more rarely. He knew his Bible well. His quotations from Genesis, Psalms, and the Gospel according to St Matthew are most numerous, but save for a few of the Minor Prophets and John I and II, every book in the Old and New Testaments is represented. If he was a zealous student of Scripture, he was also a Virgilian. His familiarity with that poet may astonish us and would certainly have shocked Gregory the Great. It is reasonable to suppose that this love for the pagan poet was first instilled by Mailduib. In short, no country in Western Europe during the seventh century could show Aldhelm's equal in intellectual achievement.

At the very time when Aldhelm had completed his studies at Canterbury, there was born in Northumbria, on territory afterwards belonging to Wearmouth and Jarrow, one who was to outshine him as a scholar as much as he surpassed his contemporaries. Bede, who was born in 673, at the age of seven was entrusted as an oblate to Benedict Biscop. Though he entered Wearmouth, he was soon transferred to Jarrow. There his life was passed, and, though it is clear from his own works that he visited Lindisfarne and York, there is nothing to show that he ever travelled farther afield than Northumbria. Ordained a deacon in 692, he became a priest eleven years later. He died in 735. For forty-odd years he laboured indefatigably as a teacher of others and as a scholar who never ceased to learn himself. His career as a writer began with school treatises on metrics, figures of speech, and orthography, and with two of his three scientific works. It ended only with the last hour of his life; for just before his death he had completed dictating a translation of the Fourth Gospel into the vernacular, a work unfortunately lost.[2] Apart from his historical books all Bede's writings are directly didactic. At the end of his *Ecclesiastical History* he has introduced a short biographical statement with a list of his compositions. This list

---

[1] For Aldhelm's sources cf. Ehwald, *op. cit.*, pp. 542–6.

[2] Bede with his last breath finished what he had set out to do; but there is some doubt whether this was to translate only a portion of the Fourth Gospel or the whole.

is extremely valuable as it enables one to set aside a number of spurious treatises which now bear Bede's name in the manuscripts. Many such were attributed to him after his time, because of his eminence as a scholar and writer in various fields.[1] He did not include in his list the short tract on the holy places (*De locis sanctis*), but he had mentioned it previously in the *Ecclesiastical History* (5, 15) and it is certainly one of his early compilations. The *Retractation on the Acts of the Apostles* is also genuine. It has been generally assumed that, because it does not appear under this name in the list, that it was composed after 731. But when he enumerates his commentaries on the New Testament, he includes 'in actus apostolorum libros II'. There can be no doubt that what he means by this is his early *Commentary on Acts* and the *Retractation*, which was probably composed between 725 and 731.[2] Only a few of Bede's works can be dated exactly by internal evidence; but it is generally possible to distinguish the earlier from the later and often the priority of one over another.[3]

The three short essays, entitled respectively, *De metrica arte*, *De schematibus et tropis sacrae scripturae* and *De orthographia*, were intended for the pupils of the monastery school and were put together by Bede when he was still a deacon. Derived wholly from earlier works, they have no special significance save for the light that they throw on the mentality of their author. They prove his thorough training in the subjects of the *trivium*, wide reading in the grammatical treatises composed in the later Roman Empire,

[1] The spurious scientific and computistical works are well treated by Charles W. Jones, *Bedae Pseudepigrapha* (Ithaca, N.Y., 1939). For the spurious commentaries on St Matthew and St John see A. E. Schönbach in *Sitzungsberichte*, Vienna Academy, phil.-hist. Klasse, CXLVI, No. 4, 1903. For some other doubtful works, not named by Bede but possibly his, see M. L. W. Laistner and H. H. King, *A Hand-list of Bede Manuscripts* (Ithaca, N.Y., 1943), pp. 154–9.

[2] On the date of the *Commentary* and the *Retractation* see M. L. W. Laistner, *Bedae Venerabilis Expositio Actuum Apostolorum et Retractatio* (Cambridge, Mass., 1939), pp. xiii–xvii; on the *De locis sanctis* cf. Laistner and King, *op. cit.*, p. 83. It was perhaps composed about the same time as the *Commentary on the Catholic Epistles*; for in both works (Comm. on II Peter, ii, 6; *De loc.*, 11) he relates in identical words the same story, based on Josephus, about Dead Sea fruit.

[3] Cf. the introductions to the manuscripts of the different works in Laistner and King, *op. cit.* For the dates of the two chronological works see Jones, *BOT*, pp. 131 and 136.

and his own enviable gift of clear exposition. One other feature is noteworthy. Whereas in Aldhelm, notwithstanding his insistence that secular literature should only be a means to an end, the artist and admirer of great poetry particularly of Virgil, over-masters the ecclesiastic; in Bede the religious teacher predominates. His poetic illustrations in the tract on metrics are taken almost entirely from Christian poets. Similarly in his second essay pagan learning supplies the rules, the illustrative citations are all derived from the Bible.

Another early work was the versified *Life of St Cuthbert*. Since Bede wished to familiarize his pupils with the miraculous powers of the saint, he may well have adopted the metrical form in order to help memorization. Again, two of his scientific treatises par-take of the character of school-texts. Both are short and both were composed about the same time. *De natura rerum* is a descrip-tion of the physical universe compiled from the elder Pliny and Isidore. The *Liber de temporibus*, completed in 703, explains the various divisions of time and the seasons. It was Bede's first attempt to explain to his pupils and others the problems of the ecclesiastical calendar and, in the words of the latest editor, 'was designed to eliminate students' dependence on Irish *computi* and the works of Isidore'.[1] Many years later (725) he composed a more elaborate work on chronology, entitled *De temporum ratione*, to which is appended an outline of world history with the chief dates since the creation of the world. In addition to the sources used in *De temporibus* Bede consulted a great number of earlier chroniclers and writers on chronology. Thus he succeeded in putting together a valuable synthesis in which divergent earlier systems of reckoning were brought into harmony. The books were used extensively after Bede's time, and through it the dating of events backwards or forwards from the birth of Christ, which Bede took over from Dionysius Exiguus and adopted in his own Easter Tables, instead of reckoning from the creation of the world, came into general use in Western Europe.

By far the largest section of Bede's collected works is made up of his commentaries on books of the Old and New Testaments. Their bulk and their subsequent influence make it desirable to

[1] See Jones, *op. cit.*, p. 132.

consider their method and content more closely than is generally done by modern critics, who have usually concentrated all of their attention on Bede's historical works. He began his exegetical labours on books of the New Testament; for the commentaries on the Apocalypse, Acts, the Catholic Epistles, and the Gospel according to St Luke were all composed prior to the commentary on Samuel, which was not finished until after 716. With the exception of the commentary on St Mark and the *Retractation* on the Acts, all his later expository works dealt with books of the Old Testament and seem to have been composed approximately in the order in which the books stand in the Bible. The commentary on Mark, though shorter than that on Luke, contains many passages that have been taken with little or no change from the earlier work. Apart from the *Retractation*, which must be separately considered, Bede's general approach and aims are the same in all his expositions. In his emphasis on allegorical interpretation he is an admiring disciple of Gregory the Great, and Gregory, together with Jerome and Augustine, is his constant guide on questions of exegesis and doctrine. Sometimes the literal and the allegorical meaning of a passage only are set side by side. For example, in commenting on the words, *qui est iuxta Hierusalem, sabbati habens iter* (Acts i, 12), he explains:

> According to the historical sense he points out that the Mount of Olives was a mile away from the city of Jerusalem; for on the Sabbath according to the Law it was not permissible to walk more than a mile. According to the allegorical sense the man who shall be worthy inwardly to behold the glory of the Lord ascending to the Father and to be enriched with the promise of the Holy Spirit, he on a Sabbath journey enters the city of eternal peace.

But at times he recognizes a threefold or even a fourfold sense of Scripture. There are many reasons why Bede's commentaries, though most of the doctrine and much of the learning that they contain are derived from earlier theologians and scholars, have a character of their own and deservedly became a model for many later exegetes. He is passionately orthodox, not merely in his support of Rome against the Celtic Church, but in his condemnation of heresy. The world has seen few men of a more kindly, charitable, and truly Christian disposition. It is also true that his strictures on many of the heresies to which he alludes in his works are, so to speak, academic and taken over from his sources; for example, his condemnation of Origen's doctrine on eternal punishment is derived from Augustine.[1] But his warnings against Pelagianism and his denunciation of Pelagius and Pelagius' chief supporter, Julian of Aeclanum, are so numerous and fierce that one must suppose that Pelagianism was a living question to him, either because there had been a recrudescence of it in Britain in Bede's own time or because it had never been completely eradicated there.[2] He had even been accused of heterodoxy himself, because he had challenged the traditional chronological reckoning from the Creation and given a different solution of the problem. Hence he attacked the computations of Victorius with severity (De temporum ratione 51; cf. also 62) and expressed himself with unusual bitterness in his Letter to Plegwin (708) and again many years later in the Preface to the De temporum ratione.[3]

Allegorical interpretation, which is the leading purpose of all Bede's commentaries and which is found in its most elaborate or extreme form in his exposition of I Samuel and of the Song of Songs, is a form of spiritual and intellectual exercise for which modern readers have neither the taste nor the understanding. Its all but universal use by monastic teachers and commentators, like the attribution of everything out of the common to miraculous intervention of the Deity either directly or through chosen instruments, forces one to realize how utterly alien to our own habits of thought, and how all but incomprehensible, were some of the workings of the medieval mind. The influence of the Antiochene school of exegesis, which had dwelt primarily on the literal or historic sense, did not wholly disappear in Western Europe, but it was slight and could make little headway against a method used by Augustine and Gregory the Great.[4] What

[1] Cf. Laistner, Bedae Ven. expositio, p. 108, 1 ff.

[2] The whole of the first book of the commentary on the Song of Songs is a diatribe against Julian. But the treatises, De amore and De bono constantiae, from which he cites and which he attributes to Julian, were composed by Pelagius himself. Cf. Clavis, Nos. 751–2.

[3] Cf. the admirable discussion of this episode in Bede's life in C. W. Jones, op. cit., pp. 132 ff.

[4] Cf. Laistner in Harvard Theol. Rev., 40 (1947), pp. 19–31.

makes Bede's commentaries more readable than most—than Gregory's *Moralia*, for example, though Bede himself would have been inexpressibly shocked to have been told so—is that his latinity is of almost classical purity, and that his wide interests and wider reading led him to introduce much other material, even though he himself considered it of secondary importance. His interest in the text criticism of the Bible was unique in his age. The Vulgate text that he used most consistently is that now represented by the *Codex Amiatinus*, a manuscript which had actually been written in the *scriptorium* of Wearmouth or Jarrow.[1] But he knew other manuscripts of the Vulgate and also at times consulted one or more Old Latin versions of the Bible.[2] He had, too, begun to learn Greek early in life, and his works are proof that he persisted in this study to the last. All his commentaries, even the earliest, contain a certain number of *Graeca*. Some indeed are derived from his sources, particularly from Jerome. But he quotes from Basil's *Hexameron*, though not in the Latin version of Eustathius, and some of his citations from Josephus do not correspond to the Latin translation made at the instance of Cassiodorus. In the *Retractation* one of his main purposes is the closer collation of the original text of Acts with the Latin translations of that book, and he had recourse again to a bilingual manuscript of the sixth century which is still extant and which he had already used when he composed his early commentary on Acts. The translation is an Old Latin version, not Vulgate.[3] He also corrects etymologies which he had put forward in his exposition of Acts, explaining frankly that he had learnt better (*sollertius ediscens*) in the interval. Some of his comments show that his contemporaries were ignorant of Greek.[4] He draws attention to erroneous renderings in the Vulgate and frequently points to a word or phrase in the Greek text which does not

---

[1] See *CLA*, III, No. 299.

[2] See *Harvard Theol. Rev.* 30 (1937), pp. 37–50.

[3] For this manuscript, *Laudianus Graecus*, 35, in the Bodleian Library, see *CLA*, II, No. 251.

[4] *Bedae Ven. expositio*, 97, 22, he warns against making *Pentecosten* a nominative; 100, 24, he explains that σκότος is translated by *tenebrae* because the Latin word has no singular. He adds that in rendering the word into Old English the singular should be kept.

appear in the Latin. In one passage he silences possible critics of
his textual studies by referring them to one of his guides, the
Greek Father, Gregory of Nazianzus; but here the quotation
shows that Bede had read him in the Latin version of Rufinus.[1]
But Bede did not know Hebrew; for it has been shown that the
occasional *Hebraica* found in his commentaries on the Old Testament are uniformly derived from Jerome.[2] No writer within the
period covered by this book had read as widely as Bede. He had
studied most of Jerome's works, much of Augustine, all of
Gregory the Great, six or seven treatises by Ambrose and most of
Isidore. But, besides these standard authors, he cites from a surprisingly large and diversified number of other writings, so that
the total number of titles with which he shows acquaintance is not
far short of two hundred.[3] Two qualifications must, however,
be made. There are not a few examples where Bede quotes at
second hand; for example, the citations in the commentary on
Acts from Martial and Sallust are, as the context clearly shows,
derived from Isidore, and he has taken over a famous sentence in
Suetonius' *Life of Claudius* from Orosius.[4] In the second place,
the list, long as it is, does not tell the whole story. The extent of
his indebtedness to his predecessors will not be certainly established until all his writings can be read in critical editions answering to the demands of modern scholarship. Undoubtedly much
that still passes as Bede's will then be found to be cited verbally
or to be adapted from earlier authors. He often refers to his
authority by name and sometimes also specifies the particular
treatise from which he quotes. But he constantly borrows from
Isidore without indicating that he is doing so, and other works
that he used without acknowledgement are Primasius' commentary on the Apocalypse, the commentary on the same book
by Victorinus of Pettau in the revision of Jerome, Cassiodorus'
commentary on the Psalms, and Salonius' allegorical exposition
of Proverbs. Nevertheless Bede was far more scrupulous than
the majority of medieval commentators in acknowledging his

[1] *Bedae Ven. expositio*, 16, 20–32; 99, 2–7.
[2] Cf. E. J. Sutcliffe in *Biblica*, 16 (1935), pp. 300–6.
[3] See my articles in *Trans. of the R. Hist. Soc.*, 16 (1933), pp. 69–94, and
in *Bede: His Life, Times, and Writings* (Oxford, 1935), pp. 237–66.
[4] *Bedae Ven. expositio*, 44, 12; 85, 20; 68, 9.

authorities. In the Preface to his commentary on Luke he specially requests those who should copy his writings on no account to omit the marginal references to his sources which he has entered in his own copy. But in the extant manuscripts such marginal source-marks are found only in two works, the commentaries on Luke and on Mark. Moreover, two generations after the death of Bede, Claudius of Turin remarks that Bede is the only commentator that he knows who indicated his sources in the margin, but that he had found such marginalia only in the two commentaries that we have named. Thus it is clear that Bede's instructions to monastic scribes were soon disregarded, if we may assume, on the strength of a single passage, that he followed the same practice in all his commentaries.[1] Yet, however great his debt to his predecessors may be, Bede does not copy uncritically. He is careful to select what will be useful and intelligible to his readers, he adds his own comments and observations, and he has knit the whole together in a way which raises his theological works well above the level of mere compilation or *catenae* and which bears clearly the impress of his own mind and personality. 'Il possède un art particulier pour agencer en une mosaïque habile les mots qu'il emprunte soigneusement à ses sources, et pour en composer un tout qui se distingue par la cohérence, l'équilibre et la pondération.'[2] In selecting and adapting so much of the teaching of the great Church Fathers for his own pupils and for those that followed after, Bede performed a service of inestimable value to medieval students of theology. Two other theological works deserve brief mention. In the list of his writings Bede names two books of homilies on texts from the Gospels. Little more than a generation after Bede's death Paul the Deacon alludes to fifty homilies by Bede. This collection survives in a few manuscripts, and these are the only homilies composed by him as such. But in the later Middle Ages the number of sermons to which Bede's name became attached multiplied greatly. Some of these, which are included in all the printed editions, except that

[1] Cf. Claudius of Turin in *PL*, 104, col. 617. For the source-marks in the two commentaries see E. J. Sutcliffe in *Biblica*, 7 (1926), pp. 428 ff., and Laistner in *Journ. Theol. Stud.*, 34 (1933), pp. 350–4.

[2] H. Quentin, *Les martyrologes historiques du moyen âge* (Paris, 1908), p. 118.

by Giles, are in fact extracts, suitable for the purpose of homiletics, culled from Bede's commentaries on Luke and Mark. But many other sermons have no claim whatever to be considered his. They were attributed to him, as other works indeed were also, because his was a famous name, in the same way that supposititious writings were fathered on Ambrose, Jerome, and Augustine.[1] Finally, the first eight questions in the *Aliquot quaestionum liber*, which until recently was regarded as spurious, are genuine. They are brief discussions of some passages in the Bible, similar in their general character to the more extended *Thirty Questions in Samuel and Kings*, and Bede may have thought them too slight to include in his list of works.[2]

But it is by his *Ecclesiastical History of the English People* that Bede is best known, and on this his reputation as an author primarily rests. It is divided into five books and the narrative is carried down to 731, the very year in which it was completed. Bede's life-long interest in two interrelated subjects, chronology and hagiography, had prepared the way for the *History*. Reference has already been made to his chronological researches and to the saints' lives that he composed. He had also compiled a history of the first five abbots of Wearmouth and Jarrow. It is severely factual and only deals fully with two of the five men, Benedict Biscop and Ceolfrid. One other work is historical in content though not in form, the letter which Bede addressed to the newly consecrated archbishop of York, Egbert, towards the end of 734, only a few months before his own death.[3] Bede never lacked friends and admirers who spurred him on to write. And, just as Acca, bishop of Hexham, was, so to speak, the godfather of many

---

[1] Cf. Laistner and King, *op. cit.*, pp. 114–18 and J. Leclercq in *Recherches de théologie ancienne et médiévale*, 14 (1947), pp. 211–18. For the *Homilies* see now *Corpus Patrum Christianorum*, cxxii (Turnhout, 1955).

[2] See P. Lehmann, 'Wert und Echtheit einer Beda abgesprochenen Schrift' in *Sitzungsberichte*, Bavarian Academy, Munich, 1919, and H. Weissweiler in *Beiträge zur Geschichte der Philosophie und Theologie des Mittelalters*, 33, fasc. 1/2 (1936), pp. 54ff. For manuscripts of this work cf. also Laistner and King, *op. cit.*, pp. 157–8.

[3] The *Historia abbatum* and the *Letter to Egbert* are included in Charles Plummer's edition of the *History*. For the prose life of St Cuthbert see the edition by Bertram Colgrave (Cambridge, Eng., 1940). The metrical life has been edited by W. Jaeger (*Palaestra*, 198; Leipzig, 1933).

of the commentaries which on completion were dedicated to him, so the prime instigator of the *Ecclesiastical History* would seem to have been Albinus, abbot of the monastery of St Peter and St Paul in Canterbury. For Chapters 1 to 22 of the first book Bede relied on earlier writers—Orosius, Prosper of Aquitaine, an early life of St Germanus, and some other hagiographical material now lost. His own work, properly speaking, begins in Chapter 23 with the mission of St Augustine. Bede explains in his preface what great pains he had taken to secure his information from reliable sources. Highly placed ecclesiastics, like Albinus himself, Daniel, bishop of the West Saxons, and others, the monks of Lastingham abbey, the priest Nothelm in London, all, Bede says, have placed him in their debt for the information that they have put at his disposal. Nothelm, when in Rome, had also consulted the Papal archives on Bede's behalf. In addition, Bede makes a general acknowledgment of earlier written sources that he had utilized. Besides this he occasionally refers in the course of his narrative to an informant, like Deda, abbot of Partney (*E.H.*, 2, 16), who has given him data about some special topic or person. There is no doubt that by his careful methods he was able to gather together much precious information and many interesting traditions, which, but for him, would certainly have been lost, about the growth of the English Church fostered by Rome and concerning the labours of the Celtic missionaries in the northern parts of the island. We are also filled with respect for the various informants who were so eager to help on a difficult undertaking and clearly so convinced of Bede's fitness for the task that they did their utmost to supply him with such material as they could muster.

Admiration for what has by general consent been accepted as a masterpiece of literature must not blind one to certain weaknesses inherent in Bede's method of combining annalistic material with hagiography. Furthermore, as has recently been shown in a penetrating study, the time references in the *Ecclesiastical History* are not wholly consistent, since their precision or vagueness depends on Bede's sources.[1] And the same critic has pointed out

[1] See Charles W. Jones, *Saints' Lives and Chronicles*, Chapters III to V, and the Appendix, pp. 161–99.

rightly that the material that Bede was able to collect was much fuller for Northumbria and the North than, for example, for Kent or Wessex. But, whether we accept the long established view that the *History* was in direct line of descent from Eusebius and later Church historians, or believe with Mr Jones that Bede's real purpose was to compose near the end of his life what was, in the last analysis, a work of edification, the *Ecclesiastical History* attained a unity which a book like Gregory of Tours' *History of the Franks* lacks, a work, indeed, to which it is superior in all respects save one, dramatic intensity. But Bede's descriptive powers were of a high order, as can be seen not only in the most familiar stories—Gregory the Great and the English boys, Oswald and Aidan, or the tale of Caedmon—but in many briefer stories.[1] The *Historia ecclesiastica* became at once, what it has remained to this day, an authoritative work and, to judge by the extant manuscripts, enjoyed a great popularity on the Continent as well. The extant manuscripts, exclusive of brief fragments, number more than one hundred and sixty, and the book is frequently met with in medieval library catalogues.[2]

[1] *e.g.*, the vivid description of Paulinus (2, 16); Wilfrith helping the starving population of Sussex which he had just converted to Christianity (4, 13); the tale of the two friends, Ethelhun and Egbert (3, 27).

[2] For the MSS. of *E.H.* see Laistner and King, *op. cit.*, pp. 93–112. The manuscript of the early ninth century, which was once at Middlehill and is marked 'untraced' in the *Hand-list*, was listed in Catalogue 77 (1948) of W. H. Robinson Ltd., London, No. 93. It is now, as Mr William H. Robinson, junior, has kindly informed me, in the private collection of Dr Martin Bodmer in Switzerland.

CHAPTER VI

The Western European Continent, *c.* 637–751, and the Missionary Labours of Boniface

Aclose union between Church and State, in which the ecclesiastical power for the most part predominated, was characteristic of Spain in the period between the death of Isidore and the Arab conquest in 711. Rigid orthodoxy coupled with a zeal for organization found expression in numerous councils, of which there were no less than fifteen between 633 and 701. The new codification of the law—the so-called *Leges Visigothorum*—completed during this period was the direct outcome of the Church's synodal activity, and represents a fusion of the enactments passed by the Temporal Power with the canons of the ecclesiastical Councils. What is known of the intellectual life of this age—and it is little enough—is centred mainly in Toledo and associated with three occupants of its see, Eugenius (646–57), Ildefonsus (657–67), and Julian (680–90). The first of these, though of no great distinction as an author, seems to have been a man of considerable culture and varied interests. He composed a treatise on the Trinity, now lost, prepared a revised edition of the Arian poet Dracontius, and was himself a prolific versifier, since the extant collection of his short poems numbers not less than one hundred. They prove that he was familiar with seven or eight earlier poets, from Virgil to Fortunatus, and although the positive merits of his verse are slight, they appear, if we may judge by the frequency with which they were cited by writers of the eighth and ninth centuries, to have enjoyed posthumous fame. Ildefonsus was both a literary biographer and a theologian. His *De viris illustribus*, continuing Isidore's book of the same name, contains brief accounts of Gregory the Great, Donatus, an African monk who became abbot of a Spanish monastery, and twelve Spanish prelates. Of his theological tracts that on the

Perpetual Virginity of the Blessed Mary is important, since it was the immediate cause and inspiration of Mariolatry in Spain.[1]

The most arresting figure, however, is Julian. During the ten years of his episcopate he was the most powerful man in Spain. For some time he was engaged in a vigorous controversy with the Papacy on the condemnation of the Monothelite heresy at the Sixth Oecumenical Council. He also regarded the suppression of the Jews as a major issue during his episcopate. Where Ildefonsus had been content to inveigh against the hated race in two chapters, Julian launched a treatise in three books. In it he attacks, often with the bitterest abuse, the claim of the Jews that hitherto there had only been five ages of mankind, while the sixth would be inaugurated by the advent of the Messiah, who was yet to come. Julian, on the contrary, maintained that the sixth age had been ushered in with the birth of Christ, sent into the world in accordance with God's promise. The thesis was not new, and Julian, in addition to numerous citations from the Old and the New Testaments, bolstered up his case by quotations from Augustine, Tertullian, Hilary, Jerome, Eusebius, Epiphanius, and Gregory the Great. His wide acquaintance with Patristic literature is further illustrated by another work, a collection of apparently contradictory passages in the Scriptures, which can nevertheless be brought into harmony. There are over two hundred of these passages, mostly arranged in twos, and the quotation of the seemingly opposed statements is followed by a short exposition reconciling them. The explanation is in many instances taken verbally from the Fathers, as the following example will show:

> Cum Psalmista dicat (Psalm xxxv, 7), 'homines et iumenta salvos facies, Domine', quomodo Paulus apostolus quasi e contrario videtur dicere (I Cor. ix, 9), 'nunquid de bobus cura est Deo?'

There follows a long passage from Augustine's commentary on Psalm cxlv. Julian's authorities in this collection are in the first place Augustine and Gregory the Great;[2] but there are also excerpts

[1] For Ildefonsus see Sister Athanasius Braegelmann, *The Life and writings of St Ildefonsus* (Washington, D.C., 1942), and *Clavis*, Nos. 1247–1256.

[2] Gregory's works were held in high honour in Spain. We saw that Ildefonsus devoted a chapter to him in his *De viris illustribus*. Taio, bishop of

from Ambrose, Jerome, Origen in Rufinus' translation, and the tract *De Trinitate et Spiritu Sancto* of uncertain authorship, though Julian assigns it to Augustine (*PL*, 96, 678C–D), and sometimes it was also attributed to Athanasius.[1] Julian's treatise on death and the future state shows a similar reliance on his predecessors. He also composed a history of the rebellion against King Wamba raised in the Narbonaise by Paul, and may probably be regarded as the author of a school-text or *Ars grammatica*. It was compiled from older grammarians but illustrated by a number of quotations from pagan and Christian poets which are not found in Julian's extant predecessors in this field. Not without reason Julian has been called 'the most competent seventh-century theologian in the West'; and his writings afford conclusive evidence that as a scholar he was no unworthy successor to Isidore of Seville, and that at the end of the seventh century the library at Toledo was still a repository of many theological and secular books.[2] Some monastic and ascetic literature was produced at this time in Spain by Julian's contemporaries, Fructuosus, bishop of Braga, and by Valerius of Bierzo.[3]

In Italy between the death of Gregory I and the age of Charlemagne there is a complete absence of names noteworthy in the history of literature or thought. But there is sufficient evidence to show that in a few cities and in some monasteries intellectual studies were not dead. It was a time of great difficulty and stress for the Roman Church and for her successive heads. The steady advance of the Lombards had not only reduced more and more territory in Italy which had once owed allegiance to the emperor

Saragossa, after he had visited Rome and obtained a copy of Gregory's works which were no longer available in Spain in his day, compiled a *liber sententiarum* of which the greatest part was culled from the *Moralia*.

[1] Cf. above, p. 77.

[2] On Julian as a theologian see F. X. Murphy in *Mélanges Joseph de Ghellinck* (Gembloux, 1951), pp. 361–73. For the *Ars grammatica* see C. H. Beeson in *Miscellanea Fr Ehrle*, I (1924), pp. 50–70. It is tantalizing to be in doubt whether Julian had access to manuscripts of Varro and Catullus (cf. Beeson, *ibid.*, p. 53). A critical text of part of this treatise has been published by W. M. Lindsay as No. XV of the *St Andrew's University Publications* (1922). Julian's theological works will be found in *PL*, 96; cf. also *Clavis*, Nos. 1258–266.

[3] Cf. *Clavis*, Nos. 1274, 1276ff., and 1869.

in Constantinople, but had destroyed the geographical continuity of the Byzantine possessions. Already by the formation of the duchy of Spoleto (*c.* 576) direct communication between Ravenna and Rome had been cut. The popes were now in effect temporal rulers of the Roman duchy, which included a part of south Tuscany, the Campagna, and the Sabine hill country to the East. The coastal regions of Campania formed the duchy of Naples. The south too—Calabria, Bruttium, and Apulia—was a part of the Eastern Empire, but between this dependency and Rome and Naples lay the powerful Lombard duchies of Benevento and Salerno. Thus Italy in the seventh century was parcelled out politically into a great number of principalities, and, although theoretically these were divided between two rulers, the emperor and the Lombard king, actually there was no continuous unity. The hold of Constantinople was steadily growing weaker, while the Lombard dukes in the south and in central Italy, and even in Tuscany, behaved in practice as independent rulers who paid little attention to the behests of the Lombard monarch in Pavia.

The great influx into Italy of Greeks and members of the Eastern Churches during the seventh century, due to the loss of Palestine, Syria, and Egypt to the Persians and Arabs, had permanent results in the south of the Italian peninsula. Bruttium and Calabria became culturally a part of the Eastern Empire. Their language and their liturgy were Greek, and their intellectual life forms a small chapter of the intellectual history of the Byzantine World.[1] Rome, too, provided a home and a refuge for many of these emigrants. There is much that is still obscure about the Eastern-Greek colony which existed there from about the middle of the seventh century, and which received many fresh members in the next century during the iconoclastic controversy. But it was one of these strangers, Theodore of Tarsus, who was chosen by Pope Vitalian to reorganize the English Church. Again, the majority of popes between Theodore I (642–9) and Zacharias (741–52) were from one or other of the countries in the Eastern

---

[1] A Greek dialect is still spoken in certain villages in South Italy. On this survival from early times cf. G. Rohlfs, *Griechen und Romanen in Unteritalien* (Geneva, 1924).

Empire. During that period the Greek liturgy was introduced in Rome. Furthermore, monks from the East performed a valuable service as translators of Greek documents. In this way Acts of councils and imperial letters, as well as homilies and saints' lives were made accessible to the Latin-speaking West.[1]

The Lombards, who on their first conversion to Christianity had been Arians, had for a while acted more ruthlessly on their arrival in Italy than any of the earlier invaders. With their gradual conversion to the orthodox faith, although there were some brief periods of Arian reaction, persecutions either political or religious ceased. The power of the clergy under Lombard rule was very restricted, and the bishops had neither the independence nor the influence in their relations with the Temporal Power which the princes of the Church were able to exercise in the contemporary Frankish or Visigothic kingdoms.

Italy at this time produced no scholars comparable to Isidore, Aldhelm, or Bede. Outside a few civic centres and the best of the monasteries education was at the lowest ebb. Surviving private deeds and documents of this age testify to wide-spread illiteracy. They are drawn up in barbarous Latin and the signatories often only affix their mark because they cannot sign their names; and in this respect many of the clergy were in no better case than the laity. In contrast to this is the evidence afforded by centres like Rome, Pavia, Milan, and Ravenna, or by monasteries such as those at Bobbio, Verona, Naples, and, after 718, Monte Cassino. At Pavia, as the historian of the Lombards records, there continued to be men like Felix, who was a learned grammarian, or bishop Damian, who is described as 'sufficiently learned in the liberal arts'.[2] Liutprand, one of the greatest of the Lombard kings (712–44), though himself illiterate,[3] founded many monasteries and churches and was the first monarch to have a private oratory in his palace. Benedictus Crispus, archbishop of Milan from 681 to 725, who became involved in a dispute with the Pope over a question of ecclesiastical privilege, is praised by Paul the Deacon

---

[1] For extant manuscripts of these translations see Siegmund, *Die Ueberlieferung der griechisch Christlichen Literatur*, pp. 171 ff.

[2] Paul the Deacon (*MGH*, Script. Langob.), vi, 7 and v, 38.

[3] *ibid.*, vi, 58—litterarum quidem ignarus, sed philosophis aequandus.

for his learning and piety, and is generally recognized as the author of a poem on Caedwalla reproduced by Bede in his *Ecclesiastical History*.[1] It is metrically correct and not unpleasing. Another Crispus, who was a deacon at Milan, is the author of a medical poem (*liber medicinalis*). It is addressed to a former pupil whom Crispus, as he says, had 'enriched with the bounty of sevenfold eloquence', a somewhat grandiose reference to the liberal arts. Its twenty-six short sections describe the remedies for various bodily ailments from a headache to gout; for the author proceeds methodically downwards from the head to the feet. He utilized Pliny, the medical writer, and Quintus Serenus, and also the Latin version of Dioscorides, thereby showing us to which earlier writers on medicine he had access. His verse is as painful to the ear as the recommended potions must have been nauseating to the palate. It is only fair, however, to attribute the harshness of the verse in part at least to the intractable vocabulary which the subject forced Crispus to employ.[2] An unknown writer of Ravenna towards the end of the seventh century produced a cosmography which is by no means without value. His main source was the so-called *Peutinger Table*, which may probably be identified with the work of Castorius to which he alludes. But he used other compilations as well, so that his book, which consists of little more than names, furnishes much useful information not to be found elsewhere concerning place-names during the early Middle Ages. The Anonymus Ravennas has often been accused of parading fictitious sources, of being, in fact, a liar. Yet in the many passages where it is possible to check his statements by comparison with other extant writings, his accuracy has been completely vindicated. And it is surely remarkable that some of his severest critics have been most ready to use his information when it suited them.[3] One is therefore justified in assigning him a place of importance side by side with Castorius and the authors of various itineraries from which we derive the bulk of our

---

[1] *E.H.*, 5, 7.

[2] The poem will be found in *PL*, 89, coll. 369–76. A better, but less accessible, text is that published by S. de Renzi in *Collectio Salernitana* (Naples, 1852), I, pp. 72 ff.

[3] Cf. Funaioli in *PW* s.v. Ravennas (1920) and the admirable remarks of Konrad Miller in *Itineraria Romana* (Stuttgart, 1916), pp. xxvi–xxix.

information about the topography of the late Roman Empire and the Germanic kingdoms.

The influence of Bobbio during the earliest period of its history is not easy to determine. It was an Irish foundation and its contacts were with the North rather than with the South. The four immediate successors of Columban were Franks, and the majority of its monks, in so far as they were not Irishmen, seem to have come from regions north of the Alps. The relations between Bobbio and what was in a sense its parent house, Luxeuil, and with Lérins were close. Even in the seventh century the library at Bobbio was respectable and a very active *scriptorium* was engaged in steadily enlarging its resources. Owing to the high cost of parchment many earlier manuscripts written in uncials or half-uncials were erased and used again for copying books of the Bible or theological and grammatical treatises. A similar practice is well attested also in the *scriptorium* at Verona, and not a few such palimpsests still survive.[1] But the hypothesis, which for a time found many supporters, that manuscripts from Cassiodorus' library in Vivarium had found their way to Bobbio and Verona has been finally disproved. In addition to the paramount importance of the Irish in the early writing-school at Bobbio, the influence of Merovingian Gaul and Spain is clearly demonstrable.[2] A seventh-century monk at Bobbio, Jonas, who was a native of Susa in North Italy, has left us an excellent example of hagiography in two books. The first contains a life of Columban, the second treats more briefly of some of Columban's disciples, including Athala and Bertulf, Columban's immediate successors in the abbacy at Bobbio. Jonas was associated with Bobbio from his earliest youth, since he entered the monastery as an oblate. His biography of Columban is detailed and seems, in the main, to be an accurate work, composed at a time when the memory of the great man was still fresh, and before reliable historical data had been submerged in a mass of legend. As Jonas himself relates, there were still many persons alive, especially in Bobbio itself,

[1] On the Bobbio palimpsests see C. H. Beeson in *ST*, 126 (1946), pp. 162–84.

[2] On Bobbio and Verona see the masterly summary by E. A. Lowe in *CLA*, IV (1947), pp. xix–xxvii.

who had known Columban, 'to relate to me not what they had heard but what they had seen'. Thus the biographer was better placed for obtaining trustworthy information than, for example, Adamnan when he wrote his *Life of Columba*. Jonas' work, moreover, is a genuine biography in which the extensive travels of the saint, his foundation of Luxeuil and other houses in Burgundy, his stay in Alemannia, and his final journey to northern Italy are described in great detail, and the miracles performed by Columban are not excessively obtruded. As a stylist, however, he is markedly inferior to Adamnan. He is inclined to be verbose, his sentences are sometimes unnecessarily involved, and here and there he even lapses into grammatical errors. Yet for his age he appears to have been well read. He cites from Cicero's *Verrines*, he was familiar with Virgil and quotes a line from Juvencus. Although one cannot assume that Jonas had perused all the writers of hagiography whom he enumerates in his opening chapter, he was certainly acquainted with some.[1] Occasionally he trips up in his allusions to Merovingian history, and he is silent about some important events in Columban's life; for, although he relates at length Columban's quarrel with Brunhild and the court, he throws no light on the saint's disputes with the heads of the Gallican Church. Nor does he advert to Columban's correspondence with Gregory the Great. But, if his work is not free from faults, it is nevertheless both for its intrinsic merits and for the interest of its subjects one of the most notable hagiographical compositions produced during the early Middle Ages.

The monastery of St Vincent on the Volturno does not emerge into prominence until the latter part of the eighth century, when, under the abbacy of Ambrosius Autpertus, it enjoyed a period of great cultural distinction. But one may guess that it was an influential religious community long before from the help it gave to the monks of Monte Cassino. The foundation of St Benedict had been destroyed in 581 during a Lombard raid. The brethren made good their escape to Rome where they found a dwelling

---

[1] The life will be found in *MGH*, Script. Merov., IV, pp. 61–156. The phrase 'quorum nos exempla temerario conatu secuti' is quite general and can hardly be interpreted as a claim that Jonas had read all the authors that he names.

near the Lateran. In 718, during the papacy of Gregory II, Monte
Cassino was refounded by Petronax of Brescia. The new community received substantial aid from Rome and from St Vincent,
and it flourished until 883. In that year, when it was destroyed by
the Saracens, the bulk of its library perished, whereas in 581 the
monks appear to have brought a goodly number of codices safely
with them to Rome. After the site had been resettled once more
in 949 by Abbot Aligernus, the parent house of Benedictine
monasticism entered on two centuries of unexampled influence
and prosperity.[1]

But already during the eighth and ninth centuries Monte
Cassino was the centre of a south Italian culture almost coter-
minous with the duchy of Benevento, a circumstance brought
most clearly before us by the use of a common script, now called
Beneventan, in all the religious communities of that area. Amongst
these centres, though not part of the duchy of Benevento, was
Naples, which had never ceased to foster the study of theology
and the liberal arts.[2] Here, even in the ninth century, Greek was
still spoken by some, though a knowledge of that language was
wellnigh extinct in the rest of the peninsula, save for the restricted
area in the extreme south, to which allusion has already been
made. It is not until the Carolingian Age, however, that notable
scholars and their works claim our attention in this region. On
the European continent the areas which in due course benefited
most fundamentally by the new Anglo-Saxon culture were the
countries lying east and west of the Rhine. In the Frankish realm
under the later Merovingian kings it was not merely the political
but the ecclesiastical organization which had declined rapidly after
the days of Gregory of Tours. The work of the Irish missionaries
in the seventh century had undoubtedly achieved results. It had
led to the foundation of new monastic centres and to the reform
of others already existing. But Irish monasticism was too rigidly
ascetic, and its organization too particularistic, to bring about a
general and permanent improvement in religious houses. It had

---

[1] On this period of florescence and the contacts between Monte Cassino
and Byzantium see Herbert Bloch in *Dumbarton Oaks Papers*, No. 3 (Harvard
U.P., 1946), pp. 165–224.
[2] On this south Italian area and its culture see E. A. Lowe, *The Beneventan
Script* (Oxford, 1914) and *Scriptura Beneventana* (Oxford, 1929).

little influence on the ecclesiastical system as a whole, being indeed incapable of arresting the rapid secularization of the Church or the steadily growing worldliness of bishops and other prelates. Nor are there at this time any productions of Irish continental scholarship to record. In truth, the literary output in Gaul—to use a convenient geographical term—between approximately 600 and 750 was deplorable both in quality and quantity. The notorious barbarism in style and language of Merovingian charters and other documents meets us also, if not in quite so pronounced a degree, in the literary remains of that age. The hagiographical literature both in the arrangement and treatment of the subject and in its latinity is exceedingly poor in comparison with the works in this genre of Gregory of Tours, Jonas, or Adamnan, and with the saints' lives written in the Carolingian period. These last may indeed be largely fictitious and inferior as historical material to the biographies composed by those three earlier authors, but at least many of them are distinguished by considerable literary merit. The *Liber scintillarum* was probably put together during the seventh century by Defensor, a monk of Ligugé. It is a carefully arranged *collectaneum* of Patristic excerpts of ethical content.[1] Apart from this, expository works, whether theological or connected with the liberal arts, are to seek, if we set aside the freakish efforts of a single enigmatic writer calling himself Virgilius Maro the grammarian. Everything that concerns this man and his work may be said to be involved in controversy. His *floruit*, though some scholars have sought to put it in the fifth, others in the sixth century, was almost certainly in the seventh. He lived in all likelihood in southern Gaul, perhaps in Toulouse. He has left us two compositions, *Epitomae* and eight *Epistles* addressed to a deacon, Julius Germanus. Both deal with grammar and linguistics, but in a manner that, as some examples will show, can only be described as fantastic. The writer would distinguish four genders and twelve different varieties of Latin! He introduces numerous verbs and other parts of speech which are pure invention, and he justifies the use of all kinds of tricks, the result being a secret language unintelligible save to the

[1] On Defensor see H. M. Rochais in *RB*, 48 (1948), pp. 137–56 and 51 (1951), pp. 63–80.

initiated. Thus, the order of letters in a word may be changed so that *lego* may be written *gelo*, and whole sentences may be broken up into their component letters and then these can be arranged together. In addition to all this Virgilius refers to many authorities. Some are the names of classical authors, like Catullus, Horace, or Lucan. Actually these names are entirely fictitious, or else they are classical sobriquets assumed by or bestowed on the author's contemporaries. There are many other names besides, including those of Virgilius' real or pretended teachers. The allusions to contemporary grammarians are as preposterous as the grammatical lore. Who can seriously believe in two grammarians who disputed for fifteen days and nights without stopping about the inchoative forms of the verb, or in two others whose argumentation concerning the vocative of *ego* lasted continuously for a fortnight? It has indeed been suggested that Virgilius may have been one of the circle of 'scholars' who kept up the study of one portion of the liberal arts in this perverted way. But even this explanation is hardly credible; for even the most precious productions of an earlier age do not approximate remotely to the extravagances of Virgilius. As regards its strangeness, the nearest approach to the cryptic character of the *Epitomae* is the *Hisperica Famina*, though the content and language are different. To take Virgilius and his work seriously as it stands is impossible, and the best explanation of his works is that they are a skit or parody on grammatical treatises.[1] Nor would they be worth even a passing mention, were it not that they found some favour with Anglo-Saxon and Irish scholars from the seventh to the ninth centuries. A far subtler parody, as will be seen,[2] is the pseudo-geographical work going under the name of Aethicus Ister. The so-called *Liber monstrorum de diversis generibus*, on the other hand, does not pretend to be anything but what it is, an account of fabulous creatures and monsters, compiled partly from earlier authors, partly from local legends gathered by the unknown compiler. His use of comparatively rare writers like Quintus

---

[1] See P. Lehmann, *Die lateinische Parodie im Mittelalter* (Munich, 1922), pp. 21–22. Virgilius' works have been edited by J. Huemer in the Bibliotheca Teubneriana (Leipzig, 1886); cf. also Kenney, p. 113 and *Clavis*, No. 1559.

[2] See below, p. 185.

Curtius and Marcellinus Comes is noteworthy and, like his distinctly superior Latin, characterizes him as a somewhat more erudite man than his contemporaries.[1]

Historical composition, finally, is represented by the so-called Fredegarius and by the *Liber historiae Francorum*. The former work, as it has come down to us, is divided into four books. But its construction is not uniform nor is it all from one hand; indeed critics have distinguished no less than three chroniclers in its pages. Only the final section from Book 4, Chapter 40 to the end, has independent value as a historical source and, in the absence of other material, cannot be neglected. The other parts of the work are derivative. The authorities used include Jerome's *Chronicle*, Hydatius, Isidore, Gregory of Tours, the so-called *Liber generationum* or *De genealogiis patriarchum* by an anonymous African author of the fifth century, and some lost works, for example, Burgundian annals. The chronicle extends to the middle of the seventh century. Its style is bald and without any literary quality. Classical Latin inflexions are kept, but many mistakes in gender and so forth occur. Also certain consonantal and vowel changes foreshadow the gradual evolution of the Romance languages from vulgar Latin. Continuations to this book were composed during the course of the eighth century. Perhaps the one interesting phenomenon for the general reader is the first recorded appearance of the legend that the Franks were of Trojan origin. Fantastic as such a belief now seems, it rapidly won popularity and it reappears elsewhere, for instance in the *Liber historiae Francorum*. The author of this compilation (*c.* 727), who did not know the so-called Fredegarius, starts off with the Trojan legend, which may thus have been generally current by then in 'learned' circles. The *Book of the Franks* is a cento derived from earlier authors, especially Gregory of Tours. Only from the point at which Fredegarius stops does it become a source for Merovingian history which cannot be overlooked. Even so its historical like its literary merits are not of a high order. Soon after its publication it was worked over by another anonymous writer. This revised or expanded book was in turn utilized by one of the writers who continued the *Chronicle* of 'Fredegarius'. In this way

[1] The work was edited by M. Haupt in *Opuscula*, II, pp. 221 ff.

some degree of fusion was brought about between two originally distinct accounts of later Merovingian history. The *Book of the Franks* was much read from the ninth century on.[1]

England, who owed her intellectual renascence partly to the Irish and partly to Rome, from the middle of the seventh century began to send out missionaries beyond her borders. Partial attempts had already been made by Frankish missionaries to effect the conversion of Frisia, when Wilfrith visited that region in 678–9. Others followed, of whom by far the most notable was Willibrord. For nearly fifty years (*c.* 690–739), and in spite of many disappointments and difficulties, caused not only by the tenacity with which the inhabitants adhered to their old beliefs but by political conditions in a country striving to maintain its independence against Frankish aggression, he laboured successfully in the regions bordering the Lower Rhine. His duties also led him to make two journeys to Rome. On the second visit he was consecrated archbishop by the Pope and became head of the new ecclesiastical province of Frisia with his metropolitan see at Traiectum (Utrecht). His biographer, Alcuin, also records an expedition made by Willibrord to convert the southern Danes. He brought back thirty-two Danish boys whom he had converted and baptized, but otherwise his mission failed. Finally, he is closely associated with the important monastery of Echternach near Trèves, with which he was presented through the generosity of several donors. Through gifts this monastery also acquired possessions in Thuringia. It thus is apparent that the influence of this remarkable and devoted man extended over a very wide area. He spent much time at Echternach in his declining years and was buried in the abbey.

Another monastic foundation (724) destined to enjoy great influence and prosperity in the centuries that followed was Reichenau (Augia maior) on a little island in the Lake of Constance in the region then known as Alemannia. Its founder and first abbot was Pirmin. His nationality has been a matter of dispute; probably he came from the Visigothic kingdom of Spain

---

[1] For the text of these historical works see *MGH*, Script. Merov., II. The most recent discussion of 'Fredegarius' is by Siegmund Hellmann in *Historische Vierteljahrschrift*. 29 (1934), pp. 36 ff.

and South Gaul which he had left when the Arabs invaded Spain in 711. Responsible later for establishing other religious communities in southern Germany, he is also known as an author. The *Dicta Pirminii* is a theological-ethical treatise; its most interesting feature is the considerable use made by Pirmin of Martin of Braga's treatise *De correctione rusticorum*. Like his Spanish predecessor he had the problem of trying to put down rustic superstitions of various kinds. However unsettled political conditions on the European continent may have been, intercommunications were not checked. We have already noted Spanish influences in north Italian *scriptoria* as well as the rapidity with which the works of Isidore found their way to England. Virgilius Maro *grammaticus* was used by Aldhelm. In the second half of the eighth century there are unmistakable signs that the library in St Gall contained Bible manuscripts written in Spain, while the writing practised in the *scriptorium* in St Gall, or rather the 'Raetic script' practised there and in some other centres shows north Italian influence.[1]

But the most eminent of the Anglo-Saxon missionaries on the Continent was Wynfrith, who was born *c*. 675 and seems to have been, like Aldhelm, a West Saxon. Dedicated at an early age by his parents as an oblate, he passed his life until he was well over forty years old as a learner and teacher. This monastic period of his career he spent first at Exeter and later at Nursling near Southampton. A compilation on grammar and one on metrics, both no doubt intended for the use of his pupils, survive, and also a number of riddles in verse, modelled on but inferior to those of Aldhelm, but some of these last were not composed till after Wynfrith had left England on his continental mission. The desire for a wider usefulness drove him in 716 to go as a missionary to Frisia. But, as the prospects of fruitful work there at that particular date were very uncertain, he returned to England. Before the end of 718 we find him in Rome. There he was well received by Gregory II, who in May 719, formally empowered him, under the new name of Bonifatius (Boniface), to proceed as a missionary to the heathen in Germany, although no special district was assigned to him for his activities. The remaining thirty-five years

[1] See K. Loeffler in *Palaeographia latina*, VI (1929), pp. 54 and 51.

of his life Boniface spent first in the work of conversion and then in the arduous task of Church organization. A collection of more than one hundred letters, composed partly of Boniface's own epistles, partly of communications addressed to him especially by successive popes, is both precious for its multifarious historical data, and, at least as far as the letters of Boniface himself are concerned, of great literary interest. Of the regions in which Boniface's work lay during the first part of his apostolate only Hesse was still all but untouched by Christianity. In Thuringia the chief task was to improve Church discipline and to correct laxity of observance. Later in his career questions of organization in Bavaria also engaged his attention; and in 739, after his third visit to Rome, he was responsible for the creation of the four sees of Salzburg, Ratisbon, Freising, and Passau, which had been projected a good many years before by Gregory II. Boniface had been consecrated bishop in 722, but not as the occupant of a particular see. Instead he had a 'roving commission' over all Germany and the countries east of the Rhine. He was in frequent correspondence with Gregory II and his successors, and in 732 received the rank of archbishop and the *pallium* from Gregory III. Finally in 739 the bishops of the four new sees became his suffragans and a little later the bishops of four older sees in Alemannia also accepted his primacy. Thus for many years Boniface strove to build up in the wide territories under his control a Church organization that was in closer touch with Rome than either the English or the Gallican Churches were at that time; indeed, down to this time 'the influence of the Pope on the Merovingian Church had been almost negligible'.[1] Many of Boniface's helpers were fellow-countrymen, and he frequently sought the advice of prelates in England, which often proved more helpful than counsels from Rome. A man like Daniel, bishop of Winchester, would be able with fair accuracy to gauge the character of the people amongst whom Boniface was active, whereas many of the problems confronting a missionary to the Teutonic peoples were remote from the experience of the Roman pontiff and his advisers. The Anglo-Saxon missionaries in turn were able to train many of their converts for the work of the Church and the ablest of them

[1] See W. Levison, *England and the Continent in the Eighth Century*, p. 89.

ended by becoming bishops of new sees or abbots of recently founded religious houses.

The death of Charles Martel in 741 had weighty consequences for Boniface. The government of the Frankish kingdom was divided between Charles' two sons, Pippin and Carloman. Carloman, between 741 and 747, when he resigned his temporal authority and took monastic vows, regarded Boniface's work with sympathetic understanding, and desired in conjunction with him to put the ecclesiastical organization of the realm on a new and sounder basis. Thus during the last fourteen years of his life, first under Carloman, then under Pippin, who became governor of all the Franks in 747 and in 751 actually their king, Boniface was brought into close relation with the successors of the Merovingian monarchs. In spite of failures and disappointments, which find expression in his latest letters, he had done a great work both as an organizer and as a promoter of culture in the countries east of the Rhine. These regions were no longer partly heathen, partly quasi-isolated Christian areas, but through his achievement their ecclesiastical organization was assimilated to that in the Frankish kingdom, of which indeed they may be said to have formed a part before Boniface's death. Again through him, and the many clerics who assisted him, Anglo-Saxon culture was transplanted to Germany; from there in the succeeding age it was to become one of the chief causes for the Carolingian renascence in the Frankish kingdom west of the Rhine. There were many monasteries or nunneries with whose creation or reform Boniface was directly connected, but none can compare in importance with Fulda. This abbey was founded in Hesse in 744 by the Bavarian Sturmi, a favourite pupil of Boniface and its first abbot. The high hopes which Boniface, who did all he could to promote the undertaking, formed of it as a future centre of literature and learning in Germany proved within less than fifty years to be justified to the full. In 751 he wrote thus to Pope Zacharias:[1]

There is a place situated amongst woods in a wide and lonely tract, yet in the midst of the nations to whom we are preaching.

[1] The best edition of the letters is by M. Tangl in *MGH*, Epist., Selectae I (Berlin, 1916). See also additions and corrections in W. Levison, *op. cit.*, Appendix VII (pp. 280–90).

There we have founded a monastery and established monks who live under the rule of our father, Benedict, who renounce flesh, wine, mead, and serving-men, and are content with the labours of their own hands ... in this spot I propose, with the sanction of your Holiness, to rest and refresh my body wearied with age, be it for some time or but a little while, and to lie here after my death. For four peoples to whom by the grace of God we have preached Christ's word are known to dwell in a circle about this place. To them, with your intercession, I can be of service, whilst life and a sound mind remain.

Boniface's wish was only partially fulfilled. In 753, after he had requested Pippin that his devoted helper, the Anglo-Saxon Lullus, might succeed him as bishop of Mayence, he was seized with a longing to take up the work of conversion once more and made his way to the scene of his earliest missionary efforts, to Frisia. He was slain with some companions near Dockum on June 5, 754, by a band of heathen Frisians. His body was subsequently brought to Fulda and there interred.

The variety of topics touched upon in the correspondence of Boniface is remarkable. There were numerous questions of discipline and observance about which Boniface consulted the Pope or his ecclesiastical friends in England or both. Sometimes both his letters and the replies that they elicited have survived. Incidentally there are many allusions to customs of the Germanic tribes which were not in harmony with the teaching of the Church. For example, what attitude should be observed towards marriages between persons who, according to the strictest interpretation of the Roman Church, were within the prohibited degrees of kinship? What shall be done with Germans who consume meats prohibited by the dietary laws of the Old Testament?[1] There are all too many references to the laxity and sometimes to the active immorality of the clergy whom Boniface found in Thuringia and elsewhere, also to the survival or recrudescence of pagan practices and superstitions in theoretically Christianized regions.[2] Sometimes light is also thrown on English customs and conditions. Thus, falconry was clearly a popular sport with English princes at this time. Boniface sends a gift of a hawk, two falcons, two shields and two spears to King Ethelbald of Mercia, while

[1] *Epist.*, 33 and 87.   [2] *e.g.*, *ibid.*, 50, 51, 80, 91.

Ethelbert II of Kent requests that Boniface may send him two trained falcons as these are scarce in his own kingdom.[1] Boniface's letter to Cuthbert, archbishop of Canterbury, in which the writer, unlike his usual practice, quotes extensively from the Bible, touches on various abuses said to be rife in his native land —luxury in dress, drunkenness, immorality—and warns against the dangers attendant on pilgrimages to Rome undertaken by women.[2] Boniface's anxiety to add to the presumably small stock of books at his disposal is often reflected in the letters. He thanks Egbert of York for a gift of manuscripts, requesting at the same time that some of Bede's commentaries be sent out to him. He makes a similar request to the abbot of Wearmouth. At another time he tries to obtain from England a copy of Gregory I's instructions to Augustine, and from Rome a selection of the same pope's letters. To abbot Duddo, besides a general petition for manuscripts, he addresses a special plea for a commentary on the Pauline Epistles, being presumably aware that Bede had compiled a *collectaneum* on them made up of extracts from Augustine of Hippo. In a somewhat pathetic note to Bishop Daniel, Boniface prays that he may be given a codex of the Prophets written in uncial characters, since with failing eyesight he will be better able to read its large letters.[3]

In conclusion, there is a passage in one of Pope Zacharias' epistles to Boniface which bears on a topic of some interest. An Irishman, Fergil or Virgil, who had become abbot of St Peter's in Salzburg and for many years (746–84) administered that see, though he was not consecrated bishop till 767, had become involved in several disputes with Boniface, so that the relations between the two men had certainly become strained. From the letter dated May 1, 748, we learn that Virgil had been accused of heresy because he had defended the belief in the sphericity of the earth and in the Antipodes. The Pope writes:[4]

> As for the perverse and sinful doctrine which he (Virgil) against God and his own soul has uttered—if it shall be clearly established that he professes belief in another world and other men existing beneath the earth, or in (another) sun and moon there, thou art to hold a

---

[1] *Epist.*, 69 and 105.   [2] *ibid.*, 78.

[3] *ibid.*, 75, 91, 76, 33, 54 (cf. also 74), 34, 63.   [4] *ibid.*, 80.

council, deprive him of his sacerdotal rank, and expel him from the Church.

The passage is brief and not free from obscurity. But, as Virgil remained undisturbed in Salzburg, evidently no further steps against him were taken, unless we are to suppose that he openly disavowed or modified his views. They were not new, for he could, and probably did, find them in one or more earlier writers, to whom he may well have had access, Macrobius, Martianus Capella, Isidore, or even Bede. Contrary to what has often been maintained, belief in a flat earth was not the commonly accepted opinion in the early Middle Ages.[1] Belief in the Antipodes was more controversial, and Isidore, who mentions it (*Etym.*, xiv, 5, 17), saves his orthodoxy by calling it a fable. In short, there has been a tendency to exaggerate the significance of an episode about which little is known; and it may be suspected that Boniface's disapproval of Virgil stemmed primarily from his dislike of what he regarded as the uncanonical administration of the Salzburg see by an Irish abbot. But there was an aftermath to the quarrel of the two men; for it has recently been shown that the *Cosmographia* of Aethicus Ister, which purports to be a translation by no less a person than Jerome of a treatise by a Greek explorer, was composed by Virgil as a skit some twenty years after his controversy with Boniface. The description of various strange and unknown countries is basically a satire on their disagreement about cosmology.[2] Virgil survived his adversary by many years. He was highly respected for his probity and learning and, in all likelihood, was the founder of the *scriptorium* at Salzburg; and he is mentioned with approval by so orthodox a man as Alcuin.

[1] See Charles W. Jones, *BOT*, pp. 366–7.

[2] See the brilliant monograph by Heinz Löwe, *Ein literarischer Widersacher des Bonifatius, Virgil von Salzburg und die Kosmographie des Aethicus Ister* in Mainz: Akad. der Wissenschaften und der Literatur; Abhandlungen der geistes- und sozialwissenschaftlichen Klasse, 1951, No. 11 (pp. 903–88 of the completed volume).

PART III

The Carolingian Age

CHAPTER VII

The Revival of Education and Learning under Charlemagne

Boniface died just before the epoch-making events which, inasmuch as they resulted in drawing much closer the bonds between the Frankish kingdom and the papacy at the cost of some subordination of the bishop of Rome to the northern monarch, would have won only his qualified approval. The year 751 was marked by two occurrences of great moment. The Pope, Zacharias, died after his diplomatic skill for more than a decade had steered the papacy between the Scylla of the Lombard kingdom and the Charybdis of Constantinople, and the exarchate of Ravenna collapsed before the attacks of the Lombard ruler, Aistulf. Moreover, this prince, by demanding a head-tax from the Romans, intimated in no uncertain terms that he proposed to exercise his overlordship over them. The new Pope, Stephen II (752–9), imitated Gregory III and appealed for Frankish aid. But whereas in 739 the reply of Charles Martel had been negative, Pippin showed himself more accommodating. After prolonged negotiations, during which the pope was the temporary guest of the Frank, and in 754 repeated the solemn act, already performed by Boniface three years earlier, of anointing Pippin as king of the Franks, and after two successful campaigns, in the autumn of 754 and again in 756, against the Lombards, the Pope was securely established as the temporal ruler of a considerable papal state. The price of the newly acquired power and of freedom from interference by either Pavia or Constantinople, was that the Pope passed under the political protectorate of the Frankish king. Nor would it seem that he even influenced the ecclesiastical reforms which Pippin continued to carry out in his realm, preparing the

way all unconsciously for the greater reorganization effected by
his son. On the death of Pippin the relations of the three States
were once again complicated by the hostility existing between the
two heirs to the Frankish dominions, Charles and Carloman, by
the marriage of a Lombard princess to Charles and her subsequent
repudiation by him, and by the preponderating influence temporarily secured in Rome by a pro-Lombard faction. With the death
of Carloman in 771 Charles became sole ruler in Frankland.
Pope Stephen III died at a critical moment when a rupture
between Charles and the Lombards was imminent. His successor
in the see of Peter, Hadrian I (772–95), from the first looked to
the Frank as a protecting ally. Two years after his accession the
fall of Pavia before the prolonged assaults of Charles brought the
Lombard kingdom to an end. Its last ruler ended his days in the
monastery of Corbie in Picardy. The further operations of Charles
in Italy and his Italian policy during the next sixteen years, which
to the world at large found its spectacular culmination in the
imperial coronation on Christmas Day, 800, within the venerated
walls of St Peter's, lie outside the scope of this book. But in 800
all Western Christendom save the Anglo-Saxon kingdom and the
narrow territories retained by Byzantium in Italy, was united
under the sceptre of Charlemagne. The two popes, Hadrian I
and his successor, Leo III (795–816), although Charles regarded
Rome and the spiritual authority of her bishop with deep veneration, were reconciled to the fact, however much it might be disguised under specious phrases, that they too were the vassals
of the king-emperor. Charles himself gave to Leo III his own
definition of the relation between his temporal power and the
papacy in the following terms:

Even as I entered into an agreement of spiritual fatherhood jointly
with the most blessed father, your predecessor, so I desire to make
an inviolable treaty of like faith and charity with your Blessedness:
to the end that, because the prayers of your apostolic Holiness have
implored the divine grace, I may in every situation (*ubique*) obtain
the apostolic blessing, and the most holy see of the Roman church
by God's help may ever be defended by our devotion. Our part is
by the help of our divine faith everywhere to defend with arms
Christ's holy church from the attacks of the heathen and the devasta-
tion of the infidel without, and within to fortify her with the

knowledge of faith. Your part, most holy Father, is, like Moses (cf. Exodus ix, 22), to raise your hands to God to aid our militant service, to the end that with your intercession, under the guidance and grace of God, Christian people may at all times and in all places be victorious over the enemies of His holy name and the name of our Lord Jesus Christ be made glorious throughout the world.[1]

It will become apparent in a later chapter that not all those who in the ninth century turned their minds to political theory were prepared to approve such dependence of the Church on the State.[2]

Several centuries had gone by during which the Church had been the sole repository of education and letters, yet with what varying fortunes in the different countries of the West we have seen in the preceding chapters. Nowhere had the decay in Church and State been more all-pervading than in Gaul under the latest Merovingian rulers. The second ruler and first king of a new dynasty, Pippin, convinced that the reconstruction of Neustria and Austrasia must have as its pivotal point the regeneration of the Church, had entered on a vigorous policy of reform. Charles, adding extensively by conquest to the lands that he inherited, was confronted also with a vaster problem of reorganization. In that empire, stretching from the Pyrenees to Saxony and from the Baltic to Central Italy, the Church was, so to say, the common denominator. Differences of race, customs, institutions, and language existed in the multiple parts of which Charles' realm was composed. But all its inhabitants professed a common creed, and the all-embracing Church was also potentially, and under Charlemagne actually, the common teacher of all.

Charles' many-sided genius was not content with possessing all the manly virtues in a pre-eminent degree nor yet with conquest. From the beginning of his reign he strove to raise the cultural level of all his subjects, and, as their number grew, so his zeal for spreading education and improving the intellectual life of his people intensified. Since none but the clergy and the monasteries could give effect to his ambitious plans, his first care was necessarily to reform Church discipline and to better the

[1] Latin text in P. Jaffé, *Bibliotheca rerum Germanicarum*, IV, p. 356.
[2] See below, p. 320.

educational qualifications of her ministers. At the same time he was active in securing a uniform liturgy and ritual in Church services. This meant more particularly that he had to bring the Gallican observance, which had developed to a marked degree on its own lines, into harmony with that of Rome; at the same time he carried further the measures taken by his father to improve choir singing in the Frankish realm and even imported fresh teachers from Rome for this purpose. It is known that Pippin's chief helper in the reform of Church music was Archbishop Chrodegang of Metz, whose cathedral school, organized on the lines of a Benedictine congregation, rapidly became famous. But Charles' policy of Romanization applied not only to the chanting but in general to the services of the Church, and this entailed a drastic revision of the existing liturgical books. This task the king entrusted to Alcuin, after Pope Hadrian at Charles' request had sent the *Sacramentum Gregorianum* to Aachen. There it was transcribed and Alcuin made corrections in the text; but, as it was incomplete, he added a section derived from some other sources, particularly from what is now known as the *Gelasian Sacramentary*.[1]

In view of the general illiteracy of even the higher Frankish clergy Charles took steps to attract prominent scholars from other countries to his court. The grammarian, Peter of Pisa, Paulinus, afterwards bishop of Aquileia, and Paul the Deacon were Charlemagne's honoured guests for several years. Two other distinguished strangers, Alcuin of Northumbria and Theodulfus, a Visigothic exile from Spain, made the Frankish kingdom the land of their adoption. In Alcuin, Charles found combined most admirably all of the qualities which were requisite for one who, with the king's support, should take charge of a thorough scheme of ecclesiastical and cultural reconstruction. English scholarship had reached its zenith with Bede. The memory and educational methods of that great man were still fresh when Alcuin was a boy; for Egbert, who became archbishop of York a few months before Bede's death, had been his pupil and his friend, and it was under Egbert's personal guidance that the school of York was

---

[1] For a fuller account of these liturgical reforms cf. W. Levison, *England and the Continent in the Eighth Century*, pp. 158–9, and Eleanor S. Duckett, *Alcuin, Friend of Charlemagne* (New York, 1951), pp. 190–7.

founded. It at once superseded Jarrow as the chief educational and literary centre in England; more than that, it was for nearly fifty years the leading home of culture in Western Europe. That there was also some decline in the cultural influence of Canterbury is probable; and, indeed, Alcuin, writing in 797 to the archbishop of Canterbury, recommends certain reforms, 'so that by your exertions the dignity of that holy see may be restored'.[1] At the same time it is likely that the intellectual and moral decline of the churches in Britain during the later eighth and the ninth century was not as marked as has sometimes been supposed.[2]

Certainly, apart from his personal qualities, the training which Charles' future 'minister of education' received could not have been bettered. Born soon after 730, Alcuin was educated at York, which at that time could also boast of an exceptionally rich library. The master to whom he owed most—for he does not seem to have come much into direct contact with Egbert, although he speaks of him with respectful veneration—was Aelbert. This man, though not, it would appear, himself a writer, was evidently a teacher of unusual gifts, in addition to having exceptionally wide interests. More especially he was indefatigable in further enriching the cathedral library entrusted to his care. Small wonder that his favourite pupil became the greatest educator of his age and cherished all his life a deep love for books. With Aelbert Alcuin went as a young man to the Continent, passing through Frankish territory and visiting both Rome and Pavia. When Aelbert succeeded to the see of York (767), the main burden of teaching in the York school passed into Alcuin's hands. To this the direction of the library was added eleven years later, when Aelbert resigned his archbishopric in favour of Eanbald. In 780 the new archbishop showed his high confidence in Alcuin by sending him to Rome in order to receive Eanbald's *pallium* from the Pope. On his return journey in the spring of 781 he passed through Parma where he was presented to Charles. He had already met the king in former years when travelling in company with Aelbert. The pressing invitation that he now received from Charlemagne to enter his service and take charge of the Palace

[1] *MGH*, Epist., IV, No. 128.
[2] See D. J. V. Fisher in *Trans. R. Hist. Soc.*, Fifth series, 2 (1952), pp. 1–19.

school was accepted by Alcuin only after he had obtained the sanction of the Northumbrian king and of his archbishop. For the rest of his life Alcuin remained in the home of his adoption, although he paid two visits, one brief, in 786, one more prolonged, from 790 to 793, to England. Charles before long showed his appreciation of Alcuin's services by conferring on him the abbacies of Ferrières and Troyes. In 796, when Alcuin, wearied of his scholastic and other duties and in indifferent health, had intimated his desire to return to the land of his birth, the king prevailed on him to remain in Neustria and bestowed on him the abbacy of St Martin at Tours. There Alcuin spent the last eight years of his life.

The long series of Charlemagne's capitularies, extending over more than a quarter of a century, is eloquent proof of his constant care for the spiritual welfare of his people. But he could not have achieved his object, had he not insisted on an educated clergy. None could hope to attain to episcopal rank or to an abbacy, whose qualifications fell short of his exacting standards. And, in truth, the galaxy of able prelates which in his time filled the higher ecclesiastical offices was little short of unique. Amongst many others there stand out especially Theodulfus, Arn, and Leidrad, who respectively occupied the sees of Orléans, Salzburg, and Lyons, and abbots like Angilbert at St Riquier, Adalhard at Corbie, and, of course, Alcuin himself at Tours. But the simple priest, too, was required, before being ordained, to pass a test of fitness, which applied not only to his moral character but to his literacy. In that way only could a reverent and intelligent conduct of Church services be ensured. Moreover, as has already been exemplified in the life-work of men like Martin of Braga or Caesarius of Arles, the importance and value of preaching to untutored medieval congregations lay not merely in exhortation to lead a religious and moral life, but in its awakening of the mental faculties. It is no surprise, then, to find Charles repeatedly stressing the need of good preachers, who, instead of always addressing their flock in the language of the Church, were permitted and even directed to use the vernacular, if their hearers were unable to follow in Latin. The *Admonitio generalis* of 789 gives expression to the wish that every member of a congregation should know by heart the Creed and the Lord's Prayer and should even be able to join in the singing of the *Sanctus* and the *Gloria Patri*. To ensure this the priest would necessarily also be the instructor of the congregation. The *Epistola generalis* (between 786 and 800) refers at length to a shortage of suitable homilies for Church use, to the corrupt text of those available, and to their employment at the improper offices; it then goes on to recommend to all the clergy a homiliary specially compiled at Charlemagne's request by Paul the Deacon, who by that time had returned to his monastic life in Monte Cassino.[1] Paul read through the treatises and sermons of divers Catholic Fathers, and, picking out the best, made a collection in two volumes of addresses sufficient for the whole ecclesiastical year, as well as free from textual errors. This work was destined to form the basis of many later homiliaries. Charles was no less anxious to raise the moral and intellectual standards in monastic houses, in many of which gross laxity and illiteracy had become prevalent in the late Merovingian period. At the same time uniform obedience to the *Rule* of St Benedict was to be secured.[2] Here again Charles' demand for a reliable text of a venerable and venerated document should be observed. On one of his visits to Italy he requested from the abbot of Monte Cassino a carefully transcribed copy of the original manuscript preserved there. When this reached Aachen, it became the exemplar from which other trustworthy copies could be made. One of these still survives. The famous *Sangallensis* 914, at the suggestion of Reginbert, the librarian in Reichenau, was copied early in the ninth century from the Aachen exemplar by his two former pupils, Grimald and Tatto. This is the most authoritative text of the *Rule* that now survives, on which all recent editions have been based.[3]

Charlemagne's zeal for monastic education, to which so many of the capitularies bear witness, found its fullest expression in a mandate addressed to Baugulf, abbot of Fulda, probably between 794 and 796. Later on, with some slight changes, it was circulated

---

[1] *MGH*, Capit., I, 22, 70 and 82; cf. also 30, 80, 25 to 81, 9.

[2] Cf. *ibid.*, 75, 37; 161, 38; 164, 16.

[3] For recent work on the *Rule* see *Clavis*, No. 1852 and Altaner, *Patrologie*, pp. 433–5.

by the abbot to bishops and certain monasteries. The original document is lost, but its text is known from a transcript made at the end of the eleventh or the beginning of the twelfth century. This transcript was destroyed during the late war, together with many other manuscripts in the Municipal library at Metz.[1] A contemporary copy of Baugulf's subsequent communication to an unknown monastery was deciphered in a manuscript now at Oxford (*Laud.* 126) by Paul Lehmann.[2] The contents of the mandate are so important that a translation may conveniently be given here:

Charles, by the grace of God, king of the Franks and Lombards and Roman patrician, to abbot Baugulf and the whole community, even our faithful vassals entrusted to your care, our clerics, in the name of Almighty God we send loving greeting. Be it known to your Devotion, which is pleasing to God, that we together with our faithful have deemed it expedient that the bishoprics and monasteries entrusted by Christ's favour to our government, in addition to the observance of monastic discipline and the practice of the religious life, should vouchsafe instruction also in the exercise of letters to those who with God's help are able to learn, each according to his capacity; seeing that, even as the monastic rule directs purity of conduct, so practice in teaching and learning directs and orders the composition of words, to the end that those who strive to please God by right living may not omit to please Him also by right speaking. For it is written (Matth. xii, 37), 'either by thy words thou shalt be justified or by thy words thou shalt be condemned'; and though it is better to do what is right than to know it, yet knowledge must precede action. In truth each ought to learn what he desires to fulfil, that, the more the tongue vies in the praises of Almighty God without the offences of untruths, the more richly the soul may understand what it ought to do. Since all men must avoid untruth, how much more ought they to abjure falsehood to the best of their power who are approved and chosen to this very end, that they should specially serve truth.

Since in these years there were often sent to us from divers monasteries letters in which was set forth the zeal on our behalf in holy and pious prayers of the brethren dwelling there, we have observed in very many of the aforesaid writings of the same persons

---

[1] MS. Metz, 226. For a list of manuscripts in French collections destroyed during the war see *Speculum*, 29 (1954), pp. 336-7.

[2] See the important study by L. Wallach in *Speculum*, 26 (1951), pp. 288-305; P. Lehmann, *Fuldaer Studien* in *SB*. Bavarian Academy, 1927.

right sentiments and uncouth language, because that which pious devotion faithfully dictated inwardly, outwardly, owing to neglect of learning, the untutored tongue could not express without faultiness. Whence it came that we began to fear lest, as skill in writing was less, wisdom to understand the Sacred Scriptures might be far less than it ought rightly to be. And we all know that, though verbal errors are dangerous, errors in interpretation are far more dangerous. Wherefore we exhort you not only not to neglect the study of letters but even with the most humble God-approved earnestness to vie in learning, so that you may prevail more easily and rightly in penetrating the mysteries of sacred literature. But, inasmuch as in the sacred pages are found embedded figures and tropes and other like forms of speech, no one can doubt that every one in reading those the more quickly understands (what he reads) in a spiritual sense the more fully he has before been instructed in the discipline of literature. Let then such men be chosen for this task as have willingness, ability to learn, and the desire to teach others. And let this be done with zeal as great as the earnestness with which we exhort you.

We would have you be, as befits soldiers of the Church, inwardly devout, outwardly learned, chaste in living a good life, scholars in speaking well, so that, whoever for the name of God and the glory of the monastic life shall seek you out to see you, even as his eyes are edified by your appearance, having been instructed by your wisdom which he shall discern in your reading and singing, may depart in gladness giving thanks to Almighty God.

And if you would have our thanks, do not omit to see that copies of this letter are sent to all your assistant and fellow bishops and to all monasteries. And let no monk dispense justice outside the monastery or go abroad to general or comitial courts of justice.

The Palace school so-called, over which Alcuin presided from 782 on, was the apple of Charles' eye. Its scholastic standards were to be high enough to incite monastic and cathedral schools to emulation; actually it became also a seminary in which many of the ablest teachers of the next generation were trained. When not absent on a distant campaign, and when the pressure of State affairs was temporarily relaxed, the king himself might attend the school, praising the diligent, reproving the sluggard, and perhaps himself engaging in a spirited dialogue with the chief master. It is to be regretted that we have no precise information concerning the organization of the Palace school. It was not a creation of Charles', for some such establishment seems to have existed since the days of Charles Martel. But before Charlemagne's reforms its purpose was more narrow and its membership more limited, existing, in fact, merely to train the royal princes and sons of the highest nobility in knightly virtues. Charlemagne's aims were far wider. It was intellectual training that he desired to stress, the very thing which before had been all but omitted, nor did he confine membership to the immediate court circle. Where the age of the pupils varied, some being adolescents and others of maturer years, it is obvious that Alcuin and other teachers, whether permanent or temporary, like Peter of Pisa, could not have followed the strict regimentation of a school intended only for boys. As to the methods of teaching, the safest guide is furnished by Alcuin's own writings. They are all, except his little treatise on orthography,[1] in dialogue form. The information that they impart is distinctly elementary and, in the main, is derived from the stock authors of an earlier age. Donatus, Cassiodorus, Priscian, Bede, Isidore, and Phocas were used in the treatises on grammar and orthography. The little manual about virtues and vices, addressed to Wido, is compiled from Isidore, Gregory, and Cassian. The *De rhetorica*, which has lately been classed with the Carolingian 'Mirrors for princes' though its form differs from other extant examples of this genre, relies primarily on Cicero's youthful work, *De inventione*, with additions from Julius Victor and probably from Cassiodorus.[2] These authors were also used for *De dialectica*, which in the first instance is based on Boethius and Isidore. There are, too, additions from the so-called *Categories* of Aristotle, a book included amongst the spurious works of Augustine, Cicero's *Topica*, Victorinus, and possibly Quintilian. The brief dialogue which bears the title, *Pippini regalis et nobilissimi iuvenis disputatio cum Albino scholastico*, which is also borrowed in part from earlier sources, is not a formal text-book, but illustrates the more familiar type of conversation which master and pupil might hold and which would serve to sharpen the wits of the learner. As an example of Alcuin's method we

[1] For *De orthographia* and its sources see the new edition by Aldo Marsili (Padua, 1952).

[2] For the *De virtutibus et vitiis* see L. Wallach, *Harvard Theol. Rev.*, 48 (1955), pp. 175–95. For his classification of *De rhetorica* see *ibid.*, p. 175. For other *Specula principis* see below, pp. 315 ff.

may quote a passage from this and one from the *De rhetorica*. In the *Disputatio* the young Pippin asks the questions, Albinus (*i.e.* Alcuin) replies, thus:

Pippinus. What is a letter?
Albinus. The guardian of history.
P. What is a word?
A. The mind's betrayer.
P. What creates the word?
A. The tongue.
P. What is the tongue?
A. Something which whips the air.
P. What is the air?
A. The protection of life.
P. What is life?
A. The joy of the blessed, the sorrow of sinners, the expectation of death.
P. What is death?
A. An unavoidable occurrence, an uncertain journey, the tears of the living, the confirmation of the testament, the thief of man.
P. What is man?
A. The slave of death, a passing wayfarer, the guest of a place.
P. To what is man like?
A. A fruit.[1]
P. How is man situated?
A. Like a lamp in the wind.
P. Where is he situated?
A. Within six walls.
P. Which?
A. Above, below, before, behind, right and left.
P. In how many ways does he vary?
A. In hunger and satiety, repose and labour, in wakeful hours and sleep.
P. What is sleep?
A. The image of death.

. . . . . .

P. What is faith?
A. Sure belief in an unknown and wondrous thing.
P. What means 'wondrous'?
A. I lately saw a man standing, a dead man walking, even one who never was.

[1] The play on words in this question and answer, *homo* and *pomo*, cannot be reproduced in English.

P. How can that be? Unfold to me.

A. A likeness reflected in the water.

P. Why did not I myself understand this, seeing that I have seen it so many times?

A. Since thou art a youth of good abilities and natural gifts, I will put before thee some other wonders (*i.e.* riddles). Try if thou canst guess them of thyself.

P. I will do as thou sayest; yet on condition that, if I reply other than rightly, thou mayest correct me.

A. I will do as thou wishest. A certain unknown man conversed with me with tongue and voice, one who never existed before and who will never be hereafter; and it is one whom I heard not nor know.

P. Did a dream disturb thee, master?

A. Even so, my son. Now, hearken to another. I have seen the dead create the living and the dead consumed by the breath of the living.

P. From the rubbing together of sticks fire is born which consumes them.[1]

It will be noted that variety is introduced in the second part by reversing the roles of the speakers. The answers all through betray that fondness for verbal enigmas which was so characteristic of the more educated men in the Middle Ages, while the short questions in the early part of the dialogue irresistibly recall the maddening iteration with which the very young and precocious have in all ages verbally assaulted their elders!

In the following passage it will be seen that the speakers are Alcuin and Charles himself. In the earlier part of the dialogue Alcuin asks the questions; in the portion cited, however, it is his turn to take over the exposition.

Carolus. Expound the nature of justice.

Albinus. Justice is a state of mind which assigns to each thing its proper worth. In it the cult of the divine, the rights of mankind, and the equitable state of the whole of life are preserved.

C. Unfold its parts also.

A. Justice proceeds in part from natural right, partly from customary use.

C. How does it proceed from natural right?

A. Because a certain natural force engenders its parts, namely, religion, dutifulness (*pietas*), gratitude, requital (*vindicatio*), observance, truth.

[1] PL, 101, col. 975C–D; 978B–C.

C. Explain each of these more clearly.

A. Religion is that which pays heed and rites to a nature, which men call divine, of some superior Being. Dutifulness is that through which one bestows on blood relatives and well-wishers of one's country service and loving homage. Gratitude is the quality in which is contained the remembrance of friendships and good offices of one's neighbour and the wish to reward him. Requital is that by which right and injury and everything that meets us is by defence or retribution advanced. Observance is the quality with which we deem those who are our superiors in worth worthy of a certain degree of veneration and honour. Truth is that through which what is, what has been, and what will be, is denoted.

C. How is justice which proceeds from customary use maintained?

A. By contract, by equity, by judgement, and by law.

C. I would fain hear more about these also.

A. Contract is an agreement between persons. Equity is that which is fair to all. Judgement is what is established by the opinions of a prominent man or of several. Law is right written down for all the people (stating) of what it is their duty to beware and what to hold fast.[1]

It may be conceded that Alcuin's educational treatises are not, judged by any standards, remarkable; indeed, they are mediocre. That he was, nevertheless, a very great teacher is beyond dispute. The list of those who were his pupils either in the Palace school, or, after 796, in Tours, is not only long, but contains many famous names, amongst them Einhard, Hrabanus Maurus, and Grimald, later (841–72) abbot of St Gall. Such men passed on the memory of their old teacher to the next generation, so that Alcuin in the later ninth century came to be regarded as the ideal scholar, poet, and theologian. Wherever the pupil's opinion of the master has survived, we find Alcuin spoken of in terms of affectionate and grateful admiration. With a ruler of vigorous mind, who expected his relatives and his nobles to cultivate the same wide interests as himself, and with a throng of theologians, teachers, and writers from every land present as the king's welcome guests, it was natural that the court should be the scene of great intellectual activity. But even so it is unfortunate that the name 'academy' has sometimes been applied to the quite informal gatherings of monarch, nobility, and scholars. A title of that kind is no more

[1] *ibid.*, col. 944B–C.

applicable to the *litterati* of the Carolingian court than to any other group of writers and artists brought together before or since that time by the patronage of an enlightened prince. The members of the inner circle were distinguished by nicknames taken from Biblical literature or from the great figures of classical antiquity. By these they addressed one another when they exchanged epistles in verse or prose on a variety of topics. Charles himself was called David, Alcuin Flaccus, Einhard Beseleel, Paulinus of Aquileia Timotheus, and so forth. On the more serious occasions antiquarian or dogmatic questions might come up for discussion; at other times a lighter tone prevailed. Then riddles, poems, or exchanges of witty repartee would amuse, as it would test the mental alertness of, those present. At the dinner table, too, Charles would have extracts read aloud from ecclesiastical or historical authors. He himself had a great interest in astronomy, and, after Alcuin had retired to Tours, the two continued their discussions about the stars and the calendar by letter. We shall have occasion to note, too, that certain Irish scholars with scientific interests were for a time at the Frankish court. The picture, imperfect though it be, which can thus be reconstructed from the poems and letters of Alcuin and from the poems of Theodulfus, of the intellectual amusements of the court circle— in a sense it may also be regarded as an outgrowth or by-product of the Palace school where Charles himself and other adults on occasion attended—is as attractive as it is unique.

When we turn from the Palace school to educational centres at large throughout the Frankish dominions, we find, indeed, no satisfactory proof of a plan of universal elementary education, such as has been attributed sometimes to Charlemagne. Compared, however, with conditions in the preceding centuries the extent to which education had by 814 become available was truly astonishing. It is unhappily true also that the phenomenon was ephemeral. The insistence on the instruction of catechumens, so that all persons should at least know the basic articles of the Christian faith, was one step in the direction of universal education. In certain dioceses, moreover, exceptionally enlightened bishops strove to go considerably beyond this minimum requirement. Theodulfus, for example, in Orléans ordained that in every village and on every estate priests should arrange for schools to which any Christian father might send his children without payment of a fee. The Council of Mayence in 813 recommended the sending of children to school, 'either to monasteries or outside to priests'. An even stronger recommendation, that 'each person should send his son to learn his letters, and that the boy abide there with all diligence till he emerge well trained', is attested for Bavaria. The bishop of Lyons, Leidrad, in reporting how he has laboured to carry out the various ordinances or wishes of the Emperor, amongst other things records the establishment of schools. Scattered as such allusions in contemporary writings undoubtedly are, they at least serve to show that Charles was able to inspire his episcopate with much of his own enthusiasm. More advanced studies, whether theological or secular, were taught in cathedral schools and in the monasteries. The immediate aims of these two types of educational centre were not the same; for in the cathedral or collegiate churches the primary purpose was to train a sufficient number of young persons, so that there should be no lack of clergy, singers, and readers. Moreover, we find Alcuin in a letter addressed to Eanbald, archbishop of York, advocating that pupils be separated into three groups, each with its proper teacher, namely, into readers, singers, and copyists or scribes, 'lest the boys, enjoying leisure, stray unattended all over the place, play foolish games, or are free to indulge in other silly tricks'.[1] He makes a similar recommendation to the archbishop of Canterbury. Since Alcuin gave this advice to an archbishop of York, it seems clear that the classification which he recommends was not in force when he himself was a pupil there. We may suppose that his experience with larger educational problems in the Frankish kingdom had taught him that with the material with which he had to work, and adequately to satisfy the different needs of the churches, specialization was the best solution. Certainly this method had weighty consequences. It meant that after the elements, which would be the same for all, had been learnt, the pupils concentrated on becoming expert in one field. This plan was also followed successfully in some monasteries. Thus the cathedral school at Metz and the abbey of St Vandrille were noted

[1] *MGH*, Epist., IV, No. 114; cf. No. 128.

for their singing, the former being the chief music school in the Empire. While the copying of manuscripts was from Charlemagne's time sedulously practised in many places, certain monastic houses were distinguished above the rest for their *scriptoria*. But, although the tuition in the monasteries might in some respects fulfil the same purposes as that in the collegiate schools, the most important part of it, nevertheless, had a different end. The monastic life aimed at Christian perfection not in, but apart from, the world. And, though it was not unessential to educate the young who had been dedicated to the religious life, so that they became efficient copyists or could take their part properly in the musical portions of the liturgy, it was mainly the monasteries which were the centres of higher learning and especially of theology. Expressed in another way, it might be said that the aim of the cathedral schools was more definitely vocational or practical; the monastic schools, while they did not neglect that side of education, in preparing their pupils had a more spiritual purpose.

When Alcuin became abbot of the monastery of St Martin at Tours he was well past sixty; his health was indifferent and his eyesight failing. In addition to his work at the Palace school, his literary output was considerable. He had written tracts and letters against the Adoptionists, also some of his Biblical commentaries, and his general correspondence had grown steadily through the years; and it has been shown that he was Charlemagne's adviser in ecclesiastical controversies.[1] When he retired to Tours, although his life for much of the time was quieter than it had been when he was at court, his fame and that of St Martin's brought constant visitors as well as many disciples. And there were still many matters to occupy his mind and to sap his strength. He kept up a vast miscellaneous correspondence with the Emperor, with friends, and with many former pupils; and his dogmatic treatise on the Trinity was composed towards the end of his life. The library at Tours had his constant attention. Evidently when he came there its books were relatively few. With Charlemagne's permission therefore he dispatched some of his monks to York, so that they might obtain, from what was still the best library in

[1] See L. Wallach in *Traditio*, 9 (1953), pp. 127–54.

Western Europe, copies of many works which the Frankish library lacked. The history of the writing-schools in the collegiate church of St Martin and in the neighbouring abbey of Marmoutier before Alcuin's time is obscure; but from such extant manuscripts as are known to have been written there one must conclude that Tours in the eighth century was surpassed by several other Frankish *scriptoria* and only attained its pre-eminent position in the ninth.[1] That the writing-schools at Tours were greatly active during Alcuin's abbacy is clear; how far he himself was responsible for reforming the script of Tours, which in the following generation exercised so wide an influence on other *scriptoria*, is still a matter of controversy. Certainly he had difficulties to contend against. An adequate system of punctuation had to be introduced, and his allusion to 'daily fights with the rusticity of Tours' shows that his task was no easy one.[2]

Another undertaking of far-reaching consequence with which Alcuin's name has been associated is the revision of the Vulgate, carried out by Charlemagne's orders. Innumerable corruptions had crept into the Sacred Texts owing to the ignorance of Merovingian clergy and scribes. The task of collation and correction undertaken by the king's command was the more difficult because the venerable codices that had to be read were for the most part written in unfamiliar uncial hands. The correct punctuation would present difficulties also, and often enough words faded to the point of illegibility would still further complicate the copyist's task. Finally, it has to be remembered that there existed different textual traditions at this date, so that there was, for instance, considerable disparity between Irish and Anglo-Saxon Bibles and those in use in Spain, while all three exhibited striking differences from the Italian. In part this lack of uniformity resulted from the slowness with which Jerome's version was adopted in the West, and from contamination with the Old Latin translations which continued to survive and were sometimes used long after Jerome's Bible was in official use. A letter of Alcuin, dated 800, relates

[1] Cf. E. A. Lowe, *CLA*, VI, pp. xxvii–xxix.

[2] The earliest extant *codex Turonensis* is assigned to the first half of the eighth century by E. K. Rand, *The earliest script of Tours*, page 4, and by Lowe, *CLA*, V, No. 682. The quotation is from a letter written in 799 (*MGH*, Epist., IV, No. 172).

that he is busy amending the Old and the New Testament. The following year he dispatched to the Emperor 'a gift of the sacred books brought together into one holy and noble volume and carefully emended'. There have also survived from his pen verse dedications to four Bibles written under his direction.[1] A little more than a generation later Angelomus, a monk of Luxeuil, reports that he has seen at Aachen a Bible copied and corrected for Charlemagne under Alcuin's direction.[2] When it is remembered that Alcuin was Charlemagne's chief adviser not only in educational but in theological and liturgical questions, it is surely not rash to assume, even if the direct evidence is slight, that he took a sufficiently important part in this labour of textual criticism to justify the name 'Alcuinian recension', which has so often been applied to this undertaking of the Carolingian Age. Existing manuscripts of later date prove that uniformity had not been attained; indeed such a thing would have been impossible in Alcuin's day. But the Carolingian revision did arrest the progress of corruption and established a norm; those two achievements were of the utmost value.

[1] *MGH*, Epist., IV, Nos. 195 and 205; *MGH*, Poet., I, pp. 362 ff.
[2] *PL*, 115, col. 160C–D; Laistner in *Harvard Theol. Rev.*, 46 (1953), p. 35.

CHAPTER VIII

Carolingian Education
and the Seven Liberal Arts

Although there is such abundant general testimony to the zeal for education of Charlemagne and, in a more restricted degree, of his successors during the ninth century, precise information about educational practice is often lacking. Where fuller information about this or that aspect of the subject is available, it applies too often only to a single institution. Obviously there is a danger in generalizing from too few particulars; for, although it may truly be said that the aim of all the monasteries and of their schools was in a broad way the same, we cannot postulate even approximate uniformity of procedure in educational matters. Still less would it be true to assume that there existed then, any more than there exists now, a uniform standard of achievement.

The regulations and admonitions of Charles the Great applied, as we saw, to every type of school. A well-known capitulary of Louis the Pious, promulgated in 817, on the other hand lays down expressly that 'in the monasteries there shall be no school save for those who are oblates'.[1] This regulation by which teaching in religious houses was confined to those who were vowed at an early age to the religious life, was only one of the many measures which together made up Benedict of Aniane's programme of monastic reform. Yet twelve years later we find the bishops making a united appeal to the same monarch at the imperial Diet of Worms to establish three *scholae publicae*, because of the perceptible decline in education throughout the Empire. The meaning of this has been much disputed. The proposed provision can hardly have been for purely ecclesiastical purposes. Three

---

[1] *MGH*, Capit., I, pp. 344 ff., para. 36.

establishments would be quite insufficient for the training of priests; besides, the needful provision for training the clergy continued to be made at the more important cathedral centres. It seems most natural to interpret *scholae publicae* to mean three imperial schools similar to the Palace school of Charlemagne. In fact the proposal is of slight importance historically, since it appears to have been ignored by the king. In 826 a Roman synod issued the following ordinance respecting lay education:

> From certain places it has been brought to our notice that there is an absence of teachers and of interest in the study of letters. Consequently, in all bishoprics and the parishes subordinated to them, and elsewhere that it may be necessary, careful and diligent measures shall be taken to appoint teachers and learned persons who, being conversant with letters, the liberal arts, and sacred theology, are regularly to teach these subjects, because in them above all the divine ordinances are made clear and manifest.[1]

This direction seems to echo the *Admonitio generalis* issued nearly forty years earlier by Charlemagne. In 825 a capitulary of Lothar throws light on the difficulty of providing general education for all in northern Italy. The king fixed nine centres, in each of which pupils from a number of neighbouring towns or districts could attend school.[2] Again we do not know whether this measure could be made effective in practice, nor, if it was, whether with any degree of permanence.

In spite of all, the elaborate schemes formed by Charlemagne to provide elementary education for all had scarcely survived his death, and the sporadic efforts made in different regions by his successors to carry them on, even if they had produced lasting results, were but a poor substitute for the universality of Charles' plans. On the other hand, the restriction placed, under the influence of Benedict of Aniane's reforming zeal, on the teaching in the monasteries was ignored, or rather, was circumvented; for in some of the larger religious houses at least provision was made for instructing those who were not dedicated to the monastic life. It is possible that the term *nutriendus*, as distinct from *oblatus*, had acquired a technical meaning by this time, signifying a monastic pupil who was not an oblate. At all events it is clear from the

[1] *MGH*, Concil., II, p. 581, para. 7 ff.   [2] *MGH*, Capit., II, p. 327, para. 4 ff.

decision of 817, quite apart from Charlemagne's earlier and more general recommendations, that the monasteries before that date provided tuition for other than *pueri oblati*. In the course of the ninth century the ordinance of Louis was interpreted, at least by some monasteries, in such a way that the oblates and the other boys were kept separate and taught in different places. This arrangement is most clearly demonstrable in St Gall. There, after the completion of the new buildings, the oblate school (*schola claustri*) was inside the monastery proper and on the east, while the *schola exterior* was one of the outer buildings on the north.[1] Several of the masters are known by name. About the middle of the ninth century Iso was apparently in charge of both schools; but in 851 or soon after he handed over the direction of the inner school to Marcellus, an Irishman originally called Moengal (died 871). Later the master of the *schola claustri* was the writer and poet Notker. Did the school of St Peter, situated a little way from the abbey of Corbie in Picardy, serve only as a *schola exterior*? We must either suppose this or else assume that the rule which kept oblates, like the other religious, within the monastery walls was relaxed by the abbots of this famous convent.[2] In view of the absence of definite information it is impossible to determine how many monasteries resembled St Gall in maintaining two educational establishments. The evidence for the existence of an outer and an inner school, each with its own master, at St Hubert in the Ardennes belongs to the eleventh century. But as this monastery was re-established on the site of an older foundation in 825, its educational activities may well go back to the Carolingian Age. A further consequence of this uncertainty is that it must remain doubtful how far the curriculum in the *schola claustri* and the *schola exterior* was the same. The elementary stages would be the same for both: learning to read from the Psalter, the memorization of its contents, and the first lessons in writing. For this last purpose the Psalter commonly was also used, a practice illustrated by two surviving leaves from a manuscript

[1] See the reproduction of the ninth-century plan in *DACL*, VI, facing p. 87.

[2] The evidence is from the *Life* of Anskar (*MGH*, SS., II, p. 687), later famous as archbishop of Hamburg-Bremen. When he was a master at St Peter's, he had to go from and return to the *claustra*, *i.e.* the abbey of Corbie.

of the Psalms which were indubitably used for elementary teaching. Certain mnemonic verses which contained all twenty-three letters of the alphabet—the device itself goes back to antiquity—came into use very early and then recur frequently in manuscripts.[1] Pupils in both schools, too, would, as a preparation for the part they had to take in the church services, receive some musical instruction. At St Gall, and doubtless elsewhere, Latin had to be spoken by all except the youngest boys at all times. Lapses into the vernacular were severely punished and, in general, the discipline in both schools was severe. There are many jottings in medieval manuscripts of lines copied by boys to practise their writing, which threaten a flogging as a penalty for laziness. Thus, in a manuscript of the early twelfth century written at Durham the verse, 'afficitur plagis qui non vult discere gratis' forms the caption for a lively drawing, an initial A formed of a master birching a boy.[2] It is said that Notker at St Gall disregarded the all but universal custom of the age and dispensed with the birch as an aid to learning. Out of school hours the boys of the *schola exterior* enjoyed somewhat more latitude, since they did not live under strict monastic rules. In a later age the existence of an outer school was sometimes deplored by monastic reformers, because its members might exert an unsettling or even a vicious influence on the oblates. In a well-conducted monastery, like St Gall in the ninth and tenth centuries, the two schools and their inmates were kept strictly separate. The boys of the outer school ordinarily were not admitted within the precincts of the abbey proper.

Though the primary purpose of the *schola claustri* was to prepare for the religious life and for the study of theology, it is certain that in many convents the liberal arts were not neglected. The attitude of medieval churchmen and teachers to the literature of pagan antiquity varied greatly and the assertion commonly made that most condemned it is entirely false. No doubt there were always some who desired Gregory the Great's ban on secular learning to be put into effect, but such rigorists were a minority.

[1] In general see B. Bischoff, 'Elementarunterricht und probationes pennae in der ersten Hälfte des Mittelalters' in *Studies in honor of E. K. Rand* (New York, 1938), pp. 9–20.

[2] See R. A. B. Mynors, *Durham Cathedral Manuscripts* (Oxford, 1939), Plate 37b.

There were also enthusiasts, like Servatus Lupus, to whom the occupation with pagan authors was an end in itself. Yet Lupus was also a model abbot and sound Churchman. But the majority of prelates and teachers took an intermediate line of seeing in the study of the liberal arts a means to an end. Their attitude, we may suppose, was not unlike that of Augustine to the works of Tyconius or of Bede and Cassiodorus to heretical commentators. Bede had aptly quoted Virgil in this connexion, bidding the boys 'to pluck the flowers and fruits, but beware of the lurking snake'. Cassiodorus more tersely, if less elegantly, cited Virgil's supposed reply to an interlocutor anxious to know why the great poet read his predecessor, Ennius: 'I am looking for gold in a dung-heap.'[1] Smaragdus of St Mihiel, when urged by his pupils to illustrate his commentary on Donatus with quotations from the Bible rather than from pagan authors, did so not without protest. To him theology was one study and grammar another; there was no need for one to impinge upon the other. In the ninth century the authority of Hrabanus Maurus must have carried great weight, and his writings were widely used. He advocated the *via media*. There are two kinds of *doctrina*, the one of human, the other of divine origin. Some of 'human doctrine' is superstitious and to be condemned, because it deals with divination, astrology and pagan rites. But the rest of human learning, which is needful for daily life should be studied *quantum satis est*; and literature is a part of it.[2] Two rigorists stand out in the ninth century, Paschasius Radbertus and the Spaniard, Paulus Albarus. Yet these two severe critics of profane literature and the liberal arts were condemning, even as Tertullian and other early detractors had done, a mental discipline and portions of a literature to which they were indebted for much of their own intellectual equipment. Radbertus, in the preface to the third book of his commentary on St Matthew, puts even Virgil under the ban:[3]

We do not treat of Virgil's 'arms and a man', finding our condi-
ment in the Greek salt of fables, but from the fountain of the Holy
Spirit, as we search with Christ's help into the meaning of the
catholic fathers, we desire to expound for the ears of our people

[1] *PL*, 91, col. 1065 with quotation from *Eclogue*, 3, 92–3; Cassiodorus, *Inst.*, I, x, 8 (ed. Mynors, p. 14, 23).

[2] *De institutione clericorum*, 3, 16.   [3] Latin text in *MGH*, Epist., VI, p. 143, 6–16.

what we understand in the Scriptures. It is not with tragic dutiful-ness (*pietas*) that we soothe the reader, nor do we seek to burden him with the asses' load of the comic poets; we unlock in simple discourse, according to our natural ability, what in those same Scriptures is touched with the divine breath. Hence, even if some of our friends take pleasure in Virgil's lines, because, as they say, he would wish to signify by 'arms' virtue and by 'man' wisdom, and so on for all that follows,[1] they should find even greater delight in the matter which we are setting ourselves to handle. There the un-surpassable virtue and wisdom of God our Father, in order that they might marshal Christian soldiers against the aerial powers, first advanced from the fountain of baptism to the desert like a leader of a host setting out for battle.

Several of Paulus Albarus' letters touch even more sternly on this topic. He was acquainted with the views of Jerome, from whose letters to Magnus and to Eustochium he quotes, Augustine, and Gregory I, who would surely have approved the following passage:[2]

> Because at that time, whoever occupied himself with verse, for the beauty of the language and as a means to eloquence, was a slave to the false teaching of the gentiles; inasmuch as men read Virgil's *Aeneid*, and wept over Dido's destruction, how she compassed her death with the sword, or the insult of beauty spurned, read, too, of the honours paid to ravished Ganymede, the treacherous gift of Minerva, and the deception of cruel Juno. That Christian men might not be sullied by such errors and foulness, (the Christian poets) had forethought to sing Christ's miracles in verse.

In another letter he refers contemptuously to the *Iliad* and the *Aeneid*, to 'the milky stream of Livy', and 'Demosthenes' viper's tongue'.[3] Most remarkable of all, however, is a diatribe against all the liberal arts, which, as it is little known, deserves to be quoted in full:[4]

> In the beginning was the word and the word was with God and God was the word (John i, 1). This the learned Plato knew not, of

[1] He means the allegorizing of Virgil's epic in the manner advocated by the mythographer Fulgentius. For the particular passage cf. Fulgentius (ed. Helm), p. 87.

[2] *Epist.*, 4, 10 (PL, 121, col. 433A); cf. *Aeneid* 6, 457; 1, 27; 2, 31. For Albarus in general see now the monograph, *Paul Albar of Cordova*, by Carleton M. Sage (Catholic University of America, 1943).

[3] *Epist.*, 14, 2 (PL, 121, col. 479A). Is the *lacteus amnis* a reminiscence of Quintilian's *lactea ubertas?*

[4] *Epist.*, 5, 4 (PL, 121, col. 451B–C.)

this the eloquent Tully had no thought, into this fiery Demosthenes never inquired. The tortuous briar bushes of Aristotle have it not nor is it found in the sinuous subtleties of Chrysippus. The art of Donatus has not searched into this by the rules of art not yet has the rank discipline[1] of all the grammarians. The geometricians, named after the earth, follow what is earthy and dusty. The rhetoricians, wordy and redundant, have filled the air with empty wind. The dialecticians, bound fast by rules and entangled on all sides by syllogisms, are deceitful spinners of words rather than builders of the art of speech. The mathematicians have striven to search into the causes of numbers, but they cannot perceive their substance, how much less can they express it in words. The musicians, empty blowers, have pursued the gusty breaths of winds and have never been able to direct their pinions to the truth of that art of music. Now, too, the astrologers have wished to soar heavenwards, but so conspicuously have they failed to mount thither led by their idols that they rather placed earthly reason in heaven than heavenly reason on earth. While they have set rams and bulls, scorpions and crabs, lions and bears, she-goats and fishes in the realm of the sky, they have done naught but raise up earthly things into celestial. For they are ignorant of the nature of heaven, they have sought after fame to dispute rashly what they know not. Yet they have produced nothing worthy of fame, since they have probed into these matters with the help of a human, not a divine spirit.

The liberal arts formed themes for art and poetry. Their personification as female figures, each with her appropriate attribute or symbol, goes back to Martianus Capella's fantastic treatise. In the Carolingian Age, as it would seem, they were first represented in art, although no examples from this time have survived.[2] Theodulfus of Orléans, however, composed a poem describing the ornamentation of a circular plaque or table-top. It consisted of portrayals of the seven arts together with certain other abstractions, like *Ethica*, *Prudentia*, and *Justitia*, in human form. Each figure had its attributes; for example, Grammar was armed with whip and shears, the one to spur on the lazy, the other to prune faults. Justice appeared with scales and a sword.[3] The

---

[1] The printed text gives *oliva*, which is just possible in the sense of grey or dusky; but the true reading is probably *olida*, rank.

[2] For pictorial and plastic representation of the Arts in the Middle Ages see K. Künstle, *Ikonographie der christlichen Kunst* (Freiburg i. B., 1928), I, pp. 145–56.

[3] *MGH*, Poet., I, pp. 544–7.

poem of the Irishman Dungal on the seven arts and Medicine is usually held to depict a series of painted figures in the Palace school at St Denis. It is made up of eight stanzas, each of six elegiac couplets.[1] While Theodulfus was indebted for some of his definitions to Martianus, Dungal took his from Isidore's *Etymologies*. Among the mural paintings with which some parts of the abbey of St Gall were decorated in the middle of the ninth century by artists from Reichenau was one portraying the Divine Wisdom as a mother in the circle of her daughters, the seven arts. This is known from a descriptive poem in a St Gall codex.[2] There are other verses which do not indeed describe actual works of art, but which were composed—often no doubt as school exercises —in honour of the personified subjects of the *trivium* and *quad-rivium*. Such, for example, are eight four-line couplets on Wisdom and the seven arts which date back to the later eighth century.[3] An eleventh-century manuscript in St Gall contains, amongst other poems, some of which are probably of Carolingian date, one on the liberal arts, while one of the ninth century, now at Berne, preserves for us four long stanzas, one on each of the four subjects of the *quadrivium*. Both of these compositions are based largely on Martianus.[4] The great popularity of his *Nuptials of Mercury and Philology* is attested by its not infrequent presence in library catalogues, although the four oldest extant manuscripts belong to the tenth century. This book, which contained many difficulties of language and in the subject-matter, called forth lengthy expositions, notably by Irish scholars with whom Martianus was an especial favourite. The commentaries by Dunchad (early ninth century), John Scotus, and Remigius of Auxerre survive.[5] It is probable that Martin, one of the teachers

[1] *MGH*, Poet., I, pp. 408–10.

[2] See Künstle, *op. cit.*, p. 147. The exact site of this painting is disputed. Künstle argues that it was within the church and that the monks of St Gall were the first to introduce the seven liberal arts into a sacred edifice. This may well be.

[3] *MGH*, Poet., I, pp. 629–30. Their authorship is doubtful. The editor prints them as an appendix to the poems of Theodulfus, but notes that they are earlier than Theodulfus' time.

[4] *ibid.*, IV, 1, pp. 339–43; 249–60.

[5] The commentaries of Dunchad and John Scotus have been edited by Cora E. Lutz. See also Lotte Labowsky in *Mediaeval and Renaissance Studies*, I

in the Irish colony at Laon, in the middle of the ninth century also lectured on this author. Some of his explanations have survived, although there is no certainty that he ever wrote a continuous commentary.[1]

If we bear in mind that secular learning and literature, even when encouraged, were regarded as a means to an end, we shall not be surprised to find that not all the arts were cultivated to the same extent. The subjects of the *trivium* were much more widely studied than those of the *quadrivium*, and even of those three only Grammar received universal attention. We must, however, guard against interpreting Grammar too narrowly. Alcuin's definition, which can justly be regarded as the norm for the teachers of the ninth century, is as follows:[2] 'Grammar is the science of letters and the guardian of right speech and writing; it depends on nature, reason, authority, and custom.' He goes on to enumerate the subdivisions (*species*) of the subject. These include not merely letters, syllables, words, and parts of speech, but many others, such as figures of speech, metre, stories (*fabulae*), and history. *Grammatica*, then, had a wide connotation and embraced the study of literature and its forms as well as language. In other words, the most advanced researches of Servatus Lupus into classical literature were *grammatica* as much as the laborious efforts at mastering the Latin elements of some Donatus-grinding oblate. As school-books the compilations of Bede and Alcuin were extensively used, as well as the *Ars minor* of Donatus himself.

The *Ars maior* and Priscian's grammar were given to more advanced pupils. Priscian greatly engaged the attention of Irish scholars, so that he has been called, 'so to speak, the national Irish grammarian'.[3] Sedulius and perhaps John Scotus wrote commentaries on this grammar, while Martin of Laon transcribed the Greek quotations in it and added very faulty Latin translations. Moreover, no less than three surviving manuscripts

(1943), pp. 187–93 for a manuscript of John's commentary which was unknown to Miss Lutz.

[1] Cf. Laistner in *Bulletin of the J. Rylands Library*, IX (1925), pp. 130–8.

[2] *PL*, 101, col. 857D—grammatica est litteralis scientia, et est custos recte loquendi et scribendi; quae constat natura, ratione, auctoritate, consuetudine.

[3] By S. Hellmann, *Sedulius Scottus*, p. 100.

of Priscian are written in Irish minuscule of the ninth century.[1] Some scholars, not content with the most popular grammarians, also studied rarer treatises. The outcome of this was that they prepared grammars themselves, based on what they had read or could consult in accessible libraries, for the use of their own pupils. Such was certainly the origin of most of the ninth-century *Artes grammaticae*. Sedulius composed a commentary on Eutyches. Two other Irishmen who specialized in grammar evidently had access to a large variety of late imperial grammarians. Malsachanus—he seems to have lived towards the end of the eighth century—in his work on the verb shows familiarity with nine grammarians in addition to Donatus, Priscian, Virgilius Maro *grammaticus*, and Isidore. Clemens Scotus, who was a teacher at the Palace school during Charlemagne's later years and under his successor, doubtless wrote his *ars grammatica* primarily for use in his own class-room, dedicating the book to the young Prince Lothar. In the extant grammar going under his name probably only the last of its three sections is by Clement. He makes a great parade of learning, but it is very problematic whether he knew at first hand more than a quarter of the authors whom he cites by name. His chief debt, which is unacknowledged, appears to have been to his immediate predecessors, of whom Malsachanus was one.[2] If he was no great scholar, he may yet have been a competent teacher. His poetic gifts, as revealed by a dedicatory poem to Louis' son, were less than mediocre.

The lengthy commentary on Donatus by Clement's contemporary, Smaragdus, is still unpublished as a whole. Based on only a few earlier grammarians, it is distinguished from other Carolingian books of this class, firstly by the wealth of its illustrative quotations and, secondly, by the fact that these are predominantly taken from the Bible, Jerome, and Gregory I. Erchanbert,

[1] Martin's *opusculum* was published by Miller in *Notices et extraits des manuscrits de la bibliothèque nationale*, 29, 2 (1891), pp. 118 ff. The extant manuscripts of Priscian in Irish script are Karlsruhe, *Aug.*, 132, Leyden, 67, St Gall, 904.

[2] Malsachanus was edited by M. Roger (Paris, 1905) and Clement by J. Tolkiehn in *Philologus, Supplementband*, XX, *Heft* 3 (1928). Tolkiehn's conclusions were severely criticized by K. Barwick (*Gnomon*, 6 [1930], pp. 385–95), who showed that the last portion of the grammar, not the first, was by Clement. He also corrected Tolkiehn on Clement's sources.

a monk of Freising in Bavaria who may be identical with the bishop of the same name in that diocese, was yet another teacher who compiled his own text-book for his pupils. It was a bulky commentary on the small and the large Donatus. He utilized a very respectable number of older grammarians, a proof both of the width of his reading and of the ample resources of the library in Freising, where there was a very active *scriptorium*.[1]

Nor were metrics and orthography neglected. Several new treatises on the one or the other appeared in the Carolingian Age, but their material did not go beyond the traditional material which had already been crystallized in writers like Cassiodorus and Bede.

The other two subjects of the *trivium* were not ignored, but they did not, after Alcuin's treatment of rhetoric and dialectic, call forth any disquisitions. Most of what seemed necessary for a beginner could be culled from Alcuin and from the relevant portions of Martianus, Cassiodorus, and Isidore. For a more thorough initiation into the art of rhetoric the most widely used work was the *De inventione*, which Cicero wrote in his youth and to which he disliked references to be made in his maturer years. The *Rhetorica ad Herennium* by an unknown author, though the Middle Ages consistently attributed it to Cicero, was also known. Both treatises are mentioned by Servatus Lupus in a letter to Einhard asking for the loan of his copy of the *De inventione* and *De oratore*.[2] Mentions in the early library catalogues and direct allusions to these two books are not common; but, on the other hand, the direct evidence of surviving manuscripts shows that neither treatise was specially rare. A Paris manuscript (7774A), containing part of the Verrine orations and *De inventione* is a book of Tours. Written in the first half of the ninth century it was for a time in the hands of Lupus, who made marginal corrections in it.[3] Three other *codices* of *De inventione*, now respectively at Würzburg, St Gall, and Leyden, were copied in the same century.

[1] For the early *scriptorium* in Freising see B. Bischoff, *Südostdeutsche Schreibschulen* (Leipzig, 1940); extracts from Erchanbert were published by M. Manitius in *Philologus*, 68, pp. 396–409.

[2] Lupus, *Epist.*, 1 (ed. Levillain, I, p. 8).

[3] Cf. E. K. Rand, *Manuscripts of Tours*, No. 85, and C. H. Beeson, *Servatus Lupus* (Cambridge, Mass., 1930), p. vii *et al.*

Of the four earliest surviving manuscripts of *Ad Herennium*, that at Würzburg was written during the abbacy of Gozbert (842–55),[1] one now in Paris is of slightly later date, while the other two, in Leningrad from the abbey of Corbie and in Berne, though usually dated in the beginning of the tenth century, may be slightly older. Nevertheless, a study of authors belonging to the Carolingian Age shows conclusively that, while *De inventione*, on which Alcuin had already relied heavily, was widely used, the *Rhetorica ad Herennium* did not come fully into its own until the twelfth century and after.[2] Cicero's *De oratore* and Quintilian's *Institutio oratoria*, however, though known, were scarce and in any event were too advanced save for an exceptional scholar like Servatus Lupus.

For the study of dialectic, which to Alcuin and to his pupil, Hrabanus, was synonymous with logic, the ninth-century teachers, if they demanded more than was offered by Alcuin's little treatise, had recourse to the same sources that he had used, namely, the translations and commentaries of Boethius and the pseudo-Augustinian *Categories*. Boethius' commentary on Cicero's *Topica*, of which there was a copy at Tours, was borrowed by Lupus;[3] but few besides him appear to have known either work in that age.

On the subjects of the *quadrivium* too, few fresh works were composed. Geometry as such was scarcely known or understood. As Boethius' treatise was lost, there were only the sections on geometry in Isidore's *Etymologies* and the sixth book of Martianus to which an interested learner could turn. But the information there provided belongs rather to geography than to the mathematical sciences. Again, the knowledge of arithmetic, astronomy, and music was derived from the old, 'standard', authors. In general the occupation with these arts was determined by practical considerations. Some acquaintance with the seasons, the movements of the planets, and the constellations was necessary to determine the proper time for Church festivals and offices. The calculations required to fix these and to draw up an ecclesiastical

---

[1] See B. Bischoff and G. Hoffmann, *Libri S. Kyliani* (Würzburg, 1952), p. 133.

[2] The very slight use made of the *Rhetorica ad Herennium* before the twelfth century has been clearly demonstrated by Dorothy Grosser in her unpublished doctoral dissertation (Cornell University, 1953), *Studies in the Influence of the Rhetorica ad Herennium and Cicero's De inventione*.

[3] *Epist.*, 53 (ed. Levillain, I, p. 214).

calendar entailed a working knowledge of arithmetic. Boethius, Martianus, and Isidore among the older, Bede among more recent, writers, were the accepted authorities of the Carolingian Age. Bede's works especially were widely used. This is proved by their presence in many, if not in most, monastic and cathedral libraries and by the fact that Bede's *De temporum ratione* survives in more than one hundred and thirty manuscripts and his early *De temporibus* in over sixty.[1] Sometimes volumes of considerable bulk were put together, containing *computi*, as the tables used for reckoning out the dates of religious festivals were called, and the standard treatises on the subject, reproduced in their entirety or else in extracts.[2] An excellent example of this procedure can be studied in a manuscript of the early ninth century now preserved in the Vatican Library (*Pal. lat.* 1448). It was written partly in Trèves, partly perhaps at Mayence. In addition to various calendars, computistic tables, and lunar reckonings, the manuscript contains Isidore's *De natura rerum* and parts of the third book of the *Etymologies*, and Bede's *De temporibus* and *De temporum ratione*.[3] The number of extant *computi* from this period is considerable. Several scholars, moreover, composed fresh treatises on the proper method of compiling such, but the material in, for example, Hrabanus or in the *De computo lunae* by Helperic, a monk who taught at Auxerre about the middle of the ninth century, is wholly derived from their predecessors. Here and there a student may have been moved by a more purely scientific interest in the heavens. If so, he could turn to Germanicus' translation of Aratus' *Phaenomena* or to the little treatise by Julius Hyginus, for both works were known at that time.[4] But nearly two centuries were to elapse from the death of Charlemagne before a real advance in geometrical and astronomical theory and

[1] Cf. Laistner and King, *A Hand-list of Bede MSS*, pp. 139–47, and C. W. Jones, *BOT*, pp. 140–67.

[2] On *computi* see the authoritative introduction to Mr Jones' edition, especially pp. 105–22.

[3] There is a full description of this manuscript by W. M. Lindsay in *Palaeographia latina*, IV, pp. 22–6; see also Jones, *op. cit.*, pp. 157 and 164.

[4] Both works are found in the ninth-century catalogues of Reichenau and Murbach. Three extant manuscripts of Hyginus and four of Aratus in Germanicus' version were copied in the ninth century.

practice was made by Gerbert (*c.* 940–1003) and Hermann of Reichenau (*c.* 1013–54).[1]

The theory of music found interested students in Aurelian of Réomé (middle of the ninth century) and Hucbald, a monk of St Amand (*c.* 840–930), but the one contributed little and the other nothing to the handbooks of an earlier age. Far more significant is the treatise, *Musica enchiriadis*, composed before the end of the ninth century. Its author, according to Dom Morin's very probable conjecture, was Hoger, abbot of Werden, who died in 902.[2] By introducing a new system of musical notation which, though not adopted by later theorists as it stood, probably influenced their more lasting systems, by his discussion of harmony and polyphonic singing, possibly also by designating the notes of the octave by the first seven letters of the alphabet, though this device may be older, he can claim a place among the pioneers in the theory and practice of music.

We have seen how Isidore's *Etymologies* was, as it were, the standard book of reference on all matters connected with the arts and sciences. It was therefore a matter of some consequence when Hrabanus Maurus produced his *De rerum naturis*—the manuscripts do not warrant the title, *De universo*—which was a new and somewhat altered edition of Isidore. Hrabanus divided his encyclopedia into twenty-two, instead of into twenty books. He transposed certain parts of Isidore so that the theological sections

[1] The view long held, and summarized in the first edition of this book, that John Scotus in his philosophical treatise *On the division of the Universe* had propounded an astronomical theory which in some respects resembled that of Tycho Brahe has been shown to be mistaken. John's scheme in the main is based on certain passages in Pliny's *Natural History* and adds nothing significant to the small stock of astronomical lore that the Carolingian Age possessed. See Erika von Erhardt-Siebold and Rudolf von Erhardt, *The astronomy of John Scotus Erigena*, and their *Cosmology in the Annotationes in Marcianum*, both published at Baltimore in 1940. The authors thus sum up their conclusions (*Cosmology*, p. 43): 'Erigena's astronomy thus turns out to be a consummation of the ancient idea of the hegemony of the sun and of Plato's picture of the dance of the planets about their Master. Its character might therefore be expressed by calling it a helio-hegemonic or helio-cosmogonic system, and, for the sake of distinction, it could be named a pseudo-heliocentric system. A system and not a mere idea it certainly is.'

[2] *RB*, 12 (1895), pp. 394ff. There is a good synopsis of Hoger's work in Manitius I, pp. 449–51, with ample bibliographical references to musicological literature.

came first, and he omitted others, notably those on the liberal arts with which he dealt in a separate treatise, called *De institutione clericorum*. The only other innovation was that mystical or allegorical interpretations were sown broadcast through the whole encyclopedia, these being taken mainly from Jerome and Bede. The useful character of the revised manual and the reputation and authority of Hrabanus ensured to the *De rerum naturis* a wide popularity and use.

One important product of monastic industry and of preoccupation with *grammatica* calls for brief notice. There were obvious advantages, both for use in the schoolroom and for private reading by those whose scholarship was limited, in chrestomathies. Such collections of short, or extracts from longer, works of various types were in great demand during the Carolingian epoch. The contents might be mainly didactic, or might be intended for recreation, or might be compounded of equal portions of what was improving and what was written in a lighter vein, in prose or verse. A ninth-century manuscript of St Gall will serve as an example of the former class.[1] It is made up of Donatus' *Ars minor*, Alcuin's *De rhetorica*, some Virgilian and Leonine verses, the second book of Cassiodorus' *Institutiones*, the treatise on metres by Theodorus, a section on miracles derived from Gregory of Tours' astronomical tract and Isidore's *De natura rerum*, and a poem on an eclipse of the moon by the Visigothic king, Sisebut. The other class of chrestomathy is well exemplified by a codex which has been made the subject of a careful study by Rand.[2] It was written in the ninth century at Fleury and in its present form contains Arator's epic on Acts, Prosper's Augustinian epigrams, and some other Christian poetry, the *Disticha Catonis*, Avianus' fables, select epigrams from the *Latin Anthology* and from Martial, Avitus, and an extract from the first book of Isidore's *Etymologies*. But a good portion from the middle of the manuscript and also the end are lost. There are sound reasons for believing, as Rand has shown, that Juvencus and Sedulius' *Paschal Hymn* followed Arator when the manuscript

[1] *Sangallensis*, 855 (saec. ix); cf. R. A. B. Mynors' edition of the *Institutiones*, pp. xix–xx.
[2] See E. K. Rand in *Philological Quarterly*, I (1922), pp. 258–77.

was complete, and that the concluding folios contained the fables of Phaedrus. We shall have occasion later to note other *collectanea* of a more advanced type, devoted to the works of Latin prose authors or of the Fathers, and it has already been shown that collections of scientific extracts also found much favour.

An indispensable aid to learning, as well as a temptation to pedants, was a dictionary or glossary. The number of these is very large and they differ greatly in size, age, and value; for it would be a grave error to suppose that all these word-lists, compiled between the sixth or seventh and the tenth centuries were, so to speak, original works.[1] Actually there are a few early glossaries, and these are basic. The material that they contained was used again and again, being expanded or abbreviated and, be it added, often garbled in the process. The two oldest all-Latin glossaries are now commonly referred to, from their opening words, as *Abstrusa* and *Abolita*. According to their latest editors, they were compiled not later than the beginning of the seventh and the beginning of the eighth century respectively.[2] The origin of such glossaries is to be found in the marginal glosses with which some manuscripts of authors were supplied. Monastic teachers often copied these down in order to use them in instructing their classes. A further stage in the creation of a dictionary was reached when the teacher or his pupils put together in roughly alphabetical order, that is to say, by the first letters of the words only, several sets of such *glossae collectae*. As the process advanced still further, so that strict alphabetical order was attained, and the glossary grew in size by splitting up the longer glosses and making fresh ones, the original source of them became more and more obscured. In reality the sources from which glossaries were derived are very limited. The *Abstrusa* glossary is made up primarily of glosses taken from a manuscript containing *scholia* on Virgil; there are also a number of Bible glosses. *Abolita* drew its material from *marginalia* to Virgil and to certain plays of Terence, and from Festus' *De significatu verborum*. The most ambitious piece of dictionary-making may be regarded justly as a product of

[1] See G. Goetz, *Corpus glossariorum latinorum*.

[2] The most important of the glossaries have been published in critical editions, and with the sources indicated as far as possible in *Glossaria latina*, 1–5 (Paris, 1926–31).

Charlemagne's revival of learning. The so-called *Liber glossarum* or *Glossarium Ansileubi* was compiled in France, and very possibly at Corbie, in the last quarter of the eighth century.[1] It was a vast achievement to weld together what is in effect part dictionary, part encyclopedia. For the glossarial portion the *Abstrusa* and *Abolita* glossaries, Placidus, and marginal glosses from Virgil manuscripts are the main sources. The encyclopedia sections come primarily from the works of Isidore; but there are many extracts from Augustine, especially the *De civitate Dei*, Ambrose, Jerome, Eucherius, Orosius, and some others.

The value of these early medieval compilations is not negligible, provided their character and particularly their origin be properly understood.[2] The classicist, working cautiously, it is true, can recover some parts of early and valuable Virgil *scholia* from them,[3] while here and there he will be rewarded by a citation from some lost Latin work, although too often it has become garbled in transmission. The comparative philologist, again, will find much to interest him in classical Latin words that have changed, or are in process of changing their meanings, or in late Latin words used to explain the earlier, which by the later Merovingian period were beginning to be unintelligible to many.[4] Such examples mark an instructive stage in the transition from Latin to the Romance languages. A few instances, all taken from the *Liber glossarum*: *Alnum*, alder wood, is explained by *verna* (French *verne*). *Mentiriosus*, given as the equivalent of the classical *fallax*, survives in the Spanish *mintroso*. *Rufus*, red, is glossed *vermiculus*, from which comes the French *vermeil*. *Saumarium* (French *sommier*) explains the classical Latin *equus castratus*, a gelding, *architectus* is glossed *macio* (French *maçon*), while *seminare* (French

[1] *Glossaria latina*, I, edited by W. M. Lindsay and others. Lindsay attributed the undertaking to the initiative of Adalhard, abbot of Corbie. See *Bulletin Du Cange*, 3 (1927), pp. 95 ff. Two of the oldest manuscripts are written in the most characteristic minuscule of Corbie, and two short fragments of the glossary in the same script have survived.

[2] Cf. W. M. Lindsay's preface in *St Andrew's University Publications*, XIII (1921).

[3] Cf. H. J. Thomson, *ibid.*, pp. 46 ff.

[4] The process, of course, already began in Roman imperial times, so that, for example, *magnus* was replaced by *grandis* and *saepe* disappeared in favour of *frequenter* or *subinde*.

semer) is the synonym for the unfamiliar *serere*. These are but a few examples out of many to show that early medieval glossaries play a by no means negligible part in the history of language. No less important were bilingual word-lists. We have seen that in southern Italy Greek continued to be a living language in the medieval period. It was probably in that region and in the latter part of the sixth century that the large bilingual glossary, commonly called the Philoxenus glossary, which has only survived in a very abbreviated form, was composed. The sources, again, are not many, namely, Festus, Charisius, the four *Catilinarian Orations* of Cicero, Bible glosses, including some that come indubitably not from the Vulgate but from an older Latin version, Horace glosses, and one or two others.[1] Just as *Abstrusa* and *Abolita* were utilized for the *Liber glossarum*, so much material was taken over into later glossaries from Philoxenus. This was notably so with a group of Latin-Old English glossaries, of which one of the oldest (eighth century) is preserved in the library of Corpus Christi College, Cambridge.[2] An early example of a Latin-Old High German glossary survives in the so-called *Vocabularius S. Galli* (*Sangallensis* 913) compiled in Fulda in the late eighth century. In this the words are assembled under separate subject headings, but there is also an appendix in which the material is arranged in alphabetical order. The great size of a dictionary like the *Liber glossarum*, or even of some glossaries like the original Philoxenus, would preclude its being copied frequently as it stood. But the compilation and transcription of shorter word-lists was a customary exercise in monastic *scriptoria* and schools during the early Middle Ages, older material being used again and again for the purpose. Old notions die hard; and the assertion that these later compilations have independent value, which is completely mistaken, still persists here and there. In short, with few exceptions, in this, as in theology and in scholarship, the lettered men of the eighth and ninth centuries were traditionalists rather than innovators.

[1] For these sources see the edition by the present writer in *Glossaria latina*, 2 (pp. 125–291), pp. 130–6.

[2] This group has been studied and analysed by Lindsay in *Publications of the Oxford Philological Society*, VIII (1921). The same scholar has also published a definitive edition of the Corpus Glossary (Cambridge, 1921).

CHAPTER IX

Libraries and *Scriptoria*

The building-up of libraries and the development of writing-schools in the early Middle Ages are so closely connected that the two topics must be considered together; and it is significant that, in general, the most active *scriptoria* were in monastic and cathedral centres where there were ample book collections. The seventh and eighth centuries were a period of experimentation all over Western Europe, the problem being how best to devise book-hands that would be more economical in parchment or vellum and in the time that they consumed when in use. The evolution of scripts in Ireland and in southern Italy, the one derived from half-uncial, the other from cursive, has already been touched upon briefly.[1] The Irish scribes evolved a characteristic majuscule and also a minuscule script. The Anglo-Saxon scribes became apt pupils of the Celtic missionaries and the earliest manuscripts demonstrably written in English centres are hard to distinguish, even for the expert, from those written by Irishmen. Gradually both Anglo-Saxon majuscule and minuscule developed along their own lines. Besides, just as in matters of ritual and doctrine two influences, Celtic and Roman, were at work in the English Church from the beginning of the seventh century, so also in *scriptoria*, though the Irish influence was profound, Rome made some contributions. Manuscripts from Rome or even southern Italy found their way to England, and scribes in English centres occasionally used a true uncial script, as can be seen in the *codex Amiatinus* of Jerome's Vulgate, which was written at Jarrow or Wearmouth between 690 and 716. Typical of Irish and of Anglo-Saxon majuscule at their finest are two

[1] See above pp. 140 and 175. The best introduction to the pre-Carolingian scripts, succinct but authoritative, will be found in the Introductions to *CLA*, volumes II, IV, and VI.

famous manuscripts of the Gospels, the Book of Kells, now in Dublin, and the Lindisfarne Gospels in the British Museum.[1] Insular scribes differed from their continental brethren not only in their script and the abbreviations that they used, but also in the way that they ruled their parchment and in the number of sheets that they bound together, in short, in the technical process of book-making. The migration of Irish, and a little later of English, scholars to the continent of Europe also had momentous consequences. These men brought manuscripts with them—we have already seen Boniface's anxiety to increase his slender stock of books—and when they settled in continental abbeys they continued to use their national hands and to teach them to others. Great advances have been made during the last three decades in the study of individual *scriptoria*. The result has been to demonstrate the profound influence exercised in them by these immigrants. Many Insular manuscripts actually originated in continental writing-schools—to date there are at least a dozen centres where the presence of Irish or Anglo-Saxons can be proved—and, even when the Carolingian reform of the script was well advanced, Insular traits, either in the abbreviations or in the form of individual letters, lingered on. Thus it came about that the Insular scripts were not finally ousted by Carolingian minuscule until the latter part of the ninth century. In England, on the other hand, the national hand held its own fully until the middle of the next century; and, even after that time, when continental minuscule had been generally adopted, the older style of Anglo-Saxon writing continued to be used for copying works composed in the vernacular.

In Spain, too, a characteristic hand had been devised not later than *c*. 700. Derived from Roman cursive, with some modifications due to the study of uncial and half-uncial hands, the so-called Visigothic minuscule was not supplanted by the all-conquering continental until the close of the eleventh century.[2]

In the Frankish kingdom and other parts of the Continent,

---

[1] *CLA*, II, Nos. 274 and 187.

[2] Since the early manuscripts in Spanish collections have not yet been published in *CLA*, the reader may be referred to A. Millares Carlo, *Paleografía española*. (Two volumes: Barcelona, 1929.)

including northern Italy, there was experimentation and much variety in writing during the earliest period. An early calligraphic minuscule, based on Merovingian cursive, was evolved at Luxeuil. The latest investigator calls Luxeuil 'the first great writing-centre of Merovingian Gaul' and has listed twenty-five extant manuscripts written in this *scriptorium* whose output was at its height at the turn from the seventh to the eighth century. Most of them are written in the highly characteristic minuscule of Luxeuil, a very few in uncial or half-uncial.[1] Nor was the importance of this *scriptorium* merely local, for its influence extended to other centres in France and even to northern Italy. Amongst the most famous manuscripts written in this script is the Ragyndrudis codex of the early eighth century. It is one of three venerable manuscripts preserved at Fulda, which belonged to Boniface, and, being the very book with which he tried to shield himself when he was killed at Dockum, bears the marks of a sword to this day. The abbey of Corbie, it will be remembered, was originally founded from Luxeuil. Its *scriptorium*, which was exceptionally active during the eighth century, is of outstanding importance in the history of Western palaeography. Three distinct varieties of minuscule were in use there, and it should be noted that they do not represent consecutive stages of development, but that they overlap chronologically and were used side by side. The most peculiar of these hands lasted until the early years of the ninth century. Yet already before 778 there had been written at Corbie a Bible in several volumes by order of Abbot Maurdramnus. Its script is the earliest example of a true Carolingian minuscule.[2]

The use contemporaneously in one writing-school of several scripts, which were the result of different lines of development, illustrates both the trouble taken to devise a truly satisfactory hand and the constant intercourse between *scriptoria*, even those which were widely separated geographically. Where so many religious houses existed, it was no wonder that there was so much variation in the practice of the writing-schools, as long as these were in the formative stage. Their graphic style would be determined partly by the older models at their disposal—for instance, venerable uncial or half-uncial codices of the Bible or the Latin

[1] E. A. Lowe in *CLA*, VI, pp. xvi–xvii.   [2] *ibid.*, pp. xxii–xxvi.

Fathers—partly by the degree of intercommunication which they were able or willing to foster with monasteries elsewhere. A successful *scriptorium* would have imitators. Foundations situated near two different cultural regions or at some nodal point of important highways would be liable to be exposed and to react to a variety of influences. Thus the presence in southern French *scriptoria*, and even in a place as far from the Pyrenees as Limoges, of Spanish characteristics in writing is easily intelligible. Lyons for centuries had stood where four or five transcontinental routes converged and had been a leading centre of culture. Among surviving manuscripts from there are some of great antiquity, uncial or half-uncial codices of the fifth or sixth centuries, and, while some may have been importations from Italy, others were products of the Lyons *scriptorium*.[1] Every monastery of any pretensions made some provision for the copying of manuscripts. In the larger foundations a good many scribes might be employed in this labour, so that the writing-school became a regular centre for multiplying copies of an author and distributing them to other houses, instead of merely supplying local needs. Existing manuscripts and library lists of the later eighth and ninth centuries prove that most of the more considerable religious houses acquired good sized, sometimes remarkably large, collections of books, sacred and profane, although the sacred naturally predominated. If only a small number of libraries is singled out for notice here, it is because no useful purpose would be served by compiling a more exhaustive list. Besides, information happens to be much more ample for some than for others, and this circumstance must largely determine the nature of any selection. Nor is this misleading, provided it be remembered that chance operates very unevenly. For the period covered by this chapter, for example, far more medieval catalogues survive of the German (Austrasia, Bavaria, Alemannia) than of the French (Neustria, Aquitaine) libraries.

We have already referred to the fame of the York library. Alcuin included an all too brief summary of its contents in his poem on the bishops of York. Like most other collections at this

---

[1] For the early Lyons *scriptorium* see E. A. Lowe, *Codices Lugdunenses antiquissimi* (Lyons, 1924), and the brief summary in *CLA*, VI, pp. xiii–xiv.

date, it was richest in theological works. The list of the Fathers is long—Hilary of Poitiers, Ambrose, Jerome, Augustine, Basil, Chrysostom, Athanasius, Orosius, Leo I, Gregory the Great, Fulgentius, bishop of Ruspe, and Victorinus. One cannot assume that the works of the more prolific authors were complete, although it is probable that Jerome, Augustine, and Gregory the Great were each represented by a goodly collection of their writings; for Bede, as we have seen, had been familiar with most, if not all, of Jerome and Gregory, and with a good deal of Augustine, and the connexion between York and Wearmouth-Jarrow was close. The Greek Fathers were no doubt in Latin dress; for neither Alcuin nor any of his contemporaries would have understood them in the original. Of Cassiodorus the library would have the commentary on the Psalms and perhaps the second book of the *Institutiones*; for Book I does not seem to have been known in England at this date.[1] To these names one must certainly add Isidore, although (for metrical reasons?) he is not mentioned in the poem. Again we can safely assume a good collection of books on the liberal arts. Alcuin specifies a few. But, apart from the needs of the school, his own interest in arithmetic and astronomy makes it certain that texts on these subjects were available; in the poem, however, they are omitted. Pagan literature seems not to have been represented so well. Alcuin names Virgil, Statius, and Lucan of the poets, Cicero, Pliny (*i.e.* the Elder), Pompeius (presumably Justinus' abbreviation of Pompeius Trogus), Aristotle (*i.e.* Boethius) among prose writers. But the list of Christian poets was long.

In France, Corbie, Tours, Fleury and Lyons could all boast of a wealth of codices during the ninth century. Manuscripts might be lent by one monastery to another for copying. When that was done, it was not unusual to demand from the borrower another manuscript as a pledge for the safe return of the borrowed book. Such inter-library loans are well attested in the letters of Servatus Lupus and they can sometimes be deduced from manuscripts.[2]

[1] P. Courcelle, *Les lettres grecques en occident*, pp. 374–6, has argued that Bede knew Book I; but cf. my remarks in *Classical Philology*, 42 (1947), p. 255. For early manuscripts of Book I see Mynors' edition, pp. xff.

[2] For a probable interchange of manuscripts between Luxeuil and Rheims and Murbach cf. *Harvard Theol. Rev.*, 46 (1953), pp. 43–5.

From Corbie and Tours no early catalogues survive; but Corbie possessed early uncial and half-uncial codices and, as we have seen, its writing-school was most active from the middle of the eighth century on. A long series of manuscripts in Corbie minuscule eventually passed to St Germain and these are now in the National Library in Paris. The library at Tours grew steadily from Alcuin's time on and before the end of the ninth century must have been one of the foremost collections west of the Rhine.[1] A ninth-century list from Fleury contains mostly theological works; one from the tenth, on the other hand, is mostly made up of pagan authors and of books on the *trivium* and *quadrivium*.[2] An early monastic chronicle shows how the abbots of St Vandrille in the late eighth and early ninth century strove to build up a monastic library.[3] Extant manuscripts prove that the *scriptoria* in the cathedral and in the monasteries of St Thierry and St Remi in Rheims were extremely active, particularly during the time of archbishop Hincmar (845–82).[4] The contents of the considerable library in the monastery of St Riquier near Abbeville were predominantly theological.[5] The cathedral library at Lyons in the ninth century enjoyed a deserved fame. Unlike most medieval collections it was not subsequently scattered in different European cities, for many of its manuscripts are still in their original home. Its excellence during the ninth century was due in the first place to the real culture of its archbishops, from Leidrad (798–814) to Remigius (852–75), and to that able but acidulated scholar, the deacon Florus, whose autograph can still be studied in the *marginalia* of some Lyons manuscripts. Theology predominated in this collection, the works of Augustine taking the place of honour.[6]

Surviving catalogues and existing manuscripts attest the importance of many libraries in what is now Germany or Switzerland during the Carolingian Age. Again, only some of the more

---

[1] See E. K. Rand, *Studies in the Script of Tours*, I (1929), and II (1934).

[2] Cf. *DACL*, V, 2, s.v. Fleury.

[3] W. Levison, *Aus rheinischer und fränkischer Frühzeit*, pp. 530–55; G. Becker, *Catalogi bibliothecarum antiqui*, Nos. 1, 4, and 7; but in list 7 only items 1 to 32 belong to St Vandrille, the rest (33–84) were in the library of St Germer-en-Fly.

[4] See F. M. Carey in *Studies in honor of E. K. Rand*, pp. 41–60.

[5] Becker, *op. cit.*, No. 11.

[6] Cf. S. Tafel in *Palaeographia latina*, II, pp. 66 ff. and IV, pp. 40 ff.

notable can be considered. The cathedral library in Cologne grew steadily, since its *scriptorium* was very active for over a century from 795 onwards, and a number of its products still exist today.[1] Similarly it is possible from extant manuscripts to obtain a good notion of the resources of the library at Mayence. It possessed, for example, a fine collection of Augustine's works. A copy of the *Retractations* there had all those writings marked—forty-eight in all—which were available on the spot. The most noteworthy absentee is the *De doctrina Christiana*, though in the ninth century there were copies of this treatise in Fulda, Lorsch, Würzburg, Reichenau and St Gall. At Würzburg, as at Lyons, many of the old books are still preserved where they were first collected or copied. The remains of a catalogue written at the turn from the eighth to the ninth century contains thirty-six items. They are mostly Biblical or liturgical texts or theological works and there are one or two rarities, like the younger Arnobius and Junillus. A fuller catalogue of the later tenth century with two hundred and nine entries also survives.[2] The monastery of Lorsch in Hesse was a comparatively late foundation, for it was established in 764 by Chrodegang of Metz. From the first, however, it enjoyed royal favour, with the result that within less than fifty years it was one of the richest abbeys east of the Rhine. The library in the ninth century was worthy of its leading position as a religious house. The extant catalogues, though not complete, enumerate nearly six hundred works arranged in sixty-three sections, and there is no other Carolingian library for which we have so full a list. No less than eighteen sections are assigned to the works of Augustine and six to those of Jerome, a clear proof of the superlative importance of these Fathers in a well-appointed monastic library. Other dogmatic or exegetical authors are well represented. Nor was profane literature neglected at Lorsch, since Virgil, Lucan, Horace, some speeches and letters and the *De officiis* of Cicero, some essays of the younger Seneca, Pliny the Elder, and later authors, like Solinus and the mythographer

---

[1] See L. W. Jones, *The Script of Cologne* (Cambridge, Mass., 1932).
[2] For Mayence see W. M. Lindsay and P. Lehmann in *Palaeographia latina*, IV (1925), pp. 15 ff. For the two catalogues from Würzburg see Bischoff and Hoffmann, *Libri Sancti Kyliani*, pp. 143 and 151.

Fulgentius, figure in the list. Among extant manuscripts of classical authors are the chief codex of Seneca's *De beneficiis* and *De clementia*, the oldest manuscript of Sidonius' *Letters*, and one containing Juvenal and Persius now in Montpellier.[1] Finally, Lorsch was well supplied with treatises on grammar, rhetoric, and metrics, all of which would be important for instruction in the school.

It is unfortunate that only fragments exist of early catalogues from Fulda. The most considerable records one hundred and ten titles, mostly of Bible manuscripts and Patristic literature, notably Augustine and thirty-six Jerome items. But, although theology and exegesis may have been the primary occupation of the Fulda scholars in the ninth century—witness the many compilations of Hrabanus Maurus in this field—and the library was in consequence well stocked with the relevant literature, it could also boast of an unusually fine series of classical and late classical authors. There were to be found such rarities at that date as Suetonius' *Lives of the Caesars*, Ammianus Marcellinus, Columella, probably parts of Tacitus, the *Letters* of the younger Pliny, and many others. The total list of secular works of all kinds whose existence in Fulda during the ninth century can be postulated with fair certainty is long, so that the role played by its library and *scriptorium* in the transmission of classical and post-classical Latin writers may fairly be called unique.[2] Although the beginnings of St Gall reach back to the early years of the seventh century, more than three generations passed before it grew to a considerable size. It is usual to date its rapid rise into the forefront of medieval monasteries from the time of Gozbert (816–36). During the later years of his abbacy and under his immediate successors the

---

[1] For Lorsch see W. M. Lindsay in *Palaeographia latina*, III (1924), pp. 5 ff. The number of extant manuscripts from Lorsch is considerable, the greater part being now among the *Palatini* in the Vatican Library. P. Lehmann (*SB*, Bavarian Academy, 1930) has identified four Lorsch manuscripts of the ninth century that are now in the British Museum (*Harleian* 3024, 3032, 3039, 3115). The manuscripts mentioned in the text are *Pal. lat.*, 1547, Oxford, *Laud. lat.*, 104, and Montpellier, 125.

[2] On Fulda see P. Lehmann in *Bok-och Bibliotekshistoriska Studier tillägnade Isak Collijn* (Uppsala, 1925), pp. 47 ff., and his essay, 'Fulda und die antike Literatur', in the memorial volume, *Aus Fulda's Geistesleben* (Fulda, 1928), pp. 9–23. A list of other articles bearing on Fulda by the same writer will be found in Note 1 of *SB*, Bavarian Academy, 1950, Heft 9.

monastic buildings were gradually rebuilt and much enlarged. A contemporary plan of the reconstructed abbey survives. Already during the course of the eighth century St Gall had acquired a fair collection of manuscripts from outside. At the same time its own scribes were active. The best known of them, Winitharius, the first of that name, was an elderly man *c.* 760, so that his *floruit* falls in the thirty years before that date. Six manuscripts still preserved in St Gall were written wholly or partly by him.[1] In a humble way he appears also to have been an author, since short passages by him are inserted in codices which he copied. The pride of the artist, not without a trace of pedantry, rings out in the colophon at the end of a large collection of Biblical and theological citations which he had assembled:

> Here ends the book which Winitharius, a sinner and a priest un-deservingly ordained, wrote. With God's help he brought it to completion by the labour of his own hands; and there is not here one leaf which he had not secured by his own efforts, either by purchase or by begging for it, and there is not in this book one *apex* or one *iota* which his hand did not trace.[2]

In the ninth century the growth of the library was phenomenal. This can be seen from a contemporary catalogue, which is supplemented by lists of acquisitions made in the abbacy of Grimald and of his private collection as well as that of his successor, Hartmut. Finally a list of nearly thirty large volumes, copied while Hartmut was head of the monastery, bears testimony to the active labours of the writing-school.[3] The catholic character of the library is noteworthy. On theology and exegesis there was a wide selection of works by the four 'doctors', Isidore, Bede, and

---

[1] See the notable study of the early *scriptorium* in St Gall by Karl Löffler, *Palaeographia latina*, VI (1929), pp. 5–66. For its manuscripts consult *SMAH*, II. For Winitharius cf. Löffler, pp. 52 ff. with Plates 8 to 10 and *SMAH*, II, p. 18 with note 24, and Plates II above and III right. Bruckner points out that two manuscripts, one in Zürich and the other in Vienna, which have been ascribed to Winitharius, were not written by him. For the plan of the abbey see *DACL*, VI, facing p. 87. I have not seen Hans Reinhardt, *Der St. Galler Klosterplan* (St Gall, 1952) with a reproduction of the plan in eight colours.

[2] Latin text, from *Sangall.*, 238, in Löffler, *op. cit.*, p. 54.

[3] All these catalogues and those of Reichenau will be found, admirably edited, in P. Lehmann, *Mittelalterliche Bibliothekskataloge Deutschlands und der Schweiz*, I (Munich, 1918).

Alcuin; Cassiodorus was represented by his commentary on the
Psalms and by the *Tripartite History* compiled under his direction.
Other historical works included Eusebius, the Latin Josephus,
Orosius, and Gregory of Tours' *History of the Franks*. Among the
rarities we may count the commentary on the Apocalypse by
Tyconius, a manuscript now unfortunately lost. Furthermore,
there was a varied collection of hagiographical writings and of
monastic rules; an important series of legal compilations, including the *Theodosian Code*; a large and miscellaneous selection of
grammars and other books on the subjects of the *trivium*, with a
few on those of the *quadrivium*; and all the chief Christian poets.
Although, with the exception of Virgil and Vegetius, the Roman
poets and prose writers do not appear in these lists, it is clear from
what is known of the school teaching from the later ninth century,
that Virgil was not the only pagan author who was studied.

The fifty books which Pirmin is reputed to have acquired as
the nucleus of a library in his foundation at Reichenau (Augia
maior) were added to steadily. Under a succession of able and
scholarly abbots the *scriptorium* was a hive of industry. In addition
many codices were obtained by gift or purchase from far and near,
not a few being presented by visitors to what was already by
Charlemagne's time one of the foremost monasteries in the eastern
half of the Empire. From 821 to 846 the books were under the
care of a remarkable librarian. No less than five book-lists from
this period have survived. The earliest contains more than four
hundred volumes. The other four enumerate the additions made
at different times during the twenty-five years of Reginbert's
stewardship. He himself refers to the three methods of enlarging
the collection which he adopted; copying in the abbey *scriptorium*,
gifts, and purchase. In the books that he himself copied—for he
was a skilled scribe, as well as a custodian of books—he inscribed
twelve hexameter lines, concluding with a friendly admonition to
the reader:[1]

> Observe, sweet friend, the copyist's heavy toil;
> Take, open, read but harm not, close, replace.

[1] Dulcis amice, gravem scribendi attende laborem;
Tolle, aperi, recita, ne laedas, claude, repone.
See W. Wattenbach, *Das Schriftwesen im Mittelalter*, p. 575.

The bulk of the surviving *codices Augienses* are still kept together and form the most valuable part of the manuscript collection in the Landesbibliothek at Karlsruhe. The general character of the library at Reichenau in the ninth century was very similar to that at St Gall. Here as there religious works in great variety formed the largest class. Besides these there was a notable array of legal codes and grammatical treatises. A catalogue written in the second half of the ninth century is chiefly of interest because it enumerates an impressive series of classical writers, as follows: Persius and Juvenal, Ovid's *Art of Love* and *Metamorphoses*, Silius Italicus, Statius, Macrobius, Chalcidius' translation of Plato's *Timaeus*, the *Letters* and *Natural Questions* of the younger Seneca, Hyginus, Sallust's *Catiline*, Justinus' abridgement of Pompeius Trogus, and Claudian. The abbey of Murbach in the Vosges had been founded from Reichenau in 725 and close relations between the two abbeys continued. A Murbach catalogue of the ninth century shows that by *c.* 850 its library was substantial and even possessed authors who at that date were rarities, like Lucretius and Frontinus.[1]

We may end the list of libraries with Bobbio. Reference has already been made to its library and *scriptorium* during the Lombard period.[2] The earliest catalogue to survive was compiled in the later ninth century.[3] By that date the monastery had acquired a collection of unusual richness. The extant list is long, embracing between six and seven hundred titles. There is a noble array of sacred and profane authors. Among the latter are Terence, Lucretius, Virgil, Horace, Lucan, Persius, Juvenal, Martial, Ovid, Valerius Flaccus, Claudian, and Ausonius. Prose of the classical period is rather poorly represented by Cicero's *Catilinarian Orations* with the *Topica* and *Partitiones*, the elder Seneca, and Pliny's *Natural History*. All the more varied and numerous were the works bearing on each of the liberal arts and the collection of Christian poets. The largest part of the library was the theological and hagiographical section, but this need not be described in detail.

[1] The Murbach catalogue has been published by Hermann Bloch in *Strassburger Festschrift zur XLVI Versammlung deutscher Philologen* (1901).

[2] See above, p. 173.

[3] Becker, *op. cit.*, No. 32. For the date see M. Esposito in *Journ. Theol. Stud.*, 32 (1930/1), pp. 337ff.

Marginalia and colophons of manuscripts often throw interesting sidelights on monastic life. Irish monks sometimes reveal their presence in an abbey by comments in their vernacular or in their peculiar script, or both, in extant manuscripts known to have belonged to that particular foundation. Where silence was a strict rule, as was usual in *scriptoria*, a written conversation might still be carried on between two neighbouring scribes, commenting on the coldness of the weather or the hairiness of the vellum used for writing on.[1] The scribe at Fleury who referred to his monastery as a humble prayer house, inserting a couplet (of his own composition?) in the middle of computistical selections, must have had an 'off' day.[2] Entries at the beginning or close of manuscripts are not uncommon, though they are not often as long as that of Winitharius nor as well composed as Reginbert's. Another exceptionally detailed example occurs in a manuscript written in 823 and now in Munich (*Clm.*, 14437). It reads as follows:[3]

> I, Baturicus, bishop at Ratisbon, in the name of God had this book copied for the salvation of my soul. It was written in seven days and revised on the eighth in the same place, in the seventh year of my episcopate and the year 823 of our Lord's Incarnation. Moreover, it was copied by Ellenhard and Dignus, while Hilduin supervised the correctness of the writing. Pray for us.

Entries of this kind, even if brief, are invaluable to the palaeographer. Thus, some manuscripts from the *scriptorium* in Cologne bear a notation that they were copied in the time of Hildebald. The cathedral at Rheims and the monasteries of St Thierry and

---

[1] Cf. W. M. Lindsay, *Palaeographia latina*, II, p. 24.

[2] In *Harleian* 3017, written at Fleury in the later ninth century. The manuscript is made up of computistical material with some extracts from Isidore and Bede. The couplet is at the foot of folio 87r., and reads:

> Haec sursum mittit buttis quos colligit ignes
> Ut querulas fugiat lacrimas haec parva prose(u)che.

The last three words are repeated and glossed in the margin 'parva domus'. Another curiosity of this *codex* is the confession (*ordo paenitentiae*) inserted on fol. 181v. to 182r. Its wording is nearly identical with that in *Vallicell*, D5, published by H. J. Schmitz, *Die Bussbücher und die Bussdisziplin der Kirche* (Mainz, 1883), p. 88.

[3] Latin text in W. M. Lindsay, *Notae latinae*, p. 468. Baturicus was bishop of Ratisbon for thirty years.

St Remi received books by gift from archbishop Hincmar, and manuscripts at Lyons still bear the *ex voto* of Leidrad or one or other of his successors.[1] Exhortations to the reader, like that of the scribe who wrote, 'turn the pages gently, reader, wash your hands, hold the books so, and lay something between it and your dress' are not so frequent.[2] But the best-known type of such entries is that which indicates the monastery or chapter library to which the book belongs; appended very often is a curse on any thief or would-be thief. Most commonly the concluding formula is simple: 'Whoever shall steal this book, may he be accursed.'[3] But it is not unusual to find scribes writing down more elaborate imprecations. A ninth-century manuscript of Juvenal and Persius has an *ex libris* note, *codex Sancti Nazarii Martiris Christi*, which tells us that it belonged to Lorsch. This entry is followed by a twice-repeated couplet, which may be rendered in English:

> Whoe'er this book to make his own doth plot,
> The fires of Hell and brimstone be his lot.[4]

At St Gall Hartmut composed a series of short poems for his manuscripts, some of which imprecate possible thieves.[5] Sometimes these entries are in prose, and two fairly elaborate examples may conclude this chapter: 'This is the book of St Maximin, which Hatto caused to be written for the glory of God and St Maximin, with such intent that, whoever shall take it from this place, intending not to return it, may he be damned in company with the devil.' 'If sudden death, which God forbid, shall overtake our intimate friend, I implore him by Almighty God into whose hands this volume of Augustine on the Holy Trinity shall pass, to see that it is restored to Saint Kylian.'[6]

[1] Cf. L. W. Jones, *The Script of Cologne*, p. 18; F. M. Carey, *Studies in honor of E. K. Rand*, p. 49; S. Tafel, *Palaeographia latina*, IV, pp. 51-3.
[2] Wattenbach, *op. cit.*, p. 284.
[3] Qui hunc librum furaverit, anathema sit.
[4] Qui cupit hunc librum sibimet contendere privum,
Hic Flegetonteas patiatur sulphure flammas.
Cf. W. M. Lindsay, *Palaeographia latina*, III, p. 12.
[5] *MGH*, Poet., IV, pp. 1109-12.
[6] Bischoff and Hoffmann, *Libri Sancti Kyliani*, p. 97 with Plate 15.

CHAPTER X

The Study of Greek

Much has been written in modern times on the knowledge of Greek in Western Europe during the earlier Middle Ages. Opinions on the subject have sometimes diverged widely. In general, however, the older writers, it must be emphasized, were in the habit of absurdly overestimating the extent to which this language was studied and understood. Their attitude was uncritical because the mere occurrence of occasional Greek words in an author seemed to them sufficient proof that he was something of a Hellenist. The first scholar who, in dealing with this as with so many other topics, opened up a new approach to a difficult subject was Ludwig Traube. Whilst warning against the assumption of his predecessors, he argued that the Irish were virtually the only students of Greek, and that the occurrence of *Graeca*, Greek words or tags, in a manuscript pointed to Irish authorship or influence. There has been in turn some reaction to these views in recent years and a distinct tendency to underestimate the contribution made by the Irish. But Traube's thesis is still sound, if by Irish we understand those who came to the Continent from Columban's time on; for there is no satisfactory evidence that they could have acquired any Greek, apart from a few ecclesiastical terms, in their homeland.[1] The old view, though entirely lacking in proof, is still met with from time to time, chiefly because those who propound it repeat what earlier books had asserted, without themselves investigating what is to be understood by 'a knowledge of Greek'. If by that phrase is meant the ability correctly to understand a Greek author theological or secular, or the Greek Bible, then assuredly competent Hellenists

[1] By far the best recent contribution to this subject is the essay, 'Das griechische Element in der abendländischen Bildung des Mittelalters', by Bernhard Bischoff in *Byzantinische Zeitschrift*, 44 (1951), pp. 27-55.

of the eighth and ninth centuries can be counted on one hand. If, on the other hand, it merely implies acquaintance with the Greek alphabet, with a few passages from the Greek liturgy, or with a few isolated Greek words or phrases, generally from the Old and New Testament, then the sum of the accomplished will be somewhat greater, though still small in proportion to the total number of literate men. It has been a radical fault of many modern discussions of the subject that little or no distinction has been drawn between the first and the second class that we have indicated. It would logically be as absurd to class a tyro, who had painfully mastered six chapters of Chardenal, and a holder of a University chair together by vaguely saying of both 'that they knew French'.

Bede, as we have seen, at least in his later years had acquired a sufficient mastery over Greek to carry through an important work of collation and textual criticism on a part of the New Testament; and the occurrence of *Graeca*, even if often derived from his sources, in his earliest commentaries on the Bible, shows that his interest in the language went back to his youth. Since the commentary on the Psalms, written in Irish minuscule of the eighth century and containing part of a Latin version of Theodore of Mopsuestia's commentary together with one by Julian of Aeclanum has now to be excluded from the list of writings once attributed to Columban, there is no evidence on which to attribute to him any knowledge of Greek.[1] The appearance here and there of Greek words in Adamnan proves no more than that he, like others later, had learnt the alphabet and picked up a certain stock of words and phrases. It has been asserted that Alcuin was something of a Grecian. His own works, which have been held to prove this, actually demonstrate the contrary; indeed they afford us a very instructive explanation of the true state of affairs in his own writings and those of other eighth- and ninth-century authors. Comparison with Alcuin's sources shows that the Greek words and their explanation in his Biblical commentaries and elsewhere were generally taken from Jerome. Similarly, technical terms and their definitions in his school treatises come from earlier grammarians that he used. In one place (*PL*, 100, 777B) he gives

[1] See above, p. 143, note 1.

his readers a mystical explanation of the name Adam which he says is formed from the initial letters of the Greek words for north, south, east, and west. But this piece of allegory occurs as early as a third-century treatise attributed falsely to Cyprian and also in Augustine. In one of his letters (*Epist.*, 162) he cites from the Psalter in Greek; but no book of the Bible was more studied than the Psalms and, as we shall see, bilingual Psalters were not uncommon in Alcuin's day and after.[1] Even less than Alcuin can Hrabanus, his pupil, aspire to the honour of being called a Grecian; for the *Graeca* in his commentaries and in his treatise on the education of the clergy are uniformly derived from his sources. Walahfrid Strabo, who had been trained at Reichenau before he became for a time the disciple and amanuensis of Hrabanus, was also connected by ties of friendship with St Gall. There, if not earlier, he may have become interested in the Greek liturgy and, perhaps with the help of some Irish teacher, have acquired some Greek rudiments. In his exceptionally interesting little treatise on ritual and liturgical uses, *De exordiis et incrementis quarundam in observationibus ecclesiasticis rerum*, he shows his curiosity in linguistics, when he remarks: 'The Latins and all who employ Latin books and the Latin language have taken over from the Greeks, *ecclesia*, baptism, chrism, and the roots of nearly all words' and he adds that the Germans (*Theotisci*) similarly have borrowed from the Latins certain words of everyday use and nearly all terms used in the liturgy. And in two chapters of this work (6 and 7) he gives etymologies of Greek ecclesiastical and some other terms.[2] Yet it must be admitted that these derivations hardly go beyond what he could have found in bilingual glossaries.

Walahfrid's contemporary, Servatus Lupus, can be credited with a similar smattering of Greek. In one letter he requests Einhard to tell him the meaning of certain Greek nouns and

---

[1] The derivation of Adam from the initial letters of ἀνατολή, δύσις, μεσημβρία, and ἄρκτος is found in the tract, *De montibus Sina et Sion* (*CSEL*, III, 3, p. 108, 5 ff.) and also in Augustine on the Gospel of St John (*PL*, 35, col. 1473) and on the Psalms (*PL*, 37, col. 1236). The *Graeca* in *PL*, 100, coll. 1014B and 1025A come from Jerome, *PL*, 26, coll. 566A and 597B.

[2] There are two editions of *De exordiis*, one in *MGH*, Capit., II, pp. 474ff., the other by A. Knöpfler, in *Veröffentlichungen aus dem Kirchenhistorischen Seminar*, München, No. 1 (1890). The passage quoted above is in Chapter 7.

Greek phrases employed by Servius. He discusses the quantity of the second syllable in *blasphemus*, knowing that it is a Greek word, and points out on the authority of Prudentius that it is long. On the other hand, he notes that *Graecus quidam*—probably an Irishman with a little Greek rather than a Greek—had argued that the syllable was short, a view to which Einhard also adhered.[1] To Gottschalk he writes, in answer to a request to explain certain words, that he is postponing his explanation because for the moment he is not sure of the exact meaning of the words asked and is too busy to go further into the matter, and he adds that he is fully aware that the precise significance of Greek words had better be sought from Greeks.[2] It looks as if the good abbot was a little disingenuous and willing to leave an impression of greater knowledge than he possessed on his correspondent. Still, it is obvious that so widely read a man as Lupus must have picked up or at least recognized as Greek a good many words in the Latin authors that he studied. When he ventures on etymology he is no better than other men of his time; what he offers was the common property of the better sort of Carolingian schoolmasters, as when he expounds the derivation of *fialas*.[3]

It must be remembered that even now manuscripts written in uncials between the fifth and the seventh century survive which contain the Psalter or parts of the New Testament in both Greek and Latin. Such were the Laudian Acts used by Bede or the *codex Bezae*, and, when the Carolingian renaissance got under way, no doubt more of these venerable tomes existed than now. They would be useful for teaching the elements of Greek; indeed,

---

[1] *Epist.*, 5 (ed. Levillain, I, p. 50); *Epist.*, 8 (*ibid.*, p. 64). The point is that the 'Greek' and Einhard pronounced *blasphemus* accentually and ignored the quantities of the vowels.

[2] *Epist.*, 80 (ed. Levillain, II, p. 54). To show how old notions die hard, I may be forgiven for referring to a long and friendly review of the first edition of this book by so distinguished a medievalist as the late Léon Levillain (*Moyen Âge*, 42, pp. 226–35). In opposition to the estimate above he maintained that Lupus, and indeed Alcuin, Hrabanus, and Einhard must have had an adequate acquaintance with Greek because it was the diplomatic language of the Byzantine Empire. Such *a priori* statements are surely without value when unsupported by evidence drawn from the extant writings of these men.

[3] *Epist.*, 8 (I, p. 66). The same derivation is found in Martin of Laon and after him in Remigius. See *Bulletin of the J. Rylands Library*, IX (1925), p. 133.

one extant Psalter evidently served this purpose.[1] At St Gall there were certainly unusual facilities for absorbing at least a beginner's knowledge of Greek; nor is it unlikely that the elementary stages, consisting of learning the alphabet and some portions of the liturgy, were mastered by a few of the brethren. The presence of Irish monks there in the eighth and ninth centuries, and the evidence of extant St Gall manuscripts written by Irish scribes, show whence came the attention given to this language. Among surviving *Sangallenses* are two bilingual Psalters and a fine volume containing the Gospels in Greek and Latin.[2] In others we find portions of the Greek liturgy, but too much must not be made of this evidence. Parts of the liturgy in Greek were used on certain stated occasions in several western European centres and even included in the Roman rite. Greek versions of the Creed, Lord's Prayer, the *Gloria*, or *Kyrie eleison*, sometimes written in Greek, sometimes transliterated into Latin characters, are not uncommon in Western manuscripts. A later ninth-century codex containing the *Pater noster* in both languages is a book of Tours, while on one page of a Reichenau manuscript the *Gloria* has been inscribed with an interlinear Latin rendering. A Harleian manuscript (5642) contains the *Gloria* and *Sanctus* partly in Latin, partly in Greek characters, while one from St Denis has the *Gloria* and *Credo* in the two languages.[3] Copyists in *scriptoria* were often familiar with the Greek alphabet and it is nothing uncommon to find Greek capitals used in writing the abbreviation of *Jesus Christus*. Or again, one finds Latin phrases, like *Deo gratias amen* or *Deo gratias semper*, but written in Greek characters, or even Greek invocations, like 'Pity me', 'Help me', 'Save me'.[4] Sometimes Greek words in a Latin Patristic author are glossed in the margin with a Latin translation, as for example in Jerome's commentaries on Isaiah (*Sangall.*, 113–15) and on Ezekiel (*Sangall.*,

[1] *CLA*, IV, No. 472, with Dr Lowe's comment at the end, based on entries on the second folio. Another bilingual Psalter is *CLA*, V, No. 520.

[2] See *SMAH*, II, St Gallen, Plates XIV and XXVI.

[3] For further examples see particularly Egon Wellesz, "Eastern Elements in Western Chant" (*Monumenta Musicae Byzantinae*, 1947), Chapters 3 and 4. For traces of the liturgical use of Greek at Metz cf. E. Kantorowicz, *Laudes Regiae* (Berkeley, 1946), pp. 27–8.

[4] Cf. B. Bischoff, *Byzantinische Zeitschrift*, 44, p. 35, note 7 and his *Südostdeutsche Schreibschulen*, p. 97.

117–18). Finally a good many bilingual glossaries and phrase-books copied in the ninth century or later have come down to us, though the material that they contain is usually much older.

The chief literary figure in St Gall in the later ninth century was Notker the poet, nicknamed Balbulus (the stammerer). His knowledge of Greek was, like that of most of his contemporaries, quite superficial, consisting of some liturgical terms and perhaps a few conversational phrases derived from glossaries, Greek liturgical pieces in manuscripts or Biblical commentaries. To state that he interspersed Greek words in his Latin, as some writers have said,[1] is contrary to fact. In his poems and in the forty sequences which, according to the latest editor, were cer-tainly composed by Notker himself, there are fewer than a dozen Greek words and these, with one exception, he could have found in a glossary. The exception is *spermologos* which, together with the interpretation of the word, Notker found in Bede's commen-tary on Acts.[2] The existence of a group of monks, contemporary with Notker and nicknamed *Ellenici fratres*, cannot be regarded as certain, since there is doubt about the authorship of the so-called *Epistle to Lantbert* in which alone they are named.[3] Ermen-rich, who was for some time at the monastery of Ellwangen and

[1] *E.g.*, J. E. Sandys, *History of Classical Scholarship*, I, p. 479, and J. M. Clark, *Abbey of St Gall*, p. 109.

[2] See von den Steinen, *Notker der Dichter*, pp. 579–80, and *Editionsband*, p. 62, for the sequence. He remarks that *spermologos* was a term of abuse which Notker evidently wished to use in an opposite sense; but he has not observed that the interpretation of *spermologos* as one who sows the seed of God's word is at least as old as Augustine. Bede on Acts xvii, 18, so interprets it in his commentary (p. 65, 26 of my edition), of which there were two copies at St Gall by the end of the ninth century (259, end of the 8th century and 260, late 9th century). Then in his *Retractation* (p. 137, 7 ff.) Bede quotes from a sermon of Augustine's (*PL*, 38, col. 808) in which Augustine *inter alia* remarks: 'Dictum est quidem ab inridentibus, sed non respuendum est a credentibus; erat enim ille re vera seminator verborum, sed messor morum.' This interpretation is found also in Arator's epic on Acts 2, 443 ff.

[3] The authenticity of the *Epistle*, which is attributed to Notker in only one of nine extant manuscripts, and that by no means the oldest, was denied by R. van Doren, *Influence musicale de l'abbaye de St Gall*, Chapter X. Von den Steinen (p. 495) abruptly rejects van Doren's arguments without further discussion, accepting the *Epistle* as genuine apparently on stylistic grounds. This, in face of the other evidence, is not convincing. The additional testi-mony of Ekkehart IV, writing in the eleventh century, is worth little; for Ekkehart, though an attractive story-teller, is not a reliable chronicler.

ended his career as bishop of Passau (865–74), had studied at Fulda, Reichenau, and St Gall. Moreover, it has been shown that all the works, sacred and profane—and there are more than thirty of them—which he used or quoted in his long and exceedingly pedantic *Epistle to Grimald* were available in the libraries of the two last-named abbeys. It was probably also at St Gall that he dabbled in Greek. His incursions into that language, in so far as they do not merely reproduce his sources, are such as he could have derived from bilingual glossaries and phrase-books.[1]

West of the Rhine there were several centres of Irish influence —Liége in the time of Sedulius, Laon, Rheims, while John Scotus taught there—and it is in these that we find some evidence for the active study of Greek. A smattering may have passed also through Heiric's influence to Auxerre, while Stavelot, or at any rate one of its teachers, Christian, may well have had contacts with Sedulius and Liége. A Greek Psalter, now in the library of the Arsenal in Paris (MS. 8047), was copied by Sedulius, as we learn from the Greek subscription; 'I, Sedulius Scottus, wrote it.' The surviving specimens of *Graeca* by Martin of Laon, in his *Scholica Graecarum Glossarum* and in a manuscript now in the municipal library at Laon (MS. 444), suggest that even the Irish for the most part lacked a thorough understanding of the language.[2] Yet these efforts at mastering it were decidedly more ambitious than those of their pupils. It was certainly a task of some difficulty to render the Greek quotations in Priscian into Latin, especially the Homeric tags. It must be admitted that Martin often blundered badly. But a generation later Remigius, the pupil of Heiric, to judge by his commentaries on Martianus and on Boethius' *Consolatio*, knew even less.

Christian of Stavelot's occupation with Greek appears to have been entirely in the interests of Biblical exegesis and of a better understanding of the Bible by comparing the Greek with the

---

[1] The *Graeca* occur especially in the versified passages. A line like *Oenon paleon pimelin gallan eleon* (*MGH*, Epist., V, p. 569, 31), glossed *vinum butyrum bibe lac oleum*, is just a string of vocables from a word-list forced into the semblance of a hexameter. He also repeats the mystical meaning of Adam which he probably found in Alcuin. See above, p. 240, note 1.

[2] For the *Scholica* see *Bulletin of the J. Rylands Library*, VII (1923), pp. 421–56, and for *Laudunensis*, 444 Bischoff, *Byzantinische Zeitschrift*, 44, p. 40, with note 2.

Latin version.[1] A similar use of Greek for theological ends occurs in a letter penned by an unidentified Irishman about the middle of the ninth century. He is concerned with the translation and textual criticism of the Psalter and quotes a number of passages from it in Greek. He also appends brief explanations of the critical signs, five in number, that were found in ancient manuscripts of the Psalms. He makes use of earlier authorities, particularly Jerome, but there can be no doubt that his comparisons of the two languages are based on some personal knowledge.[2]

Peculiar interest attaches to two translations made in the ninth century of an unusually difficult Greek author. It was probably near the end of the fifth century of our era that an unknown writer, possibly of Syrian origin, composed four treatises and ten letters, in which he strove to build up a system of Christian mysticism to combat that of the Neoplatonists. He was himself deeply imbued with Neoplatonic doctrines and in fact relied heavily on the last of the Neoplatonists, Proclus, from whose writings he sometimes copied verbally. He called himself Dionysius, claimed to be a pupil of St Paul, and in his works introduced by name sundry persons who flourished in the first century after Christ, thereby trying to strengthen the impression that his books were genuine products of the sub-Apostolic Age. He was more successful in making posterity believe this unabashed fiction than he had perhaps dared to hope. As early as the sixth century his identity with Dionysius the Areopagite (Acts xvii, 34) was generally assumed in the East, although Hypatius of Ephesus in 533 openly declared the works a forgery. In the West, too, they were accepted as genuine from the first, and in spite of the doubts expressed by Laurentius Valla and Erasmus, their authenticity remained virtually unquestioned until the seventeenth century. In the West, moreover, a curious complication was introduced by the identification at the beginning of the ninth century of the Parisian martyr Dionysius (St Denys) with the pseudo-Areopagite. For giving not merely currency but authority to this

---

[1] See *Harvard Theol. Rev.*, 20 (1927), pp. 142–5. The reference in note 49 to the *Ellenici fratres* should be deleted.

[2] *MGH*, Epist., VI, pp. 201 ff. The writer probably lived in northern Italy; cf. Kenney, p. 569.

ingenious, if glaring, fiction, abbot Hilduin and the monks of
St Denis were apparently responsible.[1] The first record in the
West of the Greek original of the pseudo-Dionysius is found in a
letter sent by Pope Paul I to Pippin in 758, together with a manu-
script of the treatises. In 827 the Byzantine emperor Michael,
amongst other valuable gifts which he sent by an embassy to
Louis the Pious, included a fine uncial codex of the pseudo-
Dionysius. This manuscript survives and is now in the National
Library in Paris (*MS* gr. 437). From it not later than 835 a Latin
version was made under the direction of Hilduin. Since the
Greek original was written in uncials, the words were not
separated and there are few accents, with the result that errors in
reading could easily be made. The translation was a work of
collaboration between two or three persons; for some of the
mistakes made can only be explained on the assumption that one
monk would read the Greek text aloud, and that the translator
and copyist occasionally misunderstood what they had heard.
This earliest Latin version of the *Corpus Dionysiacum* is preserved
in several extant manuscripts and was used by Hincmar and
Paschasius Radbertus.[2] It was, however, extremely literal and
clumsy, and so a generation later John Scotus was commissioned
by Charles the Bald to undertake a fresh translation. It included
both the letters and the four treatises and seems to have been
completed not later than 862. A comparison of the two versions
makes it certain that John had before him not only the Greek
manuscript but Hilduin's translation, though he does not refer
to his predecessor. This silence, though it may conflict with
modern notions about literary property, need occasion no surprise. The medieval scholar thought differently on this subject
and it is the exception rather than the rule for him to indicate his
sources, unless he is merely assembling a *collectaneum* of passages
on a given topic from his predecessors. John's translation was
then basically a revision, but it was thorough and he had the
Greek original constantly before him. Although he too occasionally lapsed into error, his translation is a far more accurate

[1] G. Théry in *Moyen Âge*, 25 (1923), pp. 111 ff., and in *Mélanges Mandonnet*,
II (Paris, 1930), pp. 23–30.
[2] See G. Théry, *Études dionysiennes*, two volumes (Paris, 1932–7).

presentation of the pseudo-Dionysius and at the same time it is more intelligible because expressed in better Latin. For some mistakes John cannot rightly be blamed. It happens that the Greek manuscript used by him and Hilduin is extremely faulty and also shows some *lacunae*, so that some mistranslations are due to errors in the original text. A further consequence is that, as John's version not only superseded Hilduin's, but was for several centuries the source from which the West derived its knowledge of the pseudo-Dionysius, Western scholars were misled on some aspects of Dionysiac theology until the thirteenth century.[1]

John made other translations from the Greek. Again at the king's request he produced a Latin version of the *Ambigua* by Maximus Confessor (died 662). This work was made up of difficult passages from the homilies of Gregory of Nazianzus together with a commentary. Since Maximus used the pseudo-Dionysius for his exposition, John in preparing his Latin version was on ground that was already in part familiar. He also translated, wholly or in part, the treatise *De opificio hominis*, a discussion of Genesis i, 26, by Gregory of Nyssa. He calls it *Sermo de imagine* and seemingly confused Gregory of Nazianzus with Gregory of Nyssa. Parts of a Latin rendering of Epiphanius' *Ancoratus* may also be attributed to John with great probability; but there is more doubt about an extant Latin version of the *Solutiones* of Priscianus Lydus. The Greek original of this work, which was composed in the sixth century and deals with various topics of natural science and natural history, is lost; the translation has been attributed to John but is probably not his.[2] The commentaries which John composed to elucidate further the meaning of the pseudo-Dionysius, and here and there also to justify his own translation, afford additional proof that his linguistic equipment was very respectable. Especially noteworthy, moreover, in an epoch when allegorical interpretation was all but universal, is the fact that he assigns to this quite a subordinate place in his

[1] For the thorough revision or 'translation' of John's version made by Jean Sarrazin in the twelfth century see now G. Théry in *Studia mediaevalia in honorem . . . R. J. Martin* (Bruges, 1948), pp. 359–381.

[2] See M. Cappuyns, *Jean Scot Erigène*, pp. 148–9.

commentaries. Finally a few specimens of Greek verse composed by John survive.

The only man in the West whose knowledge of Greek was comparable to John's was Anastasius. After a stormy career he had become Papal librarian during the papacy of Hadrian II. He states that he had learnt Greek in his youth and subsequently he had excellent opportunities for improving his mastery of the language, since he attended the Eighth Council of Constantinople in 869 as an official delegate. Yet his numerous translations do not impress one with any peculiar excellence. They include versions of some Greek saints' lives and of the Acts of both the Seventh and the Eighth Councils of Constantinople. His *Chronographia tripartita* is a continuation of Cassiodorus' *Tripartite History* and shows that Anastasius' primary interest was in the doctrinal disputes which were causing increasing friction between East and West. The *Chronographia* is an abbreviated adaptation of three Byzantine historians, Nicephorus, Syncellus, and Theophanes, and the translation is sometimes so free as to become a mere paraphrase. His turns of phrase from one language into the other are frequently clumsy and sometimes betray an incomplete understanding of the original. In short, his limitations as a translator were marked and he does not deserve the reputation of a great Hellenist with which he has sometimes been credited. There is therefore a certain irony in the fact that Anastasius presumed to criticize the translation of the *Corpus Dionysiacum* by John Scotus.[1] In a letter of 875 addressed to Charles the Bald he expresses surprise that John, *ille vir barbarus* from a remote part of the world, should have attained such mastery of Greek.[2] Indeed, John is singularly blest, since it is the Holy Spirit which has inspired him to fulfil his task. After such patronizing praise Anastasius proceeds to carp at John's translations on account of their excessive faithfulness to the original and their occasional obscurity. This criticism is to some extent justified. But to imply, as Anastasius does, that John himself was

---

[1] The letter which Pope Nicolas I is supposed to have written to Charles the Bald in 859, complaining that John's translation had not been sent to him for approval, is a later forgery. See Cappuyns, *op. cit.*, pp. 155–7.

[2] *Epist.*, 13 (*MGH*, Epist., VII, pp. 430–34).

confused, is absurd. As his own philosophical *magnum opus* proves, he himself had mastered the meaning of the pseudo-Dionysius, even though he could not always make it simply intelligible to others in a Latin translation. Anastasius did not carry out a revision of John's work; but he added some *scholia* taken from Maximus and John of Scythopolis and also some glosses. Some of this material is preserved in several extant manuscripts, but it is still unpublished.[1] One cannot help feeling that he was piqued that there lived in Neustria one who was a better Greek scholar than himself, and his assumption of modesty in several letters must not be taken too seriously. He admits that his own translations were literal. He expects to be criticized, but comforts himself with the modest reflection that his fate will resemble St Jerome's. Yet one must sympathize with him when he expresses the hope that any critic of his work will come out into the open against him instead of 'lacerating his brother's flesh behind his back with the tooth of envy'![2]

An attempt has been made to appraise fairly the evidence provided by authors and manuscripts of the Carolingian Age. The conclusion to be drawn is as decisive as it is unflattering to the pretensions of some writers of that epoch. John Scotus and Anastasius were both capable of making serious errors. Nevertheless they must be put in a class by themselves as Greek scholars. Far more limited was the acquaintance with a second language of men like Sedulius, Martin of Laon, and a handful of others. Yet their purpose was serious, even if their performance fell greatly short of accurate understanding or translation. A long way behind them is the little band of those whose Greek amounted not even to an elementary knowledge of the *language*, but only to familiarity with the alphabet and with a sprinkling of common words or phrases. To repeat a small portion of the Greek liturgy was no more than a feat of memorization; that it was a mechanical process is suggested by the more or less phonetic transcriptions into Latin characters that still survive. To some the introduction

---

[1] Cf. Cappuyns, *op. cit.*, pp. 160–1, and A. Siegmund, *Die Ueberlieferung der griechisch christlichen Literatur*, pp. 191 ff.

[2] *MGH*, Epist., VII, p. 442, 19—nec post dorsum fratris carnes invidentiae dente decerpat.

of a Greek word in a Latin treatise or even a poem was a mark of culture and elevated style. The writer who aspired to these qualities would make the most of the few tags that he had acquired from his teachers or culled himself from some Latin author, like Jerome, or from some glossary to which he had access. This mannerism gave its user a semblance of learning to which he was not entitled. His contemporaries were sometimes misled by outward appearances. Others in more recent times have fallen into the same error, but with less excuse.[1]

[1] In the Byzantine enclave in southern Italy and in Rome, where many Greek monks had found a refuge during the Monothelite disputes of the seventh century, there was considerable activity in translating Greek saints' lives, homilies, and some dogmatic works, as well as Acts of Eastern councils, into Latin. Cf., for example, A. Siegmund, *op. cit.*, pp. 195 ff.

CHAPTER XI

The Literature of the Carolingian Age

(a) The Study of Classical Latin Literature

Like some uncharted comet, the Irishman Sedulius appeared in Liége about the middle of the ninth century, to vanish again after a decade (*c.* 848–58) as mysteriously as he had come. Evidently an attractive personality, endowed also with a certain gift for composing occasional verse, he enjoyed the good-will and friendship of royalty and nobility no less than of his ecclesiastical superiors. As a scholar he was versatile though hardly profound. But, apart from his excursions into Biblical exegesis and political theory and his poetic efforts, which will be considered in subsequent chapters, he was one of a very small group of men who ventured into the more advanced branches of *grammatica*. The main interest of his *Collectaneum*, or collection of excerpts, lies in the wide variety of authors with which he had some acquaintance. Of these, if we leave aside Patristic selections, the more rare at that date were the treatises on warfare and tactics by Vegetius and Frontinus, Valerius Maximus, the Augustan History, and Macrobius' commentary on the *Dream of Scipio* from Cicero's *De republica*. Still more remarkable is the Irishman's rather extensive knowledge of Cicero; for he made extracts from the *De inventione, Paradoxa*, the fourth and fifth books of the *Tusculan Disputations*, the *Philippics*, and the orations, *Pro Fonteio, Pro Flacco*, and *In Pisonem*. That Sedulius had access to no less than seven works by Rome's greatest prose writer is a very noteworthy circumstance, when it is remembered that few scholars of the Carolingian Age knew more than two or three. Although the total number of Ciceronian writings then known was considerable, many libraries had only single works and only a few were better stocked.[1]

[1] Cf. M. Manitius, *Handschriften antiker Autoren in mittelalterlichen Bibliothekskatalogen*, pp. 19 ff.

The purpose which Sedulius had in view in making these short excerpts from classical and post-classical authors was to assemble in a brief compass what might be regarded as pithy observations and moral maxims. In consequence neither questions of textual criticism nor, often enough, the subject-matter of what he was reading had any compelling interest for him. Indeed, he does not hesitate to ignore the context of, for example, passages in a Ciceronian speech appropriate to a particular case, since he is intent only on what, in isolation, would pass as sentiments of general validity. Most of the excerpts are short; but his concern for ethics led him to include a few longer selections from the *De inventione* and from the fourth book of the *Tusculan Disputations*. He was, moreover, not without some understanding of philosophical questions other than ethical. In addition he had a practical interest in the style of his authors, noting down sentences that contained a striking phrase or turn of expression, such as he or his readers could use to advantage in their own literary efforts.

Propter se ipsam appetenda sapientia! This sentiment, occurring in a letter full of youthful enthusiasm, yet couched in terms of respectful admiration, which Lupus addressed to the venerable Einhard, then abbot of Seligenstadt, might well have been chosen by him as the motto of his life; for, compared with other men of the Carolingian Age, he achieved as solitary a pre-eminence in the field of humanistic studies as his contemporary John Scotus did in philosophy.

Lupus was born during the last decade of Charlemagne's reign and was educated at Ferrières. In this abbey the Alcuinian ideals and methods must have been preserved for several generations; for Sigulfus, who became abbot in 796, had been Alcuin's pupil and is credited with the establishment of a monastic school there. And, just as the abbacy passed from Sigulfus to his pupil, Adalbert, so in 822 a disciple of Adalbert, Aldric, entered into the succession. When Lupus was being educated in Ferrières the scholastic resources of the monastery do not seem to have been great. He implies that the study of the seven liberal arts was not looked on with favour, just as, some years later, he lamented the growing decline in culture in more general terms. The poverty of Ferrières compared with many other religious houses in Neustria was doubtless a contributing cause, if only because the library there, until Lupus became abbot, appears to have been small. When he was about twenty-five and had already been ordained deacon, he was sent by Aldric to Fulda in order to complete his studies. Nothing shows more perspicuously how within a quarter of a century the centre of Higher Education had shifted from the western to the eastern half of the Frankish Empire. During the years that Lupus spent in Fulda, he enjoyed the tuition and friendship of the greatest teacher of the day, Hrabanus, who had become head of the abbey in 822. Lupus corresponded with Einhard and somewhat later visited him at Seligenstadt, and he made many friends who in later years became, like himself, the heads of religious houses. With them he kept up a regular correspondence on literary and theological subjects after he had returned to Ferrières in 836. Six years later he succeeded Odo as abbot. During his twenty years' tenure of this office he was an extremely busy man.[1] Besides performing his duties as abbot, he had frequently to attend at court; he was obliged on several occasions to take part in the campaigns of Charles the Bald; more than once he was called upon to act as an emissary of the king; and he attended no less than ten ecclesiastical synods and three diets. It is well to bear these facts in mind in order better to appreciate the greatness of his achievement as a teacher and scholar. However busy he was with affairs, his enthusiasm for humanistic studies and his industry never flagged. That we are so well informed about his literary and other activities is due to the survival of one hundred and twenty-seven letters written by him between 830 and 862, and those that deal with his scholarly pursuits are unique in that age.[2] One particular interest of his, moreover, can now be further illustrated with the help of extant manuscripts that were once in his hands. First in importance,

[1] The latest letter that can be dated was written in 862. In the same year Lupus' name appears in the Acts of the Synod of Pistes.

[2] The best edition of the letters is by Léon Levillain in two volumes (1927–35). Of 133 letters there printed 126 are by Lupus. To these should be added the letter printed in *MGH*, Epist., VI, p. 115. As C. H. Beeson has shown (*Studies in honor of E. K. Rand*, pp. 1–7), it can safely be assigned to Lupus. References below are to Levillain's edition.

since it was copied throughout by Lupus, is a codex of Cicero's *De oratore* now in the British Museum (*Harleian* 2736). The date at which he wrote it is not established with complete certainty, but it is not unlikely that he made his copy from a manuscript which he had borrowed from Einhard in 835 or 836.[1] Certainly he was an expert scribe before this date, since he had, while still at Fulda, written and illuminated a large manuscript, in which five Germanic law codes were brought together. In addition there are at least a dozen other codices which were revised or annotated by Lupus. Amongst them are the Valerius Maximus at Berne (No. 366), Aulus Gellius (Vatican, *Regin.*, 597) and Ti. Claudius Donatus' commentary on the first six books of the *Aeneid* (*Regin.*, 1484), and four manuscripts now in Paris, Cicero's *De inventione* (*Lat.* 7774A), Livy, Books VI to X (*Lat.*, 5726), the *Letters* of Symmachus (*Lat.*, 8623), and Macrobius' *Commentary on the Somnium Scipionis* (*Lat.*, 6370). It is significant, as showing the close connexion between Ferrières and Tours in the time of Lupus, that four of these manuscripts (Paris, *Lat.*, 5726, 6370, and 7774A, and Vatican, *Regin.*, 1484) are *libri Turonenses*.[2] In a codex of Augustine's sermons, now in the Vatican (*Vat. lat.*, 474), there is an entry on folio 95r to the effect that the manuscript up to that point had been collated with the exemplar and punctuated by Lupus, and a manuscript containing certain of the philosophical works of Cicero (Vienna, 189) was once Lupus' property.[3]

The contents of his correspondence are astonishingly varied. The letters illustrate the abbot's unceasing care for his monastery and the labours of the brethren in orchard and field, as well as in the school, oratory, and *scriptorium*. The abbey had expert craftsmen too, for we find Lupus sending an ivory comb to the bishop of Poitiers and finely cut and polished jewels to the king.[4] The difficulties and dangers of travel were great owing to robbers

[1] *Harleian*, 2736 has been published in facsimile by C. H. Beeson under the title *Servatus Lupus as scribe and text critic* (Cambridge, Mass., 1930).

[2] E. A. Lowe lists thirteen 'Lupus' manuscripts, but one of these is doubtful. See *Persecution and Liberty: Essays in honor of G. L. Burr* (New York, 1931), pp. 63–4.

[3] See C. H. Beeson, *Classical Philology*, 40 (1945), pp. 202 and 219. The Vienna manuscript, which is not in Lowe's list, is the oldest codex containing the so-called Leyden corpus of Cicero's philosophical works.

[4] *Epist.*, 23 and 124.

and pirates; indeed, Ferrières more than once was in danger from Norman sea-raiders. It was not always safe to send manuscripts from one library to another. Lupus is afraid to send Bede's *Collectaneum on the Pauline Epistles* to archbishop Hincmar in Rheims, 'because the book is so large that it cannot be concealed in the folds of one's dress nor conveniently stowed away in a wallet'.[1] There are many allusions to the constant campaigns of Charles the Bald and the participation of Lupus and some of his monks in them, as well as to the abbot's various missions. On one such occasion he was sent to Burgundy and was unfortunate enough to lose ten horses, on another he visited Brittany.[2] But the dominant and recurring theme in the letters is literature and kindred topics. Lupus was indefatigable in increasing the resources of his library. He borrowed manuscripts from Einhard, from Tours, Prüm, Fulda, and other monasteries; he even wrote to Altsigus of York and to Pope Benedict III. When he took steps to get a copy made at Ferrières of some book that its library lacked he was doing no more than was done by many scholarly abbots and librarians of his time. What is unparalleled is his unflagging eagerness to obtain a second manuscript of some work that he already possessed in order to collate the two and improve his own copy. Sometimes his own codex was defective so that he sought another in order to fill up *lacunae*. In such circumstances he applied to Benedict III for Cicero's *De oratore* and for Quintilian.[3] His own manuscripts of these treatises were incomplete and his previous efforts to obtain the book from York (*Epist.*, 87) had evidently been unsuccessful. The list of secular authors with which he was familiar is notable. Of Cicero he knew, besides *De inventione* and *De oratore*, the eight works in the Vienna manuscript,[4] the *Tusculan Disputations, De officiis, De senectute*, the *Verrine Orations*, a collection of letters, and the translation of Aratus' *Phaenomena*. He borrowed copies from Ansbald of Prüm so that he might amplify his own defective copy of the *Aratea*, and that by comparing two manuscripts of the letters he might establish an improved text.[5] Virgil, the *Rhetorica ad Herennium*,

[1] *Epist.*, 108.   [2] *Epist.*, 45 and 83.   [3] *Epist.*, 100.
[4] i.e., *De natura deorum, De divinatione, De fato, Timaeus, Topica, Paradoxa, Lucullus, De legibus.*   [5] *Epist.*, 69.

some Livy—how much we do not know, but the Paris manuscript that he revised contains only Books VI to X—Sallust's *Catiline* and *Jugurtha*, Caesar's *Gallic Wars*, Valerius Maximus, Suetonius, Aulus Gellius swell the series of classical authors. Whether he knew any Horace directly is very doubtful; for one tag that he quotes he found in Jerome and the other may have come from a similar source or from a grammarian.[1] He also quotes Martial twice in an early letter, but here again it is likely that he cites at second hand.[2] Caesar he calls no historian and adds that only *De bello gallico* is extant, but that, after Caesar's death, Hirtius composed another set of commentaries.[3] Further, Lupus certainly had a wide acquaintance with grammarians and commentators, although those actually named or quoted by him are not specially numerous.[4] Besides the *De arithmetica* and the commentary on Cicero's *Topica*, Lupus knew also the *Consolatio* of Boethius, and he was familiar with the Latin Josephus.

Admiration for the unusual quality of Lupus' classical scholarship has led most modern writers to ignore or minimize his attainments as a theologian. It is true that apart from two brief saints' lives and a sermon that has only recently been printed,[5] his only contribution to theological literature was a single treatise supported by a *collectaneum* of relevant passages from the Fathers. In this *Liber de tribus quaestionibus* three topics are discussed, the nature of free will, predestination, and redemption. But by writing it Lupus not only took part in the most lively ecclesiastical controversy of his age, but also, by the method of his treatment, showed himself a skilled dialectician at a time when dialectics were still very imperfectly developed.[6] From the *collectaneum* and from abundant references and quotations in his

---

[1] *Satires*, I, 10, 34 quoted in *Epist.*, 1, and in a Jerome extract in *De tribus quaestionibus: collectaneum*, p. 256 (ed. Baluze). In *Epist.*, 31, *non potest vox missa reverti* recalls *Ars Poetica*, 390.

[2] *Epist.*, 8.   [3] *Epist.*, 95.

[4] He may, for example, have known Nonius Marcellus' dictionary, for in *Epist.*, 121 he uses *succussatura* and *tolutim*. The former occurs in our copies of Nonius, the latter in the *Glossae Nonii* in C.G.L. vol. V., 651, 46.

[5] By W. Levison, *Aus rheinischer und fränkischer Frühzeit*, pp. 557 ff.

[6] Hence Grabmann (I, p. 198) included him among the forerunners of Scholasticism.

letters in which he occasionally discoursed on theological questions, a clear picture emerges. He knew his Bible intimately; for in the letters alone there are more than one hundred and fifty quotations from or reminiscences of the Old and New Testament and of deutero-canonical books like Wisdom, Ecclesiasticus, and Tobit. He had read widely in theological authors from Ambrose to Alcuin and Hrabanus, and the list of his reading includes less-known works like a Latin version of Chrysostom on Hebrews, Philippus on Job, and Faustus of Riez's treatise on Divine Grace and free will. If, then, we would have a whole, not a partial view of Lupus as an intellectual force in the ninth century, it is essential to take into account his occupation with a branch of knowledge in which he did write one book, as well as his devotion to classical literature, which he signalized in none but only in his correspondence.

The topics on which he touched in the letters and the queries of others to which he sent replies are remarkably varied. At one time he discusses metrical and grammatical points in answer to an inquiry from Adalgaudus, abbot of Fleury, illustrating his remarks with citations from Virgil, Priscian, Servius, and Juvencus;[1] at another he informs Altuin, a monk at Mayence, of the proper scansion of *bibliotheca* and *statera*, and explains the formation of certain unusual words, like *nundinae* and *sistrum*.[2] The last-named correspondent on the same occasion received a disquisition on comets from his learned friend together with references to Virgil, Justin, and Josephus. To Gottschalk Lupus writes for the purpose of elucidating a passage in Augustine's *City of God* (22, 29) concerning the appearance of Christ in bodily form after the Resurrection.[3] With the help of a Servius quotation he seeks to enlighten another friend on the meaning of the words *pater patratus*.[4] Citing a sentence from Valerius Maximus, he would explain to Charles the Bald that the secret of Rome's success as an imperial power was the high sense of public duty exhibited by her senatorial rulers.[5] His method in the extant manuscripts on which he worked as scribe or textual critic is not without interest.[6] In the

---

[1] *Epist.*, 21.   [2] *Epist.*, 8.   [3] *Epist.*, 80.   [4] *Epist.*, 125.   [5] *Epist.*, 37.
[6] For fuller details of Lupus' procedure see C. H. Beeson, *Servatus Lupus*, pp. 21–40, and the article by E. A. Lowe quoted above, page 254, note 2.

Harleian manuscript he left vacant spaces wherever a word was missing in his exemplar or where he suspected a corruption. The *lacunae* he planned to fill in as far as possible when opportunity of comparing another codex offered. He also frequently marks places where there is no omission in the manuscript, if he fails to understand the text, or if he thinks that it contains some error, or even if he merely desires to note for future use some point that interests him. There is, moreover, a good sprinkling of marginal or interlinear corrections and variant readings in the margins of the various Lupus manuscripts; and his method of dividing one word between the end of one line and the beginning of the next deviates from the usual practice of scribes. In the Harleian Cicero, the Berne Valerius Maximus, and the Vatican Gellius he entered specially in the margin many words which for one reason or another seemed to him noteworthy.[1] Some he may have regarded as useful to enlarge his own literary vocabulary, others he may have intended to explain to his pupils when lecturing on the authors in question, or, more generally, when teaching them the finer points of Latin composition. One aspect, or rather result, of Lupus' literary work must not be overlooked. In his earliest letter to Einhard (*Epist.*, 1) he appears to imply that even as an adolescent pupil in Ferrières he was already a keen Ciceronian. No better proof of the thoroughness with which he had studied and absorbed many of Cicero's works can be adduced than his own literary style. No writer since Bede was a master of such pure latinity as Lupus, although the styles of the two men are quite dissimilar. Cicero certainly had a large share in forming Lupus', but the influence of the Vulgate is also very apparent. There is nothing very surprising in the fact that his mode of expression varies to some extent according to his correspondent. To near and dear friends, like Marcward of Prüm, he writes in a simple straightforward manner; in addressing Charles the Bald or some eminent ecclesiastic whom he knows but distantly, he employs a more elevated style. He indulges in more citations, especially from the Scriptures, and does not disdain occasional flights of pure rhetoric. Even then, however, his ear and his taste are too good

---

[1] For a long marginal insertion written by Lupus see E. K. Rand and L. W. Jones, *Earliest Book of Tours* (Cambridge, Mass., 1934), Plate XLIX.

to let him lapse into the turgid and often tortuous periods affected, for example, by his contemporary, Anastasius.

Lupus, who lamented in general terms what he believed to be the degeneracy of the times, and particularly deplored the decline in scholarship, was one of the men to whom the revival of letters under Charles the Bald was mainly due.[1] Nor did his influence die with him. Something of his ideals and methods doubtless lived on in many of his pupils, who in turn passed on what they had learnt to a third generation. Yet so imperfect are our records that the handing on of this tradition can only be illustrated in a single instance. Few of Lupus' disciples are even known by name, but one of them was Heiric (c. 841–76). Entering the monastery of Auxerre as a young boy he received his early education there. As a young man he continued his studies for a while at Ferrières, Laon, and Soissons. The combination is important; for it meant that a second tradition, differing from Lupus', helped to mould Heiric's mind, that of the Irish monks at Laon. Heiric's chief claim to literary fame is a long poem on St Germanus of Auxerre, but he also left behind certain other works which are a direct outcome of his studies under Lupus at Ferrières. In several manuscripts there is preserved a collection of extracts, some of considerable length, from Suetonius and Valerius Maximus. They were taken down by Heiric from the lectures and dictation of Lupus, whose detailed study of these authors has already been noted. Other writers excerpted by the monk of Auxerre were the *Sententiae philosophorum* of Caecilius Balbus, itself a collection of moral maxims from various sources, Solinus, and Petronius. He also appears, when established as a teacher at Auxerre, to have studied and lectured on the Roman satirists. Reminiscences in his poem, moreover, make it plain that he was

---

[1] Cf. *Epist.*, 31, 45, and 120; and the outburst in the *Life of St Maximin*, Chapter 4—Sed, o nostri temporis mores degeneri! omnes pene iam nervi pristini roboris conciderunt. Levibus terroribus fracta cessit constantia. Pluris pecunia quam iustitia aestimatur. Quis iam imperatoribus divinorum praeceptorum reserare salutarem severitatem non reformidet? Quis eis sua pericula, zelo divini timoris accensus, absque fuco adulationis aperiat? Incidentally, this passage with its Ciceronian thunder would be sufficient by itself to establish Lupus' authorship of this piece of hagiography. The sympathy of Charles to Lupus' efforts to stimulate afresh the study of the liberal arts is reflected in *Epist.*, 122.

acquainted with the *Odes* and *Epodes* of Horace.[1] His fame as an educator and scholar was deservedly great, and the two streams of cultural influence, from Ferrières and from Laon, which were united in him, were transmitted on to many pupils. Of these the best known were Hucbald and Remigius. The latter seems to have succeeded his master for a while at Auxerre; but in 893 he and Hucbald were called to Rheims. There the two worked to improve the school and its educational standards which seem to have declined after the death of John Scotus and archbishop Hincmar. During the last years of his life Remigius taught at Paris, where amongst others he instructed Odo, destined in later life to be the second abbot of Cluny. Untiring as a teacher, Remigius found time also for a vast quantity of writing. He was an indefatigable commentator whose lengthy disquisitions on more than a dozen different authors enjoyed greater popularity than their contents or their methods deserved. In connexion with the liberal arts he expounded Donatus, Phocas, Eutyches, Priscian, the *De arte metrica* and perhaps also *De schematibus*[2] by Bede, and above all, Martianus Capella. The secular writers who engaged his attention and gave employment to his pen were Juvenal, the *Disticha Catonis*, Sedulius, and perhaps Terence and Boethius' *Consolatio*. His theological studies comprised a treatise on the Mass, and commentaries on Boethius' *Tractates*, and on several Books of the Bible. There are some other works whose authorship is more doubtful, but their general tenor suggests that at least they were products of Remigius' school. Only a portion of this enormous output has survived and of this only a fraction has been published. One is left with the impression that the didactic zeal of Remigius greatly outstripped his natural gifts. Furthermore, it would have taken an intellectual giant to combine so prolific an authorship with great originality or marked profundity of thought and method. His reading had been wide not deep. He borrows wholesale from his predecessors and commonly omits to indicate the source of his indebtedness. Yet, in spite of all, the fact remains that, while he did not as a rule probe very far, he crowded so much information, miscellaneous and not

---

[1] See *MGH*, Poet., III, p. 424 with note 3.
[2] See J. P. Elder in *Medieval Studies*, 9 (1947), pp. 141–50.

always well digested though it was, into his own writings, avoiding at the same time prolixity in his own additions, that some at least of his expositions, especially those on Donatus and on Martianus, drove earlier commentaries out of the field.

(b) History and Biography

It is scarcely surprising that the study of history and geography fared rather poorly in the early Middle Ages. If historical writing was to be treated, as it was by the majority of Greek and Roman authors, as a form of literary art, then it required a degree of culture and expertness in style and composition to which none of the subjects of Charlemagne and his successors could aspire. If, on the other hand, the artistic side be disregarded, and the only criterion by which to judge historical works is taken to be an accurate presentation of events and a proper understanding of their interrelation, together with an intelligent appraisal of the part played by the human actors in them, then the character of the times and the circumstances in which histories or annals were composed were too often unfavourable to the attainment of even approximately high standards. Penetrating analysis of historical data presupposes either deep and wide reading, coupled with a vivid imagination, or else, especially if the field covered be narrower, at least a personal experience of affairs. Where a writer had at least the second qualification, as, for example, Nithard did, the result was a presentation which, even if stylistically mediocre, had undoubted merits as an outspoken and shrewd record of important events. But there was one factor which made even Nithard's achievement a rarity amongst writers of contemporary history, namely the fear of authority or a partiality for ruling princes. The second of these detrimentally affected even Einhard, so that what was amiable in the man became a fault in the biographer.

A great body of annalistic literature compiled in the eighth and ninth centuries has survived. Unhappily the appraisal of its historical value is inseparably linked with the origin of the different annals and the nature of their interdependence, and there is still no sort of unanimity amongst modern critics regarding the intricate problems involved. From early times it had doubtless become customary in monastic houses to jot down in the briefest possible form any noteworthy occurrences, whether local or affecting a wider area, on the monastic calendars used for calculating the correct date of Easter. Such Easter tables, moreover, might be copied in this or that abbey for the benefit of another. When they began to contain historical *marginalia*, those were copied as well and perhaps augmented in their new home. Such would be the genesis of the simplest annalistic records. But Easter tables were based on lunar reckoning and, being calculated on different recurring cycles of years, had shown great variation. When a new method of calculation was adopted in any area, based on another cycle, the tables previously in use would be discarded and annalistic jottings that they contained would tend to be lost at the same time.[1] Surviving annals of late Merovingian and of Frankish times are many. The earlier group begin at the end of the seventh century, like the *Annales Mettenses priores*, or at the beginning of the eighth, like the *Annales Sancti Amandi* or *Annales Mosellani*, and they are brief and sketchy. As the eighth century progressed several developments can be observed: continuations were composed, the notices under successive years become fuller, and additions in one set of annals were made by incorporating material from another set or sets. Distinct from these compilations, which are to some extent local, though the place of their composition is more often than not still a matter of dispute, are the longer, or as they are now usually called, the *Royal Annals*, which are identical with the compilation formerly known as the *Annales Laurissenses maiores*. Their character precludes the possibility of their composition at Lorsch or in any other monastery. They have the king as their central figure and they chronicle his campaigns and the chief measures of his government. They begin in 741 and extend to 829. Great diversity of opinion has reigned in modern times with regard to their authorship. More particularly efforts have often been made to prove that Einhard was the author of some portion. The different, and for the most part mutually destructive, theories which have been voiced,

[1] Cf. Charles W. Jones, *Saints' Lives and Chronicles*, pp. 9–15, and the list of Easter tables given on pp. 202–3.

attributing this or that section to the biographer of Charlemagne, when marshalled together read like a *reductio ad absurdum* of criticism. It may be safely said that Einhard cannot have had any hand in their composition.[1] More important, but also controversial, is the relation of the *Royal Annals* to the shorter annals composed in the eighth century. Attempts have been made, especially by Halphen, to demonstrate the priority of the *Royal Annals*. He has argued with great ingenuity that the various shorter annals, which he would arrange into five or six groups, were all derived to a greater or less degree from the *Royal Annals*. His researches have thrown much light on an intricate problem, but his main contention cannot be accepted, and the older view, that the *Royal Annals* drew some of their material from the earlier among the shorter annals, still holds the field.[2]

It is clear that not one but several authors were responsible for the several sections into which the *Royal Annals* fall. The so-called *Annales Bertiniani* form a continuation of the *Royal Annals* and extend to the year 882. The writers of almost the whole of that compilation are known; for the section from 835 to 861 was put together by Prudentius, bishop of Troyes, while for the continuation, extending from 862 to 882, the redoubtable archbishop of Rheims, Hincmar, was responsible. This last section has an interest of its own; for, so far from being reasonably objective, it reflects the strong personal feelings which Hincmar entertained against some of his political and ecclesiastical opponents. The *Annals of St Vaast* at Arras, which cover the years 874 to 900, are specially valuable from the year in which the *Annales Bertiniani* stop.

A portion of the *Royal Annals* was also worked over and amplified. This version has come to be known under the separate title of *Annales Einhardi*. Again there is no sort of warrant for the name, since Einhard was certainly not the author of this revision. But that it should have been attributed to him is not wholly surprising, since in one class of manuscripts containing Einhard's *Life of Charlemagne*, the biography is preceded by the

[1] Cf. L. Halphen, *Études critiques sur l'histoire de Charlemagne* (Paris, 1921), pp. 61–8.

[2] See *ibid.*, pp. 3–59. For the priority of the shorter annals see now Wattenbach, Levison and Loewe, *Deutschlands Geschichtsquellen im Mittelalter: Vorzeit und Karolinger*, Heft II (Weimar, 1953), pp. 182–3.

revised *Annals*. The revised version makes more pretensions to literary form than the original *Royal Annals*; they also add a number of details which are missing in the earlier compilation. For example, in the *Royal Annals* the Saxon war of 782 is very briefly noticed. There is a bare reference to 'rebellious Slavs', and the military operations which followed are summarized in a few words. The author of the revision, on the other hand, gives topographical details of raids carried out by the Slavs and stresses the magnitude of their devastations. He also recounts the military operations with considerable fullness. Indeed, his preoccupation with Saxon affairs in various passages has led to the quite improbable assumption that he was himself a Saxon. Very striking, too, is the narrative of the end of the Spanish war in 778 in the two versions. The earlier account merely states that after the destruction of Pampeluna and the subjugation of the Vascones and of Navarre Charles returned to Frankland. The reviser, however, gives a short but graphic account of the disaster at Roncesvalles:[1]

> Charles levelled the walls of Pampeluna to the ground so that the place might not revolt. Then, deciding to return, he entered a pass of the Pyrenees. At its summit the Vascones had set an ambush, and having assaulted the rear column of the Frankish army threw the whole body into the greatest confusion. And, although it was seen that the Franks were a match for the Vascones both in armature and in courage, they succumbed because of the mountainous locality and the unequal nature of the contest. The infliction of this disaster overshadowed a great part of the success of the Spanish campaign in the king's heart.

The *Royal Annals* provide the reader with a brief, unadorned narrative; but, being restricted in scope, they leave him in the dark on many topics connected with the political, diplomatic, and military history with which they deal. Nor must one expect analysis of motives or a deeper understanding of cause and effect in a plain annalistic record of events. Nevertheless the *Royal Annals* must be regarded as the most important single source for the reign of Charlemagne, and must form the basis of any historical reconstruction of that momentous era in European history.

[1] *MGH*, SS., I, pp. 158–9.

Of the longer annals recounting the course of events from the point where the *Royal Annals* break off, the *Annales Fuldenses* must be named in addition to the *Annales Bertiniani* and *Annals of St Vaast*, which form the continuation of the *Royal Annals*. The name which has become attached to the *Annales Fuldenses* once more is inappropriate, since they seem to have been compiled at Mayence, not at Fulda. The most valuable section covers the period from 838 to 887. It appears to be an independent source, the work of a single writer, whose style and approach to his subject have a characteristic quality of their own, even though the accuracy of his statements must be checked by reference to other extant works. He had a particular interest for affairs in the eastern half of what had once been Charlemagne's empire; for, as his narrative proceeds, East Frankish politics and wars engage his attention more and more. His style shows him to have been a man of superior literary gifts. Another hand, probably that of a Bavarian, added a continuation to 901, and there also appears to have existed a version, no longer preserved, which carried the narrative down to 911. The style of this part is inferior and the account itself betrays a political bias which is missing in the preceding portion. The continuation, moreover, from 887 has ceased to be purely annalistic. By putting speeches into the mouths of the principal actors in the historical drama the writer has fashioned a hybrid thing, annals masquerading as formal history.

Apart from the longer and shorter annals and local records kept by monasteries, historical composition had few exponents in the eighth and ninth centuries. Three writers made a serious attempt to imitate Bede by putting together a chronicle of world history. Freculph, who died in 853 as bishop of Lisieux, was a friend and contemporary of Hrabanus Maurus. From their correspondence it appears that Freculph at the beginning of his episcopal career (*c.* 825) found a pitiful absence of books and of education in his see. He must have remedied the former of these two evils with some success, for in his chronicle he shows acquaintance with a fair variety of sources. Its first part in seven books treats in brief compass the creation of the world and the early history of the Jews, the Assyrians, Medes, Persians, Greeks, Ptolemaic Egypt, the Maccabees, and Rome to the end of the

Republic. Freculph then decided to add a second part in five books. In it he sketched the history of the Roman Empire and its dismemberment to the pontificate of Gregory I and the establishment of the Lombard kingdom in Italy.[1] Judged absolutely, Freculph's achievement is modest enough. For the earlier part he relied on portions of Augustine, Alcuin's commentary on Genesis, Josephus, the chronicle of Eusebius with Jerome's continuation, Florus, and Orosius; for the later he used Orosius, Aurelius Victor, Rufinus' version of Eusebius' *Ecclesiastical History* with Rufinus' additions, Jerome's *De viris illustribus*, Cassiodorus' *Tripartite History*, the Gothic and Roman histories of Jordanes, and Bede. His chief stand-by, as natural, was Orosius. Nevertheless, the list of authors that he had read is varied and betokens width of reading, even if some of them were of small merit as writers of history. Freculph's familiarity with Florus, the *Epitome* of Aurelius Victor,[2] and Jordanes is of some interest, since these authors up to that time seem to have been little known in Western Europe. The bishop of Lisieux was evidently *persona grata* at court. He dedicated the second half of his book to the Empress Judith, and, years later, he sent to Charles the Bald a copy of Vegetius' treatise on warfare, which, since the manuscript was exceedingly corrupt, he had revised and corrected to the best of his power. It is also to be reckoned a merit in Freculph that he was not content to make his history a mere collection of extracts from his sources, but took the trouble to give it a more readable and literary form by skilfully joining the different excerpts and introducing transitional passages of his own composition. A generation after Freculph, Ado, bishop of Vienne (859–75), put together his *Breviarium Chronicorum*, a compilation from Adam to 869. For the earlier sections he relied mainly on Orosius, Isidore, and Bede, for the later parts he had recourse to some monastic annals and Einhard's *Life of Charlemagne*. He was also the author of a martyrology. His credibility for events near his own time is highly suspect; for in the

---

[1] The chronicle will be found in *PL*, 106, coll. 917 ff.

[2] Freculph, Lupus, and others in the ninth century knew only the *Epitome*, not the genuine Aurelius Victor whose *De Caesaribus* was exceedingly rare and survives in only two manuscripts.

Martyrology he introduced entries which he said he had taken from an ancient martyrology brought with him from Italy, but which were in fact forged by himself, and in the *Breviarium*, where he dealt with the affairs of his episcopal see, he was also guilty of falsifications. The third compiler of a general chronicle was Regino, who was abbot of Prüm in Lotharingia for seven years (892–9), and then of St Martin's at Trèves until his death in 915. Seven years before, he published his *Chronica*, dedicating it to the bishop of Salzburg. This chronicle begins with the birth of Christ, and the seven centuries and a half from that date to the death of Charles Martel are included in the first book. The second records the course of events from 741 to 906. The form of Regino's book was determined by his sources; for the occurrences of the earlier centuries are arranged according to the reigns of successive emperors, but the later part is annalistic. His chronology is extremely confused, and even for a short sketch the presentation of facts before the later part of the eighth century is very incomplete. He neglects almost everything in the earlier period which does not bear on the history of Christianity and the Church, while in describing the centuries nearest his own time, though the treatment becomes fuller, he is one-sided because he confines his attention almost wholly to the march of events in the western half of the Frankish Empire. His sources for the first four centuries were Bede's *Chronicle*, the Acts of the Apostles, some martyrologies and the *Gesta pontificum*; for the remainder of Book 1 he utilized a good deal of hagiographical material, as well as a Spanish collection of canons and decretals, the *Gesta regum Francorum*, Paul the Deacon's *History of the Lombards*, and some early annals. The early portions of Book 2 depend almost wholly on the *Royal Annals*; but for his account of the ninth century, which is the most valuable part of the *Chronica*, he appears to have consulted annals of Prüm, now lost, and probably some other annalistic sources which can no longer be identified, as well as some official documents. Freculph's *Historia* appears not infrequently in medieval catalogues, Ado's *Breviarium* and Regino's *Chronica* rarely. But extant manuscripts of all three works are not rare, and Ado, and particularly Regino, were well used by subsequent writers during several centuries, so that each of these compilations can be said to have been popular during the Middle Ages. The fact that they were composed, like the diversity and multiplicity of annals, betokens a lively and widespread appreciation of historical narrative. In particular, the consciousness that what they might well regard as a new era had begun in the eighth century led them to focus their attention with special interest on events nearest to their own time. Besides, it was a sign of wider comprehension, whatever the shortcomings of their performance, when a Freculph tried to supply his contemporaries with a background to the age in which they lived, and a Regino essayed to bring out the continuity of history by presenting his account of the ninth century not in isolation, but merely as the latest, if to him the most absorbing, development in human affairs. As he himself remarks: 'when I came nearer to our own time, I treated the story of my narrative with more elaboration. For, as Jerome observes, it is one thing to relate what one has seen and another to relate what one has heard. What we know best, we can best describe.'[1]

The achievement of Paul and of Nithard was of a different kind. Paul, son of Warnefrid, commonly called Paul the Deacon, whom we have already met as one of the notable scholars temporarily domiciled at the court of Charlemagne, was born about 720. The scion of a noble Lombard family, he was educated at the Lombard court and for some time after continued to live in Pavia, possibly filling some official position. In middle life he took monastic vows and retired (c. 774) to Monte Cassino. In 783 he visited the Frankish kingdom primarily to intercede with the king for his brother, who had been taken prisoner seven years before in a rebellion at Friaul against Frankish authority. Although his request was probably granted and his own reception by Charlemagne was most cordial, he did not stay in the North for more than a year or two. Then he returned to Monte Cassino where in his last years he composed a history of his people which was unfinished, or at least unrevised, at his death.

At all periods of his life Paul was devoted to scholarship and literature. The grounding that he had received from his teacher, Flavianus, must have been exceptionally good for that time, and

[1] *MGH*, SS., I, p. 566.

this, combined with his own further efforts to increase his knowledge, produced one of the best educated men of the day. His
own writings touched many fields—poetry, *grammatica*, theology,
and history. It was assuredly no light task to fashion an abridg-
ment of Pompeius Festus' dictionary, *De verborum significatu*,
with its abundance of Old Latin words and its miscellaneous
information about religion, antiquities, and law; and, since much
of the original work is lost, it is to Paul's shorter version that
modern philologists have to turn. Paul's first historical work was
an edition of the *Breviarium* of Roman history by Eutropius, which
he amplified by passages from Jerome, Orosius, and some other
writers. He then added a continuation down to Justinian, which
was based on seven or eight different sources. Fortunately it is
not necessary to judge his powers by this rather carelessly executed
Historia Romana; for his *Historia Langobardorum*, the work of his
maturity, enables one to form a very different estimate of his
historical talent. In the form in which it has come down to us it
comprises six books, tracing the fortunes of the Lombards from
their quasi-legendary beginnings to the death of King Liutprand
in 744. For the groundwork Paul utilized two earlier sketches of
Lombard history, which are now lost. He further relied for
different sections of his book on a variety of earlier authors, from
Pliny to Gregory of Tours, Isidore, and Bede. He had access, as
he himself explains (2, 20), to an old list of the Italian provinces
which he consulted when composing his chapters on the geography
of the peninsula.[1] Details were added from his own experience
or observation. He did not despise oral tradition and folk
legends, but allowed them a place here and there in his narrative.[2]
From such receptivity it was but a step to sheer credulity. But,
in view of the practice of many medieval and some ancient
historians, criticism of Paul for recording omens is disarmed. He
is weakest in chronology, so that the arrangement of his narrative
is sometimes exceedingly confused. He is often content to introduce a new occurrence with some vague phrase, like *circa haec
tempora* or *hac tempestate*, even if the preceding part of the narrative

---

[1] *Hist. Langob.* (ed. G. Waitz; Hanover, 1878), 2, 15–23.

[2] *ibid.*, 1, 5; 1, 2; 1, 6; 1, 15; and the story of Rodulfus and Rumetruda
in 1, 20.

took place some years before or after.[1] Apart from chronological vagaries, his story progresses in simple and unadorned language. Yet with all this economy of means Paul could pen a vivid description and could enliven the sometimes tedious succession of wars and intrigues by some passage of marked dramatic power. We see him at his best in the narrative of the war between Cunincpert and Duke Alahis or in the description of Aripert II who, like Harun ar Rashid, used to go about in disguise amongst his subjects at night.[2] As a specimen of Paul's art we may quote the story of the boy Grimoald.[3]

Now the Avars and their king having entered Fréjus pillaged everything that they could find. They burnt the city itself and led off as captives all persons whom they had discovered; yet, intending treachery, they held out to the prisoners the promise that they would settle them on the frontiers of Pannonia, the country from which they had set out. When on their way home they reached the region called *campus sacer*, they decided to put to the sword all the adult Lombards, while they divided the women and children by lot as slaves. But Taso, Cacco, and Raduald, the sons of Gisulfus and Romilda, divined their evil intent; so they straightway mounted their horses and took to flight. One of them wished to kill his brother Grimoald, a mere lad, thinking that he was too small to keep his seat on a galloping steed, and deeming it better to put him to the sword than to let him endure the yoke of captivity. Now when he raised his lance to pierce him the boy wept and cried out, saying: 'Do not run me through, for I can ride.' Thereupon grasping the boy by the arm, he lifted him on a horse without a saddle and encouraged him to keep his seat if he could. The boy, snatching the horse's reins, followed his fleeing brothers. On discovering what had happened the Avars quickly mounted and chased them. While the other fugitives escaped in swift flight, boy Grimoald was taken by one of the Avars who had ridden faster than he. However, his captor was loath to put him to the sword on account of his tender years; so he kept him intending that he should become his slave. Seizing the bridle of the boy's horse and turning him about in the direction of the camp he led him back and boasted of the noble spoil that was his; for the lad was well built and had brightly shining eyes

[1] Thus, for instance, the chronology of *Hist. Langob.*, 4, 1–24 moves hither and thither in the most distracting way. Again, in 4, 41, Columban's foundations at Luxeuil and Bobbio are introduced after the expulsion of Adaloald and the accession of Arioald as king in 626.

[2] *ibid.*, 5, 38–41; 6, 35.   [3] *ibid.*, 4, 37.

and masses of fair hair. He, on his part, as he was lamenting that he was being led off a prisoner, was 'turning over in his inmost heart a valiant resolve'. He drew from its sheath his sword, which was of a kind suited to his age, and, using all his strength, struck the Avar who was carrying him off on the crown of the head. Straightway the blow penetrated to the brain and the enemy fell from his horse. But boy Grimoald, turning his steed about, fled away with gladness in his heart and in due course rejoined his brothers. And he filled them with immeasurable joy at his escape and at the tale he told besides of his enemy's death.

Paul's *History of the Lombards* was an immense success. It appears frequently in medieval catalogues,[1] the number of extant manuscripts exceeds one hundred, and it was much used and imitated by medieval writers from the ninth to the fifteenth century. It was composed just in time when the fall of the Lombard kingdom was still a very recent memory. But for Paul the earlier *compendia* of Lombard history, the so-called *Origo gentis Langobardorum* and the chronicle of Secundus, both of which he used, and a great deal of traditional material which he incorporated in his book, would have been completely lost, and our knowledge of the latest of the Germanic invaders of Italy would be not a tithe of what it is. All of Paul's historical works dealt with past history. It is regrettable that he did not bring his narrative down to 774; for we cannot doubt that he would have given us an illuminating picture of the political events that occurred during his own youth. Yet it is possible that he never intended, being a Lombard of noble birth, to chronicle the painful story of the kingdom's final collapse.

The ninth-century historian Nithard deserves to rank as the most successful chronicler of contemporary events during the Carolingian Age; but because of its limited scope and slight interest for later generations his work was little read.[2] Nithard was of noble extraction, being the son of an irregular union between Angilbert, the lay-abbot of St Riquier, and Bertha, one of the daughters of Charlemagne. He evidently received what in those days was an exceptionally good education for a layman.

[1] Cf. M. Manitius, *HSS antiker Autoren*, pp. 351-4.

[2] The work survives in only one manuscript of the late ninth century and in an incomplete copy of this manuscript made in the fifteenth. The best edition, with notes and a French translation, is by Ph. Lauer (Paris, 1926).

Subsequently, as a staunch supporter of Charles the Bald in the political dissensions between the sons of Louis the Pious, he played an important part in the events which form the main theme of his history. He undertook to write it at the behest of Charles; but he tells his readers how he would have preferred to leave his task unfinished, first, because of the invidious nature of the subject, and secondly, because of his desire to have done with worldly affairs.[1] The first of the four books, which is introductory, sketches the troubled political history of Louis' reign; the other three give a more detailed account of the period from 839 to March 843. Nithard appears frankly as a partisan of Charles the Bald, whilst Lothar II in his conduct to Charles and to their brother, Louis the German, is the villain of the piece. At the same time the historian was an eyewitness of much that he relates; where he depended on the testimony of others he shows great discrimination. And, though he was the devoted henchman of Louis' youngest son, he does not write as a courtier but as an independent though sympathetic supporter. It is a great pity that the last book, which ends so abruptly as to make it probable that it was left incomplete, does not include a description of the Partition of Verdun. Nithard's interpretation of the events that he narrates, and especially his very unfavourable portrait of Lothar,[2] have stood the test of modern historical criticism and are accepted as substantially accurate. His narrative is severely plain, his style lacking in elegance, and he dispenses with all superfluities. Yet he has an eye for a picturesque detail, where it is strictly relevant. This is seen, for example, in the graphic account of Lothar's messengers arriving before Charles, when that prince was on the point of leaving his bath (2, 8). Again, he knows how to emphasize the importance and solemnity of a diplomatic agreement by actual quotation of the oaths taken by the contracting parties. Indeed, the description of the pact concluded by Charles and Louis II at Strassburg on February 14, 842, is of unique interest, because the historian has reproduced

---

[1] See the prefaces to Books 3 and 4.
[2] Cf. *Hist.*, 2, 7—Lodharius, uti praefatum est, dolo an vi Lodhuvicum aut subdere aut, quod mavult, perdere posset, tota mente tractabat. See also 4, 1, with a catalogue of Lothar's misdeeds.

the oaths taken by the two rulers and by their supporters in the two vernaculars. The version in the *lingua Romana* is the oldest extant specimen of a Romance language and this particular tongue was the immediate precursor of Old French.[1]

So far no mention has been made of biography, which was cultivated with varying success in the Carolingian era. As a work of literature Einhard's *Life of Charlemagne* occupies a class by itself. We have seen how the author, who was born in the Maingau about 770 and received his early education in Fulda, was sent to the imperial court where he was for a time a pupil of Alcuin. He became one of the members of the learned society surrounding the monarch whose favour and confidence he won; for he went as Charles' emissary to the Pope in 806 and was perhaps entrusted with other missions. He had developed a special interest in architecture and in consequence was charged with the general superintendence over all buildings erected in the capital by royal command; and he is said to have been the first to recommend Charlemagne to make his son, Louis, co-emperor in 813. His influence at court became even stronger under Louis the Pious and marks of royal favour continued to come to him. He became the lay-abbot of several abbeys, and it was to one of these, Seligenstadt, that he finally retired in 830, having up to that year spent some time annually at the court. He died in 840 and Hrabanus Maurus composed his epitaph.

He was a finished product of the schools of Fulda and of Alcuin. He had thoroughly mastered a learned language, his native tongue being Frankish (Old High German) and not the *lingua Romana* of the western half of the Empire which was the direct descendant of vernacular Latin. No early medieval writer more successfully imitated classical models than he; yet, like his only peer, Servatus Lupus, he also shows in his style the basic influence of the Bible and ecclesiastical Latin. The classical writer to whom he was especially indebted in the *Life* was, as was very natural, the biographer of the Caesars, Suetonius, whom he had probably read first when he was a student in Fulda. His imitation was thorough. It consists in the first place in the use of Suetonius' vocabulary

---

[1] *ibid.*, 3, 5. There is a facsimile of the page in the manuscript containing the oaths in Lauer's edition between pp. 100 and 101.

and characteristic idioms. This is most apparent in the later chapters of the biography where Einhard is portraying the character and private life of his hero; and, though with a conscious desire of juxtaposing the founders of the old and the new Roman Empire he draws most freely on the *Life of Augustus*, he borrows also from the other biographies, notably those of Tiberius, Vespasian, and Titus. But he does more than this; for he follows Suetonius also in grouping his material, and in the order in which he describes the various episodes of Charles' reign and the different aspects of the king's many-sided activity. Einhard's historical reading was, however, far from being restricted to a single author. In writing his prologue he clearly had in mind the introduction to the *Life of St Martin of Tours* by Sulpicius Severus; in the biography itself there are reminiscences of Caesar, Livy, Tacitus, Florus, Justin's abridgement of Trogus, and Orosius. Without doubt Einhard had made the most of his opportunities at Fulda, where the library was, as we have seen, unusually rich in historical authors.

The *Life of Charlemagne* was probably composed a good many years after the emperor's death. All that is certain is that it was completed before 830, the year in which Lupus mentions having seen it in the first of his extant letters to Einhard.[1] That it is a notable piece of literature and amongst the best of medieval biographies cannot be disputed. But its value as a historical document has been the subject of much dispute among modern critics. It contains a good many errors of detail and of chronology. The notion that too close adherence to his model led Einhard perhaps unconsciously to distort Charlemagne's character and habits by forcing him into the likeness of Augustus is indeed somewhat illusory; for Einhard was steeped in Suetonius as a whole, not merely in the *Life of Augustus*. In other words, there was enough variety in vocabulary and in description in the biographies of twelve Caesars to enable Einhard, who must have known them wellnigh by heart, to find all that he needed without falsifying, for the sake of a neat phrase, the portrait of the

---

[1] The best editions are by Holder-Egger (*Scriptores rerum Germanicarum in usum scholarum*, 1911) and by Halphen (*Classiques de l'histoire de France*; ed. 2, 1938).

emperor. On the other hand, it is undoubtedly true that partiality for Charles, and insufficient information about his earlier years and some of his more distant campaigns, may have led Einhard to omit or gloss over certain episodes and to confuse others. To expect complete impartiality is to demand the impossible. Einhard's long acquaintance with the emperor, and his many years of residence at the court, had peculiarly fitted him in some respects to act as biographer; but there was also one inevitable disadvantage, especially as he continued to be *persona grata* at the court for many years after 814. The trusted friend of Charles and Louis may surely be forgiven if he exhibits an occasional bias. Yet, for example, he admits that Charlemagne could be ruthless to his enemies.[1] Moreover, a number of episodes in the king's career, on which Einhard touches so lightly that some have thought him guilty of deliberately suppressing the truth, belong to the earlier period of Charles' life. It is therefore possible to assume that the narrative there is unsatisfactory because Einhard had insufficient data. Matters like Charles' quarrel with his brother, Carloman, or his relations with and subsequent suppression of the last Lombard king, whose sister he had repudiated after marriage, were topics of which the king himself was perhaps the only person who could have given a complete account. Yet even a close friend was wise to refrain from catechizing Charles on such intimate questions! There are other passages where Einhard's defective narrative cannot reasonably be excused; others, again, which have been needlessly called in question. In short, the *Life* should be no more exempt from historical criticism than any other source, and its statements must be tested in the light of all the available evidence.

It is a far cry from Einhard to other biographers of the Carolingian Age. The life of Louis the Pious engaged the attention of two contemporaries. The one, Theganus, a rural or suffragan bishop in the diocese of Trèves, composed his biography two years before Louis' death; the other *Life* is by an unknown author

---

[1] Cf. Chapter 8 (Saxon war) or 13 (campaign against the Avars) where we find this outspoken passage: 'Quot proelia in eo gesta, quantum sanguinis effusum sit, testatur vacua omni habitatore Pannonia et locus in quo regia Kagani erat ita desertus ut ne vestigium quidem in eo humanae habitationis appareat. Tota in hoc bello Hunorum nobilitas periit, tota gloria decidit.'

who wrote it some years after 839.[1] Theganus' work from every point of view is an exceedingly poor production. His style is bald and disfigured by numerous solecisms and grammatical errors. His material, which was fairly ample, was never properly digested by him; the individual facts are strung loosely together without any attempt on the part of the author to weld them into an organic whole. Over and above these grave faults, the tone of uncritical adulation of the monarch and of undignified railing against his opponents are highly distasteful. It is a sad reflection that Theganus, with such an example as Einhard's *Life* before him—and he borrowed some phrases from it and adapted them to his own hero—could not do better.[2]

The anonymous biography is a worthier composition in every way. It is better written and arranged, though it is not a work of any originality. Its chief value lies in the fact that the earlier part of the narrative was drawn from an unusually qualified witness, the monk Adhemar who was brought up in the same convent as Louis. It is not certain whether the author obtained his information orally from Adhemar or whether the monk, as is not unlikely, had composed a historical narrative now lost. For the rest the 'Astronomer' relied on annals and on Einhard's *Life of Charlemagne*.

(c) Hagiography

The example set by the Venerable Bede in writing the lives of the abbots of Wearmouth and Jarrow found many imitators. At the request of bishop Angilram, Paul the Deacon compiled a history of the bishops of Metz. A generation later it was consulted by Einhard when he was writing his *Life of Charlemagne*.[3] The lives of the archbishops of Ravenna were described by Agnellus (c. 805–54). This work is chiefly noteworthy because the author assembled a large variety of official documents, inscriptions,

---

[1] The writer has been dubbed Astronomus, the astronomer, because he reproduces a conversation on astronomy between the emperor and himself in 838 when a comet was visible in the sky. The information is not without value, since it shows that the author was in close touch with the court. Text in *MGH*, SS., II, pp. 604ff.

[2] Text in *MGH*, SS., II, pp. 590ff. and *PL*, 106, coll. 405–28.

[3] Cf. *Vita Caroli*, 2, 15, 18, and 20. Text of the *History* in *MGH*, SS., II, pp. 260ff. Agnellus' book in *MGH*, Script. Lang., pp. 275ff.

letters, and epitaphs, and incorporated them in his narrative. Consequently, although the book is devoid of literary merit, it is a historical source of unusual value. The *Gesta abbatum Fontanellensium* was composed by an unknown monk and completed shortly before 840. Superficially it resembles Bede's *Lives of the abbots*, since it deals with successive heads of the abbey of St Vandrille in Normandy. But the author did not confine his interest to the abbots of his foundation. He adds details about other inmates of the monastery, about the growth of the library and the provision made for instruction, so that the *Gesta*, not without justice, has been described as the 'first monastic chronicle of the West'.[1] In addition to earlier historical and hagiographical works, he made some use of monastic archives. Other writers were content to make the life of a single prelate the theme of their biographical writing. Amongst the best of these works in its kind is the *Life of Boniface*. Written by Willibald, an English priest, it is, apart from the intrinsic interest of its subject, a competent and adequate work, where the author relies on contemporary evidence; but there are also some striking omissions in it. An exceptional portrayal of an exceptional man is the *Life of Anskar*, once a monk at Corbie and in the daughter house in Westphalian Corvey and later bishop of Hamburg-Bremen, by his successor in that diocese, Rimbert. Besides being a sober, clearly written narrative, this biography deserves special attention because it throws precious light on conditions in the Scandinavian countries, with which, owing to the geographical position of his see, Anskar was frequently brought into contact.[2] Other examples of straightforward narrative, in which the miraculous and legendary find no place are the *Life of Sturmi*, first abbot of Fulda, by Eigil, who became abbot of that monastery in 817, and the accounts of Baugulf, the second abbot, and of Eigil by the monk, Bruun.[3] Save for the fact that the subjects of these

---

[1] By W. Levison; see *Aus rheinischer und fränkischer Frühzeit*, pp. 530–50. For the date cf. P. Grierson in *Engl. Hist. Rev.*, 55 (1940), pp. 275 ff.

[2] Best edition by G. Waitz, *SS. rerum Germanicarum* (Hannover, 1884). The *Life* is extant in a longer and a shorter version. W. Levison, *op. cit.*, pp. 567–609, has shown that the longer is the original.

[3] *Life of Sturmi*, MGH, SS., II, pp. 365 ff.; *Life of Eigil*, MGH, SS., XV, pp. 221 ff., the *Life of Baugulf* is lost.

biographies were religious leaders one would hardly classify them as hagiographies. The *Epitaphium Arsenii*, composed by Radbert of Corbie, falls into a special category of its own. It describes the career of Wala, abbot of Corbie (died 836), who had been involved in the political affairs of his time. He had many enemies and his reputation had suffered. Radbert wrote the first book of the *Life* in 836, the second not till some fifteen years later. Since the controversies in which Wala had played a part were of very recent date, his biographer introduced his real characters under fictitious names. Wala became Arsenius, Louis the Pious Justinian, and Judith Justina, and the emperor's sons and some other personages were similarly disguised. The form of the book is also unusual, since it is composed as a dialogue. Once it is understood that the *Epitaphium* is not a plain biography but frankly intended to rehabilitate the good name of the dead abbot, its historical worth is considerable, even as the literary device adopted by Radbert is unique at that date.[1]

The remarkable development in hagiographical literature characteristic of the ninth century was in part at least the outcome of the steadily increasing popularity of relics and the worship of saints. The attitude of Charlemagne, expressed both in the *Libri Carolini* and elsewhere,[2] was patently determined by a wish to restrict a form of worship which, being in harmony with the widespread credulity of laity and clergy, might easily lead men away from the fundamental truths of Christianity and become debased into superstition. At the same time it was natural that in an age distinguished by improved education and a great literary

---

[1] Critical edition of the *Epitaphium* by E. Dümmler in *Abhandlungen*, Prussian Academy, for 1900, II, pp. 18 ff.

[2] Cf. the following passages from capitularies of 794 and 813: ut nulli novi sancti colantur aut invocentur nec memoria eorum per vias erigantur; sed hii soli in ecclesia venerandi sint qui ex auctoritate passionum aut vitae merito electi sint (*MGH*, Capit., I, p. 77, para. 42). Quid de his dicendum, qui, quasi ad amorem Dei et sanctorum sive martyrum sive confessorum ossa et reliquias sanctorum corporum de loco ad locum transferunt ibique novas basilicas construunt et, quoscumque potuerint ut res suas illuc tradant, instantissime adhortantur? Ille siquidem vult, ut videatur quasi bene facere seque propter hoc factum bene meritum apud Deum fieri, quibus potest persuadere episcopis: palam sit hoc ideo factum, ut ad aliam veniat potestatem (*ibid.*, p. 163, para. 7).

revival a form of literature which had long been esteemed should receive renewed attention. It is no accident that so many leading writers, beginning with Alcuin himself, at some period of their career tried their hand at religious biography. The restrictions of the king-emperor, supported as they would be by the leading Churchmen, did not remain without effect. But it was only for a time; for Charlemagne's successor had neither the will nor the power to maintain and enforce them. The protests of lesser men, for example, the fulminations of Claudius of Turin, found no sympathetic echo elsewhere. On the contrary, from the time of Louis the Pious the desire to obtain relics of saints increased rapidly. Distance and the hazards attendant upon the transport of such precious remains were no obstacle. The relics, or what were reputed to be such since fraud was by no means unknown, of saints and martyrs were brought from Italy to all parts of the Frankish Empire, from France to Westphalia, even from Jerusalem to the West.[1] The installation of the holy bones in their new resting-place was attended everywhere by all the pomp and solemnity which monks and clergy could devise, and by the fervent participation of the laity of all classes. Nor did such sacred proceedings remain unchronicled; for the surviving accounts of such Translations are numerous and form a far from negligible branch of hagiographical literature. Einhard, who had been responsible for the translation of Saints Marcellinus and Petrus from Rome to Seligenstadt in 827, three years later composed a detailed account of the whole episode and of the miracles performed by the saints as soon as they had been inducted into their new sanctuary. Another example of considerable literary merit is the *Translatio S. Alexandri*—the remains were brought from Rome to Wildeshausen—begun by Rudolf of Fulda soon after 851 and completed by his pupil, Meginhard.[2] Apart from their immediate value for understanding cult practices and popular beliefs in the Carolingian Age, such records incidentally throw light on other matters of interest. They may illustrate methods of

[1] Cf. Hauck, *Kirchengeschichte*, II, pp. 772–6, and the most valuable article by Albert Bruckner, 'Einige Bemerkungen zur Erforschung des frühmittelalterlichen Heiligenkultes in der Schweiz' in *Studi in onore di Cesare Manaresi* (Milan, 1952), pp. 31–52.

[2] Text in *MGH*, SS., XV, pp. 239 ff., and II, pp. 673 ff.

travel and its attendant dangers, or bear witness to the literary training of the chronicler. Rudolf, for example, introduced considerable extracts from Tacitus' *Germania*, without acknowledgement, into the beginning of his narrative.

The lives of saints, martyrs, and eminent Churchmen cannot all be classified under a single head. It has been seen that a small but important group of lives, being written by contemporaries, generally friends or disciples, and intended as an accurate record of events, belong to ordinary biographical literature. But in a majority of these lives it is not a more or less authentic historical presentation which makes up the greater, or even a considerable portion of, the *Vita*. Expressed in another way, it is the essence of hagiography, as distinct from biography, to present supernatural features recorded of the subject during his lifetime. In Western Europe the most influential, though not the earliest, work in this genre was the *Dialogues* of Gregory I. The primary purpose of hagiography is edification, although other motives also sometimes influence the writer. It is, for example, by no means rare to come upon passages that were clearly introduced to justify the claims of a monastic house to independence of episcopal control, or to certain lands or other material possessions. Even so short and unpretentious a sketch as Eigil's *Life of Sturmi* contains no less than three paragraphs emphasizing the rights and immunities of Fulda.[1] Again, the *Life of Gallus* by Walahfrid Strabo relates episodes designed to show how attempts by the bishop of Constance to make his jurisdiction over the abbey effective were miraculously frustrated by the saint.[2] In fact St Gall did not become independent till 818. In extreme instances a whole *Vita* or record might be forged to serve worldly ends; and the inventor would try to uphold the fiction that his narrative was authentic by stressing that the absence or destruction of documents in wars and raids had compelled him to rely on such oral traditions as he could assemble. A similar tendency is found in visions of the Hereafter. They form a special class of hagiographical literature, their literary prototype being again Gregory's *Dialogues*. They also were used to promote political

---

[1] *MGH*, SS., II, Chapter 12; p. 375, 5–2; 375, 45; 376, 2.
[2] *MGH*, Script. Merov., IV, Book 2, chapters 15–17.

ends even by so highly placed an ecclesiastic as Hincmar of Rheims.[1]

Some *Lives* composed in the ninth century purport to have been written in the sixth and seventh, and they must therefore be counted as wilful fabrications. These must, however, be carefully distinguished from genuine attempts to deal with events considerably earlier than the author's own time or to make the best of insufficient material. Hucbald's good faith should not be called in question when he relates how he hesitated to compose a life of St Rictrudis, first abbess of Marchiennes near Douai, owing to the absence of written materials, until the nuns showed him some records that were in general accord with what they themselves remembered. This does not, of course, exclude the possibility that he was himself the victim of pious deception.[2] Lupus, in his *Life of St Wigbert*, justifies himself for treating the events of the past by citing, characteristically enough, the examples of Sallust, Livy, Jerome in his *Life of Paulus*, and Ambrose in his *Passion of St Agnes*.[3]

There was a feeling in the ninth century that many of the older Lives and Passions were composed in crude, semi-literate Latin. It became a common practice to prevail on some man with a gift for writing to work these over so as to produce a more readable and elegant piece of literature. Thus the *Life of St Maximin* by Servatus Lupus was based on an older *Vita*. Walahfrid had access to two older accounts of Gallus to form the kernel of his own. The Saint's life became a recognized genre of literary composition. Its general structure and the sequence of events became typified. Certain features, too, were indispensable characteristics of the saint—the serious outlook on life even in early youth, showing itself in disinclination to join in the amusements of other children, youthful precocity, the gift of prophecy or at least a certain superhuman foreknowledge of events, and self-depreciatory modesty and hesitation to accept material advancement or worldly responsibility. Even the scene at the death-bed, and the last words of exhortation and consolation, tended to be written down according to a formal scheme. Some

[1] See W. Levison, *op. cit.*, pp. 229–46.   [2] *PL*, 132, col. 829.
[3] *MGH*, SS., XV, p. 38.

of these traits are found in early *Lives* and indeed in Christian *Pseudepigrapha*. But in the ninth century the pattern of hagiography became set and standardized. This is not meant to imply that these religious biographies were devoid of all individual traits. The more authentic the record was, as when it was written down by a disciple of the saint or at least by one who could converse with older men who had known the deceased, the more likely it is to find not a few individual characteristics set down side by side with what was typical. Contrariwise, the more purely legendary the account, the more completely would it conform to type and nothing more.

It is noticeable that in the hagiography of the ninth century ascetism and martyrdom are stressed but little, whereas they form a feature of ever-growing importance in the *Lives* composed during the tenth and early eleventh centuries. This change of attitude may reflect the altered political and social conditions, which were never more unstable and distressful than in the tenth century. It is significant, too, that this class of literature was widely and successfully cultivated in that age when historical and some other forms of writing languished.

The lives of saints, martyrs, and outstanding figures in the Church owed their popularity to many causes. Their historical accuracy counted but little with the average reader who found in them a good story. If the adventures of the saintly hero conformed to pattern, that was assuredly not regarded as a fault. Even so in fairly recent times a certain class of popular novel was cast to a mould. The main features reappeared in each successive work of the fortunate author whose sales ran into many thousands of copies. He would have lost his public, had he, in a sudden craving to be original, deviated from the accepted plot, or failed to endow at least his leading figures with the virtue, manliness, modesty, chastity, or deep-dyed villainy characteristic of each. There is in most men a love of the marvellous. In the early Middle Ages this was the more intense because fortified by the sanctions of religion. When belief in miracles and in frequent manifestations of Divine approval or displeasure was all but universal, becoming stronger and stronger, as the veneration of saints, relics, and images now fostered and encouraged by the ecclesiastical authorities grew apace, what more attractive literature could there be than some hagiography in which the supernatural played a determining part in the hero's life and made even more manifest his powers after death? In these *Lives*, too, men might read of the customs, manners, and scenery of foreign lands, or of hairbreadth escapes, like those of Findan from his Norman captors when he set out to ransom his sister.[1] Nor are episodes of a humorous nature wholly lacking. As the worship of saints grew, even local patriotism might find satisfaction in reading circumstantially about the local saint, whose miracle-working powers surpassed, or even perhaps discomfited, the efforts of one in a neighbouring district. Much of the hagiographical literature reflects, like some mirror, not merely the beliefs, but the hopes and fears, the daily labours, pleasures, and sorrows of the people. Yet many inquirers into the life and spirit of the Middle Ages, deterred by a certain uniformity in these records, and still more swayed by the rationalism of a supposedly more enlightened age, have totally neglected this unique body of evidence. They have done so at their peril; for, in setting aside what they deemed unworthy of serious notice, the self-declared enemies of 'superstition' have closed for themselves one of the main avenues to enlightenment.

(d) Geography

Geography need not detain us long; for so slight was the interest in this subject that only two brief treatises have come down to us from the Carolingian Age, and only one of them contains anything that is new. Taken as a whole, both the *De mensura orbis terrae*, completed in 825 by the Irish monk, Dicuil, whom we have already met as the compiler of an astronomical work, and the tract, *De situ orbis*, written soon after 850 by an anonymous author, are mere *collectanea* from earlier scholars. Dicuil's book is, however, decidedly superior to the other for two reasons. He shows some interest in textual problems as he uses his authorities, and he adds a very few geographical data applicable only to his own day. Otherwise both books are mere school *compendia* of

[1] See the anonymous *Life of Findan* in MGH, SS., XV, pp. 512 ff. It was composed in the ninth century by an Irishman at Reichenau.

ancient geography; in other words, their descriptions are bounded
by the territorial limits of the later Roman Empire. The Anonymus
was not familiar with Dicuil's treatise and worked with somewhat
different sources. The Irishman relied primarily on Solinus, the
first five books of Pliny's *Natural History*, Julius Honorius, and
the fifth-century *Mensuratio orbis terrae* undertaken by order of
Theodosius II. He makes more occasional use of four or five
other writers. The author of the *De situ orbis*, on the other hand,
relies mostly on Pomponius Mela, at that time a little-known
writer, Solinus, and the sixth book of Martianus Capella. There
are also passages from Isidore, Orosius, and the *Cosmographia* of
Aethicus Ister, which was really the work of Virgil of Salzburg.[1]
The monotony of Dicuil's *rechauffé* from imperial Roman writers
is relieved in two or three passages by observations based on oral
information. He was the victim of a traveller's tale, when he
accepted the story, told to his teacher Suibneus by another monk
in Dicuil's presence, of a journey from Palestine to Egypt; for
the relator asserted that he and his fellow-pilgrims had sailed from
the Nile into the Red Sea. He had previously admired the pyra-
mids which he called 'the seven granaries built by Joseph according to the number of years of abundance'. Later on he desired to
inspect the marks of Pharaoh's chariots in the Red Sea, but the
sailors were disobliging enough not to stop for the purpose.[2]
Three other stories in Dicuil refer to the Far North. In his youth
he had perhaps stayed for a time on Iona; at all events he knew of
the Hebrides, Shetlands, and Orkneys, and of islands off the Irish
coast. He had lived in some and visited or seen others. Furthermore, a priest had told him of certain islands which could be
reached in two days and two nights with favourable winds by
sailing due north from Britain. They had once been inhabited by
hermits, but owing to the Norman raids were deserted in
Dicuil's time save for numberless sheep and sea fowl.[3] He added

---

[1] See above, p. 185. Dicuil has been edited by G. Parthey (Berlin, 1870),
De situ orbis by M. Manitius (Stuttgart, 1884). Pomponius Mela appears very
rarely in medieval catalogues before the fifteenth century. The extant text
depends on a single manuscript of the later ninth century, other manuscripts
being very late and of little value. Cf. Manitius, *Geschichte*, pp. 677–8 on
Mela in the Middle Ages.

[2] *De mensura*, 6, 12–18.   [3] *ibid.*, 7, 6; 7, 14–15.

that he had found no allusion to these islands (which must be identical with the Faroes) in any author. Most interesting of all, however, is his report on Iceland:[1]

It is now thirty years since some clergy, who stayed in that island (Thile) from February 1st to August 1st, related to me that not only at the summer solstice but a little before and after, when the sun sets in the evening, it disappears, as it were, behind a tiny hillock. The result is that it does not grow dark anywhere, but a man can do whatever he wishes even to picking lice off his shirt, as though the sun were still shining. Indeed if they had been on the top of the mountain in the island, the sun would perhaps never have disappeared from their view.

He then controverts the statement of those who asserted that the sea round Iceland was frozen and that six months of continuous night alternated with six months of continuous daylight. But he adds that one day's sail brought his informants to a frozen sea. If only Dicuil had been able to emancipate himself from geographical lore which had little but antiquarian interest in his time, and had collected reports from other travellers and missionaries, who had explored Central Europe and beyond, what a uniquely valuable brochure he could have left to posterity! As it is, neither of the geographical treatises, apart from Dicuil's references to northern Europe, have any scientific worth. Their sole significance lies in the manner in which they reflect the book-learning acquired by their two compilers.[2]

---

[1] *ibid.*, 7, 11.

[2] In the first edition of this book (pp. 203–5) Hadoard was included in the select company of ninth-century Ciceronian scholars. But in one of the last articles that he wrote (*Classical Philology*, 40 [1945], pp. 201–27) the late C. H. Beeson reviewed the earlier literature on Hadoard's *Collectaneum* and then showed conclusively that the manuscript of Cicero's philosophical works, which Hadoard excerpted in the first instance, is an extant manuscript at Florence (*San Marco, 257*) of the tenth century. He also confirmed that the manuscript of the *Collectaneum* in the Vatican Library (*Regin., 1762*) was Hadoard's autograph. Finally he gave strong grounds for believing that the centre where Hadoard was librarian about the middle of the tenth century or a little later was Tours.

CHAPTER XII

The Literature of the Carolingian Age: Theology

(a) Controversial and Dogmatic Writings

There is one feature which the Carolingian era had in common with the fourth century: both were periods during which acute dogmatic disputes gave rise to vigorous controversial literature. One of the doctrinal questions, and the most hotly discussed of all, was Predestination, which had remained quiescent ever since the Gallican opposition in the fifth century to the full consequence of Augustinian teaching. But already in the second half of the eighth century two other causes for theological contention had arisen. Spain, distinguished by the rigid orthodoxy of its Church since the Fourth Council of Toledo, was the last country from which a heresiarch might have been expected to spring. It is significant, nevertheless, that throughout the seventh century Christological questions had occupied a foremost place in the deliberations of successive Councils, a sufficient proof that guidance for the clergy and at the same time refutation of possible schismatics were felt to be urgently needed. Furthermore the Spanish (Mozarabic) liturgy contained some phraseology which might easily lead to unorthodox beliefs regarding the relation of the Second to the First Person of the Trinity, in other words, to Adoptionism. In the Acts of the Sixth Council of Toledo (638) we find a long definition of orthodox belief in the Trinity. The Eleventh Council expressly warned against Adoptionist error.[1] The Fifteenth appealed to the authority of Nicaea, Constantinople, Ephesus, and Chalcedon in formulating

---

[1] Mansi, *Concilia*, X, 661–2; XI, 133: Hic etiam Filius Dei natura est Filius, non adoptione, quem Deus Pater nec voluntate, nec necessitate genuisse credendus est.

its *professio fidei*, while the Sixteenth (693) defined the doctrine of the Trinity most elaborately and included an exposition of the will, a clear echo of the controversy raised by the Monothelites.[1]

The teaching of Elipandus, archbishop of Toledo, and of Felix, bishop of Urgel, once more gave rise to acute contention in the West concerning the nature of Christ. Elipandus, whose position as primate of Spain gave him a degree of power incommensurate with his abilities, had already taken a very independent line against Pope Hadrian, before he openly professed the heresy with which his name is associated. On Spanish soil his opinions were actively opposed by Beatus of Liébana and Etherius, subsequently bishop of Osma. With the entry of Felix into this dogmatic dispute, the controversy assumed a wider significance. His see was on territory which by then formed part of the Frankish Empire, so that propagation of his views became a matter of immediate concern to Charlemagne. Furthermore, he had been known as a man of exemplary piety and great learning, a fact which, if it raised the tone of the dispute, also made the heretical writings more dangerous. Felix was cited before the Synod of Ratisbon in 792, where his teaching was condemned. He made his submission and later repeated his recantation at Rome before the Pope himself. The subject of Adoptionism, however, was one of the dogmatic questions laid before a numerous assembly of clerics at the Synod of Frankfurt in 794. Charles himself presided and took part in the conference, and it has recently been shown that Alcuin played an important part in these deliberations,[2] which were unanimously opposed to the Trinitarian teaching of Felix and Elipandus. After a few years Felix reverted to his error. The treatises in which he strove to justify himself are almost wholly lost, but his arguments can be reconstructed to some extent from the works of his adversaries; for now condemnation and refutation came upon him from several sides. Pope Leo III, after receiving the writings of Felix, condemned them as heretical. Paulinus of Aquileia, *c.* 800, composed a treatise against the heresiarch, which was warmly approved by Felix's most notable

[1] For the Fifteenth Council see F. X. Murphy in *Mélanges Joseph de Ghellinck* (Gembloux, 1951), pp. 361–73.

[2] See L. Wallach in *Traditio*, 9 (1953), pp. 129–41.

literary opponent, Alcuin. Probably in 797 Alcuin had drawn up a short *Libellus adversus Felicis haeresin*, following this up in the next year with a long and detailed refutation, *Libri septem adversus Felicem*. He also corresponded with Beatus of Liébana on this subject, as is now known from a letter which has only been recovered in recent years.[1] In 800 Felix was once more obliged to appear before a synod, this time held at Aachen. He was condemned and ended his days in the honourable custody of his friend Leidrad, archbishop of Lyons. Alcuin also wrote a refutation of Elipandus in four books. The energetic action of Charlemagne and Alcuin had rooted out Adoptionism in the Frankish Empire. In Spain the position of Elipandus gradually weakened owing to the growing opposition of the Spanish prelates. The essence of the teaching of the Adoptionists was that Christ was according to his Human nature the Son of God *gratia* or *adoptione*, not *natura* or *genere*. This doctrine Alcuin, who saw in it a close parallel to the Nestorian heresy,[2] set himself to rebut. The tone of his treatises is one of studied moderation mixed with genuine regret, since the erudition and exemplary life of Felix had long been known to him and had filled him with admiration.[3] His presentation of orthodox teaching and his refutation of the Adoptionist errors rest entirely on the authority of the Fathers. His theological reading had been extensive and included not only Latin writers from Hilary to Leo I and Gregory the Great, but Latin translations of Greek theologians, Athanasius, Cyril, Gregory of Nazianzus, and some others. Some of this Greek material, as we have seen, had long been available in Latin dress. Other Greek excerpts, in view of marked correspondence, were derived from a Latin version of the Eastern councils, especially from the Acts of the Council of Ephesus; and, since it is probable that Alcuin edited the *Libri Carolini*, his acquaintance with contemporary and earlier Greek theology in Latin translations must have been considerable. Early in the ninth century Agobard of Lyons and Benedict of Aniane also entered the lists against the

[1] See W. Levison, *England and the Continent in the eighth century*, pp. 314-23. Alcuin's treatises will be found in *PL*, 101. His praise of Paulinus occurs in a letter to Arn of Salzburg (*MGH*, Epist., IV, No. 208).

[2] *PL*, 101, col. 88A.   [3] *MGH*, Epist., IV, Nos. 5 and 166.

adherents of heresy by assembling and publishing series of passages from the Scriptures and the Patristic authors in support of orthodoxy. Southern France was always open to influence from Spain, where, in spite of the rapid decline of Elipandus' authority, Adoptionism lingered on fitfully for some time.

A second dogmatic controversy around another aspect of the Trinitarian question was of singular importance because it was, and continued to be, a matter of contention between the Eastern and the Western Churches. The doctrine that the Holy Spirit proceeded from the Father and the Son had become the accepted belief of orthodox Christians in the Frankish Empire during the eighth century, as can be seen, for example, in the confession of faith made by Lullus on receiving the *pallium*.[1] The dispute with the East arose both before and during Charlemagne's reign, but on these occasions this dogmatic question was quite over-shadowed by the disagreements arising out of the iconoclastic controversy. This last matter Charles may have hoped to have settled once and for all; nevertheless, in a more restricted form it was resurrected in the early years of Louis the Pious. The discussion respecting the Procession of the Holy Spirit remained quiescent for nearly a century, until the action of an Eastern patriarch led the Pope to invoke the literary aid of Frankish scholars.

Before Charlemagne's time the attitude of the Popes in general had been sympathetic to the worship of images, and indeed had been one of the causes for the steadily growing estrangement between Rome and the Eastern emperors during the later seventh and eighth centuries. At the Synod of Gentilly (767), summoned by Pippin, the condemnation of image-worship promulgated at Constantinople thirteen years before was not accepted, but the practice was approved. A change in the reigning prince at the Byzantine capital brought with it a change of doctrine. Irene, widow of Leo IV and regent for her son, Constantine VI, was opposed to iconoclasm, and through her action an oecumenical council so-called met in the historic city of Nicaea in 787. Legates of Pope Hadrian were indeed present, but the Frankish Church was unrepresented. The prohibition of 754 was rescinded, and

[1] Cf. Levison, *op. cit.*, p. 239, line 9.

image-worship received the fullest sanction. This important decision was made—and it was intended to hold good throughout Christendom—although the Frankish Church had been neither consulted nor represented at the council. Charlemagne was confronted with a *fait accompli* and received a version of the Acts of the Council translated into indifferent Latin. If his subsequent conduct was dictated to some extent by political motives, it also arose in part from a genuine dislike of a type of worship which, in the extreme form practised and permitted in the Eastern Church, seemed to him, and to a majority of his subjects, idolatrous. The Acts of Nicaea were submitted to his theological counsellors, among whom Alcuin was probably the chief; for the so-called *Libri Carolini*, though no doubt a work of collaboration, seem to have been compiled under Alcuin's editorship.[1] The position adopted in that compilation was midway between the extremes of iconoclasm, as imposed in the East by the decision of 754, and the equally unreserved acceptance of image-worship sanctioned by the recent oecumenical council. The essential part of the argument was to the effect that, while the saints are deserving of veneration and should receive it, their images are placed in churches only as a reminder of their good deeds, and to beautify the churches with works of art, plastic or pictorial. Religious worship, on the other hand, is for God alone. The Pope himself, after a spirited resistance, was compelled to approve the reply to the Nicene Acts formulated by Charles and his theological advisers; and Charles' claim to be head of Western Christendom, which Byzantium had ignored so signally in 787, was more than vindicated. There the matter rested for the remainder of Charles' reign. But *c.* 820 the outspoken 'puritanism' of Claudius of Turin led to literary warfare. He condemned not only the veneration of images and relics, but the adoration of the Cross, pilgrimages, and the intercession of saints. At the request of Louis the Pious, the Irishman, Dungal, then residing in Milan, and Jonas, bishop of Orléans, undertook to refute the arguments of Claudius, who was held to be guilty of heretical opinions. Both these writers adopted the intermediate position of the *Libri Carolini*; both also followed the usual procedure of excerpting Patristic authors. But

[1] See Wallach, *op. cit.*, pp. 143-9.

Dungal added a novel feature when he introduced numerous quotations, some being of great length, from the poetry of Prudentius, Paulinus of Nola, and Fortunatus. All three had sung in praise of martyrs and saints, thus providing Dungal with much useful material for his purpose. More than half of the *De cultu imaginum* by Jonas is composed of citations from Claudius' *Liber apologeticus*, in which the heterodox views of Claudius had been expounded in rather intemperate terms. It is intelligible, therefore, and even excusable, that Jonas replied with some heat.[1]

The differences between Frankish and Eastern theologians regarding the Procession of the Holy Spirit had been touched on at the Synod of Gentilly and again in the *Libri Carolini*. About 802 Alcuin brought out his chief dogmatic work, *De fide sanctae et individuae Trinitatis*, in which his definition of the Holy Spirit was quite unequivocal.[2] The *symbolum* used in the Frankish churches, moreover, had long described the Holy Spirit as proceeding *a patre filioque*; and the *Quicunque vult*, thought not yet accepted generally, is found complete in manuscripts of the eighth and ninth centuries, and its phraseology is precise.[3] In 808 the Synod of Aachen formally approved the addition of the words, 'and from the Son' to the definition of the Holy Spirit in the creed which was henceforward to be the orthodox confession in the West. Pope Leo, though he did not disapprove words that had already been sanctioned by his great predecessor, Gregory I, was not prepared to make the addition to the *symbolum* then used in the Roman service. The formal inclusion of the words, *filioque*, was made at Rome soon after his time. Besides the more general treatise on the Trinity by Alcuin, *collectanea* from the Fathers in support of the Frankish definition of the Holy Spirit were compiled by Theodulfus, and by an unknown author whose disquisition was included by the older editors amongst the works of Alcuin. In a briefer communication Smaragdus upheld the

---

[1] Cf. the Prefaces to the three books of Jonas' *De cultu imaginum* (PL, 106, coll. 305–88), and the acidulated passage, *ibid.*, 312C. For Claudius' 'iconoclasm' see also E. J. Martin, *A History of the Iconoclastic Controversy* (S.P.C.K., n.d.), pp. 262–73.

[2] Cf. *PL*, 101, coll. 14D, 16C, 16D and 20A.

[3] 'Spiritus sanctus a patre et filio, non factus nec creatus nec genitus, sed procedens.'

same thesis by the authority of the Bible itself.[1] This dogmatic definition then was immutably fixed for the West; nevertheless the 'errors' of the Greek Church became once more a target for dialectic shafts in the time of Charles the Bald.

In 867 Pope Nicolas I turned to the Frankish theologians for a refutation of what he chose to regard as charges levelled against the whole Western Church by Photius, patriarch of Constantinople, in a famous encyclical and by the Council of Constantinople held in the summer of that year.[2] The answer supplied by Odo, bishop of Beauvais, at the request of Hincmar, the metropolitan of Rheims, has not survived; that by Aeneas, bishop of Paris, is extant but negligible, being no more than a cento of Patristic quotations. Very different was the long reply to the Greeks (*Contra Graecorum opposita*) elaborated by Ratramnus, a monk of Corbie; for, besides quoting extensively from the Fathers, Ratramnus showed the same sturdy independence of thought which he displayed, as we shall see, in his other notable contribution to dogmatic theology. In the first three books he methodically rebuts the Greek view of *Processio* from the Bible, from the Fathers in general, and from Augustine in particular. So far he followed the traditional method, though with unwonted learning, and a more consequential arrangement of his material than is generally found amongst his contemporaries. The fourth and last book historically is the most interesting; it is also the most original in content. In it Ratramnus examines a number of other points of dispute between the two Churches. He seeks to trace the genesis of these differences, whilst staunchly arguing that the Greeks were wrong on every point. He ends with a passage of which the purpose is to demonstrate that the patriarch of Constantinople is inferior to the Pope.[3]

The fearless spirit of Ratramnus had previously been shown in his controversy over the Eucharist with Radbert, a brother monk

---

[1] See *PL*, 105, coll. 259–76, and 101, coll. 65–82. For Smaragdus see *MGH*, Concil., II, pp. 236 ff.

[2] That Photius' encyclical was not directed at the whole Western Church but only at Latin missionaries in Bulgaria has been shown by Fr Dvornik, *The Photian Schism* (Cambridge, 1948), pp. 119 ff. For the Latin replies, *ibid.*, pp. 279 ff.

[3] The treatise will be found in *PL*, 121, coll. 225–346.

in the abbey of Corbie and for a few years its abbot. In the history of the dogma of Transubstantiation, which was not definitely formulated until the Lateran Council of 1215, the books of Ratramnus and of Radbert, both entitled, *De corpore et sanguine Domini*, are a landmark. The question of the Real Presence in the Eucharist had never before been the theme of a formal treatise. Inseparably connected with it in general belief, and very prominently in Radbert's book, was another liturgical act, the sacrifice of the Mass. Indeed this quite overshadowed the communion service in liturgical importance. The re-enactment of Christ's sacrifice on the Cross in the sacrifice of the Mass had long been accepted as the central act of Christian worship. And, since the words of consecration spoken by the priest celebrating the Mass, as he raised up the Host and the chalice, converted the bread and wine into the very body and blood of Christ, the same miracle necessarily was enacted also at the eucharistic celebration. It is clear that the belief in the Real Presence had long been generally held as a matter of faith. But men accepted it as a miraculous occurrence without questioning or seeking to probe into its transcendental nature. Even Amalarius of Metz, whose observations in his liturgical works leave no room for doubt that he believed in the Real Presence, did not attempt to penetrate more deeply into the mystery. Both Ratramnus and Radbert appealed primarily to the authority of Augustine. That they reached very different conclusions was partly no doubt subjective, and Radbert was clearly influenced deeply by traditions accepted in his day. But the disagreement between the two men also shows that Augustine's transcendentalism was susceptible of very divergent interpretations. Radbert upholds the belief, generally accepted in his day, in the miracle repeatedly enacted whenever the Mass was celebrated. The consecrated elements are changed into the same body of Christ which had been born of the Virgin, had suffered on the Cross, and had risen from the dead. But he taught that this mystery can only be apprehended by the worshipper through an act of faith, since it was not perceptible in any change apparent to human senses. He draws the same distinction between the outward semblance and the spiritual reality when he considers the act of communion. The former is the bread and wine, which is consumed by the communicant, since it would be improper to eat and drink the body and blood of Christ in humanly visible form. Nor would there be room otherwise for the faith of the communicant, which is necessary for him in order that he can accept the spiritual reality that he has partaken of Christ's body and blood. To these explanations the views of Ratramnus form a striking contrast. He, too, taught that there was in the Eucharist a mystery that could only be apprehended by faith. But he differed radically from Radbert in distinguishing between the mortal body of Christ and His spiritual body. The words, 'body and blood', he said, are used figuratively and refer to Christ's spiritual body; it is of this last that the communicant partakes, whereas the elements at the communion remain bread and wine and are only symbolical.[1] Ratramnus does not specifically discuss the Mass, but there can be no doubt about his interpretation. He regards the daily sacrifice of the Mass as a memorial of the real sacrifice which had taken place once only, on the Cross.[2]

The two expositions of Radbert and Ratramnus were irreconcilable, but no controversy ensued and discussion of the Eucharist remained in abeyance for two centuries, in short, until the prolonged disputes precipitated by the teaching of Berengarius of Tours in the middle of the eleventh century. Yet we can be sure that the treatise by Radbert, which essayed a philosophical interpretation of a mystery which most men were content to accept without question, was also approved by the great majority of theologians. The opinions of Ratramnus seem, indeed, to have coincided with those held by Hrabanus and John Scotus; otherwise they were disregarded until his book, at that time wrongly attributed to John Scotus, was condemned by the Council of Vercelli in 1050 and burnt.

But the question which caused the greatest stir in the ecclesiastical world during the ninth century and provoked the most extensive controversial literature was Predestination. In the

[1] *PL*, 121, coll. 159B–160A; a little later (161C) he cites Augustine as follows: 'sed quod pertinet ad virtutem sacramenti, non quod pertinet ad visibile sacramentum; qui manducat intus, non foris; qui manducat in corde, non qui premit dente'.

[2] See particularly *ibid.*, col. 170A.

country which had once been the main stronghold of Semi-pelagianism the teaching of Augustine on this subject, in spite of his unrivalled authority, was never propounded in its full rigour. In the Carolingian Age, when the works of Augustine were perused and excerpted by many, both for carrying on dogmatic disputes and for the purpose of exegesis, the number of those who penetrated to the heart of his philosophical or theological system was very small. And it is open to doubt whether a topic of unusual complexity, like Predestination, would have been canvassed at all, but for the action of one man. At the same time it was regrettable that, as it happened, a dogma involving questions of the utmost gravity for Christian men should have become entangled with a persecution, deplorable in itself, which diverted attention from the metaphysical problem to the sufferings of its newest investigator and so tended to obscure the real issue.

Gottschalk, of Saxon parentage, was dedicated to the religious life as a child and brought up at Fulda. On attaining to manhood he demanded to be released from the monastic vows taken on his behalf by others. This request was first granted and then refused, after Hrabanus had appealed against the decision; but Gottschalk was permitted to leave Fulda for another monastery. He seems to have stayed a while at Corbie, where he was a pupil of Ratramnus. Next we find him in the abbey of Orbais, a little south-west of Épernay. There he became very active as a teacher and at the same time was deeply absorbed in the study of Augustine. At length, after being ordained priest, he visited Italy, spending several years there in promulgating his doctrines, until he was finally expelled the country. After further wanderings, he made his way back to Germany. In 848 he appeared before the Synod of Mayence—whether perforce or voluntarily is not clear—in order to defend his views. He was condemned and handed over to Hincmar, archbishop of Rheims, for safe custody. A second synod, held in the following year at Quierzy, pronounced a second sentence of unjustifiable severity. Apart from the doctrines that he maintained, Gottschalk had made himself liable to ecclesiastical discipline, because he had left his monastery without authorization, and because his ordination, carried out by a suffragan (*chorepiscopus*) instead of by the bishop of the diocese, had been irregular. His punishment, however, was vindictive, and the whole episode has left a blot on the fair fame of Hrabanus, whose attitude had been strangely harsh from the first, and of Hincmar. Gottschalk was unfrocked, severely flagellated, and then imprisoned in the abbey of Hautvillers on the outskirts of Épernay. For a while he was allowed to devote himself to study, and the recovery of some of his prose writings in recent years confirms the fact that he was a man of unusual erudition.[1] He corresponded with his old teacher, Ratramnus, and with Servatus Lupus. But after 850 his custody became more severe. Steps were taken to prevent communication on his part with the outer world, and he was perhaps condemned to perpetual silence. Yet he lived for another fifteen or twenty years, adhering unswervingly to his opinions and resolutely declining to recant.

In the interval his views and his sufferings had given rise to a heated controversy and extensive literary warfare within the kingdom of Charles the Bald and beyond. The approved doctrines of the Frankish Church at this time respecting Divine Grace and free will were those which had been confirmed by the Synod of Orange in 529. That Synod may be said to have marked the end of the Semipelagian controversy in Gaul. Its findings were a compromise. The Predestination theory of Augustine was circumvented as far as possible, while the Predestination of the wicked to damnation was explicitly rejected. During the three centuries that followed the Synod of Orange the question of Predestination remained dormant because no scholar appeared who had mastered the full import of Augustine's anti-Pelagian writings or was prepared to challenge the prevailing doctrines of the Church. Gottschalk achieved the one and was fearless enough to dare the other. His essential arguments were as follows: there is a twofold Predestination, for God by His grace has predestined some to eternal life and others by His justice to everlasting death. After Adam sinned by his own free will no one has been able to exercise his free will for good but only for evil. The result of the Predestination for evil is that man sins against his will (*invitus*), but is compelled to pursue his evil life without hope of being cleansed from error and sin. Although God foresees both good

[1] See Dom Lambot in *Spicilegium Sacrum Lovaniense*, 20 (1939).

and evil, He only predestines good, which is of two kinds, bestowal of grace and justice. By the former He predestined some to everlasting life, but by the exercise of His justice He predestined the wicked to eternal punishment. The sacraments do not avail to save the wicked. Even as no one who is predestined to punishment can be saved, so no one who is predestined to good can be lost. Christ did not die for all men, but only for those predestined to be saved.

Gottschalk's contentions aroused an abundant literature in which various shades of opinion are expressed. Those who, like Hrabanus, Hincmar, and Amalarius of Metz, adhered most closely to the traditional doctrines of the Church, rejected the dogma of double or dual Predestination outright. On the other hand, there were not a few who were impelled to read or re-read Augustine and who came to side with Gottschalk in arguing for a *gemina praedestinatio*. Such were Prudentius, bishop of Troyes, archbishop Amolo of Lyons, the deacon Florus, Amolo's successor, Remigius, and Ratramnus of Corbie. Lupus of Ferrières, too, in his *De tribus quaestionibus*, accepted a dual Predestination, although he differed from Gottschalk on a number of other points. Thus he, and indeed all the other Carolingian divines, tried to vindicate the freedom of the human will.[1] The treatise, written by John Scotus at the request of Hincmar, falls in a category by itself. Composed in 851 as a refutation of Gottschalk, it provoked fully as much disapproval as the theories of the Saxon monk. The treatises of Prudentius and Florus were directed primarily against John's *Liber de praedestinatione*;[2] and the Synods of Valence (855) and of Langres (857) rejected it, applying to it the contemptuous description, reminiscent of St Jerome, 'old wives' tales and Scots' porridge'.[3] The opponents of Gottschalk generally impugned the arguments by which he had brought Divine Foreknowledge (*Praescientia*) and Predestination into close conjunction and made them operate concurrently. They, on the

---

[1] Prudentius, *PL*, 115, coll. 1009 ff.; Florus, *PL*, 119, coll. 101 ff; Ratramnus, *PL*, 121, coll. 13 ff.; Remigius, *PL*, 121, coll. 985 ff.

[2] *PL*, 122, coll. 355–440.

[3] 'Aniles paene fabulas, Scotorumque pultes puritati fidei nauseam inferentes' (Hefele, *Conciliengeschichte*, 4, p. 456). Cf. Jerome (*CSEL*, 59, 4, 30), referring to Rufinus (or Pelagius?), 'Scottorum pultibus praegravatus'.

other hand, separated the former, assigning it temporal priority, from the latter, and argued that, whereas God has a foreknowledge of both good and evil, He predestines only the good. John, in common with his contemporaries, attacked Gottschalk's position with what may seem to us undignified virulence. But he approached the whole subject from a philosophical standpoint, which was as incomprehensible as it seemed perilous and heretical to his fellow-theologians. He denied the *gemina praedestinatio*; for to him the Being of God was simple, although man was unable to apprehend it in this way, but distinguished different attributes, such as wisdom and knowledge, in the Divine Being. Thus humanly Divine Predestination was merely one more humanly conceived aspect of God, so that to speak of dual Predestination was to postulate divisibility of what was simple and indivisible. Again, according to John, sin and punishment are closely interrelated, and the trend to evil which is a negative thing has nothing to do with God but proceeds entirely from the human will, or rather, from its abuse. It will be seen later that in his chief philosophical work the whole conception of sin and punishment was at variance with the ordinarily accepted, quasi-materialistic interpretation of both. Much of the odium at first directed against Gottschalk was shifted to the Irishman. The final outcome of a long and rather arid controversy was that the definitions, already formulated by Hincmar and approved by a synod at Quierzy in 853, which were upset at Valence two years later, were reaffirmed in 860 at the Synod of Toucy. These pronouncements were four: There is only one Predestination of God. God wills all men to salvation. Christ's sacrifice took place to save all men. Man's free will is restored by grace. The last proposition was explained to mean that, as man's free will was lost through the action of Adam, so it was given back through Christ's sacrifice.

(b) Exegesis; Pastoral and Liturgical Writings

If the authority of the Fathers dominated the literature produced by the doctrinal disputes of the eighth and ninth centuries, reliance on Patristic authority was still more universal in the field of Biblical exegesis. The general similarity in method of approach and in content of most of the commentaries makes it superfluous to consider each one singly. Only a very few theologians essayed the arduous task of expounding a large portion of the Scriptures, the majority being content to concentrate on the elucidation of one or two books. Again, while some from the first might compose their commentaries with a wide circle of readers in mind, others were constrained to do so to meet the needs only of their own pupils. In spite of the activity of *scriptoria*, the standard works of earlier centuries sometimes were still difficult to obtain, so that the conscientious teacher tried to fill a want by supplying the monastery with one or more exegetical works from his own hand. Nor must it be forgotten that an author like Augustine or Jerome was often too advanced for beginners. Two examples are instructive. Angelomus, a monk of Luxeuil, at the request of his own teacher and an ecclesiastical superior, composed a commentary on Genesis. Having finished this task with some success he next yielded to the entreaties of several fellow-monks in Luxeuil and some other persons and undertook to explain Samuel and Kings. We are expressly told that the Luxeuil library owned no complete commentary on these historical books. A local reputation was succeeded by a wider renown; for in 851 the Emperor Lothar invited Angelomus to compose a book on the Song of Songs.[1] Christian of Stavelot, a younger contemporary of Angelomus, tells his readers explicitly why he was led to compose a commentary on Matthew. He found that his pupils, after they had twice received oral instruction in that Gospel, had forgotten what they had learnt. He therefore decided to write down his explanation. He adds, lest he be thought presumptuous to undertake again what had already been well done by Jerome, that Jerome's exposition was often too difficult for those beginning the study of Scripture.[2] It may further be noted how that great theologian, Radbert, being struck with the fact that no commentary on Lamentations existed, supplied the want by composing one of considerable length.[3]

---

[1] On Angelomus see my article in *Harvard Theol. Rev.*, 46 (1953), pp. 27–46.

[2] For Christian see *ibid.*, 20 (1927), pp. 129–49.

[3] *PL*, 120, coll. 1063 ff. Cf. also his letter to Odilmannus in *MGH*, Epist., VI, pp. 136–8.

The most prolific commentators were Claudius of Turin and Hrabanus. Claudius compiled expositions of Genesis, Exodus, Leviticus, perhaps Numbers, Joshua, Judges, Ruth, Kings, Matthew, and the Pauline Epistles. They were little more than collections of excerpts from earlier authorities, so that a recent critic justly calls them the first examples in the Western Church of those *catenae* which had been popular in the East for some centuries.[1] Hrabanus commented on the Heptateuch, Ruth, Samuel and Kings, Chronicles, Proverbs, Judith, Esther, Jeremiah, Ezekiel, Wisdom, Ecclesiasticus, Maccabees, Matthew, and the Pauline Epistles. Before the output of these two the achievement of others pales. Alcuin's most valued work of exegesis was a commentary on the Fourth Gospel; but he also dealt more briefly with Genesis, the Song of Songs, Ecclesiastes, Titus, Philemon, and Hebrews. Sedulius Scottus assembled a *collectaneum* on the Pauline Epistles. Perhaps its most interesting feature is the fact that Sedulius among other works used the original commentary by Pelagius, of which he had a good manuscript.[2] The Pauline Epistles also engaged the attention of Florus of Lyons, who based his work on Bede's (still unprinted) *collectaneum* drawn from the works of Augustine. Sedulius also was the author of a *collectaneum* on Matthew, and Radbert composed an elaborate commentary on this Gospel, as well as a disquisition on Psalm xl. Remigius of Auxerre expounded the whole Psalter, while John Scotus wrote an exposition of the Fourth Gospel, for which, besides Augustine, he consulted Greek sources. The list could be prolonged by the addition of many other names, but it will suffice to mention two commentaries on the Apocalypse. Both belong to the later eighth century. The one was by Ambrosius Autpertus, abbot of St Vincent on the Volturno (died 784?), whose sources were the commentary of Victorinus as revised by Jerome, Primasius, Book XX of Augustine's *City of God* and Gregory the Great.[3] Autpertus also seems to have

[1] See Dom Bellet, *Estudios Bíblicos*, 9 (Madrid, 1950), pp. 209–23.

[2] See A. Souter, *Pelagius' Exposition of Thirteen Epistles of St Paul*, I, pp. 336–9, summarizing an earlier article.

[3] For these sources see S. Bovo, *Studia Anselmiana*, 27–8 (1953), pp. 372–403. Autpertus' acquaintance with Tyconius seems to have been indirect, *i.e.* through Primasius.

commented on Psalms i to lxx. The second commentary on the Apocalypse was by the Spaniard, Beatus of Liébana, whom we have already met as the correspondent of Alcuin. This work also is a compilation from various earlier sources. Such value as it has—and this is true generally of the Biblical commentaries of the Carolingian Age—lies in the evidence it provides for the transmission of learning from one age to another. The most valuable feature of Beatus' book is that it preserves portions of the commentary by Tyconius, the contemporary of Augustine.[1]

With few exceptions all this mass of Biblical exegesis has certain common features. Many parts of the Bible were completely neglected by the commentators. Only Hrabanus and Haymo of Auxerre (died *c.* 850) paid any attention to the prophetic books. Even more noticeable is the exclusive attention paid to Matthew, while Mark and Luke were passed over. It is true that the works of Ambrose and Bede on these two Gospels were regarded as authoritative; yet, since local needs could produce expositions of Genesis and Matthew, in spite of the existence of earlier commentaries on these books, one is led to suppose that the study of the First Gospel was considered basic, and that the others were expounded in connexion with Matthew. This assumption is supported by the commentary of Christian of Stavelot; for there we find in a number of citations that he has added details from Luke, or that he actually quotes Luke's words instead of Matthew's before explaining a given episode in the Gospel story. In the second place there is a general similarity of sources used, though some writers had better library facilities than others. An extreme form of indebtedness confronts us in the commentaries of Hrabanus; for they are made up of extracts of varying length from other writers. Still, though his own additions form a small part of the whole, he fused the combined material so well that his exegetical works are true commentaries and not mere *collectanea*. His main debt is to the four Latin Doctors, Isidore and Bede, but there are many other authors, including some pagan, whom he copies on occasion. His own references to his sources are incomplete, since he sometimes makes extensive

[1] Critical edition by H. A. Sanders in *Papers and Monographs of the American Academy in Rome*, Vol. VII (1930).

use of a book without indicating to the reader that he is doing so; and the marginal entries showing authorities cited, which we find in manuscripts of Hrabanus and for which he was doubtless responsible himself, are not always complete. Thus in his commentary on Matthew he has borrowed from Claudius of Turin. In expounding Genesis he makes no allusion to Bede, although he uses him throughout; and in the commentary on Samuel and Kings he has incorporated about two-thirds of Bede's *Triginta Quaestiones* and nearly the whole of *De Templo Salomonis*, again without mentioning his source. Medieval custom did not condemn this practice. Indeed it was the custom of the time, and it is therefore futile and quite beside the point to label Hrabanus a plagiarist. But the modern student, who would determine how much of his own ideas a particular writer has set down, is sometimes faced with a task of almost hopeless complexity.[1]

There may have been a special reason why Hrabanus suppressed the name of Claudius of Turin; for there were many who regarded that prelate as not a little tainted with heresy. He has suffered for this in medieval and modern times; for, apart from the commentary on Matthew, his works do not appear to have been widely known in the Middle Ages, and most of them are still unprinted.[2] Claudius speaks with exemplary modesty and even diffidence of his performance. He had undoubtedly read very deeply in theological literature; but, though he was endowed with an original mind, he did not allow it scope in his commentaries. His own disappointment must have been bitter, for at first his exegetical labours had met with wide recognition amongst his contemporaries, including that of the emperor himself.[3] His knowledge of Augustine, whom he regarded with reverent awe, was profound; and we may guess that his Augustinian studies owed much to his residence during his early life at Lyons, where the

---

[1] For the interrelation of some of these commentaries see my article in *Harvard Theol. Rev.*, 46 (1953), pp. 27–43. The best and fairest estimate of Hrabanus is by Paul Lehmann. See his 'Zu Hraban's geistiger Bedeutung' in *St Bonifatius: Gedenkgabe zum zwölfhundertjährigen Todestag* (Fulda, 1954), pp. 473–87.

[2] In *PL*, 114 will be found only the commentaries on Kings, Galatians, and Philemon, and some Prefaces to other commentaries.

[3] See his letters in *MGH*, Epist., IV, pp. 590–613.

library, as we have seen, was unusually rich in the works of the African Father. In the task of collecting his material Claudius appears to have worked entirely single-handed, whereas Alcuin and Hrabanus on their own showing had the assistance of pupils.

Almost universally the method of interpretation was that approved by the high authority of Gregory and Bede; that is to say, in putting together their commentaries or *collectanea* on a Biblical Book the Carolingian scholars chiefly had in mind the allegorizing of the Scriptures. Claudius of Turin claims to have explained Genesis historically and allegorically.[1] Yet with him, as with others, everything else was subordinated to the main work of setting out the spiritual sense; for in the ninth century and after there are very few traces of the Antiochene school of exegesis whose teachers had assigned the chief place in their works to the interpretation of the literal or historical sense. In practice the Carolingian divines usually attempted only a twofold interpretation in a given passage, the literal, and either the allegorical or the tropological. But some at least knew of three, or even four, methods of interpretation. Thus Claudius, although he is usually content with the *litera* and the *spiritus*, also alludes to the threefold classification into physical, allegorical, and ethical sense.[2] Hrabanus, in addition to the three familiar to him from Gregory, also names the anagogical; but it is remarkable that in his commentary on Samuel and Kings the passages that he omits from Bede's *Triginta Quaestiones* and *De Templo* are uniformly pieces of allegorizing. It looks as if he found Bede's preoccupation with the spiritual sense in his later commentaries excessive. Angelomus in the preface to his exposition of Samuel and Kings discusses seven senses in which the Scriptures can be expounded, but in the commentary itself he restricts himself to the usual three.

Radbert is in a different class. That he was a profound and original thinker he showed, as has been seen, by the contribution that he made to the literature of the Eucharistic controversy. Such a man might be expected to differ as an expositor from the mass of contemporary writers. His most elaborate commentary was that on Matthew. He seems to have been engaged on it for

---

[1] See *ibid.*, p. 592, 2–4.   [2] *ibid.*, p. 594 29–30.

many years, a considerable interval having elapsed between the composition of the first four books and the remaining eight. He was not content to string his sources, which were many and varied, together, but took the utmost care both in the selection and in the disposition of his borrowed material. Particularly notable is his use of an anonymous Latin version of Origen's Matthew commentary and of Hilary of Poitiers, an author who in the other commentators of the age either plays quite a subordinate role or none at all. The methods of the good teacher are apparent throughout, but especially in the early books. Linguistic and grammatical usages receive much attention, also historical occurrences and even very occasionally pagan mythology. Radbert now and then cited classical authors, and it is evident that he was well versed in the liberal arts. But he also indulges in sharp strictures against profane authors, thereby showing that he was on the side of Gregory I on the vexed question of pagan literature and its proper use.[1] At a time when many of his contemporaries were prepared to compromise, Radbert was more outspoken and forgot that his own training had not been wholly theological. It was, however, characteristic of his active mind that he was not afraid of being controversial even on Scriptural passages and their interpretation. There is something refreshingly unusual to find a commentator in that age willing to criticize his authorities. Radbert's animadversions are not confined to those who, like Origen, were tainted with heterodoxy; for he ventures to disagree with such revered writers as Hilary and Jerome.[2] Another remarkable exception to general rules is furnished by the Matthew commentary of Christian of Stavelot. He lays the emphasis on the literal or historical interpretation of the Gospel and subordinates the allegorical. Besides this he adapts rather than copies such authorities as he used. His chief guide was Jerome. His historical reading was respectable, but, with the exception of Josephus, restricted to authors of the late imperial age, namely, Solinus, Eutropius, the Epitomist of Aurelius Victor,

---

[1] Cf. the passage quoted above, page 211.

[2] For a detailed investigation of Radbert's commentary, together with a source analysis of typical passages see A. E. Schönbach in *SB.*, Vienna Academy, 146 (1903), pp. 142–75.

and Orosius. Everywhere his commentary, which is written in a simple and unadorned style, bears witness to the hand of an experienced teacher. Yet this sane exposition of the First Gospel, because it differed so much in its approach from generally approved methods, appears to have enjoyed little posthumous popularity. Only four manuscripts of it have survived; its use by later writers has so far not been demonstrable.[1]

It would be a grave error to undervalue the work done by these exponents of the Bible, because they only reproduced other men's ideas and added little or nothing of their own. Some were men of wide learning, others of more modest attainments; but all were alike in regarding the writings of their predecessors, down to and including Bede, as so classic or canonical, that only ignorant presumption would have dared to go beyond their teaching or to question what they taught. What the Carolingian scholars did must be judged in the light of the intellectual conditions and the intellectual and spiritual needs of the time. Only a very few men in that era had either the opportunity or the capacity for making a prolonged study, or for acquiring a comprehensive knowledge, of the classics of theological literature composed in the third and fourth centuries. As for the less familiar works their use may sometimes have been accidental. Thus Angelomus would hardly have made extensive use of so little known a writer as Aponius, if the Luxeuil library had not happened to have a manuscript containing the first six books of his commentary on the Song of Songs. And, though they may have left little trace in the literature of the ninth century, some of the Biblical *Pseudepigrapha*—for example, the *Letter of Barnabas*, the *Book of Adam and Eve*, and the *Transitus Beatae Mariae*, which was known already to Bede— aroused interest and were read, as surviving manuscripts prove. Men like Alcuin and Hrabanus and their pupils put succeeding generations eternally in their debt by bringing together what seemed to them the best and the most readily assimilated utter ances of the Fathers and making this wisdom accessible to a

---

[1] That Walahfrid Strabo was the author of the *Gloss* has been proved a legend, and that huge compilation, though containing some earlier material, is of much later date. For an excellent account of the growth of the *Gloss* see Beryl Smalley, *The Study of the Bible in the Middle Ages* (ed. 2, 1952), pp. 46 ff.

greater circle of monks and clergy. In thus upholding authority and tradition, and transmitting to others the thoughts of those chiefly responsible for fixing the one and formulating the other, the Carolingian theologians were performing what they regarded with full justice as the highest of missions.

An interesting, though not a large, group of writings is made up of works dealing with the monastic or clerical life, including those of a devotional or hortatory character, or with ritual and the liturgy. Because of its wide influence and the variety of its contents the treatise in three books by Hrabanus Maurus, *Concerning the education of the clergy* (*De institutione clericorum*), deserves pride of place. What has been said of his methods of compiling Biblical commentaries applies also to this book. It is culled from earlier authors, ecclesiastical and secular. Its contents may be briefly summarized. In the first book Hrabanus devotes successive sections to the different ecclesiastical grades, to the various vestments, to the proper procedure respecting catechumens, and to the sacraments. The second book describes the offices, the chief festivals of the Church, and the parts of the liturgy. Finally the proper education of the clergy, together with a short survey of the liberal arts and a somewhat fuller treatment of the training of the preacher, forms the theme of the concluding book. The contents of the first and second books are derived almost entirely from Isidore and Bede, with occasional insertions from other writers, such as Augustine, or Cassian, or from Councils. It is only rarely that we find a passage of any length that is apparently Hrabanus' own.[1] The third book is even less original. Most of it is transcribed direct from Augustine's *De doctrina Christiana* and the *Regula pastoralis* of Gregory I. There are a few brief additions from the second book of Cassiodorus' *Institutiones*, Alcuin, and Gregory's *Moralia*; a few definitions are borrowed from the *Etymologies* of Isidore. Hrabanus' own contribution in the last book are of the slightest. He makes some comments of his own in the chapters on the liberal arts, the purpose of which is to

---

[1] Cf. 1, 27 (on catechizing) or 2, 28 (on alms) in the edition by A. Knöpfler (*Veröffentlichungen aus dem Kirchenhistorischen Seminar*, München, No. 5, 1901). The editor prints all borrowed material in italics, but warns the reader that he may not have succeeded in identifying it all.

defend their use and recommend their study as a means to an end. We can hardly doubt that he wrote in this way with the express purpose of silencing those who wished to rule out secular studies entirely. Thus, he emphasizes the need for *grammatica* and also for some acquaintance with metrics, pointing out the distinguished poets who have 'pleased God by their use, namely, Juvencus, Sedulius, Arator, Alcimus, Clemens, Paulinus, Fortunatus, and many others'.[1] He also introduces the simile of the captive woman from Deuteronomy (xxi, 11 ff.), doubtless a conscious reminiscence of a passage in Jerome's famous letter (70) to the *rhetor*, Magnus.[2] His praise of dialectic, which introduces a long quotation from *De doctrina Christiana*, is especially eloquent:[3]

> This then is the discipline of disciplines, this teaches you to teach, this teaches you to learn. In it reason itself shows and makes clear what it is, what it wills, and what it can. . . . By it we understand what it is that does good and what is a good deed, what is the creator and what the creature. By it we inquire into truth and lay hold of falsehood; by it we argue and discover what results, what does not result, and what is contrary in nature, what is true, what has the appearance of truth, and what is utterly false in disputations. In this discipline also we seek out each thing intelligently, and define it truthfully and discuss it wisely. Wherefore it behoves the clergy to know this most noble art and to ponder assiduously on its laws, so that by it they may be able to distinguish the subtle and crafty devices of the heretic and confute his poisonous words with true syllogistic conclusions.

The arts of the *quadrivium*, too, receive a few words of commendation. These passages add nothing to the knowledge of the subject, but they demonstrate that Hrabanus was a faithful pupil of Alcuin and a product of Charlemagne's educational reforms. His attitude to the study of secular literature is pragmatic. If his approbation is more outspoken than that of his teacher, he followed the guidance, and did not attempt to go beyond, the views of Jerome and the earlier Augustine, as we find them in the second book of *De doctrina Christiana*. Though not compiled with any great degree of skill, the *De institutione clericorum* is a

---

[1] *op. cit.*, 3, 19. Like Alcuin in his poem on the bishops of York, Hrabanus calls Prudentius by his cognomen, Clemens.

[2] Cf. above, p. 49.   [3] *op. cit.*, 3, 20.

clear and succinct manual. Written comparatively early in his life (819) it affords a perspicuous index of Hrabanus' practice as a teacher, abbot, and bishop. And the untiring manner in which at all periods of his career he strove to further education, and especially to raise the intellectual standards of the clergy at Fulda and more generally throughout eastern Frankland, fully justify the sobriquet applied to him, *praeceptor Germaniae*.

Monastic reform and uniformity of observance were matters that had engaged the attention of successive Carolingian rulers and their ecclesiastical advisers. The *Rule* of St Benedict was to be followed universally, and we have seen the steps taken by Charlemagne to procure a reliable text of it, free from interpolations.[1] But the *Rule* was very brief and its provisions required elucidation and amplification, if they were to be observed not merely loyally but intelligently by the brethren. Thus there was room for a fuller exposition of Benedict's ordinances and their purpose, based on actual experience of conventual life. The earliest commentary was composed by Paul the Deacon at Civate for his fellow-monks between *c.* 774 and 779. A little more than half a century later Hildemar of Civate dictated the observations of Paul to his pupils, making some additions of his own, chiefly on linguistic points. His commentary cannot, therefore, be regarded as a separate work; it is merely a new edition of Paul's. The explanations were intended for reasonably advanced students. Hence the book is not a running commentary on the *Rule*, but resembles a series of lectures which are interrupted from time to time by the questions of pupils. The whole is thus a combination of continuous discourse and dialogue. Much attention is paid to the opinions of older scholars concerning Benedict's meaning in obscure passages, and also to variant readings in the several manuscripts which Paul collated, including the original text preserved at Monte Cassino. The detailed exposition by Smaragdus, abbot of St Mihiel, who did not know Paul's work, was undertaken independently soon after 817. It was written under the

---

[1] The classic study of the pure and the interpolated texts of the *Rule* is still Ludwig Traube's *Textgeschichte der Regula S. Benedicti* (Second edition revised by H. Plenkers in *Abhandlungen*, Bavarian Academy; philosophisch-philologische und historische Klasse, 25, 1910). For more recent literature see *Clavis*, No. 1852.

influence and in the interest of Benedict of Aniane's reforms. The author explains in his preface how very necessary it was to expound the *Rule*. He points out that many religious had only an imperfect understanding of it, so that an interpretation intelligible to the ordinary inmate of a monastery was an urgent need. Smaragdus' treatment, in consequence, is more elementary in character than Paul's; in particular it disregards questions of textual criticism. The *Diadema monachorum* by Smaragdus is a devotional reading book made up of extracts from the Fathers and was composed some years before the commentary on the *Rule*. The abbot's purpose was that his monks who read a chapter from the *Rule* of St Benedict each morning should similarly peruse a chapter from his *collectaneum* each evening. He also compiled extracts from earlier commentators on the Pauline Epistles, in which, like Sedulius after him, he quoted from a pure, not an interpolated, text of Pelagius.[1]

The Church under Charlemagne and his successors was fortunate in possessing many prelates to whom their pastoral duties were a matter of constant and earnest care. Two examples will serve to illustrate this. Agobard of Lyons strove his hardest to remedy existing institutions which he regarded as abuses. He wrote a pamphlet addressed to clergy and laity in which he roundly condemned trials by ordeal. In an address to the emperor he calls upon him to abolish the duel as a means of deciding a dispute judicially.[2] From other tracts by Agobard we see that superstitions and heathen customs, whose eradication had troubled leading Churchmen in earlier times, and had engaged the attention of Charlemagne and his ministers, were still rife. The archbishop of Lyons was as active in working for their suppression in the interests of true religion, as his predecessors had been.[3] In all these writings the authority of the Bible and the Patristic authors were constantly invoked. Agobard's letters and tracts combated specific evils or abuses. The *De institutione laicali* was composed by Jonas, bishop of Orléans, in answer to a request

---

[1] See A. Souter, *op. cit.*, I, pp. 333–6.
[2] *PL*, 104, coll. 249–67; *MGH*, Epist., V, pp. 158 ff.
[3] Cf. *PL*, 104, coll. 147 ff., 179 ff.; also the address against image-worship, *ibid.*, 199 ff.

made by a nobleman in his diocese to write a disquisition on Christian marriage. Jonas was not content to explain this matter alone, but put together from the Bible and many early Christian writers what may fairly be called a handbook of Christian ethics. Although he adds little of his own, he confirms the impression, also conveyed by his book on monarchic government, that he was an unusually learned man. Besides Augustine, Jerome, Gregory I, and other widely known writers, he was also acquainted with and quoted from a number of less obvious sources. Such were the tract on dice-playing (*De aleatoribus*), composed *c.* 300 and wrongly included amongst the works of Cyprian, the book by Pomerius on the contemplative life, which, in common with most medieval writers, he attributes to Prosper of Aquitaine, and the *Homilies* of Caesarius of Arles. In the first book Jonas treats of baptism and the remission of sins, prayer and church-going, purity of life and the danger of evil living whilst professing Christianity. The second book opens with a long disquisition on marriage; this is followed by sections on the relations that should exist between clergy and laity, and on swearing, lying, false-witness, and inquisitiveness. In the third and last book the reader is instructed about the virtues of charity, humility, and patience, and the vices of pride, hatred, and envy, about the eight major sins, alms, visiting the sick, death and burial, resurrection, the day of judgment, the eternal punishment of the wicked and the reward of the good.[1]

The greatest liturgical authority of the ninth century was Amalarius of Metz. A pupil of Alcuin, he attracted the favourable notice of Charlemagne. He was designated bishop of Trèves and occupied that see for a short time. Then, in 813, the emperor sent him on an important diplomatic mission to the Emperor Michael I. After his return from Constantinople in the following year he ceased to hold his bishopric, since his nomination had never been confirmed by the bishops of Toul, Verdun, and Metz. Amalarius then disappears from view for over twenty years. What his ecclesiastical position was during that period is obscure, but it was then that his liturgical works were composed. The longest and most important was the *Liber officialis* in four books,

[1] PL, 106, coll. 121–278.

in which he set himself to interpret the inward meaning of the
Mass and of the festivals of the ecclesiastical year.[1] The disciple
of Alcuin, and already imbued deeply with the tradition, taken
over by his master from Bede and handed on to the next generation,
of allegorizing or reading a mystical significance into the Bible,
Amalarius applied this method of interpretation to the sacrament
of the Eucharist and to other parts of the liturgy. To do so most
effectively he made a profound study of Patristic literature, as well
as of all the liturgical books to which he could gain access. It is
evident that the efforts made by Chrodegang of Metz and then by
Charlemagne's advisers, to attain uniformity in ritual, and more
especially to secure full adherence to the Roman rite, had only
partially succeeded. How much variation still existed in the time
of Amalarius, even where it might be least expected, can be illustrated by one experience that he relates. Among the liturgical
books obtained by him in France was an *ordo Romanus*, which he
not unreasonably regarded as authoritative. But on visiting Rome
he discovered that the actual usage there at that time differed
substantially from what was laid down in that volume.[2] He
followed up his big work by putting together a new antiphonary
to be used at Metz, a composition now unhappily lost. Because
of the dissimilarity between the many existing antiphonaries he
desired to provide one which, based on the soundest ascertainable
tradition and practice, might be accepted thereafter as standard.
The surviving treatise, *De ordine antiphonarii*, had a double purpose: it justified his procedure and was also a commentary on the
new antiphonary. The lost service-book was a conflation of an
antiphonarium Romanum from the time of Hadrian I (772–95),
which he obtained, not in Rome, where he searched in vain, but
at Corbie, and that previously followed at Metz. It was perhaps
unfortunate that in 835 Amalarius was called to Lyons, probably
with the rank of suffragan (*chorepiscopus*), to take charge of that
diocese during the exile of Agobard. At all events he took steps
to introduce his new antiphonary there, but met with the bitterest
opposition, especially from Agobard's faithful henchman, the

---

[1] The works of Amalarius have been finely edited by J. M. Hanssens. See
his *Amalarii episcopi opera liturgica omnia* in *ST*, 138–40 (1948–50).

[2] Preface to *De ord. antiph.* (*ST*, 140, pp. 13 ff.).

deacon Florus. The sequel was that the whole of Amalarius' liturgical teaching became the object of an attack culminating in a summons before a Synod at Quierzy in 838 to answer charges of heresy. His views were condemned and he was forced to leave Lyons; but no further action against him seems to have been taken. He was impeached at the Synod on five major and several minor counts. Four of the major charges, which concerned the canon and sacrifice of the Mass, were made possible chiefly because of the somewhat unguarded language that Amalarius had used, and which was easily liable to be misinterpreted. For example, in stating that 'the body of Christ is triform and tripartite', he had in mind the then established ritual. When the consecrated wafer was broken, one portion of the Host was placed in the chalice, one was reserved for communion, and one remained on the altar. This triple division, Amalarius taught, had a mystical significance.

> By the portion of the wafer placed in the chalice is meant the body of Christ which has already risen from the dead; by that portion which is eaten by the priest and congregation is meant Christ who still walks on earth; by that which remains on the altar is meant Christ lying in the tomb. . . . And that portion stays on the altar to the end of the Mass, because to the end of the world the bodies of the saints shall lie at peace in their graves.[1]

It is not difficult to see how an embittered opponent, like Florus, could speciously charge Amalarius with teaching that Christ had three bodies, assuredly the gravest of heresies. The violent language of Florus can still be studied in a manuscript of the *Liber officialis* which he annotated in the margins with every kind of abusive expression, 'savage and insulting notes', as the latest editor of Amalarius calls them.[2] The fifth of the major accusations against Amalarius was a general indictment of his allegorical interpretations, on the ground that what was legitimate or even appropriate in explaining the Old Testament, in order to demonstrate its prophetic character and its promise of the coming of Christ and His Church, was wholly inappropriate and even

---

[1] *Liber off.*, 3, 35 (*ST*, 139, pp. 367–8).
[2] 'Furibondae ac contumeliosae notae.' Fr Hanssens has printed Florus' *marginalia* in *ST*, 139, pp. 567 ff.

mischievous when applied to the New Testament. Its meaning was clear and to be accepted literally; any attempt to interpret the words esoterically would result in blurring the central fact of Christ's mission on earth and all that followed therefrom. In spite of the prelates who condemned Amalarius, his method, though it occasionally went to extremes, was the one which the Middle Ages as a whole regarded with most sympathy. Indeed, the views implied by the judgment of Quierzy were those of a minority; and one may legitimately wonder whether those members of the Synod, if any such attended, who voted entirely without personal bias or any ulterior motive to hasten the restoration of Agobard to his see, had not been influenced by the writings of the Antiochene school of exegesis.[1] The authority of Amalarius was not permanently shaken. Extant manuscripts of the *Liber officialis* are many and Fr Hanssens has shown that there were three editions of it, the third being revised by Amalarius between 831 and 835. There are also codices of it containing changes made after his time, and it is clear that Amalarius was studied and excerpted by a succession of writers from the tenth to the twelfth century. Amalarius based his exegesis on an abundance of earlier material. We meet in his pages with extracts from Ambrose, Ambrosiaster, Cyprian, Chrysostom on Hebrews in the Latin version of Mutianus, the Latin translation of Origen's homilies on the Pentateuch, Augustine, Jerome, Hilary, Orosius, Cassiodorus' *Commentary on the Psalms* and *Historia Tripartita*, Gregory, and Bede; he made use also of a great number of liturgical books. In short, Amalarius made the first systematic attempt to interpret the liturgy as a whole, a circumstance of vital worth to the Middle Ages, which explains the attention he received from later specialists in liturgical questions. To the modern investigator of the history of the liturgy, familiar with the Roman rite as it now is, the works of Amalarius are an important landmark. They are, moreover, of utmost value for the precise information that they afford about the Church ritual in use at Metz during the ninth century, and the narrowing differences at a critically

---

[1] Cf. *Harvard Theol. Rev.*, 40 (1947), pp. 19 ff., and the important fresh evidence published by B. Bischoff in *Sacris Erudiri*, VI (1954). See particularly pp. 190 and 210 ff.

formative period between north Frankish and Roman usage, from which the universally accepted Roman rite finally emerged in a later age.

Compared with them the pamphlet of Walahfrid with its awkward title, *De exordiis et incrementis quarundam in observationibus ecclesiasticis rerum*, was a slight performance. Yet it is interesting that the author, though he consulted Amalarius, did not follow him in his mystical interpretation of various rites and institutions. He confined himself to a short investigation of their historical origins. The little book, indeed, contains a good deal that is of interest both to the archaeologist and to the student of language.[1]

[1] Cf. page 240 above.

CHAPTER XIII

The Literature of the Carolingian Age

(a) Political Ideas

It was a salutary thing, such as betokened a time of intellectual awakening, when men turned their minds to political theory, especially to the relation between Church and State. This question clearly must have presented itself to the minds of men who, like Alcuin and Hrabanus, were for much of their life involved in political and ecclesiastical affairs; and some of Alcuin's ideas on the subject are stated in simple form in the dialogue, *De rhetorica*, to which reference was made on an earlier page. Five other works deal more specifically with the problem. There is first a brief address in epistolary form written by one, Kathvulf, to Charlemagne.[1] Between 812 and 815 Smaragdus of St Mihiel composed his *Via regia* for Louis the Pious.[2] The *De institutione regia* of Jonas, bishop of Orléans, was written in 834. The *De rectoribus Christianis* by Sedulius Scotus appeared about twenty years later.[3] Latest of all was the treatise of Hincmar of Rheims, composed for Charles the Bald and entitled, *De regis persona et regio ministerio*.[4] Of these works only that by Jonas was clearly inspired by specific political events. It was called forth by Louis' unhappy dispute with his sons and his ignominious abdication, and was written for the young king, Pippin, so that he might avoid the misgovernment which had been his father's undoing.[5]

There are certain characteristics common to all those who in

[1] *MGH*, Epist., IV, pp. 502 ff.

[2] *PL*, 102, coll. 933 ff. For the date and addressee cf. my note in *Speculum*, 3 (1928), pp. 392–7.

[3] Jonas in *PL*, 106, coll. 279 ff.; Sedulius edited by S. Hellmann, *Sedulius Scottus* (Munich, 1906), pp. 19–91.

[4] *PL*, 125, coll. 833 ff.

[5] See Jonas' prefatory letter to the king, especially col. 283A–D.

this epoch reflected on the problem of government. There is, in the first place, a common background, namely, Patristic authority, and especially that of Augustine. All alike were Churchmen, and consequently all approached the questions at issue through theology. On the other hand, none, least of all those who, like Hincmar, were earnest students of civil and canon law, could remain uninfluenced by the society and institutions of their day. But in the law and government of Charlemagne and his successors two very different elements, the Roman and the Germanic, were represented, and the fusion of the two had not yet been completely effected. Hence the Roman-Christian concepts, which the political thinkers of the ninth century had taken over from Christian writers of the later imperial period were, to a greater or less degree, modified by concepts derived from the society in which they lived and forming a direct contrast to them. The opposition between what, for the sake of convenience, may be termed the Roman and the Germanic theory is most apparent when the relation of the ruler to the law is under consideration. The Roman emperors, at least in later imperial times, had been the sole source of law, and were thought of themselves as in some manner above the law. But amongst the Germanic peoples the monarch could claim no such absolute powers; for, although a strong king could generally enforce his will in legislative matters, he did not issue his ordinances without the acquiescence of the leading men in Church and State. In promulgating them he coupled their names with his, or even with that of his people as a whole. It follows that, even as the legislative power was not concentrated solely in his hands, so also he could not be regarded as above the laws, but, like his subjects, was bound by them.[1] A sentiment, such as is expressed by Sedulius, 'the wise ruler summons wise men to his council and does nothing without their advice, but the foolish ponders with himself and does what his momentary wishes bid without the advice of others',[2] indeed

[1] Cf. the full discussion with quotations from contemporary legislation as well as from the theorists in A. J. Carlyle, *A History of Mediaeval Political Theory in the West*, I, pp. 229–39. A briefer but useful survey will be found in C. H. McIlwain, *The Growth of Political Thought in the West*, Chapter V, but he omits the theorists of the ninth century.

[2] Page 38, 16–18, in Hellmann's edition.

lacks precision and applies to all, not merely to the legislative functions of the king. But the legally trained mind of Hincmar was more explicit. His essay, *De regis persona et regio ministerio*, it is true, is little more than a cento of extracts from Ambrose, Augustine, and Gregory. But the treatise *Ad proceres regis et de ordine palatii* contains contemporary judgments side by side with the authority of tradition. Most of this book is an adaptation of an earlier *De ordine palatii* by Adalhard of Corbie, the contemporary of Charlemagne. But clearly Hincmar agreed with Adalhard, and his treatise is valuable for its portrayal of the court and court procedure under Charlemagne, which Hincmar regarded as a model. His pronouncement concerning the monarch and the law is so notable that it deserves to be cited as it stands:[1]

> Even as it has been said concerning ecclesiastical laws that 'no priest may be ignorant of their canons nor yet do aught that might obstruct the rules of the fathers', so also the sacred (*i.e.* Roman) laws have decreed that 'no man may be in ignorance of the laws or scorn existing statutes'. When it is stated, 'no man may be in ignorance of the laws or scorn existing statutes', no person in any class of men is excepted, so that he is not bound by this pronouncement. For monarchs and ministers of the state have laws by which it is their duty to govern the inhabitants of every province, they have the capitularies of Christian kings and of their forebears, which these proclaimed with the general consent of their faithful subjects that they would observe in accordance with law. Concerning these the blessed Augustine says, 'men may exercise their judgment on these laws when they institute them; but when they have been instituted and confirmed, it shall not be lawful for judges to judge about them but only in accordance with them'.

It must be remembered that the treatises of Smaragdus, Jonas, and Sedulius are essentially hortatory, a type of composition to which the name *Mirrors for Princes* (*Fürstenspiegel*) has often been applied. They contrast the good and the bad ruler; in enumerating the virtues that make up the good ruler and the duties that devolve upon him, if he is to remain a just king, they reproduce examples from the Bible and citations from earlier writers of authority. It has already been seen that the tract on the twelve

---

[1] *De ordine palatii*, 8, in *MGH*, Leg., II, 2, p. 520, 25-35.

abuses of the age by an unknown Irishman was favourite literature with the Carolingian scholars. Both Jonas and Hincmar
quote the chapter on the just and the unjust monarch in full.
Jonas introduces other lengthy citations from Isidore's *Sententiae*,
Augustine's *City of God*, and Fulgentius of Ruspe. Sedulius
devotes considerable space to the king's treatment of his relatives,
servants, and nearest friends and counsellors. The king's task
is a threefold one: 'He must in the first place rule himself;
next he must rule his wife and children and their servants; in the
third place he must rule his people, committed to his care, with a
reasonable and exalted governance.'[1] He also discusses in some
detail the monarch's conduct in relation to his enemies. The
Christian ruler must trust in divine aid rather than in his own
courage and that of his troops; he must implore it even in the very
clash of battle. He must be clement to his opponents and avoid
pride over his victory manifesting itself in tyrannous treatment of
the vanquished.[2] All these chapters Sedulius has filled out with
numerous illustrations. They are drawn partly from the Bible,
partly from Roman history, for which he has taken his examples
from the *Scriptores Historiae Augustae* and from the *Tripartite
History* of Cassiodorus. In certain respects there is a marked
difference between the discourses of Smaragdus and Jonas on the
one hand and Sedulius' book on the other. All three works, and
also Kathvulf's open letter, bear a general resemblance, because
they are all, as it were, manuals of Christian ethics for Christian
rulers. But Sedulius is more diffuse and less consequential in his
treatment of the main theme. He is sometimes in danger of for-
getting his argument amid the wealth of illustrations which he
provides. While abbot and bishop cared little for literary form
but were genuinely concerned to guide the steps of still youthful
princes, in the versatile Sedulius the would-be artist in prose is
constantly throwing the moral teacher into the shade. One or two
special features are worthy of note. None of these writers pondered seriously and independently over human society as a whole.
They accepted what they were familiar with, and, where general
questions arose, they were content to reproduce the verdict of the
Fathers. In one point Smaragdus differed from other thinkers of

[1] Hellmann, *op. cit.*, p. 34, 2–4.   [2] See Chapters 14 to 17.

his age; he appeals to Louis to condemn outright the institution of slavery and urges him to prohibit enslavement in his realm.[1]

The basic problem which was to agitate the Christian world so often in the later Middle Ages, that is to say, the relation between the Temporal and the Spiritual Power, is first tentatively mooted in the ninth century. Many years were still to elapse before the aphorism of Fulgentius of Ruspe, which was frequently cited in the Councils of the late eighth and of the ninth centuries, was seriously or effectively challenged, to wit: 'as far as concerns this life on earth it is agreed that in the Church no one is greater than the pontiff, and in the Christian world no one is higher than the emperor'.[2] Smaragdus and Hincmar in De regis persona on this matter provide little beyond extracts from earlier authorities. Sedulius' attitude to the Temporal Power is summed up in the following words from the first chapter of his book:[3]

Inasmuch as the good ruler recognizes that he has been appointed by God, in so much he watches with pious anxiety how he may before God and men arrange and weigh all things in good order according to the scales of righteousness. For what are the rulers of Christian people save servants of the All-powerful? Further, each servant is satisfactory and faithful who with sincere devotion shall do the bidding of his master and lord. Hence the most pious and renowned princes feel it a greater glory to be called and to be the servants and slaves of the Most High than the lords and kings of men.

Towards the end of his book Sedulius writes:[4]

For it behoves the ruler beloved of God whom His divine ordinance has desired to be, as it were, His vicar in the governance of His Church; and has bestowed on him authority over both orders, namely, prelates and subjects, to the end that he may decree to each several persons what is just, so that under his dispensation the former order may take the lead in good teaching and good works, and the latter may in devoted obedience be faithfully submissive.

The good ruler must see to it that 'the heads of the Church occupy their places legitimately'; he must support them in

[1] PL, 102, col. 967A—ne in regno tuo captivitas fiat; cf. also generally Carlyle, op. cit., p. 209.

[2] PL, 65, col. 647D—quantum pertinet ad huius temporis vitam constat quia in ecclesia nemo pontifice potior, et in saeculo Christiano nemo imperatore celsior invenitur.

[3] Hellmann, op. cit., p. 22, 14–22.   [4] ibid., p. 86, 5–10.

exercising their office 'according to the mandates of God and the institutions of the sacred canons', and 'let not the secular powers hinder them'. We see, then, that there is no statement which makes the king in any way subordinate to the ruler of the Church; on the contrary, the king is called the vicar of God, a phrase found already in Ambrosiaster, and it is suggested that the Temporal Power may be used to prevent irregularities in the Church. But in the main the ruler and the ecclesiastical authorities are pictured as working hand in hand for the common good. In a word, the point of view expressed by Sedulius was that generally held by the contemporaries of Charlemagne.[1] Jonas, however, is a more outspoken defender of ecclesiastical claims. At the beginning of his book he observes:[2]

> All the faithful must know that the Church universal is the body of Christ and the head thereof is Christ, and in the Church universal there are chiefly two outstanding persons, the priestly and the royal. The priestly is in so far more excellent inasmuch as he shall render account to God for kings themselves.

This is a restatement of the famous dictum made by Pope Gelasius to the Emperor Anastasius,[3] which Jonas goes on to quote verbatim. He also cites the passage from Fulgentius to which we have already referred. In his second chapter he deals with the priestly power and authority; the very fact that he discusses it before passing on to a more detailed study of the Secular Power is an index to his attitude on the question. First amongst the duties of the king, moreover, is to be the 'defender of the churches and servants of God'. In certain of Hincmar's addresses, too, a similar insistence on the superiority of the bishop in spiritual matters appears. Thus we must set against those writers who, like Sedulius, seem to assign first place to the king-emperor, others who enunciate the principle that in his specific sphere the head of the Church stands higher than the ruler of the State,

---

[1] Cf. above, p. 190.   [2] *PL*, 106, col. 285B.

[3] *PL*, 59, *Epist.*, 12, 2—Duo quippe sunt, imperator auguste, quibus principaliter mundus hic regitur: auctoritas sacrata pontificum et regalis potestas, in quibus tanto gravius est pondus sacerdotum, quanto etiam pro ipsis regibus hominum in divino reddituri sunt examine rationem. For a valuable discussion of Gelasius' letter and its implications see Hendrik Berkhof, *Kirche und Kaiser* (Zürich, 1947), pp. 210–12.

because even the monarch is not exempt from ecclesiastical cen-
sure, if he transgresses against the Christian religion. The more
independent line taken by Jonas and Hincmar was due at least in
part to changed political conditions. The supremacy in both
Church and State to which Charlemagne laid claim in his later
years and which in fact he was able to exercise perished with him;
and it is significant of the instability which characterized much of
the political history of the ninth century that the princes of the
Church could, in theory, and sometimes also in practice, arrogate
to themselves authority such as fifty years earlier not even Hadrian
or Leo could enforce against the ruler of the Franks. On the
other hand, in the ninth, as in the eighth century the Temporal
Power did intervene in certain ecclesiastical affairs, for example,
when important posts in the Church had to be filled. Such
intervention was accepted as normal and proper. Contrariwise,
the dividing line between temporal and spiritual questions was
narrow and might easily become blurred. Agobard defied even
the emperor, although the question of Jewish disabilities or rights
in Lyons, however it might be disguised by appeals to the
Scriptures, was primarily economic.[1]

It is therefore evident that throughout the Carolingian era
men's ideas on government were still in a fluid and unsettled
state. What they thought at any given time was determined
chiefly by existing conditions. A generally held belief in a dual
control exercised by Church and State, by the one over spiritual,
by the other over secular matters, did not lead them to formulate
any political theory in which the relations of the one or the other
were sharply defined, still less one in which, what after all was
only a single, if very important, problem was merged in a wider
philosophical analysis, embracing the structure and progress of
human society, law, and government.

(b) Philosophy

Previous chapters will have made abundantly clear the essential
character of the Carolingian Revival. The age of Pippin had come

[1] On Jewish disabilities cf. S. Katz, *The Jews in the Visigothic and Frankish
Kingdoms of Spain and Gaul*, pp. 84-7, 100 ff., 129-30.

upon the Western world like a spring, to be succeeded by the long and radiant summer of Charlemagne's reign. Then the autumnal decline which set in soon after his death was for a space arrested by a short but brilliant Indian summer under Charles the Bald. The civilizing agent on which these princes relied—and there could have been no other—was the Church. The means to carry out their cultural mission her leaders and teachers found in the classical learning which the Church had preserved, and in part transformed, through the centuries, and in that theology which also was a heritage from earlier times. Great as the resultant achievement undoubtedly was, the almost unvarying adherence to tradition that characterized both the secular and the theological literature of the Carolingian Age set very definite limits to the development of thought. This is not to say that the eighth and ninth centuries were totally lacking in originality. But the degree to which writers of that epoch, whatever their field of study, could formulate new concepts or initiate a new approach to an old problem was severely restricted by the overmastering hold exercised by authority and tradition. It is true that there were not wanting men who displayed a freedom of judgment which a century or two later would have exposed them to sharp penalties. Such were Agobard and Claudius of Turin, and, in at least one of his works, Ratramnus. But it is surely proof of a certain enlightened liberalism on the part of the Church and of the secular government that, with the unmerciful exception of Gottschalk, such independent spirits brought on themselves no more than a literary warfare, or, at the very worst, inconsiderable temporary disabilities. On the other hand, it is hardly surprising that speculative philosophy should have secured no more than one faithful disciple; indeed, the total absence of any metaphysician in that era would be less remarkable than the solitary phenomenon of John Scotus. The liberal arts as then understood and taught opened no obvious avenue to philosophy; for even dialectic as expounded by the unchallenged authority of Alcuin was, as we have seen, no more than the simplest elements of logic designed to aid the teacher of literature or theology or the expositor of the Sacred Text. We have, indeed, a curious example of dialectic in a letter of Fridugis, Alcuin's successor at Tours, to certain members of the Frankish court.[1] In it the writer tries to explain the meaning of *Nihil* (Nothing) and *Tenebrae* (Darkness), and to demonstrate the reality of the one and the corporeal, that is, material nature of the other. It is hard to see in the misplaced ingenuity of his arguments more than an attempt to apply to what the ordinary pupil would regard as abstractions the simple dialectic learned from his master, Alcuin.[2]

It was only John Scotus who, having mastered the dialectic method in a manner quite unapproached by any medieval thinker before the great days of Scholasticism, proceeded to build up a philosophical system as impressive as it was unique. To classify John as a philosopher, as has usually been done, is justified, though his latest and best biographer would rather describe him as a theologian.[3] It is true, as Dom Cappuyns points out, that John was not a 'philosophe profane' and that it is mistaken to label him rationalist or even pantheist. Yet Augustine himself, when refuting a Pelagian opponent, had referred to 'our Christian philosophy, which alone is the true philosophy'.[4] Any attempt to distinguish too sharply between philosophy and theology when studying John's works borders on an anachronism; and his terminology is derived in great part from philosophy and particularly the Neoplatonism which he found in his Greek sources. Furthermore, it is convenient to differentiate John from his contemporaries in this way, because to them theology consisted either of exegesis or of controversial writings dealing with the truth or falsity of a particular dogma.

The early life and training of this versatile genius are entirely unknown. He seems to have come from his native Ireland to western France *c.* 850. He is generally believed to have been a

[1] *MGH*, Epist., IV, pp. 552 ff.

[2] The letter continues to interest scholars. Cf. A. J. Macdonald, *Authority and Reason in the early Middle Ages* (Oxford, 1933), pp. 29–35; L. Geymonat in *Rivista di Filosofia*, 44 (1952), pp. 280ff., and C. Mazzantini, *Atti della Accademia delle Scienze di Torino*, 87, 2, pp. 170–96.

[3] M. Cappuyns, *Jean Scot Erigène*, pp. 384 ff.

[4] *PL*, 44, col. 774: obsecro te, non sit honestior philosophia gentium quam nostra Christiana, quae una est vera philosophia, quandoquidem studium vel amor sapientiae significatur hoc nomine. This is still some way from the eleventh-century teacher who remarked: 'denique ipsa philosophia Christus'; see H. M. Rochais, *Medieval Studies*, 13 (1951), pp. 244–7.

layman since he is never referred to as either a monk or the holder
of any ecclesiastical rank. He lived for some twenty years in his
adopted home and died there soon after 870. Years later various
legends about him came into circulation, the best known being
the story, told by William of Malmesbury, that he came to
England and there in due course was stabbed to death by the pens
of his angry pupils. The ultimate source of this unusual form of
martyrdom is a poem by Prudentius; when the story was fathered
on John we do not know exactly.[1] In spite of the opposition or
even active hostility aroused by some of his writings John retained
to the end the friendship and admiration of Charles the Bald.
His labours as a translator and as a commentator on both sacred
and profane works have already been considered, as also the
isolated position that he occupied in the controversy over Predestination. In the treatise that he composed on that occasion,
that is, at the end of 850 or early in 851, he had already aired
certain of his peculiar views. But some twelve years elapsed
before the *magnum opus*, wherein his transcendental philosophy
was set out in its entirety, was given to the world.[2] Its Greek
title, περὶ φύσεως μερισμοῦ, with the Latin sub-title, *De divisione
naturae* (*On the division of the universe*), was characteristic of the man
whose ideas were formed far less by the Latin Fathers, not ex-
cluding Augustine, than by the writings of the pseudo-Dionysius
and Maximus Confessor. Nor was his acquaintance with Greek
theologians confined to these two. He had read in the original
portions of Epiphanius and Gregory of Nyssa. Occasional
quotations from Gregory of Nazianzus, whom, like Isidore before
him, he seems to have confused with Gregory of Nyssa, he took
over from Maximus. For certain works by Origen and by John
Chrysostom he relied on Latin versions, presumably because he
could not get access to the Greek text. He knew no more than
other men of his time of Plato and Aristotle, namely, a Latin
translation of the *Timaeus* and Boethius' versions of *De interpretatione* and the *Categories*.[3]

[1] *Peristephanon*, ix; for other legends cf. Cappuyns, *op. cit.*, pp. 252 ff.

[2] Dom Cappuyns (*op. cit.*, pp. 188–9) gives good reasons for putting the
completion of *De divisione naturae* between 862 and 866.

[3] Although Cicero's translation of the *Timaeus* was known in the ninth
century, since it is found in two extant manuscripts of that date (Vienna, 189

John begins by dividing 'nature', that is, Reality or the totality of all things, into four classes, as follows:[1]

Methinks that the division of the universe by four differentiations (*differentias*) produces four kinds (*species*). The first division is into that which creates and is not created; the second into that which is created and creates; the third into that which is created and does not create; the fourth into that which neither creates nor is created. Of these four each one of two pairs is opposed to the other; for the third is opposed to the first and the fourth to the second. But the fourth is classed amongst impossibles, since its difference is that it cannot exist.

A second classification drawn up by John distinguishes 'things which are' from 'things which are not'. By the former are meant all those things which can be apprehended by the intellect or by sense, while the latter are incomprehensible because they are outside sense perception and cannot be grasped by the intellect. In the third place John follows the pseudo-Dionysius in his twofold division of theology into the affirmative (καταφατική) and negative (ἀποφατική). The four divisions of 'nature' are not to be understood as four separate groups but as four different aspects of one cosmic process. The first and fourth are comprehensible of God alone, for in the former aspect God, the creating, not created, is regarded as an essence or as the first principle of the universe, in the latter, that which neither creates nor is created, God is conceived as the end to which all things return, in whom all things are at rest. The second division is concerned with first causes, the ideas or prototypes of all created things, the third with all things in the created world or world of sense. John explains the relation of these two when he observes:[2]

For whatever things seem in the processes of their natures to be separated and divided in multiple fashion are united and are one in the primordial causes. And, destined to return to that unity, they will abide in it everlastingly and immutably.

The Divine Being is incomprehensible. He is the beginning, middle, and end of all things. All classifications that we may use

and Leyden, Voss. F. 84), I should now agree with Dom Cappuyns that John probably used the better known version by Chalcidius. See Cappuyns, *op. cit.*, p. 392, note 4.

[1] *PL*, 122, col. 441B.   [2] *PL*, 122, col. 527A.

are not properly applicable to God, but are merely forms of thought which we must use because our intelligence is finite. Similarly, nothing can properly be predicated of God, and John at great length sets out to show that none of the ten categories is applicable to the Divine Being.[1]

Affirmative theology may speak of God as Being, or equate Him with Divine Wisdom, Divine Justice, and so forth. But God is more than Being, more than wise. And to each of these qualities there is an opposite, so that by predicating wisdom, justice, and so on, of God, we also bring Him into the sphere of opposites. Consequently only negative theology can correctly define Him. Any definition that can be made is ultimately negative. Thus John writes:[2]

> He who says that God is superessential does not say what He is but what He is not; for he says that He is not Being (*essentia*) but more than Being. He does not explain what that is which is more than Being when he states that God is not one of those things that are, but is more than those things that are. What that being (*i.e. superessentia*) is, he in no way defines.

God is thus both superexistent, non-existent, and the only Reality; and it may be added that in one passage God is actually described as *Nihilum*, Nothing. From Him emanate the primordial causes, the nine classes of angels, and the material universe. Man himself is, as it were, a microcosm.

> For it is agreed amongst philosophers that in man every creature is contained. He understands and reasons, like an angel; he is sentient and has a care for his body like an animal; and thereby every creature is intelligible in him. There is a fivefold division of all creatures: for a creature is either corporeal (*i.e.* inanimate objects), or vital (*i.e.* plants), or sensible (*i.e.* lower animals), or rational (*i.e.* man) or intellectual (*i.e.* angels).[3]

John himself was satisfied that he had brought his idealist philosophy into accord with Christian theology as ordinarily understood in his day. But it will be seen at once that on his contemporaries his philosophical adjustment of theological dogma would necessarily make a less satisfactory impression. His doctrine of the Trinity is an essential part of his exposition of the

[1] *PL*, 122, coll. 463A to 524B.   [2] *ibid.*, 462C.   [3] *ibid.*, 755B.

creation process; for the primordial causes or divine ideas, the sum of which is equivalent to the *Logos*, are eternally created by the Father in the Son.

> God the Father is the cause of both the Son and the Holy Spirit. The Son is the cause of the divine ideas of prototypes created in Him by the Father. The Holy Spirit is the cause of the distribution of the same causes (*i.e.* the divine ideas).[1]

Immediately after this summing-up John enters into the question whether the Father alone was the cause of the Holy Spirit or the Father and the Son. His answer that the Holy Spirit proceeded from the Father *through* the Son brought him into line with the teaching of the Eastern Church and into opposition to the formulation officially approved for Western Christendom by the Synod of Aachen.

We meet the principle of triple division in other parts of John's system, and it, as it were, runs parallel to the Divine Trinity. He expresses the function of the Trinity in one passage by saying:[2]

> The Father wills, the Son creates, the Holy Spirit perfects. Nor does this appear contrary to theology which says, 'the Father has created all things in the Son'. For the Father's willing all things to be and His creating all things in the Son are not two separate things, but the Father's willing and creating are one and the same. For the willing is this action. And we must understand this similarly of the Son and the Spirit. Their operation is nothing other than Their will. Nor is there one will of the Father, one of the Son, one of the Holy Spirit, but it is one and the same will, one love of three substances of one existent (*essentialis*) goodness, by which the Father causes Himself to create all things in the Son and to perfect them in the Holy Spirit.

Now the human soul is triple, consisting in intellect, reason, and interior sense (διάνοια), as distinct from external sense perception (αἴσθησις), and it is, as it were, an image of the Trinity, even as man himself is a microcosm. The highest concepts are created by the intellect in the reason and these are separated and distributed into the visible world by 'sense'. In another definition 'sense' is said 'to occupy the last place of the human soul, rightly, since it moves around (*circumvolvitur*) the effects, visible and invisible, of the primordial causes'.[3] The number three meets us

---

[1] *ibid.*, 601B.   [2] *ibid.*, 554A–B.   [3] *ibid.*, 570C.

also in another connexion, when John expounds that all intellectual (*i.e.* angels) and rational (*i.e.* men) natures have being
(*essentia*), power to act (*virtus*), and action (*operatio*), which are
incorruptible and eternally binding.[1]

In conclusion, we must allude once more to John's exposition
of a central question in orthodox theology—the fall of man, sin,
and punishment. His detailed treatment of the opening chapters
in Genesis is, as one would expect, purely allegorical. Sin is
entirely negative and is the result of an abuse of free will, this
last being in itself good. The cause for the abuse cannot be discovered. Yet man fell immediately after his creation.

> A creature (*i.e.* man) is not evil, nor yet his knowledge, but the
> perverse motion of the rational soul is bad. Through this he
> abandons contemplation of his Maker and turns himself with death-
> bringing steps and with lustful and unlawful desire to a love of
> material objects of sense. Thence he cannot return unless he is first
> set free by Divine Grace.[2]

Punishment, again, proceeds from the will, not from nature.
What we call the punishment of the wicked consists in the
anguish of the perverted will when in the final consummation it
will not find that which it desired in earthly life. By making thus
much concession to orthodox theology John really deviated from
consistency; for even an eternal punishment such as he envisages
is an excrescence on his main theological system, in which the
cycle of divine creation is perfected by the return of all things to
God. A highly mystical delineation of the eight stages by which
the final reunion of the many in the One will be accomplished
brings John's treatise to a conclusion.

A system, based on John's interpretation of the Neoplatonic
ideas that he found in Augustine and even more on the combination of Christian theology and Neoplatonism found in the
works of the pseudo-Dionysius and Maximus Confessor, was too
alien from the understanding of Western Christendom in his day
to receive approval or even serious attention. John only resembled his contemporaries in this, that he, too, obtained his
material from others, and that ultimately his appeal also was to
authority. But, unlike his fellow-theologians in the West, he so

[1] *PL*, 122, col. 486B.   [2] *ibid.*, 844D.

mastered the teaching contained in his sources, and so fused and even transmuted it, that the result was a work of some originality in its substance and highly individual in its style; for this last, though difficult and sometimes unwieldy, is essentially John's own. Attempts have been made to trace the influence of John's masterpiece on a variety of thinkers from the eleventh to the thirteenth century, but they are not convincing. With few exceptions, and those chiefly in obscure heretical writers, the supposed similarities of thought are too general and too vague to make indebtedness to the *De divisione naturae* even probable. The treatise was finally condemned in 1225 by a bull of Honorius III. And, though manuscripts of the work at that date seem to have been fairly numerous, the fact that its condemnation had not been pronounced officially long before suggests that the book had been little studied. Indeed, it is open to doubt whether Papal action would have been taken at all, if the condemnation of Amalric of Bène and his followers had not drawn attention to it. To class John as a forerunner of Scholasticism or even as 'the first of the scholastics' is mistaken. Apart from his skilful use of dialectic, which, knit, as it is, into the very fabric of the *De divisione naturae*, the effect being heightened by the use of the dialogue form, might seem on a superficial view to justify this classification, there is no common ground between John and the Schoolmen. As a metaphysician he was an isolated figure and it would not be easy to find another thinker of equal intellectual stature whose contribution to human thought aroused so few echoes either amongst his contemporaries or with posterity.

CHAPTER XIV

The Literature of the Carolingian Age: Poetry

The first impression made on the mind of the reader who peruses the four massive volumes of Carolingian poetry in the *Monumenta Germaniae Historica* is inevitably one of fatigued disappointment.[1] True, the variety of subjects deemed worthy of poetic treatment is not small. But there is a monotonous conformity to certain models. From the trammels imposed by these, genuine inspiration or originality of thought were able to disentangle themselves but seldom. Against the overmastering authority of the classical poets of Rome and of the Christian poets of the later Empire free poetic fancy could not often prevail. At the same time it is only fair to observe that, if the bulk of the poetry composed in any other century were brought together in four or five folios, the superficial effect would be hardly more favourable; for, inevitably, mediocrity would command undue attention and would overshadow real talent or even genius. And it is well to recollect that even in the greatest ages of poetic literature, which, like the Athenian in the fifth century, are now judged by a small number of masterpieces from the hands of the greatest authors, there would be much indifferent verse which, in that instance, has not survived. As far as form, as distinct from content, is concerned, the greatest innovation of the ninth century was a great increase in the use of rhythmic verse, sometimes even by writers who generally adhered to the quantitative scansion of their classical or late-classical models. Rhythmic verse was nothing new, even if hitherto it had been sparingly used. But the so-called hexameters in the *Carmen apologeticum* by

---

[1] *MGH*, Poet., Vol. V, so far as published, contains poetry of the Ottonian period, but Vol. VI, Part 1, published in 1951, is a supplement to Vols. I to IV.

Commodian (fifth century?) depend more on word accent and on stressed and unstressed syllables than on quantitative scansion. Hymn writers ever since the fourth century had used octosyllabic lines which were scanned accentually but which imitated the quantitative trochaic or iambic dimeter, and Bede concluded his early school treatise on metres with a section, De rhythmo.[1] The earliest extant poem in rhythmic lines of fifteen syllables was composed at the end of the eighth or beginning of the ninth century.[2] Thereafter octosyllabic or quindecasyllabic rhythmi become increasingly common, although within our period quantitative verse easily predominates; for it is not until the tenth or even eleventh century that rhythmic poetry becomes more popular than poetry with quantitative scansion.

It is undoubtedly true that the Carolingian epoch produced no poet to rank with the immortals; but it is also true that there were four or five who, both as literary craftsmen and as poets, stand high above the crowd of their versifying contemporaries. Again, one must not forget that the writers who can be identified were monks or Churchmen. Hence there is a preponderance of narrative and elegiac poetry, which is either purely religious or at least has a didactic purpose. Much of this, too, runs to inordinate length. The poem by Milo of St Amand (c. 810–71), On sobriety, is composed of 2,118 hexameter lines.[3] The lament on the death of Hathumoda, first abbess of Gandersheim, by Agius, which is cast in the form of a dialogue between the poet and the nuns of the convent, extends to 359 elegiac couplets or 718 lines in all.[4] The poem De fide catholica, by Hrabanus Maurus, is composed of 608 rhythmic octosyllabic verses with a single, double, or even triple rhyme in every couplet.[5] The saints' lives are even longer. Almost invariably they are versifications of prose lives, so that they have no independent value for the historian or student of hagiography. Milo was the author of a life of St Amandus; Heiric of Auxerre chose St Germanus as his hero. With the prefatory verses Milo's poem runs to nearly 2,000, Heiric's to almost 3,400 lines.[6] An unidentified monk of St Gall put together

---

[1] H. Keil, Grammatici latini, VII, pp. 258–9.   [2] MGH, Poet., I, pp. 79 ff.
[3] ibid., III, pp. 613 ff.   [4] ibid., pp. 372 ff.   [5] ibid., II, pp. 197 ff.
[6] ibid., III, pp. 561 ff. and 427 ff.

a metrical life in 1,800 hexameters of the abbey's venerated founder.[1] An almost necessary consequence of their origin—adaptation of biographies in prose—was that their poetic merits were usually slight. Even metrically they are sometimes halting or incorrect, either because of the writer's lack of skill or by reason of his pious desire to preserve, as far as possible, the language of the prose life that he was forcing into unwilling verse. Panegyric and historical narrative poems, again, which form a by no means negligible group, often assumed wearisome proportions. Ermoldus Nigellus, not content with singing the praises and exploits of Louis the Pious in four books of over three hundred couplets each (c. 826), addressed two shorter panegyrics to Louis' son, Pippin.[2] The poetic annals of Charlemagne by the Saxon poet in four books of hexameters and one of elegiacs are longer by several hundred verses than Ermoldus' major work.[3] The first and second books of the epic written by Abbo, a monk of St Germain, shortly before 900 describe the Norman attack on Paris of the year 885–6 in more than 1,200 verses of singularly difficult and artificial Latin.[4] Of far greater merit than any of these is the epic *Waltharius*, which, exclusive of the much disputed prologue, runs to 1,456 hexameters.[5]

Of the shorter poems also by far the greatest proportion, irrespective of the contents, was composed either in hexameters or in elegiac couplets. The occupation with earlier poets, especially Virgil and Ovid, and the assimilation, with variable success, of their poetic idiom, meet the reader at every turn. Under Virgilian influence, too, the eclogue form was much favoured, even when the subject was not specially suited to treatment in dialogue. The *Epicedium Hathumodae* illustrates this defect. The alternation of long exhortations and enumeration of the dead woman's virtues by the poet with the equally protracted

---

[1] *MGH*, Poet., II, pp. 428 ff.

[2] The best edition of Ermoldus is by E. Faral in *Les classiques de l'histoire de France au moyen âge*, Vol. 14 (Paris, 1932).

[3] *MGH*, Poet., IV, pp. 7 ff.

[4] Best edition by H. Waquet in *Les classiques de l'histoire de France*, Vol. 20 (Paris, 1942). For the third book which does not deal with the siege and which Waquet omits see my note in *Bulletin Du Cange*, 1 (1924), pp. 27–31.

[5] *MGH*, Poet., VI, 1, pp. 24 ff.

responsiones of the nuns is quite alien from the spirit of the bucolic idyll with its rapid movement and the contrasted personality of the speakers. One of Alcuin's more pleasing poems is a little eclogue on the cuckoo, the speakers being Winter and Summer in the presence of a young and an old shepherd. The last-named concludes the contest by siding with Spring and praising the coming of spring-time whose harbinger the cuckoo is.[1] This pretty trifle is still genuinely in the bucolic tradition. Sedulius Scotus also was not unsuccessful in a charming example of this genre of fifty lines. It is the rose and the lily who compete for first honours while Spring is the arbiter.[2] On the other hand, the prolix poem by Walahfrid on the statue of Theodoric, which had been transferred from Ravenna to Aachen in 811 by order of the emperor, would probably have gained in effectiveness if it had been composed as a continuous narrative. Instead it is cast in the form of a dialogue between the poet and Scintilla, a personification of his own poetic fancy. The introductory lines, with their rather conventional praise of rustic scenery, accord little with the main theme of the poem. This begins with an attack on the Ostrogothic king because he was an Arian. Then Walahfrid passes on to a panegyric of the ruler of the orthodox Franks, Louis the Pious, who is compared to Moses, and of other members of the royal houses, as well as of Hilduin, Einhard, and Grimald.[3] The eclogue by Modoin is a conversation between an old man and a boy. The boy sings in praise of poetry, with allusions not only to the ancients but to members of the Carolingian 'academy'. The old man tries to dissuade him from cultivating the Muses when he were better occupied tilling the fields:[4]

> Quis te musarum tantus seduxerat error?
> Rura colendo fuit melius tibi stiva tenere
> Agricolam patrio cantando imitarier usu.

But the most elaborate example of a poem in eclogue form is the *Eclogue of Theodulus*. It is a contest between Pseustis and Alithia, while Fronesis acts as arbiter. The author, though he has

---

[1] *ibid.*, I, pp. 270 ff.   [2] *ibid.*, III, pp. 230 ff.   [3] *ibid.*, II, pp. 370 ff.
[4] *ibid.*, I, pp. 384 ff. The lines quoted are 68 to 70.

taken the Greek words for 'liar', 'truth', and 'thought' or 'reflection' for the names of his characters, makes Pseustis male and assigns him the character of a goat-herd, thereby giving the conventional bucolic setting. The metrical scheme is regular, each of the two contestants alternately uttering four lines. The hexameters are rhymed and monotonous, because, with one exception, the caesura always comes in the same place, in the middle of the third foot. Pseustis begins by praising the story of Saturn and the golden age, and then proceeds to dwell on other stories from Greek and Roman mythology. Alithia counters each pronouncement of her rival by telling some episode taken from the Bible. The author obtained his mythological material chiefly from Virgil and Servius' commentary, Ovid, and Martianus Capella; there are also reminiscences from Sedulius and Prudentius. Formally the arrangement is not without interest, because it appears to be the first systematic attempt to set out parallel examples from pagan and Biblical sources. Who the author was is unknown; for in spite of the name, Theodulus, which is an almost exact reproduction in Greek of the German, Gottschalk, it seems impossible to attribute the poem to the champion of double predestination. The date of its composition is also disputed; for, though it has been commonly assigned to the ninth century, a strong case can be made out for placing it in the tenth.[1] There is, however, no doubt about the immense popularity of the *Eclogue* throughout the Middle Ages. It became a favourite school-book at least from the end of the eleventh century onwards, it appears frequently in library catalogues, and the number of twelfth-century or later manuscripts is great.[2]

Few Carolingian poets experimented with classical verse forms other than hexameters and the elegiac couplet. This is what one would expect from the generality of versifiers, seeing that the most popular models were Virgil and Ovid, and of more recent writers, Juvencus, Sedulius, and Venantius Fortunatus. The

---

[1] Cf., K. Strecker in *Neues Archiv*, 45 (1924), pp. 18–23. Of recent writers Curtius (*Europäische Literatur*, p. 264, note 2) follows Strecker in dating the eclogue in the tenth century, De Ghellink, *Littérature latine au moyen âge*, I, p. 180, favours the ninth.

[2] On the use of the *Eclogue* in the Middle Ages see G. L. Hamilton in *Modern Philology*, 7 (1909), pp. 169 ff.

Satires and *Epistles* of Horace, too, were far better known than the *Odes*, whilst the most popular works of Prudentius were those composed in hexameters, not the hymns with their remarkable variety of lyric metres. Moreover, even moderate success with a lyric metre requires considerably greater skill and knowledge than are needed to devise indifferent hexameters and pentameters. Yet it is surprising to find that one of the most skilful metrists of the age, whose familiarity with earlier poetry was unusually wide, namely Theodulfus, wrote only four short pieces in hexameters and only three times tried his hand at sapphics. All the rest of his poetry, filling some one hundred and twenty pages in the *Monumenta Germaniae Historica*, is composed in elegiacs.[1] The sapphic stanza was, however, handled expertly by Walahfrid and by Sedulius Scotus; indeed, Sedulius is unique in the period for the variety of his lyric metres, all being scanned by quantity. Anapaestic and iambic verse, asclepiad, trochaic tetrameter, and other schemes, besides sapphics, hexameters and elegiacs, all flowed smoothly from his pen, so that he can claim to be the most versatile metrical artist since Prudentius. His one attempt at writing rhythmical verse is so agreeable a trifle that one could wish that he had composed more in this form. It is addressed to a friend, probably a cleric, named Robert, and thanks him for a gift of wine. The poem opens gaily with a grammatical declension of the donor's name:[2]

> 'Bonus vir est Robertus,
> Laudes gliscunt Roberti,
> Christe, fave Roberto,
> Longaevum fac Robertum,
>
> Amen salve, Roberte,
> Christus sit cum Roberto'—
> Sex casibus percurrit
> Vestri praeclarum nomen.

After singing his praises and the praises of wine through

[1] *MGH*, Poet., I, pp. 445 ff. It is very doubtful whether the sapphics in No. 77 are by Theodulfus, since the scansion is partly quantitative, partly accentual, a scheme found nowhere else in his poetry.

[2] *MGH*, Poet., III, p. 215 (No. 58).

ten four-line stanzas Sedulius concludes with very unorthodox
levity:

> Qui tristibus Falerna
> Largiri gaudes dona,
> Poteris fonte vitae
> Alma sanctorum sorte.
>
> Nec tanta de Siloa
> Grata manant fluenta.
> Haec suxi—non negabo,
> Haec sugam: sicera, abi.

The bulk of Walahfrid's poetic writing is in elegiacs or
hexameters; but he, too, experimented with sapphics, hendecasyllabics, glyconic, trochaic, and anacreontic lines. In short, the
more notable poets adhered to classical models and therefore
rarely composed anything other than quantitative verse. But they
allowed themselves certain licences which, though not sanctioned
by Virgil, Horace, or Ovid, had abundant and early authority
elsewhere, such as the shortening of final 'o' in nouns and in the
ablative of the gerund. One may also note the occasional use of
rhyme within the line, particularly between the first and second
half of the hexameter; but the fully developed leonine hexameter
only came into regular use in the late tenth or eleventh century.

To enumerate all the poets and poetasters of the eighth and
ninth centuries—and there were comparatively few figures in that
literary world who did not at some time try their hand at verse—
would be tedious and unprofitable. It will suffice to concentrate
first on the leading poets and then to bring forward a few typical
examples drawn from the rest. In this way it will also be possible
to illustrate somewhat further the general observations which were
outlined at the beginning of this chapter.

Following a roughly chronological order one may begin with
Paul the Deacon. His poetic output was not great. Besides two
longer compositions—one of 154, the other of 64 lines—in praise
of St Benedict, there are upwards of twenty pieces, all short. A
few are epitaphs; some illustrate the foible of Carolingian scholars
for exchanging versified notes and riddles, Paul's correspondents
being Peter of Pisa and Charlemagne. Some of their replies have
survived also. Two poems not merely stand out from the rest

of his work, showing that Paul had moments of real inspiration, but deserve to be classed with the finest examples of Carolingian poetry taken as a whole. The first is a charming description of Lake Como, familiar to the poet in the days that he spent at Civate.[1] In language, which is all the more effective for being unadorned, he brings vividly before our eyes the lake fringed with olive groves and with laurels, whose sombre colours are here and there relieved by the deep red fruit of the pomegranate. The orchards are full of peaches and citrons whose scent together with myrtle fills the air. No other lake save only the Galilean can compare with it. From the lines that follow it is clear that Paul had also seen the waters of Lake Como upheaved by one of those sudden squalls common on inland seas, especially in hilly country:

> Fluctibus ergo cave tremulis submergere lintres;
> Ne perdas homines fluctibus ergo cave.
> Si scelus hoc fugias, semper laudabere cunctis;
> Semper amandus eris, și scelus hoc fugias.

In the other poem, which is full of pathos, he pleads with Charlemagne to set his brother at liberty and allow him to recover his ancestral home, succouring his wife and children who are in beggary:[2]

> Septimus annus adest, ex quo nova causa dolores
> Multiplices generat et mea corda quatit.
> Captivus vestris extunc germanus in oris
> Est meus afflicto pectore, nudus, egens.
> Illius in patria coniunx miseranda per omnes
> Mendicat plateas ore tremente cibos.
> Quattuor hac turpi natos sustentat ab arte,
> Quos vix pannuciis praevalet illa tegi.

Here assuredly we see great art born of heart-rending sorrow!

Amongst his contemporaries, and especially in the court circle, Alcuin was esteemed as one of the outstanding poets of the age; nor, judged by the standards of the time, was such an estimate without warrant. His diction is fluent, affording ample proof of his wide reading. His lines move smoothly with a certain grace, although they are by no means free from metrical errors. He had

---

[1] The best edition is *Paulus Diaconus* by Karl Neff (Munich, 1908). The poem on Como is No. 1, the lines cited are 23–6.

[2] No. 11, lines 5–12.

an enviable gift for saying the appropriate thing in verse on any occasion. The following lines of exhortation to young students combine elegance and felicity of expression in a remarkable degree, and are a good example of Alcuin's manner:[1]

> O vos, est aetas, iuvenes, quibus apta legendo,
>   Discite: eunt anni more fluentis aquae.
> Atque dies dociles vacuis ne perdite rebus:
>   Nec redit unda fluens, nec redit hora ruens.
> Floreat in studiis virtutum prima iuventus,
>   Fulgeat ut magno laudis honore senex,
> Utere, quisque legas librum, felicibus annis,
>   Auctorisque memor dic: 'miserere deus'.
> Si nostram, lector, festucam tollere quaeris,
>   Robora de proprior lumine tolle prius:
> Disce tuas, iuvenis, ut agat facundia causas,
>   Ut sis defensor, cura salusque tuis.
> Disce, precor, iuvenis, motus moresque venustos,
>   Laudetur toto ut nomen in orbe tuum.

Among his few longer poems that on the history and cathedral of York is perhaps the best, although its chief value lies in the subject-matter. His shorter poems were addressed to a very wide circle of persons, ranging from the king and the members of the royal family to friends across the Channel, from Pope Leo III and high dignitaries in the Church to his own pupils. The contents are almost equally varied. In addition there are many specimens of metrical inscriptions composed for altars and churches, riddles, and acrostics. But the modern reader perusing Alcuin's work, especially if his own youthful training included Latin verse composition, will feel most of the time that he is looking at a series of unusually competent fair copies. Real inspiration is rare; and when it does appear, Alcuin fails to maintain a consistently high level throughout. The poem in which he takes leave of his cell begins with a dozen or so truly beautiful lines, but the rest is commonplace. Even the ode to the nightingale, which shows Alcuin at his best, is disfigured by one prosaic couplet of intolerable bathos:

> Non cibus atque potus fuerat tibi dulcior odis,
>   Alterius volucrum nec sociale iugum.[2]

---

[1] *MGH*, Poet., I, p. 299 (No. 80, 1).   [2] Nos. 11 and 61.

Very different were the character and attainments of Theodulfus, whose manifold activities as bishop and theologian have already engaged our attention. He was not merely one of the most cultured members of Charlemagne's circle; he was also its most distinguished poet. Apart from the formal excellence of his verse, apart also from an abundance of classical, especially Ovidian, echoes which are for the most part felicitous, not forced, there are many features which show Theodulfus' originality as a thinker and his marked individuality as a poet. He had a true appreciation of beauty whether in natural scenery or in works of art. He could lovingly describe a finely written or illuminated manuscript, a painting, or a plastic decoration, or in a couplet bring before our vision the essential features of a landscape.[1]

> Saxosa petimus constructam in valle Viennam,
>   Quam scopoli inde artant, hinc premit amnis hians.[2]

What could be more vivid than this, or than the little poem on the tomb of St Nazarius containing a brief allusion to his own visit to Lorsch in winter-time, the bleak landscape and falling snow contrasted with the cheerful sight of the monastery building where a kindly welcome awaited him?

> Aulica silvestris delubra in rure locasti,
>   Martyr, et in vacuis syrtibus aula micat.
> Nazarium vocitat hunc florem natio cuncta,
>   Nam Nazar Hebraea flos bene lingua vocat.
> Hunc ego Wangionum veniens festinus ab urbe
>   Dum peterem, vidi nube nivem cadere.
> Pisciflui Rheni transivi in robore ripas
>   Ut citius possem eius adire locum.[3]

Elsewhere he draws a charming picture of another monastery —the fields and stream, the chapel, the refectory, the kitchen, and the novices' quarter, all are there.[4] Interwoven with his descriptive passages there is often a strong dramatic element. While we meet this even in his slighter pieces, like that which describes a fox who, after robbing the monastic hen-roost, is himself unexpectedly trapped,[5] it is most marked in certain of the longer

[1] Cf., for example, Nos. 41, 2; 43, 46, 47.   [2] No. 28, 125–6.
[3] No. 49, 7–14.   [4] No. 30, 51–64.   [5] No. 50.

poems where it is combined with a pretty gift for satire. In a poem of 122 couplets addressed to Charles, and in a shorter one to an unidentified friend, the poet draws an unforgettable portrait of the king surrounded by his courtiers, and by learned men, poets, and poetasters.[1] The various characters bear the sobriquets customarily employed by the members of the 'academy'; hence it is not always possible to identify them. We gather from the second of these poems that there were some versifiers at court whose pretensions far outstripped their abilities, and whose intrigues might also cause annoyance. The special aversion of Theodulfus appears to have been an Irishman who has recently been identified as a certain Cadac who assumed the name of Andreas.[2] Theodulfus compares these pretenders to birds not noted as songsters![3] But it is the individual sketches which will chiefly delight the modern reader. Here we meet Alcuin, always surrounded by young men, for whom, as well as for himself, he always replies as befits one clad in authority and years, ever ready to speak on theology and to utter edifying maxims, and withal showing himself a good trencherman:[4]

> Et pater Albinus, sedeat pia verba daturus,
> Sumpturusque cibos ore manuque libens.

Einhard, little in stature, but great in mind, bustles hither and thither, like an ant.[5] Bishop Hildebald of Cologne piously blesses the dishes as they succeed one another, while the cupbearer, bald Eberhard, is busy with his vintages.[6] Over all, unruffled, in regal dignity, Charles presides as he deals out huge portions to his guests:[7]

> In medio David sceptro regit omnia, largas
> Disponens epulas ordine pacifico.

Nor must we forget that 'mountain of flesh', the peer of Falstaff, Knight Wigbod, fuming at Theodulfus' poems and lumbering forward heavily when summoned to the royal presence:[8]

> Audiat hanc forsan membrosus Wibodus heros,
> Concutiat crassum terque quaterque caput.

[1] Nos. 25 and 27.
[2] See B. Bischoff, *Historisches Jahrbuch*, 74 (1955), pp. 92–8.
[3] Cf., No. 27, 1 ff.　　　　[4] No. 25, 131 ff., 190 ff.; 27, 35 ff., 109 ff.
[5] No. 25, 155 ff.　[6] No. 27, 75 ff.　[7] *ibid.*, 73–4.　[8] No. 25, 205 ff.

> Et torvum adspiciens vultuque et voce minetur,
> Absentemque suis me obruat ille minis.
> Quem si forte vocet pietas gratissima regis,
> Gressu eat obliquo vel titubante genu.
> Et sua praecedat tumefactus pectora venter,
> Et pede Vulcanum, voce Iovem referat.

The satire of Theodulfus owes its effectiveness and charm largely to the fact that it is devoid of malice. There is in it nothing of the sardonic bitterness which nearly a century later impelled John Scotus to compose a two-line epitaph on Hincmar of Rheims while that archbishop was still alive:[1]

> Here Hincmar lies, a thief by avarice fired:
> His only noble deed—that he expired!

A corollary to Theodulfus' gift for satire was his pessimism. We can observe this in certain of his religious poems, notably one where he contrasts manners and ideals in the time of the Apostles with those of his own age, and in the verses composed during his last years, when he had been deposed from his bishopric and banished to a monastery in Angers.[2] Several poems are filled with a *saeva indignatio* that made him lash hypocrisy or avarice, and criticize severely the administration of justice and the undue severity of the law within the Frankish realm.[3] And lastly, although his lines on the approaching end of the world were inspired by a passage of Cyprian and treat in verse what was a commonplace of theological literature, we shall not err in believing that to Theodulfus the sentiments which he reproduced from Cyprian had a special application to his own day, the more so as the concluding couplet is Theodulfus' own:

> Dira cupido viget, sordes, periuria, luxus,
> Livor edax, falsum, iurgia, rixa, dolus.[4]

The difference in spirit between Theodulfus and Walahfrid, which is so palpable to any one who reads their poetry, was partly due to temperament, partly to external fortune. Walahfrid

---

[1] *MGH*, Poet., III, p. 553:
> Hic iacet Hincmarus, cleptes vehementer avarus,
> Hoc solum gessit nobile, quod periit.

[2] Nos. 17 and 72.   [3] Nos. 6, 7, 10, and 29.   [4] No. 14, 39-40.

was reared and spent most of his life in the cloister. His nine years' stay (829–38) at the court as tutor of the young Prince Charles did not alter the nature of one who was essentially a scholar and a lover of simplicity and peace. And even the temporary misfortune owing to political partisanship on the side of Lothar, which deprived Walahfrid of the abbacy presented to him in 838, was not long and deep enough to leave any permanent scar in his mind. He was reinstated as abbot of Reichenau in 842, dying in that office seven years later.

His versified account of a vision, that had appeared to his teacher, Wetti, before his death, was written when Walahfrid was only eighteen. Nor was that his first attempt at poetry, since his transcription into hexameters of the life of the Cappadocian martyr, Mamme, appears to have been made the year before. Another hagiographical poem on the Irish martyr, Blaithmaic, and his De cultura hortorum were composed not much later. At Fulda, whither he went to complete his studies under Hrabanus, his chief occupation was with theology; but neither at court nor subsequently did he abjure the Muses, although few of his shorter poems can be dated with precision. His earliest works at least had shown that he had been an unusually apt pupil and had made the best use of the treasures in the library at Reichenau. His own native gift of song is first fully apparent in the poem on his garden; for, though it teems with Virgilian reminiscences, it is not an artificial drawing-room piece, but manifestly the work of a young man who loved fresh air and the simpler beauties of nature.

> Haec non sola mihi patefecit opinio famae
> Vulgaris, quaesita libris nec lectio priscis.
> Sed labor et studium, quibus otia longa dierum
> Postposui, expertum rebus docuere probatis.[1]

An introduction of seventy-five lines on the purpose of gardening, the difficulties to be overcome, and the constant application required in the garden, leads up to a description of twenty-three plants in as many paragraphs, which vary in length from six to fifty-two lines. In each he first describes the plant and then explains its medicinal virtues; sometimes allusions to pagan

[1] MGH, Poet., II, p. 335, 15–18.

mythology or Christian symbolism are added. The twelfth in his list affords an admirable specimen of the poet's method and style:[1]

GLADIOLA

Te neque transierim Latiae cui libera linguae
Nomine de gladii nomen facundia finxit.
Tu mihi purpurei progignis floris honorem,
Prima aestate gerens violae iucunda nigellae
Munera, vel qualis mensa sub Apollinis alta
Investis pueri pro morte recens yacincthus
Exiit et floris signavit vertice nomen.
Radicis ramenta tuae siccata fluenti
Diluimus contusa mero saevumque dolorem
Vesicae premimus tali non secius arte.
Pignore fullo tuo lini candentia texta
Efficit, ut rigeant dulcesque imitentur odores.

The poem concludes with a dedication to Grimald, that most excellent man and abbot of St Gall, and pictures him seated in the orchard of the monastery and reading his young friend's work, while his own boy pupils play and pick fruit hard by. For simplicity and charm it would not be easy to find the equal of these verses:[2]

Haec tibi servitii munuscula vilia parvi
Strabo tuus, Grimalde pater doctissime, servus
Pectore devoto nullius ponderis offert,
Ut cum consepto vilis consederis horti
Subter opacatas frondenti vertice malos,
Persicus imparibus crines ubi dividit umbris,
Dum tibi cana legunt tenera lanugine poma
Ludentes pueri, scola laetabunda tuorum,
Atque volis ingentia mala capacibus indunt,
Grandia conantes includere corpora palmis:
Quo moneare habeas nostri, pater alme, laboris,
Dum relegis quae dedo volens, interque legendum
Ut vitiosa seces, deposco, placentia firmes.
Te deus aeterna faciat virtute virentem
Immarcescibilis palmam comprendere vitae:
Hoc pater, hoc natus, hoc spiritus annuat almus.

Amongst the poems of his maturer years are many addressed to persons of rank and to notable Churchmen. The emperor

[1] *ibid.*, 217–28.   [2] *ibid.*, 429–44.

himself, the Empress Judith, Walahfrid's own pupil, Prince Charles, Hilduin, abbot of St Denys, Hrabanus, Theganus, for whose *Life of Louis the Pious* Walahfrid wrote an introduction, Agobard of Lyons, and many others received these graceful tributes. The poetical level maintained by the poet is unusually high when we remember how often such *pièces d'occasion* fail to call forth the highest inspiration of the writer. There is little of the romantic spirit in the Latin poetry of the Carolingian Age, and the character and situation of its authors precluded the writing of amatory verse. Nevertheless several of Walahfrid's finest poems were the expression of his deep love for friends, and a note of hardly disguised passion rings through them. His poem to the friend of his boyhood, Gottschalk, whom he calls, *meae pars unica mentis*, is full of affection;[1] but it is surpassed by two addressed to a young cleric, Liutger, and one to an unnamed friend. The first of these is, besides, full of that feeling for natural scenery which characterizes Walahfrid's *De cultura hortorum*.[2]

> Dulcibus officiis et amica mente colendo
>   Liutgero Strabus paucula verba dedit.
> Parva licet fuerit nostrae dilectio partis,
>   Credo tamen memorem te satis esse mei.
> Quicquid habes dextrum gaudens volo; porro sinistrum
>   Si quid adest, doleo cordis in oppidulo.
> Unicus ut matri, terris ut lumina Phoebi,
>   Ut ros graminibus, piscibus unda freti,
> Aer uti oscinibus, rivorum ut murmura pratis,
>   Sic tua, pusiole, cara mihi facies.
> Si fieri possit, fieri quod posse putamus,
>   Ingere te nostris visibus, oro, celer.
> Nam quia te propius didici consistere nobis,
>   Non requiesco, nisi, videro te citius.
> Excedat numeros astrorum, roris, arenae
>   Gloria, vita, salus atque valere tuum.

If this little poem gives voice only to Walahfrid's deep abiding love, in the next his passion is mingled with despair at being parted from his friend:[3]

> Care, venis subito, subito quoque, care, recedis:
> Audio, non video, video tamen intus et intus
> Amplector fugientem et corpore, non pietate.

[1] No. 18.　　　　[2] No. 31.　　　　[3] No. 32.

Certus enim ut fueram, sum semper eroque foveri
Corde tuo me, corde meo te. Nec mihi tempus
Suadeat ullum aliud, tibi nec persuadeat ullum.
Visere si poteris, sat erit, si videro gratum.
Sin alias, rescribe aliquid, tua tristia novi
Atque dolens recolo, dolor est possessio mundi,
Quaeque serena putas, magis haec in nubila tristes
Et tenebras fugiunt; volucri qui pendet in orbe
Nunc scandit, nunc descendit, rota sic trahit orbis.

The remaining poem, although it is perhaps superior to the other two in the formal perfection of its lines, is not so vibrant and spontaneous in the outpouring of the poet's inmost soul. Its charm indeed lies in the calmer setting that forms the background to his vows of friendship and unswerving fidelity:[1]

Cum splendor lunae fulgescat ab aethere purae,
Tu sta sub divo cernens speculamine miro,
Qualiter ex luna splendescat lampade pura
Et splendore suo caros amplectitur uno
Corpore divisos, sed mentis amore ligatos,
Si facies faciem spectare nequivit amantem,
Hoc saltim nobis lumen sit pignus amoris.
Hos tibi versiculos fidus transmisit amicus,
Si de parte tua fidei stat fixa catena,
Nunc precor, ut valeas felix per saecula cuncta.

Until recently there were only seven poems by which to judge the poetic gifts of Gottschalk. The recovery of ten others is therefore very welcome. These last consist of a rhythmic poem in quindecasyllabic verses grouped in threes, which is a kind of personal litany full of melancholy but of considerable poetic power; a series of eight shorter poems in the same metre on the canonical hours; and a fragment of a prayer to Christ in hexameters.[2] Of the seven other poems, five deserve to be called religious poetry of a very high order. Two of these are composed in the Adonian metre, one in sapphics, one in the dactylic trimeter hypercatalectic, and one in rhythmic verse. Each line of each stanza ends with the same rhyme, whilst in the sapphics it appears even after each half of the first three lines. Consciousness of human sinfulness, amounting almost to despair, alternating with

[1] No. 59.
[2] For the newly discovered poems see MGH, Poet., VI, 1, pp. 86–106.

hopeful trust in the mercy of God and the intermediation of His
Son, are the themes that dominate these strangely beautiful
hymns.

> Respice flentem,
>   quaeso, clientem.
>   te metuentem
>   atque petentem,
>   te venerantem
>   quin et amantem.
> Porrige dextram,
>   erige vernam,
>   exue multam,
>   postulo, culpam,
>   tu, male tritam.
>
> *　　*　　*
>
> Semper ubique,
>   Christe tuere
>   et mihi, celse
>   tu, miserere,
>   teque timere
>   atque amare
> Per tua, sancte,
>   scripta meare,
>   corde vel ore
>   hinc peragrare,
>   perpete mente
>   hinc recitare,
> Da meditari
>   et modulari,
>   ore profari,
>   corde operari
>   et tibi regi
>   da famulari.[1]

We have quoted but five of the thirteen stanzas of this moving
litany. The spirit which runs through it finds briefer expression
in the haunting refrain,

> O deus, miseri
>   miserere servi.

which begins each of the twenty stanzas of the fifth poem.[2] The
seventh, composed in hexameters, but preceded by thirty-two

[1] *MGH*, Poet., III, pp. 725 ff.　　　[2] *ibid.*, p. 729.

anacreontics, rhyme being used throughout, is addressed to
Ratramnus of Corbie. The poet thanks him for a poem, assures
him of his friendship, and alludes to his own Confession. This he
had sent to several other theologians. There follows a brief
explanation of his views on Predestination.[1] The remaining poem
is in a somewhat different category. It is addressed to a dear young
friend who had asked Gottschalk for a poem. In it we hear that
same passionate note that we have already remarked in three
poems of Walahfrid.

> Ut quid iubes,   pusiole,
> quare mandas,   filiole,
>   carmen dulce   me cantare,
>   cum sim longe   exul valde
>   intra mare?
>   o cur iubes canere?
> Magis mihi,   miserule,
> flere libet,   puerule,
>   plus plorare   quam cantare
>   carmen tale,   iubes quale,
>   amor care.
>   o cur iubes canere?

After four more stanzas the poet changes from loving protest
to his friend at an unseasonable request to the praise of God;
after three stanzas comes the climax of the last:

> Interim cum   pusione
> psallam ore,   psallam mente,
>   psallam voce,   psallam corde,
>   psallam die,   psallam nocte
>   carmen dulce
>   tibi, rex piissime.[2]

It would be difficult to find a greater contrast to this unhappy
singer than the cheerful Irishman who for a decade was the chief
literary figure at Liége. Sedulius Scotus, besides his skill as a
metrist, possessed to an eminent degree the faculty of inditing
occasional verse. Much of it certainly is only of average merit.

[1] *ibid.*, p. 733 ff.

[2] *ibid.*, p. 731. The stanzas cited are 1, 2, and 10. In *MGH*, Poet., IV,
pp. 934 ff., is printed a poem dealing with Predestination, which has been
tentatively assigned to Gottschalk. It consists of ninety-four leonine
hexameters, but the beginning and end of the poem are lost.

But he had a variable as well as a versatile temperament, so that both in his solemn and his gay mood he produced some work of very high quality. Following the example of Martianus Capella and Boethius he introduced poetic interludes from time to time into his treatise, *On Christian rulers*. For the most part their contents have a direct bearing on the subject of the book. His poetic powers are seen at their best when, after describing at length the adversities that may come upon king and people in time of war, he bursts into lines of elemental force with the very ring of the *dies irae*:[1]

> Ventosa cum desaeviat
> Euri procella perstrepens,
> Altis tonans de montibus
> Cum nubilosa grandine,
>
> Silvae ruantque protinus
> Turbetur actus et maris,
> Minas et astris inferat
> Ventus crepanti fulmine,
>
> Ferit pavor mortalium
> Tunc corda contrementium,
> Ne sternat ira caelitus
> Propaginem terrestrium.

A good example of his serious manner in a more placid mood is furnished by the elegiac lines on Easter, when the landscape is clothed with fresh verdure and flowers, when the birds fill the air with song, and when all nature and the heavenly bodies join in a Hosanna to the newly-risen Lord:[2]

> Tellus florigeras turgescit germine bulbas,
>   Floribus et pictum gaudet habere peplum.
> Nunc variae volucres permulcent aethera cantu,
>   Produnt organulis celsa trophea novis.
> Exultant caeli, laetatur terreus orbis,
>   Nunc alleluia centuplicatque tonos.
> Nunc chorus ecclesiae hymnizans cantica Sion
>   Ad caeli superos tollit osanna polos.

---

[1] S. Hellmann, *Sedulius Scottus*, p. 71; *MGH*, Poet., III, p. 612.
[2] *MGH*, Poet., III, p. 219, 21–8.

The man who could depict the horrors of war knew also how to celebrate a victory in trumpet tones. This we see notably in a sapphic ode on a Norman defeat.[1] We have already sampled one specimen of Sedulius' lighter verse. He enjoyed good things to eat and drink, and he was not above giving his friends a broad hint or even asking outright for a sheep or a butt of wine.[2] He has, too, given us a clever example of parody; for his piece, *On a ram torn to pieces by dogs*, is a mock epic in miniature, and the grand manner is admirably sustained. The unhappy ram, at bay, breaks into a ten-line speech in the best heroic style. All the other dogs are abashed; but one, more fierce than the rest, like barking Anubis—what would Virgil have said to this?—leads a fresh attack. After the death of the gallant horned hero the poet pronounces a long eulogy on him:[3]

> Non mendosus erat nec inania verba loquutus:
> Báá seu béé mystica varba dabat.
> Agnus ut altithronus pro peccatoribus acrem
> Gustavit mortem filius ipse dei:
> Carpens mortis iter canibus laceratus iniquis
> Pro latrone malo sic, pie multo, peris.
> Quomodo pro Isaac aries sacer hostia factus,
> Sic tu pro misero victima grata manes.

The poem ends with an eight-line epitaph, in which there is more than a mere hint that the dead will grace a monkish feast. In this connexion we may refer to three poems that may be classed as forerunners of a poetic genre highly popular in the later Middle Ages, the beast fable. This literary ancestry, of course, was ancient, going back to Phaedrus and Aesop. The authorship of these agreeable and humorous morsels is uncertain. That they were not composed by Paul the Deacon, although they are found in a manuscript containing genuine poems by him, may be regarded as certain; nor are there adequate grounds for assigning them to Notker Balbulus. Indeed, it is by no means improbable that they are not all three by the same hand.[4] The first and longest

[1] *ibid.*, p. 208 (No. 45).
[2] *e.g.*, Nos. 9 and 36, as well as the poem to Robert cited above.
[3] *ibid.*, pp. 204 ff. The lines cited are 115–22.
[4] Cf., K. Neff, *Paulus Diaconus*, pp. 192–3. The poems are printed *ibid.* pp. 193–7 and in *MGH*, Poet., I, pp. 62–5. On the question of authorship see also K. Strecker in *Neues Archiv*, 44 (1922), p. 219.

relates the story of the sick lion who, as king of the beasts, is visited by all the other animals except the fox. The bear proposes that the fox should be fetched and punished. The lion gives orders accordingly; but the fox, when he is brought before the lion, appears in a most ragged condition, attributing this to his travels far and wide, pursued until at last he had found a physician who had told him how to cure the king of the beasts. The lion inquires eagerly what advice the fox had received. The reply is that the bear should be stripped of his pelt, as a warm bearskin was the only cure for the ailing monarch. The poems ends with the taunt of the fox, who has 'saved his skin', to the bear after he has been deprived of his fur:

> Quis dedit, urse pater, capite hanc gestare tyaram
> Et manicas vestris quis dedit has manibus?

The bishop's mitre and gloves, to which the fox jeeringly alludes, are the tufts of hair on the bear's head and paws, which are all that remain to him of his pelt. The moral of the tale is to beware lest in digging a pit for another you fall into it yourself! The characterization of the three leading actors is excellent. Especially is the traditional servility and cunning of the fox brought out, as he feigns the utmost reluctance to narrate what he has learnt:

> Tandem praecipuum medicum vix inveniebam;
> Sed tibi, rex, vereor dicere quae docuit.

The other two poems are much slighter. The one is a conversation between a calf and a stork; the calf laments that he has lost his mother and has had no milk for three days. The stork replies with a sneer: 'what a thing to worry about, I have had none for three years'. But the last word is with the calf who wittily enough snaps back: 'one can see by your legs the kind of food that you have been having':

> Quo sis pasta cibo, en tua crura docent.

The third is the tale of the poor man's gout and the rich man's flea who exchanged roles in the world so that both thereafter had a happier life.

Of those who are commonly considered major poets in our

period Notker, nicknamed Balbulus (the Stammerer), is before all a religious poet. Tradition regards him as the most gifted inmate of St Gall in the last decades of the ninth and the first of the tenth century. Expert and beloved as a teacher, he was also a writer of great versatility. In prose his most substantial achievement was a book on Charlemagne, *Gesta Caroli*. The worth of this as a historical source in the strict sense is small;[1] but it has a unique value and interest for another reason. It embodies a great deal of folk tradition and legend about the Frankish king, whose heroization is sensibly advanced. Composed in rather colloquial Latin that sometimes appears as a close translation from the German vernacular—in which the writer received many of his stories—and enlivened by frequent use of dialogue, the book might be likened to a good historical novel. It attained an early and lasting popularity. Notker was also the author of a number of letters in both prose and verse. Several of the most attractive are addressed to two of his pupils, Waldo, later bishop of Freising, and his brother, Salomo, who became abbot of St Gall and bishop of Constance. In two of them he lays down a plan of reading and study in Patristic and ecclesiastical literature. He compiled a brief and unimportant historical sketch or *breviarium* of East Frankish history from 827 to *c.* 881, a martyrology, and a *Life of St Gall*, composed partly in prose, partly in verse, of which only scanty fragments survive. It was, however, on his poetry that his reputation as an author rested and rests. He composed four hymns in honour of St Stephen. Examples of non-religious verse by him are not many and they are not distinguished by any marked poetic beauty. One of the best contains moral instructions addressed to his old pupil Salomo in a series of short stanzas. Their tone is exceedingly frank; at the same time they breathe a deep sincerity, as the following specimen will show; it forms the conclusion of the poem:

> Pervigil excubitor, superans noctemque diemque,
> Te docui potus immemor atque cibi.
> Omnia deposui tibimet parendo petenti:
> At nunc spernor ego, alter amatur homo!

[1] Cf. L. Halphen, *Études critiques sur l'histoire de Charlemagne*, pp. 104 ff. For the text of the *Gesta* see *St Galler Mitteilungen zur vaterländischen Geschichte*, 36 (1920), pp. 1–67.

Sin magis ille senex odiis agitatus iniquis
  Divisit socios corde furente locis,
Tum merore pari lugens et corde dolenti
  Te sequor et lacrimis strata rigabo tua.
Sed, quocumque loci casu quocumque viabis,
  Implens cuncta deus te comitetur ope.
Haec monimenta mei describito corde tenaci,
  Rumine continuo quae revoluta legas.[1]

A poem on the liberal arts, based on Martianus Capella, is a rather pedantic school-piece and its Notkerian authorship is doubtful. Even more unlikely is the ascription to Notker of a poem on three brothers who were in doubt what to do with the goat that was their father's solitary bequest.[2] It has a certain droll humour depending on the absurdity of the respective wishes by which the brothers would decide who should have the beast. But it lacks the subtlety of the fable of the sick lion, nor is it its equal metrically.

Notker's achievement as a religious poet is on a higher plane, even if some of the estimates of his genius made in recent years are exaggerated. From the time of Theodulfus and Alcuin there had been a certain revival in the composition of religious hymns. One by Theodulfus, to be sung on Palm Sunday and beginning:

Gloria, laus, et honor tibi sit, rex Christe, redemptor

was taken into general use, in spite of the unwonted metre. Paulinus of Aquileia is mentioned as a writer of hymns both by Alcuin and by Walahfrid. A rhythmic poem on Lazarus, which was meant to be chanted, can now be attributed to him. It runs to 280 quindecasyllabic lines and is one of the most impressive examples of rhythmic verse composed in the Carolingian Age.[3] Five religious hymns from the pen of Walahfrid, one on the Nativity, the others on different saints and martyrs, are good poetry, but too elaborate in language and too intricate in structure to be suitable for general adoption in the liturgy. Allusion

[1] *MGH*, Poet., IV, p. 345, 15–26; W. von den Steinen, *Notker der Dichter: Ergänzungsband*, p. 139.

[2] The poem on the liberal arts is printed among the *Dubia* by von den Steinen, p. 151; that on the three brothers (*MGH*, Poet., II, pp. 474–5) is excluded by him.

[3] *MGH*, Poet., VI, 1, pp. 208 ff.

to the unusual quality of Gottschalk's religious verse has already
been made; and there are other examples of rhythmic hymns
composed before the end of the ninth century.[1] The four hymns
to St Stephen by Notker, while even less adapted for general use
than Walahfrid's, are distinguished by a certain stately beauty
and an undeniable depth of religious feeling. The beginning of
the first hymn affords a fair example of Notker's powers:[2]

> Primus ex septem niveis columnis
> A Petro electus Stephanus beato
> Voce vel signis medicans misellis
>   Claret in orbe.
> Qui brevi verbo replicans priora
> Persecutores docuit piorum
> Esse Iudaeos probitate cassos
>   Felleque plenos,
> Nec novum quid, quod dominum furore
> Impio ad poenam crucis impulerunt,
> Cum prophetas vel patriarchas ante
>   Saepe necarent?
> Hisce pro dictis, licet angelorum
> Ille fulgeret facie decorus,
> Ceu profanum moenibus urbis altae
>   Eiiciebant.
> Saulis et curae induvias calentes,
> Ne piger forsan furor impeditus
> Tardius sanctum lacerare posset
>   Deposuerunt.
> Tum volant crebri lapides per auras
> Instar ingentis pluviae vel ymbris
> Vineae tandem sterili negandi
>   Atque nocivae.

It is undeniable that Notker was not fully at ease, as were
Sedulius and Walahfrid, when composing in classical metres. To
see him at his best one must turn to that form of liturgical poetry
known as the sequence, with which his name is especially
associated. The origin of the sequence is exceedingly obscure. If
the statement of Gregory I be correct, then Pope Damasus in the
second half of the fourth century had already introduced the
'alleluia jubilus' in the graduale; that is to say, it became customary to prolong the final 'a' of alleluia by a series of purely vocal

[1] Cf., *ibid.*, IV, pp. 447 ff.   [2] W. von den Steinen, *op. cit.*, p. 148.

embellishments (*iubili*).[1] The innovation of adding words to this religious *coloratura* appears to be much later; for at present it cannot be shown to antedate the time of Pippin or Charlemagne. Nevertheless the sequence was, even so, considerably older than the time of Notker, and he cannot therefore be regarded as its inventor. At the same time he can claim to be the father of sequence-writing in Germany and the development of this genre of religious poetry owes a great deal to him. Until lately editors and critics have shown a signal lack of agreement, when trying to determine how many of the extant sequences in Notker's *Liber hymnorum* were actually composed by him; for some in that collection are demonstrably not his. The most recent editor has, however, shown with reasonable certainty that forty sequences can be assigned to Notker himself, while a good many others belong to 'the school of Notker'.[2] To illustrate Notker's skill and inspiration as a composer of sequences two examples may be given. The first is for Ascension Day:[3]

> Christus hunc diem iocundum
> cunctis concedat
> esse Christianis
> amatoribus suis.

Christe Iesu,
fili dei, mediator
naturae nostrae ac divinae:
Terras deus visitasti
aeternus, aethera
novus homo transvolans.
Tu hodie terrestribus
rem novam et dulcem
dedisti, domine,
sperandi caelestia,
Quanta gaudia
replent apostolos,
Quam hilares in caelis
tibi occurrunt
noveni ordines

Officiis
Te angeli atque nubes
stipant ad patrem reversurum.
Sed quid mirum, cum lactanti
adhuc stella tibi
serviret et angeli!
Te hominem
non fictum levando
super sidereas
metas, regum domine,
Quis dedisti cernere
te caelos pergere!
In humeris portanti
diu dispersum
a lupis gregem unum!

> Quem, Christe, bone pastor,
> tu dignare custodire.

[1] Gregory, *Epist.*, 9, 26. [2] W. von den Steinen, *Notker der Dichter.*
[3] *ibid.*, *Ergänzungsband*, p. 52.

The other example is in honour of the saintly founder of St Gall:

Dilecte deo
Galle, perenni

Hominibusque et coetibus	Qui Iesu Christi oboediens
angelorum	arduae suasioni
Praedia patris	Coniugis curam
gremium matris,	ludicra nati
Sprevisti pauperem	et crucem gaudiis
pauper dominum sequens	praetulisti lubricis.
Sed Christus	Haec compensat,
pretio centuplicato	ut dies iste testatur,
Dum tibi nos omnes	Sueviamque suavem
filios dulci	patriam tibi,
subdit affectu	Galle, donavit,
Necnon et iudicem in caelis	Te nunc suppliciter precamur,
apostolorum choro iunctum	ut nobis Iesum Christum, Galle,
te fecit sedere.	postules favere
et locum corporis	ac tuos supplices
eius pace repleas	crebra prece subleves,
ut tibi debitam	laetabundi semper
honorificentiam	mereamur solvere,

O Galle, deo dilecte.[1]

These sequences are clearly the work of a man imbued with deep religious feeling and a master of literary expression; but that Notker was in the front rank of poets, as his latest editor would have us believe, may legitimately be doubted.

The longer epic and didactic poems by various poets, with one exception, rarely rise above mediocrity as poetical compositions, whatever their value as sources for history or hagiography. The reader has to travel over many arid places before he reaches at long intervals a poetical oasis. Even in the *Life of St Germanus* by Heiric of Auxerre, which as regards form and mastery of the metre is among the best of the hagiographical poems, it is only very occasionally that our attention is arrested by a passage of real power. There is, for instance, a vivid description of the saint's enthusiastic and clamorous reception by the people of Arles.[2] But perhaps the most impressive lines in the whole poem occur

[1] *ibid.*, p. 72.
[2] *MGH*, Poet., III, p. 483 (Book 4, 306ff.).

near the end, where the poet imagines the vision of the universe
that opens out before St Germanus after his translation to heaven:[1]

Et iam sub pedibus nubes et sidera cernit,
Despectat rosei candentia lumina solis,
Despectat gelidae rorantia sidera lunae,
Et quaecumque vagos exercet stella recursus,
Telluris molem circumfusasque tenebras
Pneumata ventorum tempestatumque tumorem,
Cur ver tranquillum, cur torrida prodeat aestas,
Autumnus uvis, faetetur bruma pruinis,
Et quicquid mundi volvit structura triquadri,
Et quicquid physicis perhibent succumbere causis.
Si qua vigent numeris, mensuris ponderibusve,
Si qua latent et si qua patent in cardine rerum:
Puro cunctorum speculatur lumine causam.
Omnis se subter, Christum super omnia cernit.
Ridet quin etiam pompas et culmina saecli,
Reges horrendos, diademata sceptra tyrannos
Et multo gazas scelerum fervore petitas,
Illusas auro tenui discrimine vestes,
Et quicquid mundana potest variare supellex.

Ironically perhaps, there is something of the same grandeur in
these verses as in the poetry of Epicurus' pagan disciple, whose
splendid poem was composed to prove the mechanical origin of
the universe and to ridicule the ordinary beliefs held in his time
about divine intervention in the affairs of men. Of the historical
poets Ermoldus Nigellus is perhaps the best. His descriptions of
warfare are vivid. He lightens his narrative here and there with
short descriptions or episodes that betray a certain pawky
humour. But he is less successful in his portrayal of persons, partly
perhaps because his mind was overstocked with the diction of the
classical poets and he lacked the genius to make his book-learning
more effective. Certainly his lines on Benedict of Aniane[2] are
stereotyped and convey to the mind little that can be called
characteristic. So, too, in the account of the royal hunt, which in
other respects is one of Ermoldus' most telling pieces, the leading personages are depicted in the traditional language of the epic
and are wanting in individual traits. The empress is *pulcherrima*

---

[1] *MGH*, Poet., III, p. 511 (Book 6, 418–36).   [2] Book 2, 533 ff.

coniunx, Lothar is *celer, florens, fretusque iuventa*; and even the boy prince, Charles, has a literary ancestor in Ascanius. The lines devoted to him are, however, so lively and characteristic of the poet's manner that they deserve to be quoted:[1]

> Quam puer aspiciens Carolus cupit ecce parentis
>   More sequi, precibus postulat acer equum;
> Arma rogat cupidus, pharetram celeresque sagittas,
>   Et cupit ire sequax, ut pater ipse solet.
> Ingeminatque preces precibus; sed pulcra creatrix
>   Ire vetat, voto nec dat habere viam.
> Ni pedagogus eum teneat materque volentem,
>   More puer pueri iam volet ire pedes.

But for originality and power the most remarkable of the Carolingian epics is *Waltharius*. The literature that has accumulated about this famous poem since Jakob Grimm published his edition in 1838 is enormous. Grimm, on the basis of a passage in the eleventh-century monastic chronicle (*Casus S. Galli*) by Ekkehard IV, thought that the author was Ekkehard I, who died in 973. It is, however, important to remember that only one of the manuscripts used by Grimm contained the prologue. Grimm's attribution remained virtually unchallenged, at least in Germany, for nearly a hundred years. Among the general reading public the belief that Ekkehard I had composed *Waltharius* was greatly strengthened by the success of Scheffel's historical novel, *Ekkehard*, published in 1855. Furthermore, many scholars supported the theory that the poem was inspired by, or even was a direct adaptation in Latin dress of, an Old High German epic now lost. But investigations conducted in recent years have shown conclusively that the poem was composed in the second half of the ninth century and that the assumption that the poet simply adapted an earlier German epic is incorrect. But, though the poet composed an original poem, there is no justification for saying that he invented the basic story. There are many signs in the poem to show that he was familiar with some of the old Germanic sagas and tales, though whether in the form of orally transmitted minstrel lays or in some other way it is now impossible to establish. It is probable that the Geraldus who wrote the prologue is

[1] Book 4, 519–26.

also the author of the epic; but we know nothing about him except that he hailed from Alemannia or Bavaria. What is of greater importance and beyond dispute is that he had a wide and intimate acquaintance with Virgil, Ovid, Statius, and Valerius Flaccus, as well as with some of the Christian poets, particularly Prudentius.[1]

The poem opens at the court of Attila, who during the course of his campaigns had taken as hostages from his opponents three royal children, the Frank, Hagen, the Burgundian princess, Hiltgunt, and the Aquitanian prince, Walter. The three young people grew up at the Hunnish court. Hagen, soon after reaching manhood makes good his escape and succeeds in returning to his homeland. Meanwhile Walter, who has become the bravest and most trusted warrior among the Huns, plans to escape with his childhood friend Hiltgunt. To this end, after a successful campaign, he gives a lavish banquet to Attila and the Hunnish nobles. The wine flows freely most of the night until the king and his companions sink into a drunken stupor. Walter and Hiltgunt, who, on Walter's instructions, had made secret preparations for their flight, escape. After forty days they reach the Rhine near Worms. The Frankish king, Gunther, who has received news of the travellers, sets out with Hagen and eleven other stalwart fighters to intercept them and rob them of the treasure that they have brought with them from the land of the Huns. They catch up with Walter and Hiltgunt in a narrow defile of the Vosges (*saltus Vosagus*). Hagen, who had opposed Gunther's project from the first, again tries to dissuade the youthful Gunther from making this treacherous attack, and refuses to take part in the fighting. The poet then describes with gusto eleven single combats between Walter and the Frankish warriors, each of whom he defeats and kills. Gunther in despair upbraids and taunts Hagen. He, torn between loyalty to his king and to his boyhood friend, finally consents to fight, and he and Gunther plan a simultaneous

---

[1] See K. Strecker in *Deutsches Archiv für Geschichte des Mittelalters*, 4 (1941), pp. 355–81, and his introduction to the poem in *MGH*, Poet., VI, 1; O. Schumann in *Zeitschrift für deutsches Altertum*, 83 (1951–2), pp. 12–40, and in the *Anzeiger* (65) to that volume, pp. 13–41, where he gives a survey of books and articles written about *Waltharius* since 1926; W. von den Steinen, *Zeitschrift für deutsches Altertum*, 84 (1952–3), pp. 1–47, who makes some shrewd criticisms of Strecker and Schumann.

attack on Walter. This final contest ends in a stalemate; for Gunther has lost a leg, Walter his right hand, and Hagen an eye and six teeth. Hiltgunt binds up their wounds and Hagen and Walter are reconciled and taunt each other in friendly fashion. Then Hagen escorts Gunther back to Frankland, while Walter and Hiltgunt make their way to Aquitaine. There they are married and Walter, after his father's death, rules Aquitaine for thirty years.

Geraldus must have known the *Aeneid* by heart, for Virgilian reminiscences are thick as blackberries. He seems to have been almost equally familiar with other poets, pagan and Christian. His debt, moreover, is not wholly confined to the language. It has been suggested that, when composing the series of single combats between Walter and his Frankish enemies, he took as his model a long passage in the second book of Statius' *Thebaid*, where Tydeus is attacked by the henchmen of Eteocles. But this theory, like so many others, goes much too far and has been legitimately criticized. The most that one can say is that, since Geraldus certainly knew the *Thebaid*, he may have drawn some inspiration from this source; but the differences between the two episodes are greater than the similarities.[1] The poet was no slavish copyist but a poet in his own right. The characterization of the three chief actors is excellent, and so is the contrast between Attila's queen, who has her suspicions of Walter and warns her lord, and Attila himself who is more trustful. The descriptive passages at their best are impressive, as shown, for example, in the banquet scene and in the final three-cornered fight between Walter, Hagen, and Gunther. Geraldus, when he wishes to produce a special effect, does not hesitate to take liberties with both prosody and language.[2] In short he has produced an epic poem unique for the age in which it was composed.

We may conclude these passages in which we have tried to illustrate the similarities and diversities of Carolingian poetry by referring to two examples of verse couched in a more popular strain. In either instance the name and personality of the author

---

[1] See F. Panzer, *Der Kampf am Wasichenstein* (Speyer am Rhein, 1948); Schumann in *Anzeiger*, 65, pp. 39–41; K. Stackmann in *Euphorion*, 45 (1950), pp. 231 ff. and W. von den Steinen, *op. cit.*

[2] See Schumann, *Zeitschrift*, 83, pp. 12–22.

are unknown. The first is an incomplete accentual poem relating
the capture of Louis II by the leaders of an insurrection at
Benevento in 871. It begins thus:[1]

Audite omnes fines terrae   errore cum tristitia,
   quale scelus fuid factum   Benevento civitas:
   Lhuduicum compreenderunt sancto pio Augusto.

Beneventani se adunarunt   ad unum consilium,
   Adelferio loquebatur   et dicebant principi:
   'si nos eum vivum dimitemus certe nos peribimus.'

'Celus magnum praeparavit   in istam provintiam,
   regnum nostrum nobis tollit nos habet pro nihilum,
   plures mala nobis fecit: rectum est ut moriad.'

Deposuerunt sancto pio   de suo palatio:
   Adelferio illum ducebat   usque ad pretorium.
   ille vero gade visum   tamquam ad martirium.

The captive prince is condemned to die, but at the critical
moment the country is threatened by a Saracen raid:

multa gens paganorum   exit in Calabria
super Salerno pervenerunt   possidere civitas.

and so Louis is released. It is an excellent specimen of a popular
chantey, being a very interesting example of vernacular Latin.
The other poem is composed in more literary diction and is full
of classical allusions. Nevertheless, the unknown author writes
simply and has succeeded in giving his poem a popular tone. It
is a song for the watchmen of Modena bidding them guard their
walls securely. As it is an excellent example of rhythmic verse, it
deserves to be quoted in full:[2]

O tu qui servas   armis ista moenia,
Noli dormire,   moneo, sed vigila.
Dum Hector vigil   extitit in Troia,
Non eam cepit   fraudulenta Graecia.
Prima quiete   dormiente Troia
Laxavit Synon   fallax claustra perfida.

[1] *MGH*, Poet., III, p. 404.   [2] *ibid.*, pp. 703–5.

Per funem lapsa   occultata agmina
Invadunt urbem   et incendunt Pergama.
Vigili voce   avis anser candida
Fugavit Gallos   ex arce Romulea.[1]
Pro qua virtute   facta est argentea
Et a Romanis   adorata ut dea.

Nos adoremus   celsa Christi numina:
Illi canora   demus nostra iubila.
Illius magna   fisi sub custodia
Haec vigilantes   iubilemus carmina.
Divina, mundi   rex Christe, custodia
Sub tua serva   haec castra vigilia.

Tu murus tuis   sis inexpugnabilis,
Sis inimicis   hostis tu terribilis.
Te vigilante   nulla nocent fortia,
Qui cuncta fugas   procul arma bellica.
Tu cinge nostra   haec, Christe, munimina,
Defendens ea   tua forti lancea.

Sancta Maria   mater Christi splendida,
Haec cum Iohanne   teothocos impetra.
Quorum hic sancta   venerantur pignora
Et quibus ista   sunt sacrata limina.
Quo duce victrix   est in bello dextera
et sine ipso   nihil valent iacula.

Fortis iuventus   virtus audax bellica,
Vestra per muros   audiantur carmina.
Et sit in armis   alterna vigilia,
Ne fraus hostilis   haec invadat moenia.
Resultet echo   'comes, eia vigila',
Per muros 'eia'   dicat echo 'vigila'.

[1] The six lines printed by Traube after this and placed by him in square brackets were added by another hand and have here been omitted.

CHAPTER XV

Vernacular Literature

(a) Poetry

No study of the intellectual life of Western Europe to the end of the ninth century would be complete without some allusion to the remains of vernacular literature. What has survived and what must come within our purview, since the year 900 has been taken as the lower limit of our survey, is not great in quantity. The oldest surviving remains of any of the Romance languages, the direct descendants of Latin, do not antedate the tenth century.[1] A few of the earliest poems in Old Norse and Icelandic are generally admitted to go back to the ninth, but in the main this great literature belongs to the tenth and eleventh centuries, while the heyday of Scandinavian prose is even later. At all events it is not feasible to separate the oldest portions of the Older Edda from the rest, and a consideration of the whole of that poetry is quite outside the scope of this book. Similarly the older Celtic literature of Ireland and Wales can only be profitably studied as a whole; and, although small portions of the surviving literature can be assigned to a very early date, the bulk of what is still extant in its existing form is the product of the tenth and following centuries. That many of the legends and tales embodied in prose or verse, whether we are dealing with Scandinavian or with Celtic literature, had their roots much farther back is true enough; but the modern student must needs investigate and appraise them primarily in the literary form in which they have been handed down and in connexion with the age in which

---

[1] For the Romance version of the Strassburg oaths see above, p. 273. The *Chant de Sainte Eulalie*, to be precise, which is the earliest monument of Old French, was composed in the last years of the ninth century. Its form is adapted from the Latin sequence.

they were so shaped. It is thus justifiable to confine our attention to the vernacular literature of England and the German-speaking portions of the Frankish Empire.

Nearly all the poetry composed in Old English which now survives is preserved in one or other of four manuscripts: a manuscript in the British Museum (*Cotton Vitellius* A XV) containing *Beowulf* and some other pieces in verse and prose; a manuscript in the Bodleian Library at Oxford (*Junius* 11); the so-called Exeter Book, which is one of the treasures of the cathedral library in that city; and a manuscript in the capitular library at Vercelli.[1] All four of these codices can be assigned on palaeographical grounds to the period 950–1000. Since most of the poems are anything from fifty to two hundred and fifty years older than the manuscripts that contain them, and there is no other information about them, specialists have had to rely on internal evidence for dating, such as dialectal forms, grammar and syntax, and metrical peculiarities. Such methods have not always been convincing and leave the way open for a considerable margin of error in assigning a date to a particular poem. Thus, for example, the fragment of *Waldere* has been dated as early as the seventh and as late as the ninth century. The *Dream of the Rood* is preserved in the *Vercelli codex*, but parts of fourteen lines from the poem are inscribed in Runic letters on the Ruthwell Cross. A majority of scholars would date this monument *c.* 700, but the Runic inscription may not be as old as the Cross itself.[2] Thus it is hazardous to adhere too strictly to dialectal and linguistic tests. It is most unlikely, in view of what is known about political and social conditions in England during the eighth and ninth centuries, that linguistic barriers were rigid, and more reasonable to assume that a poetic or literary language developed, which allowed a certain latitude to the poet in the grammatical forms that he used and which differed to some extent from the locally spoken vernaculars.

[1] For a possible way by which the Vercelli manuscript reached Italy cf. K. Sisam, *Studies in the History of Old English Literature* (Oxford, 1953), pp. 109–18.

[2] For the Ruthwell Cross see now Meyer Shapiro in *Art Bulletin*, 26 (1944), pp. 232–45.

An oft-quoted passage in Einhard's *Life of Charlemagne* (Chapter 29) reads as follows:

> Again, he wrote down the very ancient Germanic (*barbara*) poems, in which the achievements and wars of ancient kinds used to be sung, and transmitted them to posterity. He also inaugurated a scholarship of his native tongue. He assigned names in the vernacular to the months, since before that time the months amongst the Franks were designated partly in Latin, partly in German. Similarly he gave proper (German) names to the winds, whereas before it was scarcely possible to find appellations for more than four.

Then follows a list of these names—'ianuarium uuintermânôth, februarium hornung', and so forth. Scholars have held very divergent views regarding the themes of the heroic poetry mentioned by the biographer. Indeed, there seems no necessity to assume that the subjects of these lays were confined to any one heroic cycle. Legends glorifying the doughty deeds of early Frankish or Burgundian rulers may have been used side by side with others whose heroes were Gothic kings, like Theodoric (Dietrich) or Ermanaric. At least there can be no doubt of the width of the emperor's sympathies, which allowed this most Christian monarch to authorize the preservation of a vernacular literature, till then transmitted orally, whose background and tone were essentially pagan. Yet, in spite of all, it was not destined to survive. The disappearance of all this poetry, except for one short lay, is proof that Charles' successors and the Church effectively suppressed that which their Christian principles could not approve. Nor was the situation greatly different in England; for, although one long narrative poem has survived, the art of *Beowulf* presupposes a long anterior development, just as its Christian elements show it to belong to a relatively late date. Furthermore, *Beowulf* is not a lay or collection of lays handed down orally from generation to generation, but a literary epic whose author seems to have had some acquaintance with the *Aeneid*. Yet here again caution is called for. Resemblances between episodes or descriptions in *Beowulf* and Virgil's epic have often been noted, but they are general rather than specific and prove no more than that the author of *Beowulf* in the course of his education had read some pagan Latin poetry. The other remains of the Old English epic are brief fragments, though often their content may fill the reader with regret that nearly all of an abundant and imaginative literature has perished. Of popular poetry nothing survives, either in Old English or in the German dialects, save a few spells. The Church at all times set her face resolutely against the belief in magical incantations and their practice. But by transferring appeals to ward off sickness, or for the protection of the flocks, or for fertility, to the Christian saints or to the Virgin Mary the Church directed old beliefs and observances into new channels. Heathen spell poems, like two in Old High German intended respectively to bring about the release of a captive and to heal a lame horse, are exceedingly rare.[1]

Old English epic poetry comprises, beside *Beowulf*, the following shorter pieces. A fragment of forty-eight lines describes the fight, resulting from a blood-feud, between Hnaef, the Dane, with fifty-nine henchmen, and a body of Frisians in the hall of the Frisian king, Finn. It is a part of the same story of which a variant and a fuller account is related as an interlude in *Beowulf* (ll. 1068–1159). Of the poem, *Waldere*, only two fragments of thirty-two and thirty-one lines are preserved; when complete, it was probably of considerable length. The complete story is best known from the Latin poem *Waltharius*; it belongs to the cycle of heroic legends and traditions whose central figures were Theodoric and Attila (Etzel). The first of the extant fragments is a speech in which Hildegyth heartens her betrothed, Waldere, when he is weary after fighting, and bids him trust in the efficacy of his magic blade, Mimming, made by the god, Weland, himself. The second fragment is part of a dialogue between Waldere and Guthhere before their duel. The date of *Waldere* has been much disputed, but the poem may have been composed before the end of the eighth century. Certainly the recent theory that the poet took his story from the Latin *Waltharius* is untenable; for the poem cannot be as late as the end of the ninth century. There are differences in detail between the fragments and the Latin poem, and it is highly unlikely that an Old English poet would derive his inspiration for a Germanic saga from a Latin poem composed

---

[1] Cf. E. von Steinmeyer, *Die kleineren althochdeutschen Sprachdenkmäler*, No. lxii.

on the Continent.[1] Both in *Waldere* and in the *Fight at Finnsburg*, so far as can be judged from the scanty remains, the setting and spirit were heathen. At the same time neither poem is in any sense primitive; the legends are early but the treatment is the work of an educated craftsman. In short, both poems stand, like *Beowulf*, near the end of a long poetical evolution.

Beowulf, with its 3,182 lines, is the only complete epic narrative in an Old Germanic tongue, as well as the most substantial monument of Old English heroic poetry. The plot is simple and is composed of three main episodes, the third being separated from the other two by a long interval of time. Beowulf, prince of the Geats, having heard that Heorot, the hall of Hrothgar, ruler of the Danes, has been infested for a dozen years by a man-eating monster, Grendel, voyages with fourteen stalwart companions to Heorot. There he is well received and explains his desire to destroy Grendel. At night he lies in wait for the ogre, and, after a terrific fight, wounds him mortally. The second episode is the battle between Beowulf and Grendel's dam, who comes from her mere to avenge her son's death. When she has withdrawn again, Beowulf follows her and overcomes her deep down in her cavern beneath the mere. After being richly rewarded Beowulf departs for home with his comrades. The last episode takes place many years later. Beowulf, having succeeded to the throne soon after his return from Heorot, has been king of the Geats for fifty years. Then a great fire-dragon, the guardian of a treasure-hoard, ravages the land. The king goes forth to destroy the pest and succeeds, but is himself mortally wounded. The poem ends with a description of the heroic monarch's funeral rites. Besides the leading actions of which Beowulf is the central figure there are many minor incidents and digressions, such as the lay of Sigemund the Volsing (ll. 874 ff.) sung by a minstrel at the Danish court, the story of Finn, or the tale of the froward queen (ll. 1,931 ff.). The conversations between the leading characters are recorded at great, one might say at heroic, length, and there is also a good deal of repetition. Some of the speeches are amongst the finest things in the poem, even if they slow up the dramatic

[1] Cf. the remarks of W. von den Steinen, *Zeitschrift für das deutsche Altertum*, 84 (1952–3), pp. 1–47.

action. They are varied and full of *ethos*, so that, even if their general construction tends to adhere to a standard pattern, they serve admirably to convey the individual characteristics of the speakers. We need only contrast the Nestor-like address of the elderly Danish king with the briefer and more practical, yet charming, remarks put in the mouth of his spouse, Queen Wealtheow (ll. 1,698 ff.; 1,215 ff.). Of Beowulf's own speeches the finest is his reply to the churlish Dane who taunts him; almost equally impressive, but in quite another genre, are the noble lines spoken by the old hero, when he is dying (ll. 530 ff.; 2,729 ff.; 2,794 ff.). The following brief extracts will help to illustrate the varied skill of the poet. He paints a graphic picture of the good cheer at Heorot after Beowulf's arrival (ll. 611 ff.):[1]

> There was laughter of warriors, song sounded forth, the words were joyous. Wealtheow, Hrothgar's queen, went forth, mindful of court usage, and greeted, gold-adorned, the men in hall. The noble lady first gave the cup to the hereditary ruler of the East Danes, and bade him be joyful at the beer-drinking beloved by his people. He, the victorious king, partook in gladness of the feast and hall-cup.
>
> Then the lady of the Helmings went round every part of the hall, to the well-tried and to the younger warriors; proffered the costly goblet, until it came that she, the diademed queen, ripe in judgement, bore the mead-cup to Beowulf. She greeted the prince of the Geats, and thanked God, discreet in speech, in that her desire had been fulfilled, that she might look to some warrior for help from these attacks.

The queen, after the slaughter of Grendel, in winsome words commends her young sons to Beowulf (ll. 1,215 ff.):

> The Hall was filled with sound. Wealtheow spake, before the company she said: 'Have joy of this circlet, Beowulf, beloved youth, with luck, and this mantle—a treasure of the people—and thrive well! Be known for valour and be kind in counsel to these boys. For that will I be mindful of reward for thee. Thou hast brought it to pass that men will magnify thee far and near, to all eternity, even as widely as the sea surrounds the windy coasts. Be, so long as thou livest, a prosperous prince. I wish thee store of costly treasures. Be friendly to my son in deeds, guarding his happy state. Here is each noble true to the other, in spirit mild, and faithful to his lord; the

---

[1] The translation is Clark Hall's with some changes.

knights are loyal, the people all ready, and warriors primed with wine perform my bidding.'

Hrothgar's farewell to Beowulf is characteristic of the king, as it is unimpeachable in sentiment (ll. 1,840 ff.):

> Hrothgar addressed him in turn: 'The wise Lord put these speeches in thy mind. Never heard I a man talk more prudently at so young an age; strong art thou in thy might and ripe in mind, wise in thy spoken words. I deem it likely, if this falls out, that spear or combat fierce and grim, disease or knife, takes off the son of Hrethel, thy prince, the shepherd of thy people, and thou hast life, that the Geats of the sea may have no better man to choose as king, as guardian of the people's treasure, than thyself, if thou dost will to rule the kingdom of thy kin. Thy character charms me more as time goes on, beloved Beowulf.
>
> Thou hast effected that to both folks—Spear-Danes and the people of the Geats—there shall be peace in common; wars shall cease, the vengeful enmities, which they carried on of yore; that, while I govern this wide realm, there shall be interchange of treasure, many a man shall greet his fellow with good things across the gannet's bath; the ringed ship shall bring over the sea's gifts and love-tokens. I know the people are of stedfast build, both as to friend and foe, blameless in both respects, after old custom.'

That the poet was also a master of the grisly and fearful can be seen from a passage in the dragon-slaying (ll. 2,669 ff.):

> After these words, the serpent, the fell spiteful spirit, came angrily a second time, bright with belched fire, to fall upon his foes, the loathed mankind. His shield was burnt up to the rim by waves of flame, his corslet could afford the youthful spear-fighter no aid; but the young man went to it valiantly under his kinsman's shield after his own was consumed by flames. Then once more the war-king was mindful of his renown, by mean force he struck with his battle-sword so that it stuck in the head, driven in by the onslaught. Naegling snapped. Beowulf's old, grey-coloured sword failed him in the fray. . . .
>
> Then a third time the people's spoiler, the dreadful fire-dragon, was intent on fighting; he rushed upon the hero, when occasion favoured him, hot and fierce in battle, and enclosed his whole neck between his cutting jaws; he was bathed in life-blood—the gore gushed out in streams.

The 'youthful spear-fighter' is young Wiglaf, the only one of Beowulf's men who did not desert but in the hour of need stuck to his lord to the end.

Beowulf, indeed nearly all the old vernacular poetry, is composed in alliterative verse. Each line consists of two half-lines with an intervening caesura. There are usually two feet in each half-line, although the number of unaccented syllables is variable. The alliteration is between the accented portions of each half-line; it consists either of the occurrence of the same initial consonant or of any initial vowels in both half-lines. The lines very commonly run on in such a way that the end of a sentence comes at the end of the first half-line; at the same time there is a good proportion of verses where the end of the whole line and the end of the sentence coincide. Apart from the variety resulting from this, monotony was further avoided by different rhythmical or metrical types, six in number, which, while they conformed to the primary rules of accented-alliterative part and unaccented part in each half-line, produced on the ear an effect of diversity in unity.[1]

We cannot here enter into the multiple problems—linguistic, literary, archaeological—which have given rise to a vast literature about this poem. It must suffice to point out only certain leading facts or probabilities. The scene of the action is laid in Seeland, Heorot being perhaps on the site of the modern village of Leire near Roskilde, while the land of the Geats was in southern Sweden. But since the poet lived in England and utilized the heroic stories that his forebears had brought with them across the sea, we must reckon with the possibility that, although the general setting of this story may be traditional, he has added scenic details from that region of England in which he lived, be it Northumbria or Mercia.

The essential story with its fabulous monsters, and episodes like the cremation of the dead Beowulf, are purely pagan. Yet many of the ideas, especially those concerned with human conduct, are Christian indubitably. Certain allusions also, like those to the Creation or to the story of Cain and Abel, are taken from the Old Testament. In one and the same speech Beowulf remarks

[1] ll. 1240–43 will serve as an illustration:

> Beor-scealca sum
> fus ond faege   flet-raeste gebeag.
> Setton him to heafdon   hilde-randas,
> bord-wudu beohrtan.

(ll. 440–1, 455) 'he whom death carries off shall rest assured it is God's will' and 'Fate goes ever as it must'.

There are also certain historical elements in the tale. Though the hero himself cannot be identified with any person who actually lived, the names of some others mentioned in the poem seem to belong to history, notably the king, Hygelac, who perished in a raid on the Frankish coast recorded by Gregory of Tours.[1] So, too, the allusions to the bitter enmity and wars between Geats and Swedes reflect actual historical occurrences. The personality of the poet is wrapped in mystery. But, if we bear in mind that the Christian elements in *Beowulf* are not merely incidental, but that the poem in the form that it has come down to us is essentially a Christian poem with some pagan elements, and that its language and structure are the work of a cultured man, writing a literary epic on traditional themes for an aristocratic audience, we shall be disposed to picture him as a well-educated denizen of some English monastery rather than as a minstrel at the court of an English prince. His home is most usually said to have been in Northumbria, but may have been in Mercia, while the poem may be dated tentatively *c.* 750.

The poem entitled *Widsith* is held to be one of the earliest examples of Old English verse. It is not an epic, but it alludes to a variety of legends of the heroic age. Much of it indeed is a catalogue of names—Scandinavian, Frankish, Burgundian, Hun, and Gothic rulers with the peoples over whom they held sway; and it is now generally agreed that this material is older than the rest of the poem. It is couched in the first person, the minstrel, who is actually recording the list of epic stories familiar to him speaking as though he had himself wandered from court to court. It is of great interest to the student of Germanic saga, but its poetic merits are not great.

The short poem, *Deor*, has been classed both with heroic and with lyric poetry. Though there is in it passing mention of the Germanic saga of Weland, the smith, and other heroic tales, it is best classed with the elegies of which there are several other examples in Old English. The singer of *Deor* laments because his place at court has been taken by another; but he comforts himself

[1] *Hist. Franc.*, III, 3.

with the thought which recurs six times in forty-two lines as a refrain:

> That sorrow passed by, so can this of mine.

Of half a dozen other elegies that on a ruined city, because of its very simplicity, is the finest. The unknown poet brings before our eyes a picture of the utter desolation that has followed halcyon days of wealth and power. It has been suggested with some probability that the ruined site which the poet had in mind was Roman Bath:[1]

> The wide walls fell; days of pestilence came; death swept away all the bravery of men; their fortresses became waste places; the city fell to ruin; . . . the place has sunk into ruin levelled to the hills, where in times past many a man light of heart and bright with gold, adorned with splendours, proud and flushed with wine, shone in trappings, gazed on treasure, on silver, on precious stones, on riches, on possessions, on costly gems, on this bright castle of the broad kingdom.

Nothing of Old German heroic poetry survives except the short *Lay of Hildebrand* (*Hildebrandslied*). The poem is not part of a longer epic, but a self-contained lay in which the whole interest of the poet is centred on the clash of two personalities. The background of the story, which is only adumbrated sketchily, belongs to the Theodoric cycle of Teutonic sagas. Hildebrand has followed Theodoric into banishment, when Theodoric has been driven out of Italy through the hatred of Odovacar. After thirty years of warring, the exiles, with the help of the king of the Huns and his army, are hoping to be restored to their homes. The invading army is opposed by a host of defenders, one of whom is Hadubrand, the son that Hildebrand has left behind him as a small child many years before. The issue between the two armies is to be decided by single combat, and the respective champions are Hildebrand and Hadubrand. In the lay Hildebrand, inquiring, as was the custom, of his opponent about his name and style, learns that he is his own son. He tries to convince Hadubrand of

[1] Quoted from R. K. Gordon, *Anglo-Saxon Poetry* (Everyman Library), p. 92. This excellent anthology contains most of the secular and religious poetry written in Old English in prose translation. Of some of the longer religious poems, however, only selections are given.

this but without avail, as the younger man believes his father dead and suspects his present adversary of treachery:

> Thou art an old Hun, exceeding crafty; thou beguilest me with thy words and wilt hurl thy spear at me. As hast thou grown old, so dost thou ever bring forth treachery. Men seafaring westwards over the Vandal Sea have told me that war carried him off; dead is Hildebrand, son of Heribrand![1]

The duel begins and the poem breaks off, as the last few lines are lost. There can, however, be no doubt that the end was tragic. It is usually stated that the father became the slayer of the son, but this is not certain. The reverse may have been the poet's resolution of the tragedy or even the deaths of both father and son. Not only the subject but the straightforward presentation, partly in the poet's own words partly in the form of dialogue between father and son, make this short poem a work of great pathos and dignity. The language is not a homogeneous dialect, but shows Low German forms side by side with High German. Many explanations of this mixed language have been given, but it is now generally agreed that the lay was originally composed in Old High German, but that whoever wrote it down introduced Low German (Old Saxon) forms because that was the language native to him.[2]

Far more abundant both in England and in Germany is religious poetry composed in the vernacular. Only two English poets are known by name, Caedmon and Cynewulf. The story of Caedmon is related in one of the most famous passages in Bede's *Ecclesiastical History* (4, 24). Caedmon was already well advanced in years when in a dream there appeared to him a figure who bade him sing of the Creation. Next day he remembered the hymn that he had sung, although until then he had thought himself incapable of writing or reciting poetry to the harp. He was received into the monastery of Whitby, where he spent the remainder of his days, says Bede, singing

> of the creation of the world, and the origin of the human race, and the whole history of Genesis, of the going out of Israel from Egypt

[1] E. von Steinmeyer, *op. cit.*, No. i, lines 39–45.
[2] Cf. the valuable discussion of the dialectal problems in J. K. Bostock, *A Handbook of Old High German Literature* (Oxford, 1955), pp. 64–9.

and the entry into the Land of Promise, and about many other episodes of the Sacred Scripture, the Incarnation of the Lord, His passion, resurrection, and ascent into heaven, of the coming of the Holy Spirit and the teaching of the Apostles.

Besides the historian's Latin paraphrase, two versions of Caedmon's first hymn, one in the Northumbrian, one in the West Saxon dialect, have survived.[1] It is but nine lines praising the Creator and of no great poetic worth. Of what Caedmon may have composed after he entered the monastery we have no knowledge beyond Bede's statement; for the group of narrative poems with religious content, preserved in the Bodleian manuscript, are certainly not his. They are *Genesis A*, *Exodus*, *Daniel*, and *Christ and Satan*. Of these *Exodus* may be earliest in date, but the style and metre of the four poems are not uniform, so that one must suppose that they are by different authors. Whatever the precise date at which they were composed, *Genesis A*[2] and *Exodus* seem to be at least a generation older than Cynewulf. He is the only Old English poet known to us by name; for in four extant poems—*Christ B*, *Juliana*, *Elene*, and *The Fates of the Apostles*—his authorship is attested by his signature worked into the body of the poems in Runic letters. The poem, *Christ*, in the Exeter Book, which runs to 1,664 lines, is really made up of three separate poems, dealing respectively with Advent, the Ascension, and the Day of Judgment, but only the second is signed by Cynewulf. Finally, certain other religious poems have come down to us anonymously. Such are *Andreas*, *Judith*, and two poems on St Guthlac, the anchorite.

We cannot here do more than attempt a general appraisal of this poetic literature as a whole and touch upon certain of its characteristic features. The subject was derived either from the Old Testament (*Genesis*, *Exodus*, *Daniel*) or from apocryphal literature (*Fates of the Apostles*, *Andreas*), or from portions of the liturgy (*Christ A*), or from Patristic literature (*Christ B*, adapted from part of a homily by Gregory I) or from the lives of saints (*Juliana*, *Elene*, *Guthlac A* and *B*). But there is much variation

[1] Cf. E. van K. Dobbie, *The MSS of Caedmon's Hymn and Bede's Death Song* (New York, 1937).

[2] *Genesis A* consists of lines 1–234 and 851–2,935 of the extant poem. For *Genesis B* (lines 235–850) see below, p. 377.

in treatment; for example, the poet of *Genesis A* follows the Bible version very closely, whereas the writer of *Exodus* allows himself more independence. Giving his imagination free rein, he describes the various stages of the Israelite march, their army, the host of Pharaoh and its destruction in the Red Sea with so much picturesque detail that he quite loses sight of the Biblical text. In many of the poems the influence of the old heroic poetry is felt either in the phraseology or in the portrayal of the character and attributes of the leading figures. Moses and his followers in *Exodus* bear not a little resemblance to a Germanic or English chieftain accompanied by his faithful retainers. In the *Fates of the Apostles* and in *Andreas*—attributed by some scholars to Cynewulf—there are not only specific echoes of *Beowulf*, but Andrew and his fellow-Apostles are spoken of as doughty warriors, and they are accompanied by their thanes. Great stress is laid on battle scenes, and other motifs of the old epic are woven in. A similar tendency appears in *Daniel* when the poet describes Nebuchadnezzar's wars against the Hebrews. So, too, in *Judith*, which was perhaps not composed before the first half of the tenth century, the carousal of Holofernes and his supporters is portrayed in the old heroic manner. It cannot be said that this intrusion of an element quite foreign to Christian story and teaching is fortunate; for, where it occurs, the reader is bound to feel an incongruity. It is borne in on him that the poet is within the trammels of an older poetic tradition, and his attempt to combine two incompatibles has resulted in a certain artificiality. Again, where, as in *Genesis A*, the author follows his source closely, it is at the cost of poetic inspiration, and the effect is wearisome. Indeed the religious-didactic purpose being of primary importance renders most of these works, taken as a whole, rather unattractive. It is often necessary to read through many lines of tedious moralizing before one is rewarded by a passage in which spontaneous inspiration together with fine and appropriate diction has resulted in true poetry.[1]

---

[1] For example, the storm at sea in *Andreas*; the conversation between Joseph and Mary in *Christ I*; the destruction of the Egyptian host in *Exodus*; and the passage in *Elene* where the discovery of the True Cross, and how the glorious discovery was bruited abroad in the Roman world, are described.

Apart from two longer works, Old German religious poetry is small in quantity and undistinguished in quality. Among surviving poems we may mention two hymns, one celebrating St Peter, the other, St George, a paraphrase of Psalm cxxxviii, and a poetic version of the story of Christ and the woman of Samaria. The *Ludwigslied* is a hymn of victory, rather in the style of a ballad, commemorating the defeat of the Normans by Louis III in 881. In respect of metrical form it is noteworthy that all these poems are, like the poetry of Otfrid, composed in rhyming verse and not in the alliterative metre of the heroic and the Old English religious poetry. The older metre was, however, employed in an incomplete poem of 103 lines in the Bavarian dialect. The flight of the soul from the body after death, a description of and warning against the pains of Hell, and an unusually vigorous portrayal of the Last Judgment, form the subject-matter of this remarkable, if difficult, fragment.[1]

The contrast between the older and the newer metrical scheme can be studied most fully in the two poets of whose work we have more substantial remains. The unknown author of the *Heliand* (*Saviour*) made use of alliterative verse; Otfrid of Weissenburg, although he did not invent, developed a line which was also composed of two halves, but in which the final syllables of the two half-lines rhyme. That there is sometimes double rhyme is accidental and not a necessary part of the scheme. The influence of contemporary Latin poetry is palpable. *Heliand* is written in Old Saxon and runs to nearly six thousand lines. The *Gospel Book* of Otfrid was composed between 863 and 871. It runs to over seven thousand lines and is in the Franconian dialect. Both poems treat the same theme, the life and Passion of Christ, but with that the resemblance between them ends. While the author of *Heliand* took the *Gospel Harmony* of Tatian as his guide, Otfrid based his work on the Vulgate text and on those portions of the Gospel story which had been selected for use in the liturgical books of his day. He betrays his preoccupation with the current theological studies of the cloister by introducing passages of

---

[1] The *Muspilli*, as it has been named after the word, apparently meaning 'world-destruction' or possibly Last Judgment, which occurs in line 56, is No. xiv in E. von Steinmeyer's selection.

interpretation according to the moral, the spiritual, or the mystical sense. Thus he becomes a commentator along the orthodox lines approved by Gregory and Bede and their successors, but he does so to the detriment of his poetry. The exegetical books which he turned to were Hrabanus Maurus on Matthew, Bede on Luke, and Alcuin on the Fourth Gospel. Otfrid consciously strove to emancipate himself from the influence of the older vernacular poetry. This aim is made clear first of all in the Latin dedication to Liutbert, archbishop of Mayence. He explains that his poem has been composed in answer to a request from certain fellow-monks for religious verse in the vernacular in place of the 'offensive song of laymen' (*laicorum cantus obscenus*). But Otfrid's deliberate purpose is shown also by the choice of a different metre and by the tone and language of the narrative passages, not to speak of the exegetical portions of his work. Even so specialists have been able to point to occasional features in the *Gospel Book* that represent an unconscious lapse into the style of the *cantus laicorum*. Otfrid, we may observe, also explains his desire to turn his native language into a vehicle for literary expression not unworthy to be set side by side with the learned tongue in which the poets of antiquity and the early Christian poets composed their masterpieces. It is difficult to rate Otfrid very highly as a poet; for an occasional flash of inspiration is all too swiftly quenched in pedestrian paraphrases of the Gospel text or in allegorizing passages which lose none of their tedium by being written in verse. But at least one must praise and attach the highest value to his contribution towards the development of his native language.

The author of *Heliand* proceeded in a very different manner. Nothing specific is known either about his personality or the place where he composed his religious epic, though Fulda has been suggested. But its date can be fixed within narrow limits, between 821 and 840. The poet was an educated man—monk or cleric—who besides the *Gospel Harmony* of Tatian made use of the same Latin commentaries to which Otfrid turned a generation later. He must also have been familiar with some of the Old English poetry of the eighth century. Although he is handling a Biblical subject, he is so thoroughly familiar with the epic tradition and secular poetry, that, to a greater extent than in any religious poetry composed in England, the characters of Heliand are cast in the heroic mould. Jesus himself has the characteristics of a Teutonic ruler; His disciples are nobly born; their relation to the Saviour is described in terms applicable to the relation between thane and king, and they are designated 'bold warriors'. The setting of the Sermon on the Mount is such that it unmistakably recalls a heroic assembly, with the king addressing his faithful followers and subjects. Episodes, like the arrest of Jesus and Peter's assault on Malchus or the marriage feast at Canaan, afforded the poet an opportunity of depicting with much wealth of detail a fight and a cheerful carousal in the best heroic style. On the other hand, where an incident in the Gospel story is, like Peter's betrayal of his Master, irreconcilable with the manners of the heroic age—in that instance, the fidelity owed by the warrior to his lord—the poet goes out of his way to give a plausible explanation of it. Besides this the author of *Heliand* treats the Gospel story with a good deal of freedom. With true poetic insight he seized on those parts which seemed most suitable for picturesque elaboration even if they were concerned only with minor characters or episodes. For example, the dispute between Elizabeth and the Jews (Luke 1, 59 ff.) about the naming of her child is worked up into a most graphic scene with dialogue.

In conclusion we must mention an Old Saxon poem on Genesis, of which only 337 lines survive in a manuscript of the ninth century, now in the Vatican Library. In the same codex are preserved seventy-nine lines of *Heliand*. The Genesis fragment is of special interest for the literary relationship existing between Old Saxon and Old English religious poetry. The Old Saxon Genesis was translated into Old English. Of this version more than six hundred lines survive; for they were inserted in the Old English poem on Genesis (*Genesis A*) preserved in the 'Caedmon' manuscript at Oxford. *Genesis B*, as it has come to be called, describes in a graphic and vigorous style the Fall of the Angels and the Fall of Man. Between the Old Saxon *Genesis* together with *Genesis B* and *Heliand* there are many resemblances in style and manner. These two poems, with the Old English *Dream of the Rood*, attain the summit of achievement in religious poetry composed in the vernacular tongues.

(b) Prose

Remains of Old English prose prior to the middle of the ninth century are scanty. Some ordinances of Ethelbert of Kent, who died in 616, and of other Kentish rulers are preserved only in a manuscript copied early in the twelfth century; but the linguistic forms seem to point to an exemplar written in the eighth. The laws promulgated between 688 and 694 by the West Saxon monarch, Ine, have only survived in the form in which they were incorporated two centuries later by Alfred in his own code. A glossary now preserved in the library of Corpus Christi College, Cambridge, is an early example of a bilingual dictionary designed to facilitate the reading of Latin authors. Though the manuscript itself was not written until the end of the eighth century, the glossary has close affinities with another which was copied at least fifty years earlier, so that the original compilation may go back to the seventh century.[1] Several extant Bible manuscripts of early date contain interlinear glosses in Old English, but these belong to the late ninth and the tenth centuries.[2] It is a matter for deep regret that the translation of part of the Fourth Gospel on which Bede was engaged at the end of his life has perished; for, in view of his exceptional attainments as a scholar and a Latin stylist, it cannot be doubted that his translation was a work of real merit. Had his work survived, it is safe to say that he would have appeared before us as a real and worthy predecessor in this field of Alfred and his associates.

The first redaction of the *Old English Chronicle*, as it now exists, belongs to the last years of Alfred's reign. But if the theory be correct that there is embedded in it an earlier version extending to the death of Ethelwulf (858) and completed shortly after, then this oldest chronicle, composed before Alfred came to the throne, would justly rank as the one outstanding example of Old English

[1] Cf. W. M. Lindsay, *The Corpus, Epinal, Erfurt and Leyden Glossaries* (London, 1921), p. 2. For the manuscripts cf. *CLA*, II, No. 122 (saec. viii–ix) and VI, No. 760 (saec. viii[1]).

[2] Namely, the Lindisfarne Gospels (*CLA*, II, No. 187), a Psalter (*ibid.*, No. 193), and the Rushworth Gospels (*ibid.*, No. 231). The glosses in the Psalter are assigned by Dr Lowe to the late ninth century, those in the other two manuscripts to the tenth.

prose before the revival of letters with which the great king's name is so closely associated. The *Chronicle* was composed in the West Saxon kingdom, presumably at Winchester. The compiler used Bede's *History* and a lost Latin chronicle as the basis of his work to the end of the eighth century. The narrative of this earlier part is, in general, very brief; here and there an episode is treated a little more fully, but there is a possibility that these passages are interpolations of Alfred's time. When the chronicler approaches nearer to his own times the treatment becomes appreciably fuller. The narrative is unpretentious in form and diction, and only very occasionally goes beyond the bare entries of an annalist. Two examples will afford some insight into the author's method and into the solid merits of this straightforward record which, as has often been pointed out, is, next to Bede, the most important source for English history before the Norman Conquest:

A.D. 794.[1] In this year pope Adrian and king Offa died; and Aethelred, king of the Northumbrians, was slain by his own people, on the thirteenth day before the Kalends of May (April 19th); and bishop Ceolwulf and bishop Eadbald departed from the land; and Ecgferth succeeded to the kingdom of the Mercians, and died the same year. And Eadberht succeeded to the kingdom in Kent, whose other name was Praen. And the aldorman Aethelheard died on the Kalends of August (August 1st). And the heathens ravaged among the Northumbrians, and plundered Ecgferth's monastery at Done-muth (Wearmouth); and there one of their leaders was slain and also some of their ships were wrecked by a tempest, and many of them were drowned, and some came to the shore alive, and they were forthwith slain at the mouth of the river.

* * *

A.D. 855 (856). In this year heathen men first took up their quarters over winter in Shepey. And in the same year king Aethel-wulf chartered the tenth part of his land over all his kingdom (West Saxon), for the glory of God and his own eternal salvation; and in the same year went to Rome with great pomp and dwelt there twelve months, and then returned home; and Charles, king of the Franks, then gave him his daughter[2] for queen; and after that he

---

[1] Thorpe's translation. All manuscripts of the *Chronicle* date these events two years too early, as they occurred in 796. Cf. *Handbook of British Chronology* (London, 1939), p. 17, s.v. Offa.

[2] Judith, daughter of Charles the Bald.

came to his people, and they were rejoiced thereat; and two years after he came from France, he died, and his body lies at Winchester, and he reigned eighteen years and a half.

At the very end of our period we come to a literary renascence brought to birth by the personal example of Alfred and matured by his unwearying zeal, supported by such devotion as he was able to inspire in a few of the leading Churchmen within his realm. The significant fact of far-reaching consequence was that it was especially the moulding of the vernacular tongue into an effective literary medium which the king had at heart. To promote this end translations of certain Latin books, then considered standard, were prepared. But Alfred after his victory over the Danes (878) strove also to improve the education of at least a portion of his subjects. His biographer relates how the king instituted a school in which the sons of many nobles and even of common men were educated with his own children. Of persons holding office under the monarch it was required that they should be able to read and write in their own tongue. But correct knowledge of Latin had also sadly declined since the days of Bede and Alcuin. And not the least disastrous result of the havoc wrought by the Danish invasions had been the desolation of many monasteries, virtually the only centres of education and learning. In the preface to the translation of Gregory the Great's *Pastoral Rule*, which Alfred himself dictated to a scribe or scribes, he laments the decay of learning and the destruction of books before his reign and sets out his own aims:

Then I recalled how the Law was first devised in the Hebrew tongue, and again, how when the Greeks learned it, they turned it all into their own language, and all other books too. And again in like manner the Romans, when they had learned them, they turned all of them by wise interpreters into their own language. And also all other Christian peoples translated some part of them into their own tongue. Therefore it seems better to me, if it seems likewise to you, that we too turn some books which are most needful for all persons to know into the tongue which we can all understand; and that you act, as we very easily can with God's aid, if we have quiet, to the end that all the youth now in England of free men who have the wealth to be able to apply themselves to it be set to learning so long as they are no use for anything else, until the time when they can read English writing well; let those afterwards be instructed further in the Latin language, whom one wishes to instruct further and whom one wishes to advance to a higher rank.

Another work by Gregory I that seemed well adapted to the ends present in Alfred's mind was the *Dialogues*. The translation of these was made by Waerfrith, bishop of Worcester (873–915) the king only contributing a brief introduction. The other so-called translations are in a somewhat different category; for in these Alfred allowed himself considerable freedom in handling the text. For example, in the Old English version of Orosius some passages of the original bearing on human vices and follies have been omitted, to others additions have been made to enhance the importance of the Christian life. Important interpolations have also been introduced to illustrate the more extensive knowledge of geography available in the ninth century about Germany and northern Europe. The best known of these insertions describe the voyage of the Norwegian Ohthere to the Far North and the exploration of the Baltic Sea effected by Wulfstan. Again, of the three books of the Old English rendering of Augustine's *Soliloquies*, only the first reproduces the Latin original more or less faithfully. The later part of the second and the whole of the third book are Alfred's own composition, although much of the thought is a restatement of what he had studied in other Latin books, namely Gregory, Boethius, and some other treatises by Augustine. The *Consolatio philosophiae* of Boethius was also treated by the royal scholar, who evidently had the deepest admiration for this masterpiece of expiring paganism, with great freedom, with more indeed than one would gather from the preface:

King Alfred was the interpreter of this work, and turned it from Latin into English, as it is now done. Sometimes he put down word for word, sometimes sense for sense, as he could translate most perspicuously and most intelligibly, in spite of the numerous and manifold cares which often engaged him in mind and body. The cares are very hard for us to number which in his days came upon the realm that he had received, and yet, when he had learned this book and translated it from Latin into the English tongue, he afterwards wrought it into poetry, as it is now done. And now he asks and in God's name entreats every one whom it may please to read this book, to pray for him and not to lay it to his charge if he understand it more correctly than the king could. For each man, according to the measure of his understanding and according to his leisure, ought to speak what he speaks and do what he does.[1]

Throughout this work Alfred frequently turns aside from the text that he is translating in order to add observations of his own; and this habit grows upon him as he proceeds, so that in the later part, and especially in Book 5, the bulk of the Old English version reproduces the king's own thoughts inspired by the philosophy of Boethius. Alfred's simple but profound piety finds expression in prayer, in his reflections on the Divine Being, and in his discussions of dogmatic questions, like predestination. The words of the Preface and the general tone of the book hardly leave room for doubt that Alfred's adaptation of Boethius is the work of a man who feels that he is nearing the end of his life and labours.[2] Hence it seems likely that this was the king's last important literary undertaking and not, as a later chronicler asserts, the result of a collaboration between Alfred and Asser; for if that statement were true, the *Consolatio* would have to be regarded as one of Alfred's earlier writings.

Of other prose works dating from Alfred's time it will suffice to mention two, the continuation and redaction of the *Old English Chronicle* and an Old English translation of Bede's *Ecclesiastical History*, which has sometimes been attributed to Alfred. But since it is notably inferior to the other translations and also contains a number of Mercian, in place of West Saxon, linguistic forms, it is more reasonable to assume that it is the work of another hand, though possibly undertaken at the king's request.

The surviving examples of prose in one or other of the Old German dialects, though in the main interesting only to the linguist, nevertheless prove how great were the efforts made in some religious houses to fashion a book language out of the spoken vernacular. Thus glossarial material is very abundant, consisting partly of bilingual word-lists, partly of interlinear or

---

[1] The best edition of the Old English Boethius is by W. J. Sedgefield (Oxford, 1899).

[2] Some scholars have questioned the authenticity of the Preface and of the versified parts of the *Consolatio*, but without adequate reason. See the valuable discussion by K. Sisam, *op. cit.*, pp. 293–7.

marginal glosses to Latin texts, most of these being religious.[1]
The earliest centres of these lexicographical studies appear to
have been Freising, Reichenau, and Murbach. There survive also
fragments of an Old High German (East Franconian) rendering of
the *Lex Salica*, some charms and medical prescriptions, and one
or two miscellaneous short documents. In considering translations of theological works one must remember the ordinance of
Charlemagne, which required the parish clergy to ensure that the
people properly understood the essential articles of the Christian
faith. But, while the provisions of the *Admonitio generalis* of 789
were universal for the whole Empire, the need for instruction
would be especially felt, and the teaching would be less easy to
impart than elsewhere in those regions which had only recently
renounced their heathen practices. The bulk, then, of this prose
literature shows that it is the direct outcome of these two purposes, the general religious education of the people and the
facilitation of missionary work. A Weissenburg manuscript
copied in the ninth century contains two translations of the
Lord's Prayer, the Apostles' and the Athanasian Creed, the
Gloria in excelsis and the *Laudamus*, together with a bilingual list
of the deadly sins. The archaic language makes it probable that
the rendering belongs to the previous century.[2] The *Pater noster*
is first given entire and then each sentence of it is commented on
in a few sentences. Bound up with the manuscript of St Gall
(No. 911) which preserves an important bilingual word-list—
the so-called Keronian glossary—dating from the end of the
eighth century, are some sheets of another codex. On these are
inscribed the Creed and *Pater noster* in the Alemannic dialect.
Another translation of the Lord's Prayer in Bavarian appears to be
slightly later in date. Very instructive, because they illustrate the
missionary or pastoral labours of the clergy, are a general exhortation to the people (*Exhortatio ad plebem christianam*), extant in

[1] For the glosses see the classic work of Steinmeyer and Sievers, *Die
althochdeutschen Glossen* in five volumes (Berlin, 1879–1922).

[2] The text of these remains of Old German prose can be conveniently
studied in Steinmeyer, *op. cit.* or in W. Braune, *Althochdeutsches Lesebuch*
(ed. 12, revised by K. Helm, Halle, 1952). There are good facsimiles of
several of these documents in E. Petzet and O. Glauning, *Deutsche Schrift-
tafeln*, I Abteilung (Munich, 1910), Plates I to V.

both Latin and Bavarian, and two bilingual texts reproducing the vows taken by converts at baptism. The vernacular rendering of one of these is in East Franconian, the other in Old Saxon. It is notable that in addition to repeating the chief formulas of Christian belief the candidate for baptism was specifically required to abjure heathen practices. Indeed in the Old Saxon version we find the leading Germanic deities mentioned by name:

> End ec forsacho allum dioboles uuercum and uuordum. Thunaer ende Uuoden ende Saxnote ende allum them unholdum the hira genotas sint.[1]

Several vernacular renderings of the general catalogue of sins used in connexion with the confession heard by the priest at Eastertide have also survived. Extant translations of Biblical books or theological works are not especially numerous; but what survives is probably only a fraction of the total output during a century or more. Thus there are fragments of several interlinear versions of the Psalter and of an Old Dutch translation of the same; also a few remnants of a commentary on the Psalms written in Old Saxon and based, as far as the contents are concerned, on Cassiodorus and the pseudo-Hieronymic *Breviarium in psalmos*. Besides their glossarial work translators in the abbey of Reichenau were responsible for an interlinear version in Alemannic of the *Regula Benedicti* and one of twenty-one Ambrosian hymns. The collection passed to Murbach where six more hymns were added and translated. Both translations seem to have been made during the first or second decade of the ninth century. At Fulda, during the abbacy of Hrabanus a group of six scholars was engaged in translating Tatian's *Gospel Harmony*. A Latin version of the second-century Greek original, in which the more essential parts of Matthew were combined with passages from the other three Gospels, was one of the most venerable manuscripts in the Fulda library. Written in uncials before 546, it had been discovered by Victor, bishop of Capua, during the sixth century; traditionally it is one of the books that belonged to Boniface.[2] The Franconian version of this book is extremely literal. Indeed, a slavish

---

[1] Steinmeyer, *op. cit.*, p. 20.

[2] This, the so-called *Codex Fuldensis*, is now *Codex Bonifatianus* 1 in the Landesbibliothek at Fulda.

adherence to the letter is characteristic of all the translations which have been enumerated so far. The various translators had not yet learned to use their own native speech with complete freedom and control of idiom, so as to produce a rendering of the sacred text or of a portion of the liturgy which combined accuracy with literary elegance. Actual mistranslations are not rare, perhaps the worst examples being in the German version of Benedict's *Rule*. This, however, was an exceptionally difficult text to interpret.

In view of the mediocre character of most of these translations, it is all the more astonishing to find that one of the earliest extant pieces of German prose is immeasurably superior to all the others produced before the end of the ninth century. A manuscript now in Paris (B.N. lat. 2326) contains in parallel columns the Latin text and part of a German version of Isidore's treatise, *De fide catholica*.[1] Some pages of a manuscript copied fairly early in the ninth century also survive at Vienna. They contain, in addition to a few fragments of the Old High German version of *De fide catholica*, parts of St Matthew and pieces of three sermons or homilies, one by Augustine, in the two languages. The same version of Isidore is found in both manuscripts, although there is a difference of dialect; for the Paris version is in Franconian, while the other is in Bavarian. There has been much dispute both about the date of this remarkable piece of scholarship and about the monastery in which it originated. Although it has been suggested that it may go back to the time of Pippin, it is more probable that the translation was made in the last decade of the eighth century, and there is much that is attractive in the theory that it was, so to speak, a by-product of the Adoptionist controversy. Murbach, Metz, or even some monastery in Neustria have been proposed as the centre where the translation was made, but the evidence is insufficient to form any definite conclusions. The translator or translators of these works handled their task expertly, the *De fide catholica* being exceptionally well turned into the vernacular. The unknown Frankish scholar instead of

---

[1] Both de Boor in his *Geschichte der deutschen Literatur*, p. 29, and the new catalogue of Latin manuscripts in the Bibliothèque Nationale date the manuscript saec. viii/ix, but, since it is excluded from *CLA*, V, it is presumably written after 800.

confining himself to a timid, word for word, reproduction of the original text without much regard for literary form or graces, has fully mastered the meaning of the Latin and then rendered it faithfully, yet with due regard for the different idiom and linguistic limitations of his native tongue. The achievement is the more remarkable because Isidore's book abounds in abstract ideas and in the technical phraseology of Latin theological literature, as an example will show:

> Dicendo enim Christum Dei Iacob et Filium et Patrem ostendit, Item dicendo: 'Spiritus domini locutus est per me' sanctum Spiritum evidenter aperuit. Idem quoque in Psalmis (xxxii, 6): 'Verbo', inquit, 'domini caeli firmati sunt et spiritu oris eius omnis virtus eorum'. In persona enim domini Patrem accipimus, in verbo Filium credimus, in spiritu oris eius Spiritum sanctum intellegimus. Quo testimonio et trinitatis numerus et communio cooperationis ostenditur.

> Dhâr ir quhad 'Christ Iacobes gotes', chiuuisso meinida ir dhâr sunu endi fater. Dhâr ir auh quhad: 'gotes gheist ist sprehhendi dhurah mih', dhâr meinida leohtsamo zi archennenne dhen heilegan gheist. Avur auh umbi dhazs selba quhad David in psalmôm: 'druhtînes uuordu sindun himilâ chifestinôde endi sînes mundes gheistu standit al iro meghin'. In dhemu druhtînes nemin archennemês chiuuisso fater, in dhemu uuorde chilaubemês sunu, in sînes mundes gheiste instandemês chiuuisso heilegan gheist. In dheseru urchundîn ist ziuuâre araughit dhera dhrînissa zala endi chimeinidh iro einuuerches.[1]

Not until Notker the German in the late tenth and opening years of the eleventh century gave the world of his day a series of translations from standard Latin works, do we again find so high a level of performance in any extant prose work in Old High German.

[1] Braune, *op. cit.*, No. iv.

Epilogue

The tenth century has often been singled out as a period of disorganized barbarism. So sweeping a condemnation, like most facile generalizations, expresses only a part of the truth; and it is satisfactory to note that a juster estimate of that age is gaining ground.[1] Certainly, compared with the unity of Charlemagne's Empire and the qualified stability still existing under his successors of the ninth century, political, economic, and social conditions were in a state of upheaval and flux. The Church and the religious houses did not escape the common lot. Much was destroyed, discipline was relaxed, abuses crept in. Yet there were men who strove successfully to remedy abuses—Dunstan and Aethelwold in England, the Cluniac reformers on the Continent. Nor was the century devoid of notable writers. Widukind of Corvey and Flodoard of Rheims are not unworthy successors of the Carolingian historians. Aelfric, first at Cerne and later at Eynsham, and Notker the German at St Gall were men of wide learning and by their translations greatly furthered the development of their native tongues as book languages. In hagiography the tenth century surpassed the ninth in quantity and sometimes in quality. Poetic composition still claimed its devotees. Hrotsvitha, the gifted nun of Gandersheim, after reading Terence, was impelled to compose religious dramas. The unknown author of the *Ecbasis captivi*, if indeed he belongs to the tenth century rather than to the first half of the eleventh, found his material for a mock epic in beast fables. The Carolingian tradition in scholarship lingered on; in some instances we can trace a direct process of transmission. We had occasion earlier to note that Odo of Cluny was a pupil of Remigius of Auxerre. Like his teacher, he put together extracts from earlier writers. His attention, very properly

[1] Cf., the 'Symposium on the tenth century', *Medievalia et Humanistica*, IX (1955), pp. 3–29.

since he was a member of a reformed religious congregation, was given to theology, his *Collationes* being drawn from the works of the Fathers. Atto of Vercelli, again in composing his commentary on the Pauline Epistles, followed the traditional procedure of excerpting his predecessors. While some monasteries languished, others continued as before, for example, St Gall. Fleury, which renewed and extended its influence when Abbo became abbot (988), entered on a new era of prosperity. In spite of the disturbed condition of wide tracts of country, intercommunication was not permanently hampered. The migrations of manuscripts alone show this; the movements of the learned prove it also. Abbo spent two years as a teacher in England in the abbey of Ramsey. There Byrhtferth was probably his pupil. Later he in turn paid a visit to the Continent. Ratherius who was first at Liége, afterwards came to Italy. His *Praeloquia*, containing the reflections on men and manners that he put down in writing during a captivity of two years, are a work of remarkable originality. And, at the very end of the century (999), the most learned man of his age and a pioneer in mathematical science, Gerbert, was chosen to fill the see of Peter. The many extant manuscripts copied in the tenth century, finally, demonstrate that *scriptoria* continued to be very active. The tenth century was intellectually a period of transition. Nearest akin to the brilliant era that it succeeded without any abrupt change, it perpetuated sufficient of Carolingian learning to serve as the foundation for the more vigorous minds of the eleventh and twelfth centuries.

Appendix of Translations

For the convenience of the reader English renderings of the poetic passages quoted in this book are here given.

CHAPTER IV

CORIPPUS (p. 114):

There is a place cut sharply off afar in the mist of sandy wastes, whose edge the river wave, like the ocean, washes, and, as it issues forth, shuts in the lands with its bitter waters. In these regions seaweed and yielding ooze and deep slime are rank beneath an eddy. When it came to this spot, the horse sheered off affrighted from the black weeds and turned back in panic. Then, with snorting nostrils, it pricked up its two ears—a mark of panic—and reared, and maddened foamed, and rolled its eyes as it looked ahead; and it dared not make trial of the dread peril. The great-hearted leader, alas, resisting had come to the end of life and road. With shouts the crowding enemy follow, driving and harassing the hero. Then with repeated blows of the spur he stabs his horse and shakes his mighty arms. The steed driven on, leaps high, and, bearing on, tries to approach the forbidden way. Sucked down in the whirlpool it plunged itself, and on the top the fearful earth swallowed up its master in a ruthless chasm; and Fortune snatching him from his foes took him in her care that he might not stand unarmed or a humble suppliant, and gave him a tomb, lest else his body stripped had lain on Libya's sands.

ISIDORE (p. 125):

He lies who vows that he has read thee entire. What reader can possess all thy works? Thy lustre, Augustine, is reflected from a thousand tomes. The books are witness to my words. Though many be here to please thee by their writings, reader, if Augustine be at hand, he is enough for thee.

CHAPTER XIV

MODOIN (p. 333):

What great vagary of the muses has led thee astray? Better for thee to till the fields and grasp the plough-handle, to imitate the husbandman after thy father's example, than to sing.

SEDULIUS (p. 335):

        A right good man is Robert,
        High swells the praise of Robert,
        Be gracious, Christ, to Robert,
        Long-livèd render Robert.

        So be it, prosper, Robert,
        May Christ abide with Robert;
        Thy glorious name's declension
        Its course runs through six cases.

        *   *   *

        May'st thou, to whom on sad men
        Falernian gifts to lavish
        'Tis joy, drink at life's fountain
        By the saints' kindly choosing,

        Less copious from Siloam
        Gush forth the cheering streamlets.
        Thine have I sucked—yes truly,
        Thine will I suck! Avaunt, beer!

PAULUS DIACONUS (p. 337):

  Do thou beware 'neath quivering waves from sinking craft!
    Lest thou destroy men with thy waves do thou beware!
  If thou eschew this crime, all men shall sing thy praise!
    Ever shalt thou be loved, if thou eschew this crime!

        *   *   *

'Tis now the seventh year since rebellion begat manifold sorrows and shook my heart. So long is my brother a captive in your climes, heart-stricken, naked, and in need. In her home-land his wife begs with trembling lips for food from street to street. Four children she supports from this ignoble art, that scarce avails to cover them with tatters.

ALCUIN (p. 338):

Ye lads, whose age is fitted for reading, learn! The years go by like running water. Waste not the teachable days in idleness! The flowing wave returns not, the hastening hour returns not. Let early youth thrive in the pursuit of virtues that the old man may shine with the full lustre of praise! Let each read a book, and use the happy years, and, mindful of his Maker, say, 'have mercy, O God'! If, reader, thou wouldst remove our mote, first lift the beam from thy own eye! Learn, my boy, that ready speech may plead thy causes, that thou mayest defend, protect, and succour thy people. Learn, I pray, my boy, graceful movements and habits, that thy name may be praised throughout the whole globe.

ALCUIN (p. 338):

Not food nor drink, nor thy mating with another bird had been sweeter to thee than songs.

THEODULFUS (p. 339):

We make our way to rocky Vienne in the valley, locked in by cliffs on that side, hugged by a yawning stream on this.

* * *

O martyr, thou hast set thy lordly shrine in a wooded country region, and thy hall shines bright in an empty waste. Nazarius all the people calls this flower; for the Hebrew tongue fitly calls flowei 'nazar'. As in haste I came from the city of the Wangiones and sought this spot, I saw the snow falling from a cloud. I crossed in a skiff from bank to bank of the fish-laden Rhine, that I might more swiftly reach the saint's home.

THEODULFUS (pp. 340–1):

And father Albinus would sit, ever on the point of uttering pious words and freely partaking of food with lips and hand.

* * *

In the midst David presides with sceptre, dealing out mighty portions in order unperturbed.

* * *

Haply the large-limbed hero Wibod may hear this and shake his fat head three or four times. And scowling he may threaten with looks and voice, and overwhelm me in my absence with his threats. If perchance the king's most gracious majesty should summon him, he would go with bent and shaking knees. And his swollen belly would march afore his chest, a Vulcan in his gait, a Jove in voice.

* * *

Fearful greed thrives, squalor, perjury, luxury, biting envy, falsehood, quarrels, wrangling, cunning.

WALAHFRID (pp. 342–3):

It is not merely the current belief of folk that has revealed to me this lore, nor reading pursued in ancient books. But toil and industry that I preferred to long days of idleness have taught me, schooled by the test of experience.

* * *

Gladiola

Nor will I pass thee by, for whom the untrammelled eloquence of the Latin tongue has fashioned a name from the word 'sword' (*gladius*). Thou dost bear me the beauty of a purple flower, in early summer bringing a gift like to the sweet dark-hued violet, or like the hyacinth new grown beneath Apollo's high table in memory of a beardless boy, his name formed by the flower's top. The branches of thy root we dry, crush, and mix with flowing wine, and even thus with such art we assuage the bladder's cruel pain. By thy aid the fuller makes snowy linen fabrics free from creases and fragrant with a sweet scent.

WALAHFRID (p. 343):

Most learned father Grimald, thy pupil Strabo with loyal heart offers to thee this humble little gift of trifling weight for his boyhood's pupilage; that, when thou sittest in thy modest fenced-in orchard beneath the fruits shaded by leafy tree-tops, where the peach breaks up the foliage with uneven shadows, what time the sportive boys, the cheerful band of thy scholars, pluck for thee the pale fruit with tender bloom and take the mighty peaches in their palms stretched wide, striving to close their hands over the great globes, thou mayest, kind father, have wherewith to be reminded of my industry. And, while thou dost read again what I gladly entrust to thee, and, as thou readest, I pray that thou cut out what is faulty and approve what pleases thee. May God, the imperishable, in his everlasting goodness grant thee to grasp the vigorous palm of life. May Father, Son, and kindly Spirit say yea hereto!

WALAHFRID (pp. 344–5):

Courting him with sweet civilities and thoughts of friendship Strabo has sent these few words to Liutger. Though affection for us may be small, yet I trow that thou rememberest me well enough. Whate'er of good hap is thine, I gladly wish it so; but more, if aught of ill hap is thine, grief dwells in my heart's little township. Like an only child to his mother, like Phoebus' light to earth, like dew to sward, like river murmurs to meadow, like the sea-wave to fishes, even so, dear youth, is thy dear face to me. If that could be which we think can be, bring thyself to our sight swiftly, I pray. For, since I have learnt that thou art nearer to us, no rest is mine unless I see thee sooner. May glory, life, safety, and thy weal exceed the number of the stars, of dewdrops and grains of sand.

*   *   *

Dear friend, suddenly thou art come, suddenly too, dear friend, thou art gone. I hear, I see not, yet see inwardly and inwardly embrace thee escaping in the flesh, but not in devotion. For as I was in the past, so

I am and shall ever be sure that thy heart cherishes me, and mine thee. And let no occasion incline me to a different view, nor persuade thee otherwise. If thou canst visit, I will be satisfied if I have seen thy welcome self. If it be else, write somewhat; I know thy sorrows and in grief rehearse them; grief is the world's possession. What thou thinkest tranquillity, that rather flees away into clouds and dark sorrow. Who clings suspended to the fleeting globe, now rises, now falls; thus the earth's wheel drags him on.

*   *   *

When the gleam of the virgin moon shines from the upper air, do thou stand beneath the heavens, viewing in a wondrous mirror how it is lit up from the moon with her pure torch and in its gleam enfolds as one two friends, sundered yet linked in loving thought. If thy face could not behold the loved one's face, let this light at least be our pledge of love. These brief lines thy trusty friend has sent thee. If, for thy part, the links of friendship hold fast, I pray now for thy happiness and weal through all the ages.

GOTTSCHALK (p. 346):

Look down, I pray, on thy weeping servant, who fears and implores thee, who adores, yea, and loves thee. Stretch forth thy hand, raise up thy slave, strip off, I pray, his heavy guilt, correct his ill-spent life. . . . O Christ, guard me always and in every place, and, all-highest, have pity on me. Grant me to fear and love thee; to make my way, holy one, through thy writings, from them to set out with heart and lips, from them to recite with eager mind, to meditate and sing, to pray aloud, to work with my heart, and to serve thee, the king.

*   *   *

O God, have pity on thy pitiful servant.

GOTTSCHALK (p. 347):

Why dost thou bid, my little lad, why constrain me, my little son, to sing a sweet song, seeing that I am an exile far across the sea? Oh why dost bid me sing? Rather should I, my little sinner, weep, my little boy, rather lament than sing a song such as thou biddest, dearest heart. Oh why dost bid me sing? . . . Meanwhile with my lad I will chant a psalm, a sweet song, with lips and mind and voice and heart, by day and night, to thee, most holy king.

SEDULIUS (p. 348):

When the east wind's gusty gale rages boisterously, thundering down from the high mountains, the while hail falls in clouds, and straightway forests totter, and the ocean tide is upheaved, and the wind hurls threats at the stars as the lightning crackles, then fear strikes the heart of trembling mortals, lest heaven-sent wrath lay low the race of earthly men.

*   *   *

The earth makes flower-bearing bulbs to swell with blossom and rejoices to have a painted robe of flowers. Now bright-plumed birds soothe the air with song, from their young beaks they pour a song of lofty triumph. The skies exult, the earth is glad, and now re-echoes an hundredfold its notes of Halleluia. Now the church choir, singing its chant of Sion, lifts up its Hosanna to the sky's poles above.

SEDULIUS (p. 349):

Without blemish was he and spake not empty words. Báá or béé were the mystic sounds he used to utter. As a lamb enthroned on high to redeem sinners the Son of God Himself tasted bitter death. Going the road of death, torn by cruel hounds, thus good bell-wether, thou dost perish for the unrepentant thief. As a ram was made a sacrificial offering for Isaac, so thou art a pleasing victim for a poor wretch.

ANONYMOUS (p. 350):

Father bear, who gave thee this mitre to wear on thy head, and who gave thee these gloves for thy hands?

*   *   *

At length I scarce found an excellent physician. But, o king, I fear to tell thee what he taught.

*   *   *

Look, your legs show what food you've been living on.

NOTKER (p. 351):

A sleepless watcher, mastering day and night, heedless of drink and food, have I taught thee. All have I laid down in obedience to thy wishes. But now I am spurned, another has thy love. Yet, if that aged man, driven on by unjust hatred, with raging heart has torn friends asunder, then grieving with like anguish and sorrowing heart I follow thee, and will wet with my tears the road that thou treadest. But in whatever place, with whatever hap thou makest thy way, may God who fulfils all things escort thee with his aid. These memorials of me write down in a retentive heart, that thou mayest read them that have been turned over in continuous meditation.

NOTKER (p. 353):

First from among seven snow-white pillars Stephen, chosen by blessed Peter, with voice and tokens healing the wretched is famed in the world. Repeating in brief words past events, he taught that the

Jews, dishonest and full of envy, were persecutors of God-fearing men. No novelty their deed in having driven the Lord to the punishment of the cross in their unholy rage, seeing that they used oftentimes before to slay prophets and patriarchs. In requital for such words as these, though he shone beauteous with the face of angels, they cast him like some profane wretch down high from the city walls. And in Saul's care they laid their garments yet warm, lest perchance slow rage hampered might too tardily be able to mutilate the saint. Then the stones flew thick through the air like to mighty rain or a shower denied to a vine long barren and harmful.[1]

NOTKER (pp. 354–5):

Christ grant that this day be gracious to all Christian men, his lovers. Christ Jesus, Son of God, mediator between the Divine Nature and ours, Eternal God, thou hast visited the earth, a man new-made, through the air swift-moving. With their ministrations angels and clouds throng about thee as thou art about to return to thy Father. Yet no marvel is it that a star is still thy servant and the angels. This day hast thou given to earthly men a new, sweet gift of hope for heavenly things, O Lord, by raising thyself, a man true-fashioned, above the orbits of the stars, O Lord of kings. What joy fills thy apostles, to whom thou didst grant the sight of thee traversing the skies. In the skies how gladly the nine orders meet thee, bearing on thy shoulders a single flock long scattered by wolves. It do thou deign to guard, O Christ, the good shepherd!

*   *   *

O thou, Gallus, dear to eternal God, and to men, and to the angelic hosts, who, obedient to the lofty behest of Jesus Christ, didst spurn a father's property, a mother's bosom, a wife's care, a son's playful antics, poor thyself to follow the poor Lord, and didst prefer the Cross to transient pleasures! But Christ repays this an hundredfold, as this day testifies, the while He subjects us all to thee as sons in sweet affection, and has given thee, Gallus, Suevia, a suave home-land; has, too, made thee to sit a judge in the skies jointly with the band of the Apostles. Thee now as suppliants we pray, Gallus, that thou request Jesus Christ to give us his favour, and that thou fill the spot where thy body lies with peace, and that thou raise up them that supplicate thee in constant prayer, so that, full of gladness we may ever be worthy to render to thee the honour that is thy due, O Gallus, beloved of God!

HEIRIC (p. 356):

And now beneath his feet he spies clouds and stars. He looks down on the shining radiance of the roseate sun, looks down on the dewy

[1] The reader should compare Acts vii, especially vv. 55 ff.

orb of the cold moon, and the recurrent wanderings of all the planets, the earth's mass and all-enveloping darkness, the wind's breaths and swelling tempests. He sees why peaceful spring and burning summer avail, why the autumn abounds in grapes and winter in frosts; sees all that revolves in the world's three-dimensional fabric, all that men say is subject to physical causes, all that has its being in number, measure, or weight, all that is hidden and all that is visible at the hub of the universe. With vision unclouded he gazes on the cause of all things. He beholds all mankind beneath him, Christ above all things. Yea, he looks smiling too at the vanities and high offices of human life, dread monarchs, diadems, sceptres, despots, and treasures sought after with many passionate crimes, robes vainly decked with gold in delicate variety, and all the manifold forms of earthly properties.

ERMOLDUS (p. 357):

Lo, the boy Charles regarding her, wishes, like his sire, to follow; with spirited prayers he demands a steed; eagerly asks for weapons, for quiver and swift arrows, and yearns to go ahunting, as his sire himself is wont to do. But his fair mother forbids his going and lets not his wish be fulfilled. Were not his tutor and his mother restraining him as he wishes to go, the boy, boy-like would now be speeding on to go on foot.

ANONYMOUS (p. 360):

Hearken to a sin with anguish, all ye lands of every clime,
To the dastard deed accomplished by Benevento's citizens!
They have taken Louis captive, sacred, godly emperor.

To a council then foregathered all Benevento's burgesses.
Adelferius first addressed them, and their leading men spoke thus:
'If alive we do discharge him, we shall surely be undone;

Great the crime that he has plotted here against that land of ours.
He despoils us of our kingdom, us he doth esteem as nought.
He has done us wrongs too many; just it is that he should die.'

Then the sacred, godly ruler from his palace they deposed.
Adelferius him conducted straightway to the justice-seat.
But the king went forth as if to meet a joyous martyrdom.[1]

*   *   *

For a mighty horde of heathen landed on Calabria's shores.
On they came atop Salerno, masters of the burgh to be.

[1] The meaning is clear, although the first half of the line appears corrupt.

ANONYMOUS (p. 360):

    O thou, who armed dost guard yon battlements
    Beware, I bid, of slumber and keep watch,
    What time Sir Hector wakeful lived in Troy,
    It fell no prey to Greece's cunning wiles.
    When all was silent first and slumbered Troy,
    The crafty Sinon loosed his treacherous bolts.

    Down ropes they swarmed, the hidden company,
    Raided the town and kindled Pergamum.
    With wakeful voice the snowy goose did drive
    Gauls headlong from the fort of Romulus.
    Then for her prowess she, in silver wrought,
    Was worshipped, goddess-like, by Roman men.

    Ours be't to worship Christ's divinity,
    To give to Him our tuneful songs of joy.
    Trustful beneath his mighty custody,
    While watching let us chant our joyous hymn,
    'Earth's monarch, Christ, in holy custody
    Beneath thy watchful care this castle keep,

    Be thou to thine a wall impregnable,
    To enemies a foe implacable;
    With thee awatch, no doughty deeds can harm,
    Who drivest off all warlike arms afar.
    Gird thou about these muniments of ours,
    O Christ, thy warrior spear be their defence!

    And thou, his radiant parent, Holy Mary,
    Mother of God, and John, support our prayer,
    Your holy pledges here are held in awe,
    Yon threshhold, too, is dedicate to you,
    Christ leading, victory crowns our might in war;
    Without his aid, our weapons nought avail.'

    Courageous youth, bold-hearted warriors,
    O let your songs from wall to wall ring out,
    Stand by, in alternating watches, armed,
    Lest foeman's treachery assault these walls.
    To echoing call, 'Ho, comrade, be on guard'
    'Cross walls let "Ho" re-echo "be on guard!"'

Select Bibliography

Only a selection from the more recent literature is here given. Books marked with an asterisk contain ample bibliographical information. These should be consulted for works published prior to the year 1920, which, with a few exceptions, have here been omitted. For the best texts and editions of the medieval writers, and for monographs or articles dealing with special topics, the reader is referred to the appropriate notes accompanying the text of this volume.

GENERAL WORKS OF REFERENCE

*ALTANER, B. *Patrologie*. Ed. 2. Freiburg i. B., 1950.

Cambridge Mediaeval History. Vols. 1 to 3. Cambridge, 1911–22.

*CASPAR, E. L. E. *Geschichte des Papsttums*. Vols. 1 and 2. Tübingen, 1930–4.

*DEKKERS, E. and GAAR, E. *Clavis Patrum Latinorum* (*Sacris Erudiri*, III). Bruges, 1951.

Dictionnaire d'archéologie chrétienne et de liturgie. Vols. 1 to 15. Paris, 1907–53.

Dictionnaire de théologie catholique. Vols. 1 to 15. Paris, 1908–50.

*FLICHE, A. and MARTIN, V. *Histoire de l'église*. Vols. 1 to 6. Paris, 1933–9.

HARNACK, A. VON. *Dogmengeschichte*. Ed. 6. Tübingen, 1922.

*RABY, F. J. E. *A History of Christian Latin Poetry*. Ed. 2. Oxford, 1953.

*RABY, F. J. E. *A History of Secular Latin Poetry in the Middle Ages*. Vols. 1 and 2. Oxford, 1934.

STRECKER, K. *Einleitung in das Mittellatein*. Ed. 2. Berlin, 1929.

CHAPTERS I–III

ÅBERG, N. *Die Franken und Westgoten in der Völkerwanderungszeit*. Uppsala, 1922.

ÅBERG, N. *Die Goten und Langobarden in Italien*. Uppsala, 1923.

*BARDENHEWER, O. *Geschichte der altkirchlichen Literatur*. Vols. 1 to 4. Ed. 2. Vol. 5. Freiburg i. B., 1913–32.

BESNIER, M. *L'empire romain de l'avènement des Sévères au concile de Nicée*. Paris, 1937.

BUONAIUTI, E. *Il cristianesimo nell' Africa romana*. Bari, 1928.

BURY, J. B. *The Invasion of Europe by the Barbarians*. London, 1928.

CAVALLERA, F. *Saint Jérome: sa vie et ses œuvres*. Vols. 1 and 2. Louvain and Paris, 1922.

CHADWICK, NORA K. *Poetry and Letters in Early Christian Gaul*. London, 1955.

COURCELLE, P. *Histoire littéraire des grandes invasions germaniques*. Paris, 1948.

DOPSCH, A. *Wirtschaftliche und soziale Grundlagen der europäischen Kulturentwicklung*. Vols. 1 and 2. Ed. 2. Vienna, 1923–4.

*LABRIOLLE, P. DE. *Histoire de la littérature latine chrétienne*. Vols. 1 and 2. Ed. 3 revised by G. Bardy. Paris, 1947.

LAISTNER, M. L. W. *Christianity and Pagan Culture in the Later Roman Empire*. Ithaca, N.Y., 1951.

LIETZMANN, H. *Geschichte der alten Kirche*. Vols. 1 to 4. Berlin and Leipzig, 1932–44.

*LOT, F. *La fin du monde antique et le début du moyen âge*. Paris, 1927.

MARROU, H. I. *Histoire de l'éducation dans l'antiquité*. Paris, 1948.

*MARROU, H. I. *Saint Augustin et la fin de la culture antique*. Vols. 1 and 2. Ed. 2. Paris, 1949.

MURPHY, F. X. (ed.) *A Monument to Saint Jerome*. London and New York, 1952.

PIGANIOL, A. *L'empire chrétien*. Paris, 1947.

RAND, E. K. *Founders of the Middle Ages*. Cambridge, Mass., 1928.

REITZENSTEIN, R. *Augustin als antiker und als frühmittelalterlicher Mensch*. *Vorträge der Bibliothek Warburg*, 1922–3, pp. 28–65. Leipzig, 1924.

*SCHANZ, M. and KRUEGER, G. *Geschichte der römischen Literatur*. Vol. 3. Ed. 3. Vol. 4. Ed. 2. Munich, 1920–2.

SCHMIDT, F. L. *Geschichte der deutschen Stämme*. Vols. 1 and 2. Ed. 2. Berlin, 1934–8.

STEIN, E. *Geschichte des spätrömischen Reiches*. Vol. 1. Vienna, 1928.

STREETER, B. H. *The Primitive Church*. London, 1929.

CHAPTERS IV–XIV

*BALLESTEROS Y BERETTA, A. *Historia de España*. Vol. 1. Barcelona, 1919.

BECKER, G. *Catalogi bibliothecarum antiqui*. Bonn, 1885.

BEESON, C. H. *Isidorstudien*. *Quellen und Untersuchungen zur lateinischen Philologie des Mittelalters*, iv, 2. Munich, 1913.

BEESON, C. H. *Servatus Lupus as scribe and text critic*. Cambridge, Mass., 1930.

BEZZOLA, R. *Les origines et la formation de la littérature courtoise en occident (500–1200)*. Part I. Paris, 1944.

BISCHOFF, B. *Südostdeutsche Schreibschulen*. Leipzig, 1940.

400   SELECT BIBLIOGRAPHY

BISCHOFF, B. and HOFFMANN, J. *Libri Sancti Kyliani.* Würzburg, 1952.

BLAIR, P. H. *An Introduction to Anglo-Saxon England.* Cambridge, Eng., 1956.

BRUCKNER, A. *Scriptoria Medii Aevi Helvetica.* 7 vols. in 13. Geneva, 1935–52.

BUTLER, C. *Benedictine Monachism.* Ed. 2. London, 1924.

CAPPUYNS, M. *Jean Scot Erigène: sa vie, son œuvre, sa pensée.* Paris, 1933.

CARLYLE, R. W. and A. J. *A History of Mediaeval Political Theory in the West.* Vol. 1 (by A. J. C.). Edinburgh and London, 1903.

CHAPMAN, J. *Saint Benedict and the Sixth Century.* London, 1929.

*COURCELLE, P. *Les lettres grecques en occident.* Ed. 2. Paris, 1948.

CURTIUS, E. R. *Europäische Literatur und lateinisches Mittelalter.* Bern, 1948. [English translation, London, 1953.]

*DALTON, O. M. *The History of the Franks by Gregory of Tours.* Vols. 1 and 2. Oxford, 1927.

DILL, S. *Roman Society in Gaul in the Merovingian Age.* London, 1926.

*DUCKETT, ELEANOR S. *Alcuin, Friend of Charlemagne.* New York, 1951.

DUDDEN, F. H. *Gregory the Great.* Vols. 1 and 2. London, 1905.

GILSON, E. *Études de philosophie médiévale.* Strasbourg, 1921.

GILSON, E. *La philosophie au moyen âge.* Ed. 3. Paris, 1947.

HALPHEN, L. *Études critiques sur l'histoire de Charlemagne.* Paris, 1921.

*HAUCK, A. *Kirchengeschichte Deutschlands.* Vols. 1 and 2. Ed. 3–4. Leipzig, 1911–12.

HELLMANN, S. *Sedulius Scottus: Quellen und Untersuchungen zur lateinischen Philologie des Mittelalters.* i. 1. Munich, 1906.

HODGKIN, R. H. *A History of the Anglo-Saxons.* Vols. 1 and 2. Ed. 2. Oxford, 1939.

JONES, C. W. *Bedae Opera de Temporibus.* Cambridge, Mass., 1943.

JONES, C. W. *Saints' Lives and Chronicles in Early England.* Ithaca, N.Y., 1947.

*KENNEY, J. F. *The Sources for the Early History of Ireland.* Vol. I: *Ecclesiastical.* New York, 1929.

KER, N. R. *Medieval Libraries of Great Britain.* London, 1941.

KLEINCLAUSZ, A. *Alcuin.* Paris, 1948.

LAISTNER, M. L. W. *Bedae Venerabilis Expositio Actuum Apostolorum et Retractatio.* Cambridge, Mass., 1939.

LAISTNER, M. L. W. and KING, H. H. *A Hand-list of Bede Manuscripts.* Ithaca, N.Y., 1943.

LEHMANN, P. *Die lateinische Parodie im Mittelalter.* Munich, 1922.

LEHMANN, P. *Fuldaer Studien. Sitzungsberichte.* Bavarian Academy, 1925, No. 3, and 1927, No. 2. Munich.

LEHMANN, P. *Mittelalterliche Bibliothekskataloge Deutschlands und der Schweiz.* Vol. I. Munich, 1918.

LEHMANN, P. *Mitteilungen aus Handschriften.* Fasc. 1 to 9. *Sitzungsberichte,* Bavarian Academy, 1919 to 1950. Munich.

LEVISON, W. *Aus rheinischer und fränkischer Frühzeit*. Düsseldorf, 1948.

LEVISON, W. *England and the Continent in the Eighth Century*. Oxford, 1946.

*LOT, F., PFISTER, CHR., and GANSHOF, F. *Les destinées de l'empire en occident de 395 à 888*. Paris, 1928.

*LOWE, E. A. *Codices latini antiquiores*. Vols. I to VII. Oxford, 1934–56. [Three more volumes are to follow.]

LOWE, E. A. *Codices Lugdunenses antiquissimi*. Lyons, 1924.

LOWE, E. A. *Scriptura Beneventana*. Oxford, 1929.

LOWE, E. A. *The Beneventan Script*. Oxford, 1914.

*MANITIUS, M. *Geschichte der lateinischen Literatur des Mittelalters*. Vols. 1 to 3. Munich, 1911–31.

MANITIUS, M. *Handschriften antiker Autoren in mittelalterlichen Bibliothekskatalogen* (*Zentralblatt für Bibliothekswesen*, Beiheft 67). Leipzig, 1935.

MCILWAIN, C. H. *The Growth of Political Thought in the West*. New York, 1932.

*MCNEILL, J. T. and GAMER, HELENA, M. *Medieval Handbooks of Penance*. New York, 1938.

MENENDEZ PIDAL, R. (ed.). *Historia de España*. Vol. 3 (1940) and 4 (1950). Madrid.

*MOSS, H. ST. L. B. *The Birth of the Middle Ages, 395–814*. Oxford, 1935.

OGILVY, J. D. A. *Books known to Anglo-Latin Writers from Aldhelm to Alcuin*. Cambridge, Mass., 1936.

Palaeographia latina (ed. W. M. Lindsay). Parts 1 to 6. London, 1922–9.

RAND, E. K. *A Survey of the Manuscripts of Tours*. Vol. 1, text. Vol. 2, plates. Cambridge, Mass., 1929.

RAND, E. K. and JONES, L. W. *The Earliest Book of Tours*. Cambridge, Mass., 1934.

*SCHUBERT, H. VON. *Geschichte der christlichen Kirche im Frühmittelalter*. Tübingen, 1921.

*SÉJOURNÉ, P. *Saint Isidore de Séville*. Paris, 1929.

SIEGMUND, A. *Die Ueberlieferung der griechisch christlichen Literatur in der lateinischen Kirche bis zum zwölften Jahrhundert*. Munich, 1949.

SMALLEY, BERYL. *The Study of the Bible in the Middle Ages*. Ed. 2. Oxford, 1952.

STENTON, F. M. *Anglo-Saxon England*. Ed. 2. Oxford, 1947.

*TAYLOR, H. O. *The Mediaeval Mind*. Vols. 1 and 2. Ed. 4. New York, 1925. (Reprinted 1951).

THÉRY, G. *Études dionysiennes*. Vols. 1 and 2. Paris, 1932–7.

THOMPSON, A. H. (ed.) *Bede: His Life, Times, and Writings*. Oxford, 1935.

*WADDELL, HELEN J. *The Wandering Scholars*. London, 1927.

WALLACE-HADRILL, J. M. *The Barbarian West, 400–1000.* London, 1952.

*WATTENBACH, W., LEVISON, W., and LOEWE, H. *Deutschlands Geschichtsquellen im Mittelalter.* Fasc. I and II. Weimar, 1952–3. [Fasc. II extends to the death of Charlemagne.]

CHAPTER XV

*BAUGH, A. C. (ed.) *A Literary History of England.* New York, 1948. [The section on Old English literature is by Kemp Malone.]

*BOOR, H. A. W. DE. *Geschichte der deutschen Literatur von den Anfängen bis zur Gegenwart.* Vol. 1 (770–1170). Munich, 1949.

*BOSTOCK, J. K. *A Handbook of Old High German Literature.* Oxford, 1955.

BRAUNE, W. *Althochdeutsches Lesebuch.* Ed. 12, revised by K. Helm. Halle, 1952.

*CHAMBERS, R. W. *Beowulf: An Introduction to the Study of the Poem.* Ed. 2. Cambridge, 1932.

*EHRISMANN, G. *Geschichte der deutschen Literatur bis zum Ausgang des Mittelalters.* Vol. 1. Ed. 2. Munich, 1932.

GORDON, R. K. *Anglo-Saxon Poetry.* Rev. ed. London, n.d. (1955?)

HALL, J. CLARK and WRENN, C. L. *Beowulf and the Finnsburg Fragments.* London, 1950. [A prose translation of the poems.]

KENNEDY, C. W. *The Earliest English Poetry.* Princeton, 1943.

LAWRENCE, W. W. *Beowulf and Epic Tradition.* Cambridge, Mass., 1928.

PLUMMER, C. *The Life and Times of Alfred the Great.* Oxford, 1902.

SISAM, K. *Studies in the History of Old English Literature.* Oxford, 1953.

STEINMEYER, E. VON. *Die kleineren althochdeutschen Sprachdenkmäler.* Leipzig, 1916.

STEVENSON, W. H. *Asser's Life of King Alfred.* Oxford, 1904.

WHITELOCK, DOROTHY. *The Audience of Beowulf.* Oxford, 1951.

WRENN, C. L. *Beowulf.* London, 1953.

General Index

Abbreviations—(a.) abbot; (b.) bishop; (e.) emperor; (m.) monk; (p.) pope; (st.) saint.

NOTE: *Saints are listed under their respective names: the entries under 'Saint' refer to monastic houses.*

Abbo (a. of Fleury), 388
   (m. of St Germain), 332
Academy (Carolingian), 201–2
Acca, 164
Adalbert, 252
Adalgaudus, 257
Adalhard, 194, 223 n.1, 317
Adamnan, 147–9, 239
Adhemar, 276
Ado, 266–7
Adoptionism, 204, 286–9, 385
Adrianople (battle), 21
Aelbert, 193
Aeneas (b.), 292
Aethelwold, 387
Aethicus Ister, 177, 185, 284
Aetius, 23
Africa (Roman), 43, 57–60, 113–15
Agapetus (p.), 96
Agius, 331
Agnellus, 276
Agnes (st.), 127, 281
Agobard, 309–10, 311–12
Agrimensores, 124
Aix (councils or synods), 121, 288, 291, 327
Alamanni, 20
Alans, 22
Alaric, 21–2, 71
Albarus, 212–13
Albinus, 165
Alcuin, 39, 179, 185, 192, 193–4, 198–202, 204–6, 215, 218, 221, 239–40, 273, 279, 288, 290–1, 305, 307, 311, 315, 333, 337–8

Aldfrith, 153
Aldhelm, 112, 153–6
Aldric, 252
Alfred, 90, 108, 378, 380–2
Aligernus, 175
Allegorical interpretation, 41, 42, 65–6, 67, 104–6, 110–11, 121, 159–61, 221, 303, 304, 311–12, 328, 376
Altsigus, 255
Altuin, 257
Amalarius, 297, 310–14
Amalric, 329
Ambrose, 30, 52, 57, 82, 102, 106, 120, 122, 162, 169, 223, 229, 301, 384
Ambrosiaster, 40, 66–7, 313, 320
Ambrosius Autpertus, 174, 300
Ammianus, 37, 232
Ammonius, 87, 99
Amolo, 297
Anastasius (e.), 25, 320
   (of Antioch), 108
   (papal librarian), 248–9
Angelomus, 206, 299
Angilbert, 194, 271
Angilram, 276
Annals (Merovingian and Carolingian), 261–5
Annegray, 141
Ansbald, 255
Anskar, 277
Antiochene school, 65, 160, 313
Antiphonaries, 311
Antipodes, 185

Index of Patristic and Medieval Authors cited in the Text

Index of Modern Authors cited in the Notes